The Economics of Ottoman Justice

During the seventeenth and eighteenth centuries, the Ottoman Empire endured long periods of warfare, facing intense financial pressures and new international mercantile and monetary trends. The Empire also experienced major political-administrative restructuring and socioeconomic transformations. In the context of this tumultuous change, *The Economics of Ottoman Justice* examines Ottoman legal practices and the sharia court's operations to reflect on the judicial system and provincial relationships. Metin Coşgel and Boğaç Ergene provide a systematic depiction of socio-legal interactions, identifying how different social, economic, gender, and religious groups used the court, how they settled their disputes, and which factors contributed to their success at trial. Using an economic approach, Coşgel and Ergene offer rare insights into the role of power differences in judicial interactions and the reproduction of communal hierarchies in court, and demonstrate how court-use patterns changed over time.

Metin Coşgel is Professor of Economics and Department Head of the Economics Department at the University of Connecticut. He has published widely on the Ottoman Empire.

Boğaç Ergene is Associate Professor of History at the University of Vermont. He is the author of *Local Court, Provincial Society and Justice in the Ottoman Empire* (2003).

Other titles in the series are listed at the back of the book.

The Economics of Ottoman Justice

Settlement and Trial in the Sharia Courts

METIN COŞGEL
University of Connecticut

BOĞAÇ ERGENE
University of Vermont

CAMBRIDGE
UNIVERSITY PRESS

CAMBRIDGE
UNIVERSITY PRESS

University Printing House, Cambridge CB2 8BS, United Kingdom

Cambridge University Press is part of the University of Cambridge.

It furthers the University's mission by disseminating knowledge in the pursuit of education, learning, and research at the highest international levels of excellence.

www.cambridge.org
Information on this title: www.cambridge.org/9781107157637

First published 2016

Printed in the United States of America by Sheridan Books, Inc.

A catalogue record for this publication is available from the British Library.

Library of Congress Cataloging-in-Publication Data
Coşgel, Metin, author. | Ergene, Boğaç A., 1971– author.
The economics of Ottoman justice : settlement and trial in the Sharia courts / Metin Coşgel, University of Connecticut; Boğaç Ergene, Unviersity of Vermont.
Cambridge [UK] ; New York : Cambridge University Press, 2016. |
Series: Cambridge studies in Islamic civilization | Includes bibliographical references and index.
LCCN 2016037423 | ISBN 9781107157637 (hardback)
LCSH: Justice, Administration of (Islamic law) – Turkey – History. | Islamic courts – Turkey – History. | Justice, Administration of – Economic aspects – Turkey – History. | Turkey – History – Ottoman Empire, 1288–1918. |
BISAC: HISTORY / Middle East / General.
LCC KKX1572 .C67 2016 | DDC 349.956–dc23
LC record available at https://lccn.loc.gov/2016037423

ISBN 978-1-107-15763-7 Hardback

Contents

Figures

Tables

Maps

Acknowledgments

In the process of writing this book we accrued many debts, which we would like to acknowledge here. Generous grants from the American Council of Learned Societies, the Social Science Research Council, the National Endowment for Humanities, and the American Research Institute in Turkey provided both financial support and moral encouragement that sustained initial research on the project. Likewise, funding and release time furnished by our home institutions, the Department of History and the College of Arts and Sciences at University of Vermont and the Department of Economics and the College of Liberal Arts and Sciences at the University of Connecticut, have been critical for the completion of the book.

We have had the opportunity to share our ideas and findings with many colleagues, who read our papers, listened to conference presentations, or patiently endured informal conversations. It is impossible to list here all of these individuals, but we are particularly indebted to Iris Agmon, Faiz Ahmed, Jun Akiba, Beshara Doumani, Cemal Kafadar, Atabey Kaygun, Timur Kuran, Thomas Miceli, Şevket Pamuk, David Powers, and Kristen Stilt, whose expert advice and constructive criticisms helped us to refine our analysis and improve our arguments. Virginia Aksan, Yavuz Aykan, Carter Findley, and Avi Rubin read earlier versions of the manuscript and made valuable suggestions that allowed us to sharpen our reflections on our findings. We are also grateful for the insightful criticisms of the four anonymous referees. While we are fortunate to benefit from the scholarly support of our colleagues, we acknowledge all shortcomings of the book as our own.

We appreciate the encouragement we received from Chase Robinson and Alan Mikhail in the process of the book's production. Gregory T. Woolston created the handsome maps that we use in the book. Charlotte Weber's editing skills turned our technical discussion into a more elegant version of the original. We owe the title of the book to Maria Marsh, our commissioning editor at Cambridge University Press. Since assuming her position at Cambridge University Press in the spring of 2015, Maria has steered us through many stages of the publishing process, for which we are grateful as well. It was a joy to work with Dominic Stock, our content manager at Cambridge University Press, who is an exemplary professional with good humor and much patience. Without his attention to detail and commitment to our book, the last phase of the publication process would have been very difficult. We also extend our gratitude to Aishwariya Ravi and Velmurugan Inbasigamoni, our project managers at Integra, for their efforts to accommodate our needs. Helen Cooper copyedited the book for the press and Susan Sutch prepared the index. We thank them for their hard-work.

Finally, we wish to express our deep gratitude to our wives, Febe Armanios and Patricia Coşgel, who have experienced both the joys and the anxieties associated with writing this book almost as much as the authors.

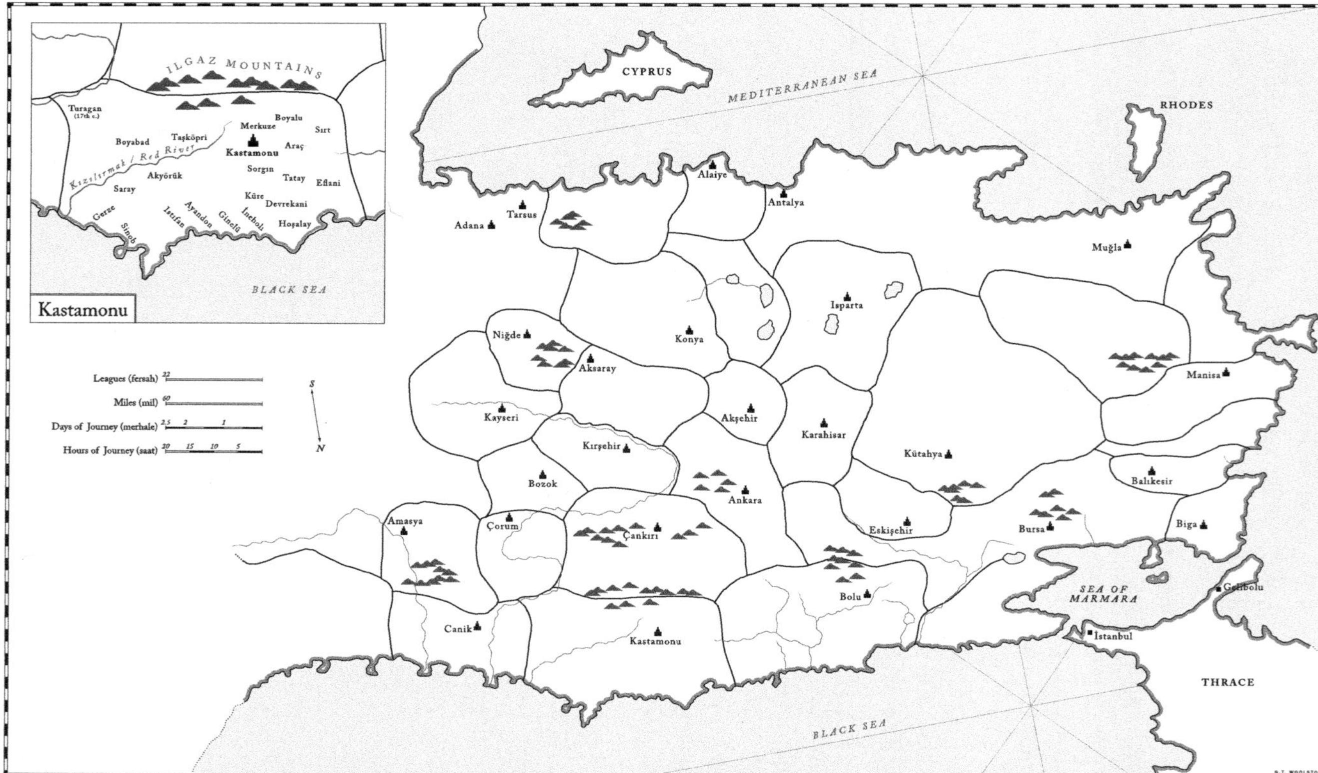

MAP 1 Kastamonu and Anatolia in the Seventeenth Century According to *Cihannüma*
Note: Location names in the map are identified and transcribed according to the information found in Baykara (2015).
Sources: Katip Çelebi (2013, 118) and Baykara (2015).

MAP 2 A Modern Map of the Administrative Boundaries in Seventeenth-century Anatolia
Source: Pitcher (1972, map XXV)

Introduction

This book studies legal practice in the Ottoman Empire. Using the court records (sing. *sicil*) of the provincial town of Kastamonu, located on the Black Sea coast in Anatolia, we investigate the legal interactions of gender, religious, and socioeconomic groups during the late seventeenth and eighteenth centuries, a period of major social and economic transformation. We combine insights from the "Law and Economics" literature with methods of historical and quantitative analysis to examine the functions of the court, and the way these functions changed over time, in this highly stratified provincial setting.

In recent years, historians of the Ottoman Empire have shown renewed interest in the seventeenth and eighteenth centuries, a period traditionally described as one of decline and degeneration. Historians now recognize it instead as an era of major socioeconomic and political transformation. The Ottoman state endured intense financial pressures in this age, mainly as a consequence of long years of warfare with powerful adversaries, changes in the technologies of warfare, escalating demographic pressures, and new international economic and monetary trends. At the same time, the empire experienced major fiscal and economic developments as short- and long-term tax-farming arrangements replaced traditional forms of prebendal revenue extraction, which accompanied the emergence of a money- and market-based economy in various Ottoman domains. In the center of the empire, new oligarchic structures diluted the sultanic absolutism of the earlier periods and contributed to the materialization of a relatively pluralistic system of governance. In the provinces, local notables took advantage of the new fiscal and economic opportunities by investing in tax-farming arrangements and commercial ventures, integrated themselves into provincial administration, and became influential in local decision-making. Historians now agree that these changes may have caused the reshaping of socioeconomic relationships in Ottoman society.

Although academic interest in Ottoman law and legal practice has grown recently, this scholarship has lagged behind economic and political historiography in producing a comprehensive portrait of the post-classical age (ca. 1600–1800). Thus far, legal research on the period has concentrated on jurisprudential issues, such as the supposed decline of state law (*kanun*), after the sixteenth century as representative of fundamental changes in the state's legislative practices.[1] Historians have also examined shifts in judicial organization, legal procedures, and law enforcement.[2] However, we still know too little about the court's operations and services to identify how the legal practice and the functions of the court changed during this period. This is one of the main objectives of the present study.

At the same time, we examine the dynamics of group relationships and experiences among court clients. In this regard, one of our main concerns is to produce a research framework that can identify group interactions in court. Until now, few studies in Ottoman legal history have attempted to characterize how court clients, as representatives of socioeconomic groups, participated in legal processes. To the contrary, most studies tend to focus on the individual court clients in isolation and make little attempt to analyze their experiences as members of a group. This tendency undermines our ability to identify the role of the court in regulating and reproducing class, gender, and religious relationships.

[1] Historians have long claimed that *kanun* legislation disappeared from the seventeenth century onward due either to intensifying sharia-minded conservatism in the government (İnalcık 1978a, 1978b; Barkan 1943; Repp 1988) or to changing economic and fiscal circumstances (Tezcan 2012, 30; Abou-El-Haj 1991b). A few researchers, however, have rejected the claim that *kanuns* declined (see Gerber 1994, 61; Ze'evi 2006, 69–71; Akgündüz 1990, 64–7).

[2] Michael Ursinus (2004) and Rossitsa Gradeva (2006) have discussed the possible emergence of a judicial hierarchy in the provinces whereby governors and high-ranking kadıs acquired appellate and supervisory responsibilities in their jurisdictions. For a critical assessment of these suggestions, see Aykan (2012). Fariba Zarinebaf, on the other hand, has argued that the Ottoman state developed an "increasing ability to discipline and punish" during the eighteenth century (2010, 111). Among other things, the state implemented surveillance tactics, such as population surveys of specific neighborhoods, as methods of social control (2010, 128–30). Also, "the aim of the penal system changed from corporal punishment to correction, isolation, and rehabilitation" (2010, 173).

The focus on the individual in the scholarship is related to the fact that court records provide limited information about the socioeconomic characteristics of court clients. While we can distinguish male clients from females and Muslims from non-Muslims, it is not easy to differentiate wealthy and socially prominent parties from the poor and underprivileged. To generalize about group experiences in court, we thus need to ascertain the socioeconomic characteristics of court clients based on indirect indicators found in the court records. This is precisely what we do in this book. We use honorific titles, religious markers, and family associations as indicators of socioeconomic prominence. This effort, justifiable based on the information available in the archival sources (see Chapter 2), provides us the tools of analysis for a group-based exploration of legal practice and the court's activities in the Ottoman context.

From a historiographical perspective, our concern with group interactions finds its roots in our desire to further shift the focal point in Ottoman legal research from the institution of the court and its legal-administrative functions to the clients of the court and their socio-legal affairs. While the body of the court and its place in the Ottoman provincial administration have received significant attention in the Ottoman scholarship, a traditionally state-centric field, it is only recently that historians have become seriously interested in provincial peoples as legal agents and have explored the court's archive to understand their legal concerns, thought processes, and activities (Rubin 2011; Agmon 2006; Peirce 2003; Ergene 2003, 2010). We contribute to this latter orientation by proposing a novel approach that allows us to consider legal practice according to the gender, religion, and class characteristics of court clients.

METHODOLOGICAL CONSIDERATIONS

This book makes two important methodological contributions to Ottoman legal studies. First, it offers a sophisticated quantitative approach for analyzing the legal information found in Ottoman court records. In this sense it represents both a continuation of and a break from earlier research based on *sicil*s. Quantitative approaches to Ottoman court records have a long history, though most quantitative studies of Ottoman *sicil*s have focused on the economic information found in court registers, rather than the legal information. Additionally, because such studies often lacked historically grounded understandings of the institution of the court and the legal-scribal processes that produced the court records, their conclusions were often simplistic, reflecting uncritical acceptance of the data contained in those records.

Since the mid-1990s, under the influence of the so-called cultural turn in the social sciences and humanities, we have witnessed the emergence of an orientation in *sicil*-based research toward the textual and rhetorical characteristics of court records (Agmon 2004b, 2006). This shift has generated a new and critical appreciation of the way institutional structures and socio-legal practices have shaped the production of the court's archival documents. It has also raised awareness of the limits of the information contained in court records as well as doubts about its reliability. As more *sicil* specialists have come to question the dependability of court records for empirically grounded research, so has the methodology used in earlier studies come under increasing criticism. Although researchers have not completely lost the temptation to use the Ottoman court records as bases of empirical information, quantifiable or not, more *sicil* specialists now doubt these documents as reliable sources for research.

The present study harks back to the earlier trend in *sicil*-based research in that it adopts an explicitly empirical, quantitative approach to glean information about legal practice. As we explain in the first chapter, we consider quantitative techniques useful because they allow us to identify patterns and tendencies that may not be visible otherwise and to test our hypotheses with statistical precision. At the same time, our study represents a methodological break with earlier quantitative research on *sicil*s because we use rigorous techniques that are designed specifically for our sources' unique legal, contextual, and linguistic characteristics. In other words, the quantitative approach proposed in this book is informed by the insights of the cultural turn. In this sense, the book aims to combine the strengths of two generations of *sicil*-based scholarship while avoiding the pitfalls that each is susceptible to. The first chapter provides a comprehensive defense of our methodological choices in conversation with existing discussions on the validity of different approaches to Ottoman court records.[3]

A second methodological distinction of our study is its employment of analytical tools associated with the discipline of economics. More specifically, we engage the Law and Economics scholarship, as developed in Western, especially North American, legal research, in our efforts to interpret the information found in Ottoman court records. This scholarship,

[3] We should also point out that quantitative studies of legal topics are exceptionally rare in Ottoman legal research. Most quantitative studies that employ court records focus on socioeconomic themes.

developed in the last century in a collaborative effort by economists, sociologists, and legal researchers, has made important contributions to the analysis of dispute resolution by treating court clients as contextually situated rational actors who choose among legal actions based on the (monetary and non-monetary) costs and benefits of available alternatives. In this study, we explore how a number of key insights developed in the Law and Economics scholarship can help us better conceptualize dispute-resolution processes in the Ottoman context.

Adopting an economic approach to Ottoman legal research is not a conventional preference, given the established tendencies in this scholarship. We have made this choice based on our knowledge regarding the analytical sophistication that the conceptual tools associated with the Law and Economics scholarship has brought to Western legal research and with the confidence that they will likewise yield fresh interpretations in our own field. This choice, however, should not be interpreted as a call to arms against more established approaches in Ottoman legal studies, or as a rejection of older methodologies. On the contrary, a successful application of economic concepts and approaches to Ottoman legal research requires a great deal of dialogue and cross-fertilization across disciplines. For this reason, we not only engage the existing literature on Ottoman legal history, but also learn from anthropological research on modern Muslim societies. We are convinced that an inclusive and multidisciplinary orientation is necessary to successfully apply the Law and Economics methodology to the Ottoman context.

A NOTE ON THE SOURCE BASE AND HISTORICAL CONTEXT

The research for this book is based on a detailed examination of the Kastamonu court's archives from three roughly ten-year periods: 1684–96, 1735–43, and 1781–90. This periodization reflects our objective to identify temporal changes in the court's functions and the ways in which different client groups utilized them. The court's archives contain ample information on judicial and administrative processes in provincial contexts. They also provide plentiful detail on the affairs and interactions of individuals from different segments of the society. While it is not clear how representative the records are in terms of reflecting major trends, tensions, and interactions among our population, a topic we return to in our discussion, the court's archive nevertheless remains one of the most important sources for research on Ottoman social, economic, and legal history. This is especially the case for a small, secluded, provincial location such as Kastamonu, for which we lack the narrative sources that are usually available for larger and more important urban centers. Ottoman court records are also uniquely appropriate for the type of history that we aim to write: One that focuses on common men and women and seeks to characterize inter- and intra-class, -gender, and -confessional relationships through a systematic exploration of large numbers of observations. We provide a detailed discussion of our source base and its contents in Chapter 3.

The town of Kastamonu, located in north-central Anatolia, was a modest-sized town with a majority Turkish-speaking Muslim population during the seventeenth and eighteenth centuries (see Chapter 2). Although the town was the legal and administrative center of the eponymous subprovince (*sancak*), it was relatively isolated, probably due to its distance from principal military and courier road networks (Heywood 1978, 738). As is the case for most small- to medium-sized townships in the Ottoman Empire, we do not know much the social, economic, and political characteristics of Kastamonu for our period. The court records indicate a relatively diverse spectrum of economic activities – including agriculture, animal husbandry, and wool, cotton cloth, and copperware production – though European travelers from the nineteenth century described a lethargic economic life in the town and the wider region. Despite being a small town in the interior, Kastamonu is ideal for this study and is representative of the Ottoman periphery in general, because it does not have any extraordinary characteristics that could distort the analysis and bias the results. Moreover, the town's court records are quite complete for this period, making them an ideal source base for analysis. Finally, recent quantitative research (Ergene and Berker 2008; Ergene and Kaygun 2011, 2012; Ergene, Kaygun, and Coşgel 2013; Coşgel and Ergene 2011, 2012) on the socioeconomic groups of the town provides us with a valuable context in which to interpret our findings.

THE PLAN OF THE BOOK

The book is divided into four parts and ten chapters, excluding the introduction and conclusion. The first part opens with a methodological discussion (Chapter 1), in which we engage the existing debates on various approaches to the Ottoman court records and make a case for the quantitative methodology we adopt in this book. More specifically, we respond to criticisms directed at quantitative studies based on Ottoman court records and explain how a carefully designed quantitative approach can make important contributions to *sicil*-based legal research. Chapter 2 provides deeper contextual information on the town of Kastamonu, its population, and the surrounding region during the seventeenth and eighteenth centuries. Given the limited information on this location in the secondary literature, we make a special effort to utilize the town's probate estate inventories (*muhallefat* or *terekes*) in order to demonstrate how its socioeconomic circumstances changed between the late seventeenth and late eighteenth centuries. Our analysis reveals not only that economic conditions deteriorated, but also that wealth distribution became more polarized. In this chapter we also justify the socioeconomic categories that we use in subsequent sections of the book. The estate inventories play an important role in this effort as well, since we use these sources to demonstrate how different groups of court clients, identified on the basis of honorific titles, religious markers, and family affiliations, among other personal and social indicators, were stacked in terms of their wealth levels and to what extent this economic hierarchy changed over time.

In Chapter 3, which is the first chapter of Part II, we introduce the reader to the court of Kastamonu and its actors. This chapter also offers a detailed discussion of the documentation found in the court's archives and how the contents of this archive changed between the late seventeenth and eighteenth centuries. Although previous research has explored variations in the functions of courts located in different regions (cf. Ergene 2003, Chapter 3), few works (if any) have examined changes in a single court's operations over time. Chapter 3 reveals the temporal nature of the court's functional characteristics by exploring how its records reflect changing socioeconomic circumstances. Chapter 4 explores how various client groups used the court (for contractual arrangements or dispute resolution), whether their legal interactions with others followed certain patterns, and how these patterns varied across decades. Through a diachronic analysis of group behavior and interaction, this chapter demonstrates dissimilar tendencies in court use among clients with distinct gender, religious, and socioeconomic characteristics.

Part III is focused on alternative methods of dispute resolution, i.e., amicable settlements (sing. *sulh*) and litigations (sing. *dava*). In Chapter 5, we survey the legal, historical, and anthropological literature on the topic and discuss from a multidisciplinary perspective how scholars have thus far characterized dispute-resolution processes in various

Muslim-majority settings. Since settlements represent an understudied topic in Ottoman historiography, we make a special effort in this chapter to define its legal bases and scope according to jurisprudential interpretations and archival sources. On the basis of this discussion, we offer in Chapter 6 an economic approach to trial-settlement decisions in the Ottoman context. Inspired by the approaches developed in the Law and Economics scholarship, this framework hypothesizes that the decision to settle or litigate a dispute was influenced by a number of factors, including the relative cost of litigation and settlement, divergent expectations among disputing parties from litigations, and their different stakes in trial results. Chapter 7 uses the empirical information found in Kastamonu court records to test the hypotheses presented in Chapter 6. More specifically, the chapter examines how the characteristics of court clients affected the likelihood that they litigated their dispute rather than settled it amicably and how these patterns changed across case-type and over time.

The final part of the book focuses on litigations. Chapter 8 provides an in-depth discussion of the procedures of litigation and evidentiary standards according to Ottoman jurisprudential sources, legal manuals, and court records. The chapter also offers information on specific tools of litigation, including jurisprudential opinions (sing. *fetva*) and legal representation (*vekalet*). In Chapter 9 we discuss how these rules and tools of litigation, along with the characteristics of litigants, could influence trial results. As in Chapter 7, we offer a formal framework, inspired by the Law and Economics scholarship but adapted to the Ottoman setting, to hypothesize how the trial outcome could depend on variations in the expectations and stakes of litigant groups and differentials in their ability to use evidentiary procedures and tools of litigation. In Chapter 10, we analyze the information on litigations found in the court records of Kastamonu to test the insights and expectations presented in Chapter 9. Our results indicate significant variations in trial performances across litigant groups, revealing, among other things, that the wealthy and privileged litigants, presumably more skilled in estimating the quality of their suits and informed about legal procedures, tended to perform better against their poorer and otherwise underprivileged counterparts. In a fashion generally consistent with the insights developed by the Law and Economics scholarship, the findings of Chapter 10 demonstrate that strategic choices and differential ability in court use influenced how litigant groups fared in the arena of the court.

EVOLUTION OF THE PROJECT AND PREVIOUS WORK

This book has been long in the making. Boğaç Ergene's exploration of the Kastamonu court records pertaining to many topics studied in this book goes back to the early 2000s (Ergene 2002, 2003, 2004, 2005, 2008, 2010). The two data sets that serve as the empirical foundation of the book, one based on probate estate inventories and the other on different types of legal interactions, are products of Ergene's long-held research interest in the Kastamonu *sicil*s. The construction of these data sets, which took years, constituted the most labor-intensive and time-consuming phase of the process that generated this book. Ergene's earlier publications with multiple collaborators explored the probate estate inventories from different angles, including economic stratification, long-term wealth accumulation and distribution, and intergenerational mobility patters in Kastamonu (Ergene and Berker 2008; Ergene and Kaygun 2011, 2012; Ergene, Kaygun, and Coşgel 2013; Coşgel and Ergene 2011, 2012). These studies provide the conceptual and analytical foundations of the socio-economic categorizations based on gender, honorific titles, religious markers and family associations used in this book.

Metin Coşgel is an economist and economic historian, and has a long-standing interest in Ottoman history. In earlier work in this field, he studied the Ottoman system of taxation, tax collection, and revenue allocation (Coşgel 2004, 2005, 2006; Coşgel and Miceli 2005, 2009). More recently, he has worked on the political economy of various Ottoman policies and institutions, such as the fiscal regime, political legitimacy, technology adoption, and law enforcement (Coşgel, Miceli, and Ahmed 2009; Coşgel 2011, 2015; Coşgel, Etkes, and Miceli 2011; Coşgel, Miceli, and Rubin 2012a, 2012b; Coşgel, Ergene, Etkes, and Miceli 2013). He was among the first to utilize the Law and Economics framework in the Ottoman context in studies that explored the relationships between Ottoman legal systems, fiscal institutions, and economic development. Based on the data sets used in this book and the socio-economic categorizations Ergene and his collaborators introduced in earlier publications, Coşgel and Ergene have produced three articles (2014a, 2014b, and 2014c). In the present book we build on the contributions of these articles and provide more in-depth analyses of the information found in the court records.[4]

[4] Author names are listed alphabetically on the cover.

Finally, we should say a few words about *how* the book was written. This book is the result of a collaboration between an Ottoman socio-legal historian with economic interests and an economist with experience in legal and historical research. The process that produced the book involved extended discussions between the two on the nature of their sources, how they should be interpreted, and the most appropriate means to explore them. Sometimes tension-filled, this process of negotiation led the researchers to continually reconsider their respective understandings of Ottoman legal processes and client interactions in the court. It also forced them to see their material from different perspectives and accommodate scholarly conventions that they did not initially identify with.

As in other humanities and social science fields, calls for multidisciplinary approaches are common in Ottoman studies. What usually remains undisclosed in such calls is how arduous such efforts can be, especially in fields that resist multidisciplinary exploration. Ottoman legal history is one such field. It is rare for researchers with different specializations to work together, in part because of the relative inaccessibility of the legal sources and also because of the time and energy required to master them. At the same time, we believe that the present study exemplifies what such efforts can accomplish. We say so not because we consider the book to be the best socio-legal exploration of Ottoman court records, but because we know from experience that it represents something more than the sum of what each of us could have accomplished on our own. Ultimately, this is why collaborative and multidisciplinary efforts, as tricky and arduous as they can be, can prove valuable. Collaboration among researchers from different disciplines has the potential to stimulate a productive, critical conversation among scholars with dissimilar skill-sets, which is rare in Ottoman history-writing. It is our hope that the type of cooperation and conversation this book represents will become more common in the future.

PART ONE

METHODOLOGY AND BACKGROUND

1

Quantitative Approaches in Research on Ottoman Legal Practice

Our book represents a primarily (though not exclusively) economic and quantitative exploration of Ottoman legal practices based on the court records (sing. *sicil*) of eighteenth-century Kastamonu. We will have opportunities in the rest of this book (specifically, in Parts III and IV) to explain our economic approach to Ottoman legal practice. Here, we discuss why a quantitative orientation toward the court records, aided by non-quantitative approaches and tools of analysis, may be a rewarding one. We accomplish this task first by engaging with existing debates over the best way to analyze Ottoman court records, providing a (belated) response to the arguments against quantitative methodologies. Second, we suggest, with the help of ideas proposed by some of the leading representatives and defenders of quantitative history, how a quantitative orientation may benefit legal historiography in the Ottoman context.

HOW TO STUDY OTTOMAN COURT RECORDS: A METHODOLOGICAL DISCUSSION

The documents housed in court archives reflect the many functions served by courts in the Ottoman Empire. As attested by previous research, Ottoman courts did not function solely as arenas of litigation. They also operated as public notaries and court officials, in particular the *kadı*s (or, in their absence, *naib*s, the deputy judges) held administrative responsibilities within their jurisdictions. Thus, in addition to hearing and resolving disputes, court officials recorded contractual agreements in the court ledgers, appraised and divided estates among heirs, received and conveyed government orders to the local populace, supervised the assessment and collection of local taxes, and participated in provincial administrative and decision-making processes alongside other government functionaries. The content of court archives ranges from litigation summaries to settlement extracts to contractual arrangements, from probate estate inventories to tax records to imperial orders.

Interest in Ottoman court records is not new. Since the 1960s, historians have used these documents primarily for social and economic research, treating them as, in Iris Agmon's phrase (2004b, 173), "a pool of information." Based on this material, historians have learned valuable information about aspects of the society not directly discernible from other types of sources. Court records have helped shed important light on Ottoman material culture, mercantile and commercial activities, wealth levels and distribution, and provincial administration. More recently, scholars have begun using *sicil*s to explore how the law was interpreted and practiced in different locales and periods, although this legal focus is still less common than socioeconomic research.

Despite the varied methodological approaches to court records employed in such works, we lack a fully developed critical literature on the relative merits of these methodologies. Given the fact that the court records contain millions of documents on every aspect of Ottoman life for virtually every period and location in the Empire, it is essential for Ottoman *sicil* researchers to think carefully about how they explore this very rich source base. This is what we aim to accomplish in this chapter: We aim to contribute to existing methodological deliberations by engaging the ideas of those few colleagues who have made important observations on the topic, which remain influential and widely acknowledged in *sicil*-based research.

In a 1996 review of Colette Establet and Jean-Paul Pascual's quantitative analysis of Damascene estate inventories (1994), Zouhair Ghazzal appears to have been the first to raise the question of how to study the material found in *sicil*s. Ghazzal's later correspondence with André Raymond (1998) in the pages of the *International Journal of Middle East Studies* helped him clarify a number of his original assertions, in particular, his criticism of quantitative approaches. It is, however, Dror Ze'evi who, in an article published in 1998, offered the first comprehensive and systematic discussion of alternative research orientations used by *sicil* researchers. Later, Iris Agmon would take on the topic in multiple studies (2004b, 2006; Agmon and Shahar 2008) and make a number of critical observations. Ghazzal would return to the issue in his 2007 book, in part to reassert and elaborate on some of his original arguments. In what follows, we critically engage the claims in these works regarding quantitative techniques in the study of Ottoman court records.

Although Zouhair Ghazzal's review of Establet and Pascual's book came first, we begin our discussion with a treatment of Dror Ze'evi's article, which remains one of the most-cited studies in the scholarship on Ottoman court records due to its explicitly methodological orientation, and continues to shape how researchers approach *sicil*s as a historical source. According to Ze'evi (1998, 38), the scholarship on Ottoman court records exemplifies "three basic categories or techniques, according to the methodology used." These are quantitative history, narrative history, and microhistory. Narrative history, as Ze'evi describes this "technique," is a fairly common approach in *sicil* studies and consists of "(1) examining the material in the court ledgers referring to the time-frame defined, (2) finding the strands that can be woven into a story, and (3) attempting to recreate a logical sequence of events" (1998, 45). The potential danger of this approach, according to Ze'evi, is the possibility of generating "a false story or a false chain of events" based on a selective and impressionistic reading of the court's archive, which is treated as a "fact quarry." Often, Ze'evi argues, *sicil* researchers "tend to discover a narrative at an early stage [of their research], sometimes by connecting two or three haphazard examples, and then try to look for evidence to substantiate [their] claim[s], while ignoring the pieces of the puzzle that do not fall into place."[1]

Another approach that Ze'evi identifies is the "microhistorical approach," which he defines as focusing "on a single detailed recorded incident, or on a series of records referring to the same narrowly defined space and time" (1998, 47). However, since microhistorical research entails an examination of detailed documentation on very narrowly defined historical phenomena (such as single event or small numbers of related incidents), court records are not particularly suited for this type of analysis. This is because these documents often lack detailed information on the circumstances surrounding the particular event(s) or the mindsets of the individuals involved (Ze'evi 1998, 48). It is also unusual

[1] Iris Agmon (2004b, 192) considers Ze'evi's description of "narrative history" in *sicil*-based research to be "vague." Although she agrees that it is common for *sicil* researchers to extract small pieces of information from court records to support their narratives in an arbitrary fashion, she considers what Ze'evi calls "narrative history" a rhetorical strategy rather than a methodology.

to find a multitude of documents pertaining to a single event or individual.[2]

Ze'evi's most comprehensive critique of *sicil* studies pertains to the quantitative approach, which historians began to adopt in the 1960s and 1970s. He suggests that "statistical processing of *sijill* data may seem the most natural use to which we can put these sources" (1998, 39). This is because

> the ledgers of the court offer great numbers of ostensibly similar cases over a period of several years. For some types of records – marriages, inheritances, sale deeds – one can easily assemble a voluminous database. What could be more precise than collecting several hundreds of, say, marriage records, and processing the data – the dower paid, the origins of the bride and groom, their social status and so on?

However, Ze'evi questions the reliability of these studies for two main reasons: "First," he suggests

> we have very few clues as to the representativeness of our sample. Seldom do we have any kind of material indicating who came to court and why. . . . The extent to which the sample obtained from court records represents any part of society is an enigma. The kinds of graphs and tables demonstrating social stratification, for example, so popular in quantitative research, might therefore be skewed to such an extent that they only represent the sample itself. (1998, 39–40)

Next, he questions (1998, 40) the ability of researchers with quantitative inclinations to accurately interpret the information found in their sources: "No less problematic for the quantitative mode is the relationship between the written record, the 'reality' it speaks about, and prevailing cultural norms. Does the record give actual prices, real values, or is there some other reasoning that determines these values?" Since the court records are opaque sources at best, which do not readily reveal the practices and thought processes that produced them, they may be deceptive. Indeed, Ze'evi insists (1998, 43), "we know almost nothing about the courtroom strategies that lie behind the *sijill* façade. . . . Without such knowledge we have difficulties interpreting the records, and should not accept them at face value."

Ze'evi admits that many researchers are aware of these problems. In this regard he cites Colette Establet and Jean-Paul Pascual's (1994) use of the probate estate inventories of eighteenth-century Damascus,

[2] According to Agmon (2004b, 194), "full-fledged microhistory was hardly employed in the field" at the time that Ze'evi published his article and since then; for an exception, see Peirce (2003).

a study in which the authors explicitly address the shortcomings of their research, particularly the uncertainty regarding the representativeness of their sample.[3] While Ze'evi calls Establet and Pascual's analysis "meticulous," the fact that their study does not satisfactorily answer the problems that he raised about quantitative research based on court records leads him to question the entire purpose of this endeavor: "[I]f that is the case [that is, if it is not clear whether the sample that Establet and Pascual's study is representative of the entire population] ... what is the point of such meticulous work? A non-statistical, impressionist approach would have served equally as well" (1998, 44; we return to the implications of this quote at the end of the chapter).

As mentioned, Dror Ze'evi was not the first scholar to criticize Establet and Pascual's study for methodological reasons. In 1996, two years before the appearance of Ze'evi's article, Zouhair Ghazzal published a review of Establet and Pascual's work, in which he criticized the authors for failing to properly contextualize the estate inventories (as found in the court records), which overlaps with Ze'evi's second, more epistemological criticism directed at quantitative research:

> Having bypassed the textual analysis of individual documents, Establet and Pascual create an enormous problem of contextualization of all their material: Each fact is first torn from its original source document (the "context"), then assigned as a variable to a data-base field, and finally associated within a broader statistical pattern or regularity. In such an approach, it is the broader statistical regularity rather than the document itself that creates the context for the fact. (1996, 432)

Ze'evi and Ghazzal's criticisms should be seen as related to what Agmon has called the "cultural turn" in *sicil* studies since the mid-1990s (Agmon 2004b, *passim*; 2006, 32), which, under the influence of the deconstructionist trends in the 1970s and 1980s (Agmon 2004b, 180), aimed to "turn court records themselves into an object of historical investigation, both as a means for a better understanding of the societies that produced them, and as a result of the understanding that court records are cultural products of these societies" (Agmon 2004b, 191). This approach, popularized by those who favor subjecting court documents to textual analysis and problematizing the processes that produced them, refuses to treat the court records as transparent windows to the past, taking them instead as social, political,

[3] Establet and Pascual's book (1994) examines about 600 probate estate inventories from late seventeenth- and early eighteenth-century Damascus to understand economic characteristics of the urban population in one early-modern Ottoman community.

and legal artifacts that need to be understood in their own terms and contexts.

We find nothing objectionable about demanding a contextually sensitive approach to the Ottoman court, its operations, and records. In fact, we believe that such efforts are bound to produce better, more historically grounded analyses of the material in court records. Nevertheless, we also feel obliged to raise a few points in regards to Ze'evi and Ghazzal's critical comments on quantitative approaches since they have become influential in the wake of the "cultural turn" in *sicil*-based research. In what follows, we first provide methodological responses to Ze'evi and Ghazzal's criticisms and then discuss how a quantitative approach can contribute to Ottoman legal history-writing.

IN DEFENSE OF QUANTITATIVE HISTORY BASED ON SICILS

The task of deciphering "reality" from the written record is a significant problem for *sicil* researchers since Ottoman court records are notoriously terse and formulaic in their descriptions of the court's actions and court clients' affairs. In this sense it is difficult to fault Ze'evi for pointing out the discrepancies between anthropological and *sicil*-based representations of legal practice. However, it is curious for Ze'evi to raise this point in his critique of quantitative research, as if it were only quantitative analysis that has the potential to be distorted by the limitations of the source base. To be clear, all methodologies (including narrative and microhistorical approaches) are vulnerable to this problem and there is no easy way to avoid it. *Sicil* researchers must constantly revisit their assumptions and question their own readings of the court records. As Ze'evi suggests, a comparative and cross-disciplinary orientation might help them to develop an alternative, initially counterintuitive interpretation of the sources, and would depend on to their becoming familiar with scholarship beyond the Ottoman context on legal phenomena and the human interaction that surrounds it. And yet the problem that needs to be tackled and resolved by *all* scholars pursuing *sicil*-based research may have little to do with the methodological choices associated with quantitative analysis.

True, Ze'evi's complaints about the representativeness of the samples used by quantitative scholars are relevant to the type of research they conduct. However, his objections in this regard do not constitute so much a critique of quantitative history as a research orientation per se as they do a critique of poor quantitative history-writing. One does not have to be a proponent of textual analysis to complain about sample representativeness or to question to what extent a dataset (e.g., one based on the estate inventories that Pascual and Establet study) can act as a proxy for the phenomenon (e.g., wealth levels at times of death) that the historian claims it stands for. In fact, these two often constitute the most common topics of discussion and disagreement among quantitative researchers.

However, when such researchers deliberate on these topics, they often discuss them with reference to *specific* studies and/or findings. They debate whether a specific quantitative study has produced sound results and/or plausible conclusions. They question whether particular calculations are likely to misrepresent the "reality" that they try to approximate. They wonder how such problems influence their conclusions, and consider the best ways to remedy them. It is such difficult, nitty-gritty technical work that requires quantitative expertise that truly improves the researchers' collective understanding of their resources and the historical implications of their research.

On the other hand, by attributing shortcomings to an entire genre of research ("quantitative history based on Ottoman court records"), rather than specific examples of it, Ze'evi shirks his responsibility to approach the topic constructively – that is, by carefully engaging individual studies on their own terms, by telling his readers why and to what extent their results may be defective, and by making suggestions for improving or correcting them. Is it the case that *all* quantitative studies based on court records are susceptible to the problem of representativeness? Given the large corpus of such studies, it is curious that the only work other than Establet and Pascual's book that Ze'evi (1998, 40, fn. 12) explicitly identifies as flawed is a short and self-consciously tentative book chapter by Judith Tucker (1991), in which the author makes observations on marriage patterns in eighteenth- and nineteenth-century Nablus, based on 107 marriage registrations as found in nine *sicil* registers spanning about 65 years.[4]

[4] One wonders, for example, what Ze'evi has to say about Ronald Jennings' largely quantitative study on Ottoman women (1975), which Ze'evi himself cites at one point in his article (1998, 36, fn. 2). Jennings' study examines more than 10,000 entries from 12 court ledgers of Kayseri that cover about 25 years from 1600 to 1625. Within this sample, Jennings identifies about 1,800 entries that demonstrate the multiple ways in which women participated in court proceedings, and subjects them to detailed statistical analysis. This is quite a large sample for an urban center with a population of about 20,000 individuals in the early seventeenth century. In addition, Jennings offers in his discussion valuable clues about the contents and shortcomings of the court records, allowing the reader to reach her own conclusions about their representativeness. Finally, the analysis of the material in Kayseri court ledgers is complemented by Jennings' observations on

Moving on to the second (epistemological) critique of quantitative research based on *sicil*s, we find in Ghazzal's objections a more articulate justification of the doubts regarding the credibility of quantitative history. According to Ghazzal, as he explains in his response to André Raymond's rebuttal of his original review,[5] the main problem with subjecting estate inventories (and, by extension, other types of court records) to a quantitative analysis is that the economic and/or demographic orientations associated with this type of research are inherently inappropriate for these sources:

Establet and Pascual confront each document with an a priori agenda and with categories that did not emerge from a questioning of probate records. Thus, for example, *tarikāt* [pl. for *tereke*; probate estate inventories that Pascual and Establet explore] records were obviously not drafted by judges and their scribes in order to keep track of currency fluctuations, or the age of deceased individuals, or their sex and occupation for that matter. Our two historians decide on an a priori basis and in a line of reasoning *exterior* to the documents themselves that such questions and statistical categories are essential for an understanding of these societies. (emphasis in original,1998, 474)

Instead, Ghazzal argues, "[w]hat is badly needed is a concept of 'political economy' for a 'non-disciplinary' society in which kinship (*qarāba*) and socio-professional and religious groupings (*ṭawā'if*) are crucial, but such an enterprise could not be done properly without massive recourse to the *fiqh* [jurisprudence] literature for 'property' (*mulkiyya*), 'money' (*māl*), 'value' (*qīma*), and other such concepts" (Ghazzal 1996, 432; cf. Agmon and Shahar 2008, 13). Ghazzal provides a more comprehensive discussion of this topic in his recent book, *The Grammars of Adjudication* (2007). Here as well, Ghazzal accuses (2007, 4) the existing literature on Ottoman socioeconomic history of being anachronistic:

It is generally assumed that a legal system operates in conjunction with a socioeconomic one. Yet ... the encounter with an "economic" sphere as such is ... problematic. In fact, and this should come as no surprise, there were no

women's involvement in legal processes in other urban centers in Anatolia (Amasya, Karaman, and Trabzon) during the same period, which is invaluable in documenting contextual variations. While it is possible to doubt some of the findings and conclusions Jennings offers in this article, it is difficult to dismiss the study in its entirety just because it is quantitative.

[5] Ghazzal's criticism of Establet and Pascual's work led André Raymond, a mentor to Establet and Pascual, to respond two years later (1998). In this rebuttal, Raymond attempted to make a case for quantitative methodology in the study of Ottoman court records, without necessarily addressing Ghazzal's methodological concerns (1998). Also see Agmon (2004b, 190) and Agmon and Shahar (2008, 12) for a discussion of this exchange.

autonomous discourses of "economy" or "political economy" in Ottoman societies. If "economics" is a form of social inquiry peculiar to capitalist societies, then it is indeed no surprise that Ottoman societies failed to produce such a literature. Yet, much of contemporary Ottoman historiography has specifically centered on what is labeled as the "socio-economic" without addressing the fundamental issue of a lack of an indigenous literature on the "economic." But considering the impossibility of such a literature, the issue then becomes of whether the "socio-economic" could be addressed on its own, as if endowed with its own rationale and mode of existence.

According to Ghazzal (2007, 4), "not only the 'economic' could not be addressed outside the 'legal,' but both spheres, in turn, cannot co-exist outside the discursive totalities of Ottoman societies." The respective roles of the economic and the legal may be considered only "in conjunction with the religious, moral, political, and hence with the linguistic components" of the society (Ghazzal 2007, 5). This is where the *fiqh* becomes relevant for Ghazzal:

> Considering that Ottoman societies did not produce an economic literature as a form of inquiry, by contrast the *fiqh* as a form of jurisprudential knowledge could pose itself as a domain whose mode of inquiry was total, even encompassing an implicit economic rationale. To begin with ... scholars who worked with the domain of the *fiqh* did so on the basis of a total experience, and with an awareness that both the juridical norms and the customary practices of a particular society could only be formulated within a linguistic framework, one which in effect begins with God's discourse (*khitab*) as a source of normative rules and open for interpretation through the multifaceted enterprise of the *fiqh*. It is within such a framework that property rights and contractual rights would find their place – one where *ex cathedra* rights had a prime importance. But property and contracts notwithstanding, the "economic" would have to be formulated through the juridical norms of the *fiqh* and the process of judicial decision-making.

For the purposes of our book, Ghazzal's points constitute a methodological challenge since they emphasize how quantitative approaches, shaped by assumptions that originate from specific (Western?) academic disciplines (in particular, economics and demography), distort the findings of *sicil* researchers who attempt to utilize them because these assumptions are not appropriate to explore the material in Islamic legal sources. On our part, there are two ways to respond to this challenge. One is to show that the techniques (quantitative or otherwise) that we utilize in this book are based on a thorough understanding of the contents of our sources and the processes that produced them, despite our interest in the research orientation associated with the Law and Economics scholarship. We accomplish this task in subsequent chapters. The second one is to critique Ghazzal's reification of the *fiqh*, which is what we attempt in the rest of this subsection. Before we do so, however, we should point out that such reifications of specific aspects of Islamic culture are common tendencies among Islamic researchers who tend to doubt most attempts of comparative and interdisciplinary scholarship that involve aspects of their fields of study. In this sense the arguments we make below have broader implications than what may initially appear to our readers.

The Grammars of Adjudication, where we find an elaborate characterization of Ghazzal's views on the topic, is a fascinating discussion of Ottoman law that draws on the work of Foucault and Geertz. Because, according to Ghazzal, the *fiqh* discursively and substantively shaped every aspect of life, a "thick description" of most aspects of Ottoman culture, be it legal, economic, or, political, can be produced only by decoding its relationship to jurisprudence. That is, by figuring out how it was constituted by and also came to reflect the norms of the Ottoman *fiqh*. In this sense, according to Ghazzal, the *fiqh* offers a language that should be used to decode the culture because it encompasses its essence.

There is no question that a competent understanding of the legal theory is necessary for a researcher to conduct research based on court records. It is, however, one thing to insist that an adequate understanding of the legal terminology and concepts is necessary for a competent use of historical documents, which is consistent with the analysis presented in this book; it is another to suggest the transcendent influence of the *fiqh* on other aspects of Islamic life and civilization, or to claim that only a primarily *fiqh*-based approach to court records can provide an accurate understanding of *all* layers of their historical meaning. A call for a methodology that is not "exterior to the documents" imagines the constitutive power of the *fiqh* as such, conceives of an Islamic "economy" or "politics" or "sociology" that is sui generis, in the way that certain interpretations of Foucault and Geertz's thought characterize societal and historical structures largely as embodiments of discursive practices and cultural meanings. It is unfortunate that Ghazzal does not elaborate on the unique characteristics of Ottoman economic thinking or demonstrate precisely and empirically how the researchers that he criticizes as being uninformed misunderstand or mischaracterize it.

It is also unclear how one can *prove* that legal/economic/political knowledge and practice were solely or even mostly a product of jurisprudence. Nor does Ghazzal elaborate on the limits of this relationship. In the case of court-prepared probate estate inventories, what about contextual variations in the legal and economic concepts that Ghazzal might be unaware of? What about the role of customary practices that are not found in classical or contemporary *fiqh* works or that have not been incorporated into (or tamed by) the formal language of the *fiqh*? What about other unaccounted, extra-judicial factors that may have influenced the court's division of estates?

How can one be certain of the relationship between the *fiqh* and historical documents without answers to such questions? Also at issue are the historian's own preferences and subjectivities, and how arbitrary one's attempts to attribute meaning to traces of the past may be. Presumably, for Ghazzal, historians who truly deserve this label possess an intimate knowledge of their sources, which guides them to a "correct" understanding of the documents and leads them to ask wise questions. But how does one come to possess this intimate knowledge? Some historians influenced by the cultural turn have implied the existence of an intuitive path to the historical, one whose legitimacy is not necessarily based on the much-derided "objectivity" or "scientific nature" of the approach. For example, Florencia Mallon (1994, 1507) explains how she deals with historical ambiguity and how she acquired historical wisdom as follows:

> I, too, want to touch the pictures of the historical subjects I struggle to retrieve; yet I, too, know that "there is no 'real [subject]' to be found." This is precisely the point. The contradictory attempt to "know" the past, to become acquainted with the human beings who made it, leads us through archival sources that refuse to yield clear pictures. But because the archives provide unique clues about power relations, and about the human, moral, and philosophical quandaries faced by the people who produced them and by the people whose shadows inhabit them, we cannot afford to do without them. In my experience, it is the process itself that keeps us honest: getting one's hands dirty in the archival dust, one's shoes encrusted in the mud of field work; confronting the surprises, ambivalences, and unfair choices of daily life, both our own and those of our "subjects." However poignantly our search is conditioned by the understanding that we will never know for sure, occasionally, just for a moment, someone comes out of the shadows and walks next to us. When, in a flash of interactive dialogue, something is revealed; when, for a brief span, the curtain parts, and I am allowed a partial view of protagonists' motivations and internal conflicts – for me, those are the moments that make the quest worthwhile.

Similarly, Arlette Farge (1989, 9–11) is adamant that one can re-imagine past realities only if she is willing to endure and overcome the capricious nature of archival documents. With patience and perseverance, and after a lot of sifting and sorting, disconnected and often contradictory bits and pieces of information can lead to the identification of general patterns and historical structures and provide answers (if partial) to questions about the past. What is striking in both Mallon and Farge's approach to historical truth is how situated, personal, and remarkably solitary they are. These researchers seem to argue that it is not the "facts" in the archival documents that determine the truth of the past but one's unique, subjective experiences with his or her sources. Reconstructing the past becomes akin to a quest for personal enlightenment, almost in a spiritual sense (it is "revealed" in a "flash of interactive dialogue" says Mallon). The historian in the archive, very much like the Sufi dervish in a cell, suffers (*çile çekmek* in Ottoman Sufi parlance) alone to achieve this enlightenment.[6] In both cases, the reward for the suffering is a glimpse of the past that is more *felt* to be true than actually known.

It is not clear that Ghazzal would characterize his relationship to historical knowledge similarly. However, it is worth noting that Geertz's and Foucault's work, which appear to have deeply influenced Ghazzal's interpretations, have been described by some as almost occult in nature. In particular, Mark Schneider (1993) considered Geertz's interpretive attempts and Foucault's discursive archeology as "enchanting" in the sense that they aimed to reveal the underlying, "sublime" aspects of the culture and, by doing so, represent the latter in intriguing and wondrous ways. In his interpretation of Schneider's work, Michael Saler (2006: 715) suggests that "Clifford Geertz's ambiguous account of 'culture as text,' Michel Foucault's reliance on the mysterious matrix of 'power/knowledge,' … differ little from the explanations offered by seventeenth-century natural philosophers, 'whose investigations sought more to preserve than to dispel enchantment.'" This is partly because, according to Schneider (1993: 23), they resist any effort of empirical verification: "The criterion [that makes enchanting endeavors appealing] is the 'depth' of the reading, not its capacity to survive efforts at verification, and real depth can only be evaluated by those with the broadest and discerning sensibilities."

Relevant to our concerns here are some critical observations made by quantitative historians in the 1980s in response to new trends in humanities scholarship. Theodore Rabb, for example, suggested that the growing influence of anthropological methods and microscopic analyses in historical research had generated "a demand for a different, and more

[6] Farge (1989, 90) suggests that even when the archive appears to "easily deliver what one expects of it, the work is [still] demanding. We must patiently abandon our natural 'sympathy' for what the archive offers us and consider it an adversary to fight; [what the archive offers] is a piece of knowledge that is not there [for us] to annex but one that functions to disrupt [our narrative]; to be able to really know it, you have to unlearn it and not assume you understand it from a first reading" (translation from the original French text).

exclusively empathetic, kind of history" (1983, 595; also see 1981). Rabb called this trend "a flight from materialism" because "comprehension [in this type of research] is thought of as intuitive and rhetorical, not concrete or dependent on rigorous proof" (1983, 595). Similarly, Morgan Kousser, another well-known defender of quantitative approach in historical research, wrote (1984: 140–1) the following about intuitively based historical wisdom generated by approaches that he associates with certain anthropological and historical orientations:

> Can claims that are not falsifiable and that entail no precise falsifiable conclusions, even in principle, really be part of scholarship? . . . While I enjoy speculation and Zen conundrums as much as the next person, I have never been able to understand the basis for the assertion that *verstehen* amounts to more than informed guesses, or to determine clear standards for deciding which historian has "the Force" with him or her . . . I am always a bit wary of calls for historians to be especially attentive to questions of hermeneutics and *mentalité* because of my fear that these slogans mask a desire to relax standards of proof. . . . In fact, because when we enter the jungle of non-quantifiable evidence we must leave such weapons as significance tests and sensitivity analysis behind, we should be particularly on guard – more anxious than at other times to make our assumptions, reasoning processes, and evidence explicit.

Going back to Zouhair Ghazzal's methodological choices, it might be the case that Ghazzal would have no objection to exclusively or predominantly *fiqh*-based economic, political, sociological approaches to or quantitative treatments of Islamic sources. There are two problems with this position, however. First, it is not evident that such approaches and treatments can be developed and until this happens the expectation might be debilitating for researchers who take Ghazzal's position seriously. Second, what if the type of inquiry Ghazzal promotes fails to answer *our* questions? This could be because the sources are not designed to meet our expectations or because their rationale and concepts reflect those of another culture, context, and mind-set. Are we supposed to abandon our research if/when this happens? Can we not force the sources to speak to our own concerns, compel them to answer our questions, as long as we make clear to our audience the choices (in the form of certain assumptions) we are making in this process? What is the worst that can happen if we do this? Is it that our findings and conclusions might be wrong?

Let us emphasize here that the alternative to the mystical quest for historical knowledge is not necessarily a positivist one, fixated on the discovery of the Truth of the past. It can be, however, a dialogic and experimental one, which considers, at least initially, *all* readings of the sources to be provisional, tentative, and subjective. While all these readings may be improved, no reading is *inherently* wrong (although it might be factually so). This approach does not aspire to represent the Truth of the past, but to produce falsifiable propositions by using available sources, which should be subject to scrutiny from future researchers and either (provisionally) confirmed or rejected. In fact, awareness of the limitations of our methods can be productive. If we agree that there can be no single authorized reading of the documents and that the value of our contributions is not based on their supposed Truth-values (but on their ability to further existing conversations on specific topics), we can take liberties in interpreting our documents, such as testing novel categories of analysis that are not immediately or instinctively justified by our sources, and applying relevant methodologies from other fields.

POTENTIAL BENEFITS OF QUANTIFICATION AS A RESEARCH APPROACH

Quantitative historians have been fighting similar battles in other fields for some time. In particular, the debates surrounding the birth of cliometrics in American historiography in the first half of the twentieth century yielded well-known defenses of quantitative analysis. It is not necessary to get into the details of these debates since the literature on the topic is vast and often unnecessarily contentious. However, it would be useful to focus on the general factors that make quantitative approaches valuable to historical inquiry – in our case, Ottoman legal history.

Quantification as a means for verifiable and not-so-obvious generalizations: According to William Aydelotte (1966, 804), "[t]he principal value of quantification for the study of history, stated in the simplest terms, is that it provides a means of verifying general statements." The ability to make verifiable generalizations is especially critical when large numbers of observations are available, since the historian's ability to processes and accurately represent the information found in a large dataset is naturally limited. It is often difficult, and sometimes impossible, for historians to notice the trends, generalities, and relationships in their dataset without the aid of formal statistical techniques. Even simple summary statistics, such as mean, median, and mode, can help identify historical tendencies and inclinations that might not be clear otherwise. Regression analysis provides the ability to hold other factors constant in our attempts to identify the nature of the relationship between two specific variables, which is especially useful in cases where dependent variables are influenced by a large number of factors. Thus, quantification offers a "way of seeing," in John Berger's words, information that otherwise remains invisible.

Quantitative techniques are also valuable because they permit historians to assess the relative strength of their generalizations. For example, the standard deviation, a simple statistic that displays the variability in a particular population, enables the researcher to determine how reliable an average should be deemed as a generalization in regard to a particular population. An average is a better summary statistic for a population that has a small standard deviation than for one with a large standard deviation, which is why, in the latter case, it should perhaps be avoided or accompanied by other summary statistics, such as mode and/or median.

For both of these reasons, assertions based on even simple quantitative techniques can help bolster many impressionistic observations that many historians rely on. "To an uncritical audience several concrete illustrations may carry more conviction than a statistical table. Yet to support an argument by only a few examples, though it may be a persuasive rhetorical device, is not logically adequate" (Aydelotte 1966, 805). Here, it is worth remembering Dror Ze'evi's suggestion that a quantitative study that cannot be unequivocally proven to be representative is not worth the time researchers invest in it: "A non-statistical, impressionist approach would have served [the historian] equally as well" (Ze'evi 1998, 44). If, however, a quantitative methodology can unearth otherwise invisible tendencies in the sources, it should be considered valuable, even if it is not clear that it will generate results that are representative. Although we might doubt the representativeness of a sample, a quantitative analysis of this data set might "yield suggestions or lead to fresh hypotheses that can be [further] tested" (Aydelotte 1966, 820).

Quantification as a means for hypothesis-testing: One particularly underutilized aspect of quantitative approaches in the Ottoman context is its use in hypothesis-testing (Rabb 1983; Aydelotte 1966, 805–6). "Hypothesis-testing" refers to the historian's ability to (1) statistically identify the impact of specific factors on a combined result; and, based on this ability, (2) ask and provide reasonable answers to counter-factual questions, such as how a specific outcome would be affected if one or more of the factors suspected to have influenced that outcome were eliminated. Regression analyses and the accompanying t- and F-tests, which help researchers to determine whether a single variable or a group of variables has a statistically significant impact on an outcome, are instrumental to this type of orientation.

A good example of this approach can be found in Robert Fogel's well-known work on the economic importance of railroads on the nineteenth-century American economy (1964). Arguing against the then historiographic orthodoxy that American economic growth in the second half of the nineteenth century was largely due to the spread of railroads that tied together different corners of the continent, Fogel was able to suggest how the American economy would have performed if railroads had not been invented. Under a number of historically realistic assumptions, Fogel demonstrated that in the absence of the railroads, the overall increase in transportation costs would have been about 3 percent of the American GDP in the 1890s, indicating that railroads were not indispensable to economic performance.[7]

Simulation of alternative realities is not an endeavor many historians are keen on pursuing and model/hypothesis-testing has been criticized as a historical approach in the debates between cliometricians and their opponents. However, asking "what if" is not particularly daring or revolutionary in historical scholarship and historians, whether quantitative or not, engage in this kind of task, often implicitly, when they assess why and how a particular factor contributed to a particular incident. The attempts of quantitative historians in this regard represent merely a formalization of such endeavors, one in which alternative models of historical reasoning/explanation are explicitly formulated, the underlying assumptions in each of these models are clearly stated, and then hypothetical scenarios are subjected to empirical verification so far as this is possible (Fogel and Elton 1983, 51). Thus, statistical hypothesis-testing provides researchers a tool that allows them to explore historical events and their consequences in an informed and systematic manner.

Quantification as a force for common language across disciplines: According to Pat Hudson (2000, 14), "numbers, graphs, and formulae should be regarded first and foremost as strategies of communication. They are designed to convey information or results in a standardized form

[7] Similarly, in a rare study in the Ottoman context, researchers were able to demonstrate that although the wealth levels of the upper classes remained flat and possibly declined in eighteenth-century northern Anatolia, structural economic circumstances would have allowed wealth accumulation among the wealthy in the absence of economic shocks associated with wars, weather patterns, and the post-1767 financial crisis (Ergene, Kaygun, and Coşgel 2013).

which can be understood across distances of culture and class where face to face trust and confidence are difficult to establish by other means." Quantitative approaches force researchers to adopt a language – the language of statistics – that makes information and the procedures followed to generate it accessible beyond the confines of a specific field. As such, quantification is a translation of field-specific knowledge and terminology into a widely shared technical and linguistic framework that enhances the possibilities of interdisciplinary communication, collaboration, and criticism.

Take the example of wealth studies in Ottoman contexts based on probate estate inventories (*tereke*s) that have proliferated in the last two decades.[8] The quantitative approaches pursued in this literature served Ottoman historiography in two ways: (1) it forced Ottoman historians to think carefully about how to characterize the contents of *tereke*s as components of wealth, as defined in other fields (in particular European and North American economic history) and the implications of this "translation"; and (2) it forced Ottoman historians to study the quantitative methods employed in similar types of research in other geographic fields and find ways to use them in the Ottoman context. One result of this endeavor has been the opening of a fruitful dialogue between Ottomanists and our counterparts in other fields, who have both offered constructive criticisms and incorporated insights from Ottoman contexts into their own work. Such dialogue has thus widened the scope of comparative scholarship that extends beyond a specific field. Obviously, no translation is perfect, at least not initially. In fact, there might be cases in which translation is impossible. Nevertheless, even in such cases the effort to explain our material and their peculiarities to outsiders in a language shared by all is potentially rewarding, as this effort requires us to think about our sources in ways that have been proven to be productive in other fields.

Before we conclude this section, let us underscore that we do not consider quantitative history to be more equipped to approximate historical Truth-with-a-capital-T than any other methodology. Although quantitative researchers themselves made such assertions at the turn of the twentieth century with reference to the supposedly "objective" and "scientific" nature of quantitative approaches, later generations came to recognize

[8] Examples include Gradeva (2005), Establet and Pascual (1994, 2011), Establet, Pascual, and Raymond (1994), Canbakal and Filiztekin (2013), Ergene and Berker (2009), Coşgel and Ergene (2011, 2012), Ergene, Kaygun, and Coşgel (2013).

how problems related to data sources and often arbitrary choices could affect their results. Nowadays, when quantitative researchers discuss the notion of objectivity, they do not identify it with the truth of the past, or what Pat Hudson calls "knowledge congruent with real." "Instead," Hudson insists (2000, 40), "objectivity [in new quantitative research] is applied to knowledge which meets criteria of validity and reliability that are held to be as free from bias as possible. It indicates the avoidance of subjectivity by following impartial rules of measurement, observation and experiment."

It is a fact that quantitative researchers (in history and other fields) have become far more self-conscious about their ability to represent the past. Robert Fogel once suggested (Fogel and Elton 1983, 27) that much of the work of quantitative researchers "has been directed to spelling out and formalizing the models implicit in traditional historical narratives and to considering the empirical validity of those models." This is still largely true. As indicated, most discussions and disagreements among the practitioners of quantitative methodologies hover around empirical questions, including whether the models used in specific studies are historically justifiable or whether the assumptions made by individual researchers are realistic. In a field that defines itself as primarily empirical, it is natural that more space is devoted to explaining how certain results are generated than what their historical implications might be.

Yet it is also true that not all historical evidence is quantifiable. In fact, quantitative approaches often force the researcher to focus on select, often limited, aspects of broader historical topics. Thus, the potential advantage of quantitative methodologies is not necessarily that they provide alternative, more reliable answers to important historical questions, but that they offer an ability to approximate greater precision by restricting focus:

> What is attempted in [quantitative] approach is to take more effective advantage of selected parts of evidence: to seize on those parts of the data that can be handled more strictly, by mathematical means, and to subject them to a more refined analysis. The procedure consists in applying close and exact attention to the limited elements of the general problem under consideration that are capable of being handled in this fashion. (Aydelotte et al. 1972, 9)

Consequently, an insistence on quantitative methodology does not mean a disregard for non-quantitative approaches: "The worst of all errors is to assume that either literary evidence by itself or quantitative evidence by itself is sufficient when they are not" (Fogel and Elton 1983, 48). Rather, historians can try to utilize different approaches in a complementary fashion. They should seek ways to produce layered narratives generated by alternative "ways of seeing" in their source materials. It may not be necessary that every researcher be skilled in every historical methodology. It is, however, desirable that dissimilar methodologies be well represented in individual fields to provide alternative and falsifiable approximations of the truth of the past.

There are also various ways to conceptualize collaboration and complementarity between various "ways of seeing." One that immediately comes to mind is employing more than one method of analysis simultaneously to answer particular questions. For example, while understanding the evidentiary procedures followed in litigations requires a textual and legal analysis of court records, one simply needs to count the numbers of litigants who submitted documents to court to figure out how often written records were used in legal hearings. Very often, however, the quantitative methodology needs to be informed by the socio-legal categories and processes revealed in detailed textual and legal analyses of the source material. This is the case if, to give another example, we would like to understand how frequently written evidence was used in court proceedings because not all documents submitted to court were intended or treated as evidence, although few researchers have seemed to pay attention to this fact (Ergene 2004; Chapter 8, this volume). Thus, it makes no sense to assume a mutually exclusive relationship between qualitative and quantitative approaches, especially in a study on Islamic law, which requires a nuanced and sophisticated legal-textual understanding of legal documents.

THE NEED FOR SOPHISTICATED QUANTITATIVE APPROACHES IN THE STUDY OF ISLAMIC/OTTOMAN LEGAL PRACTICE

There is no shame in admitting that quantitative historians who intend to study Islamic law require the services of legal and textually oriented specialists. What about the other side of the equation, however? What might be the contribution of sophisticated quantitative research to the study of Islamic law? After all, scholarly treatments of Islamic law and legal history are not limited to the interpretation of jurisprudential treatises or ideas of past legal experts on different aspects of legal theory. Indeed, some of the most recent and exciting research on Islamic law in the Ottoman context has been socio-legal in nature, seeking to delineate the ways in which the law, legal institutions, and socioeconomic structures interacted and influenced one another. In this sense, the works that constitute this literature belong as much in social and economic history, where quantitative analysis is common, as they do in legal studies.

As a matter of fact, the academic literature on Ottoman courts of law and legal practices is filled with generalizations that may be subject to quantitative verification. For example, many historians have analyzed the operations of the courts and how these influenced and/or reflected the balance of power among different social, economic, religious, and gender groups in different Ottoman communities. In this regard, most students of Ottoman court records have emphasized the relative impartiality of the courts' operations. For example, Ronald Jennings observed in multiple influential publications the "fair, speedy justice" (1975, 96) of the court in sixteenth- and seventeenth-century Anatolia, which protected women, children, the poor, and non-Muslims against the rich and powerful (1978a, 1978b). Likewise, Abraham Marcus (1989, 112) observed for eighteenth-century Aleppo that it was not only common for government officials, members of distinguished families, religious scholars, and descendants of Muhammad (*ashraf*) to lose cases against their social inferiors, but that Christians and Jews often prevailed over Muslims. More recently, Reem Meshal (2010, 212) has suggested that the courts in Egypt operated as "as equitable venues where 'a woman or a slave' could win rulings against *amir*s [military-administrative authorities] ... where *dhimmi*s [non-Muslims] preferred to have their cases heard." There are many other examples (see, for instance, Hanna 1995; Gerber 1994; İslamoğlu-İnan 1994).[9]

Although the above characterization of the Ottoman court is still prevalent, the last decade or so has also witnessed the emergence of studies that have pointed out the power differentials inherent in the legal system. For example, Fatma Müge Göçek (2005, 56) has suggested in an article on eighteenth-century Galata (in İstanbul) that the court "privileged the societal status of male Muslims over non-Muslim males, and female Muslims over non-Muslim females." Leslie Peirce has argued that in

[9] According to many historians, the relative fairness of the court's operations served to bolster the political and administrative legitimacy of the Ottoman government: The early-modern court, which functioned almost as a semi-independent branch of the government, was instrumental in keeping the provincial power-holders and non-judiciary state functionaries in check and limiting their exploitative tendencies. By guaranteeing the welfare of the common men and women the legal system ensured their faith in the legitimacy of the Ottoman system of government (İnalcık 1986, 1988a; Barkey 1996, 2008; Cohen 1994; Gerber 1988, 1994; İslamoğlu-İnan 1994).

sixteenth-century Aintab, "the law was not a level playing field" (2003, 6) for all socioeconomic, religious, ethnic, and gender groups, and "it was not an ideal of the premodern Ottoman legal system that its justice be blind" (2003: 143). More recently, Fariba Zarinebaf (2010, 160) has argued that "social status, religion, and gender were important factors in gaining better access to judicial authorities."[10]

Collectively, these works have significantly enhanced our understanding of the court's operations, its place in Ottoman society, and legal interactions among court clients. That being said, the claims they make regarding the court and its impact on socioeconomic relationships – however varied or contradictory – are often based on impressions. One wonders how it is possible to assess the "fairness" of a court or its social, political, and ideological inclinations without subjecting the court records to a systematic analysis in order to answer questions such as the following: Who went to court? How often? For what purpose? Whom did these parties encounter or engage with as allies and adversaries? Who won and lost litigations? What type of litigations? And, how might these patterns have changed over time?

In the context of our discussion, what should be considered curious is not our insistence that studies on legal practice utilize reliable and sophisticated quantitative analysis when necessary and possible, but that most such research in our field does not attempt to do this. A sound quantitative methodology has much to contribute to existing scholarship on Ottoman courts and their interaction with the society in which they functioned. Very recently, a handful of articles have appeared that attempt to develop and apply sophisticated quantitative techniques, with tantalizing results (Kuran and Lustig 2012; Coşgel and Ergene 2014a, 2014b, 2014c), although they remain exceptions in the field. This book represents the first book-length effort to bring quantitative analysis to Ottoman legal research.

[10] For a more systematic analysis of the ways in which the Ottoman legal system and its documents reproduced social (in particular, gender and religious) hierarchies in early modern Syria, see Najwa al-Qattan's pioneering work (1996, 1999).

2

Kastamonu: The Town and Its People

The present chapter serves two functions. First, it provides background information on Kastamonu during the eighteenth century. Specifically, it discusses the economic characteristics of the town and how the local population may have been affected by the major transformations that the empire experienced during this period. Second, the chapter introduces and justifies the socioeconomic categories of analysis used in the rest of the book. Due to the absence of narrative sources, socioeconomic divisions within Kastamonu before the nineteenth century are not well documented compared to larger urban centers such as İstanbul, Damascus, and Cairo. Thus, much of what we know about the region comes from archival material, although the disappearance of tax registers (*tahrir defterleri*) after the sixteenth century makes the task of finding relevant information in official sources particularly difficult for the seventeenth and eighteenth centuries.[1] Consequently, a large portion of our discussion is based on sporadic information found in the court records, especially, if not exclusively, the probate estate inventories, which provide valuable clues about socioeconomic trends and divisions in eighteenth-century Kastamonu.

1 The *tahrir*s are official surveys that provide detailed information on tax-payers and taxable resources in numerous locales in the empire, making it possible to study the economic and social history of Ottoman lands in the fifteenth and sixteenth centuries. For a discussion of the literature on these sources and a sophisticated economic analysis of the information found in them, see Coşgel (2004).

KASTAMONU IN THE EIGHTEENTH CENTURY

Location, Administrative Status, and Population

In the Ottoman provincial administrative system before the nineteenth century, provinces (*eyalet*) were divided into subprovinces (*sancak*), which were divided into multiple judicial districts or "judgeships" (*kaza*). The town of Kastamonu, along with the adjacent villages and rural settlements, constituted the district of Kastamonu, which was the administrative center of the eponymous subprovince, one of the fourteen that constituted the province of Anatolia (Maden 2012, 19). The province of Anatolia was administered by the governor (*beylerbeyi* or *vali*)[2] or his representatives. In the subprovinces, subgovernors (sing. *sancakbeyi*) or their representatives were in command.[3] *Kaza*s were administered by the kadıs or, often in the seventeenth and eighteenth centuries, their representatives (*naib*s). The Kastamonu subprovince was located in north-central Anatolia on the Black Sea coast. The town, however, was located in the interior, demarcated in the north by the İsfendiyar (Küre) Mountains, which hugged the coastline, and by the Ilgaz Mountains in the south. The Gök River (Gökırmak in Turkish), one of the branches of the Red River (Kızılırmak in Turkish) ran through the town, as it does today, and supplied the town's and the surrounding region's water needs.

In principle, the subgovernor (or his representative) was personally responsible for managing the military, fiscal, and administrative affairs of the subprovince with the help of other officials, including the kadı, as

[2] Mehmet İpşirli (1992, 69) has stated that the title "*vali*" became common from the seventeenth century onward.

[3] According to İpşirli (1992, 71), two horse-tailed (*iki tuğlu*) *beylerbeyi*s were often appointed to subprovinces after 1640 because the empire lacked the adequate number of provinces to sustain the inflated numbers of *beylerlerbeyi*s and *vizier*s at that time. *Sicill-i Osmani* indicates that the Kastamonu subprovince was occasionally granted to *beylerbeyi*s. For example, Boynueğri Durak Mehmed Paşa was appointed as Kastamonu *beylerbeyi*, presumably in the early 1640s (Mehmed Süreyya 1996, vol. 2, 422). Seyyid Ahmed Paşa was brought to this position in 1689 (Mehmed Süreyya 1996, vol. 1, 220), perhaps as a reward for commanding troops made up of *seyyid*s (descendants of Muhammad) in battle (Mehmed Süreyya 1996, vol. 5, 1503). İbrahim Paşa was made Kastamonu *beylerbeyi* in 1726/27 (Mehmed Süreyya 1996, vol. 3, 770). *Sicill-i Osmani* also contains references to Kastamonu "*vali*s." For example, Cerrah Kasım Paşa (in 1670), Gelibolulu Bahri Mehmed Paşa (in 1687), and Eyüplü Hasan Paşa (in 1703) were appointed as "*valis*" to Kastamonu (Mehmed Süreyya 1996, vol. 3, 875; vol. 2, 353 and 638). Nil Tekgül (2012, 5) has suggested that the titles of provincial and sub-provincial governors changed respectively to *eyalet mutasarrıfı* and *sancak mutasarrıfı* in the late eighteenth and early nineteenth centuries.

we will see. In 1727, revenues of the *sancak* constituted a *has* grant, typically valued in excess of 100,000 *akçe*s per year and assigned for life (*ber vech-i malikane*) (Başar 1997, 70). According to the court records, the subprovince could also be assigned as an *arpalık*[4] to high-ranking government officials. These individuals did not often assume their official responsibilities personally, but authorized agents (*mütesellim*) to supervise the affairs of the subprovince and collect the revenues due to them. Ergene (2003, 14) has suggested that the revenues of Kastamonu began to be assigned as a life-term tax-farm (*malikane mukata'a*) from the first half of the eighteenth century onward, sometimes to two or more individuals. It is possible that the tax-farmers subcontracted the subprovince's revenues to *mütesellim*s with local connections, although this is more likely to have happened in the second half of the eighteenth century.[5]

In the eighteenth century, the number of districts comprising the subprovince varied between 32 and 39 (Ergene 2003, 20; McGowan 1981, 119).[6] As is the case for many other locations during this time, the demographic trends of the region are not clear. Using available tax registers, Suraiya Faroqhi has estimated the population of the town of Kastamonu to be between 9,000 and 11,000 by the end of the sixteenth century (cited in Behar 1996, 7). Through a different set of calculations based on the same sources, Ahmet Kankal (2004, 59) has arrived at a figure of over 10,000 for the same period. Unfortunately, no tax registers are available for the seventeenth and eighteenth centuries, although historians agree that the populations of Anatolia and the Balkans generally declined during the seventeenth century (Özel 2004; McGowan 1981; White 2011). According to information found in Kastamonu court records, the number of *avarız* households for both the subprovince and district of Kastamonu was reduced by half at the turn of the eighteenth century.[7] While a tax record from 1685 gives the number of district and

[4] Literally, "fodder money." Metin Kunt (1983, 87) suggests that beginning in the early seventeenth century, *arpalık*s were assigned to out-of-office provincial governors to keep them in funds while they waited for a province appointment befitting their rank.

[5] Yaşar Yücel (1970) suggested that *mütesellim*s in Anatolia were usually chosen from local families in the eighteenth century. According to Ergene (2003, 13), however, those in Kastamonu came from outside the subprovince in the first half of the eighteenth century and were usually household members of those to whom the subprovince was assigned.

[6] Fahri Maden (2012, 20), however, gives the number of districts as high as forty-nine in the late eighteenth century.

[7] *Avarız* was initially an irregular tax collected to support military campaigns; to maintain the post system, the imperial kitchens, or the navy; to guard mountain passes; and to uphold bridges, roads, and waterworks. Beginning in the late sixteenth century, it was

subprovince *avarız* households as 525 and 4,210 respectively, another record from 1735 gives them as 268 and 2,042 (Ergene 2003, 20). It is not clear if the variations in the number of *avarız* households reflect a scribal error, a fiscal/administrative reorganization that involved a change in the number of real households that *avarız* households corresponded to, or a catastrophic decline. However, during the eighteenth century these numbers did not change much. On the other hand, while there were forty-five quarters and seventy-two villages in the district in 1684, in 1741 there were forty-one quarters and seventy-seven villages, and in 1790 there were forty-one quarters and seventy-five villages.[8]

Based on a number of surveys found in the court records, Burhan Şahin (2009, 5) puts the population of the town at around 11,000 in the early eighteenth century. According to John Kinneir, it was around 12,000 in 1814, of which 300 families were Greek and 40 families were Armenian (1818, 282).[9] The first Ottoman census of 1831 gives the male population of the district as 14,861, which implies a total population of about 29,700 (Şahin 2009, 5; Maden 2007, 163; Behar 1996, 25). Assuming that the urban population constituted about 22 to 26 percent of the census result (based on the proportions observed in fifteenth- and sixteenth-century tax registers), Kankal (2004, 78) has suggested that the town population ranged between 8,500 and 10,000 people in the early nineteenth century.[10] Finally, according to Charles Issawi (cited in Behar 1996, 33),

regularized and began to be collected annually in cash (McGowan 1981, 105–14). The amount of *avarız* tax levied on a particular locality was determined according to the number of *avarız* households in that area. Each *avarız* household consisted of a certain number of real households. However, the exact proportion of these units varied from one place to another. Each *avarız* household could comprise three to fifteen or even more real households, depending on their size and the relative prosperity of the district. Ahmet Kankal (2004, 71) has determined that one particular urban quarter in Kastamonu with eighteen real households was counted as one *avarız* household in the late seventeenth century, although, on average, four real households constituted an *avarız* household in the town.

[8] Maden (2012, 21) gives the number of villages and rural settlements in the district as 115 but, for some reason, he includes in this number the villages that belonged to two other districts (cf. Kankal 2004, 41).

[9] According to William Ainsworth, the town's population was about 48,000 around the 1840s (1842, 82), a figure that Colin Heywood deems exaggerated (1978, 738). Ainsworth also claims that about 160 Greek and 40 Armenian households existed in the city (1842, 82).

[10] Before he makes this calculation, Kankal (2004, 78) adjusts the census result for the district by adding to this figure the results for two other districts, Akkaya and Merküze, which were part of the district in the sixteenth century but not in 1831.

the town's population was around 12,000 in the 1830s, 16,000 in 1890, 20,000 in 1912, and 15,000 in 1927.

Admittedly, the demographic information available for Kastamonu does not reveal much about the fluctuations over the course of more than 200 years. But given the observations in the preceding paragraphs we may assume that the population of the town remained relatively stable during the eighteenth century.[11] A comparison of the available demographic information for Kastamonu with that of other locations (see Table 2.1) indicates that the town was a small- to medium-sized urban center by Anatolian and Balkan standards.

Economic Activities

Agriculture and animal husbandry were prevalent in the region despite the relatively rugged and mountainous landscape (Maden 2012, 35–6; Kankal 2004, 184–6). Wheat and barley growing dominated the agricultural economy. Rice, chickpea, onion, garlic, and fruit (in particular, apple, pear, grape, fig, and walnut) production was also widespread. As in most locations in Anatolia, small peasant families dominated agricultural production, but urban-dwellers also owned orchards and had access to agricultural fields (Kankal 2004, 195). Horse, mule, and donkey breeding were widespread, as was the raising of sheep, goats, cows, and buffalo (Maden 2012, 36–8; Kankal 2004, 193–5). Abundant forests in the region allowed the development of a significant timber industry.

Economically significant activities included linen-, cotton-, and woolen-cloth weaving, and which not only supplied local demand but also attracted buyers from outside. Metalware (especially copperware) production, tanning, candle-making, jewelry production and trade, soapmaking, and cloth-dying were also important (Eyüpgiller 1999, 45–6; Maden 2012, 41–6; Kankal 2004, 93–102, 116–63). According to Suraiya Faroqhi (1984, 131–5), hemp was produced in the neighboring districts of Küre and Taşköprü during and after the sixteenth century and provided the raw material for the rope-making industry in the

[11] Kemal Eyüpgiller (1999, 383–4), who studied the urban history of the town, does not regard the period as one of major construction or expansion, although he suggests that many public buildings were restored in the eighteenth century. He also claims that the boundaries of the town by the end of the nineteenth century were not much different from those in the sixteenth century.

TABLE 2.1: *Population Estimates for Select Ottoman Towns*

	17th Century	18th Century	19th Century
Adana		25,000[b]	12,000–30,000
Aleppo		100,000–120,000	70,000–150,000
Amasya			12,000
Ankara			23,000–35,000
Antalya			13,000
Baghdad			105,000
Balıkesir			16,800
Bayburt	3,500		
Bursa	20,000–35,000[a]	55,000–70,000[a]	32,000–100,000
Damascus			79,866–154,000
Diyarbakır		80,000–100,000[a] 30,000–50,000[c]	35,000–54,000
Edirne			87,000–110,000
İstanbul	600,000–1,000,000	500,000–600,000	391,000–1,115,946
İzmir	24,000–90,000	65,000–128,000	44,000–200,000
Kayseri	15,000–20,000[a]	25,000–40,000[a]	26,000
Konya			28,000–44,000
Malatya			12,000–30,000
Manisa	18,000–20,000	20,000–25,000[a]	
Mosul			65,000
Muş			7,000–27,000
Niğde			6,700
Salonika			80,000
Samsun			4,000–11,000
Sarajevo			65,000
Sofia			50,000
Trabzon			35,000–55,000

Note: Although we have attempted to compile only figures provided for town populations, some of the estimates likely include the population of adjacent villages and settlements, which may explain the large variations in the figures for specific locations.
Sources: a Canbakal and Filiztekin (2013). *b* Tamdoğan (2008, 58). *c* Aykan (2012). The rest of the estimates are from Behar (1996).

region. Rope-making continued to exist in the eighteenth century and supplied the needs of the imperial fleet (Eyüpgiller 1999, 44; Maden 2012, 45; Kankal 2004, 161–2). Maden (2012, 150–1) counts about 150 different trades and artisanal occupations in the court records of the late eighteenth century, most of which were geared to meet local demand. According to Evliya Çelebi, there were about 1,000 trades and artisanal occupations in the empire during the seventeenth century (Maden 2012, 47).

Copper-mining was a major economic activity, especially in the neighboring district of Küre. In the late seventeenth and eighteenth centuries, the imperial government regularly auctioned the rights to extract copper (Yaman 1941). In the sixteenth century, the extracted copper was either sent to İstanbul or transported to the south toward Syria via the route of Amasya, Tokat, and Sivas (Faroqhi 1987, 175). In the seventeenth and eighteenth centuries, the imperial canon foundry (*Tophane-i Amire*) in İstanbul claimed the vast majority of the production (Yaman 1941; Maden 2012, 58; Kankal 2004, 122–3). Nevertheless, copperware producers in Kastamonu, Sivas, Amasya, Tokat, and Erzurum and Iranian merchants also purchased copper from the mines during and after the sixteenth century (Kankal 2004, 123). Although copper mines generated employment for the local population, copper was extracted mainly by slaves (Maden 2007, 153; 2012, 58).

In the sixteenth century, two routes that were used to transport sheep from Diyarbakır in the southeast and Erzurum in the east to İstanbul passed through Kastamonu (Faroqhi 1984, 225–7; also see Kankal 2004, 199). Mehmet Genç observes that during the seventeenth and eighteenth centuries the town was still a notable stop on the trade routes that connected eastern and southern provinces to İstanbul (as cited in Karagöz 2009, 299). According to Mehmet Karagöz, Kastamonu also had commercial ties with urban centers in central Anatolia, mainly Kayseri and Ankara (2009, 266). One would imagine that the town's proximity to the important Black Sea ports of Sinop and İnebolu must have also contributed to its economic and commercial life and attracted merchants and transit trade from other locations (Maden 2012, 57). According to court records, traders from or with connections to Rumelia, Crimea, and Iran regularly visited the town (Maden 2012, 49–51). Ainsworth reports that cotton arrived from Adana in the early nineteenth century, and was used to produce sailcloth by women, which was then sent to İstanbul via the Black Sea (1842, 82; cf. Maden 2012, 49). However, neither Kinneir nor Ainsworth mentions any major interregional trade activity in or around the town that resembled, for example, the mohair industry in Ankara, located about 250 kilometers south of Kastamonu. In fact, according to Colin Heywood, the town was a relatively obscure and isolated location during Ottoman times (1978, 738).

The economic literature on the eighteenth-century Ottoman Empire is dominated by discussions of the fiscal changes implemented during this period, in particular the increasing use of tax-farming for revenue and the institutionalization of life-term tax-farming in 1695. In life-term tax-farming, the government farmed out revenue sources on a lifetime basis in return for a one-time lump-sum payment at the beginning of the contract and subsequent annual payments. In this way the government used "tax-revenues as collateral and borrow[ed] on a large term basis. In comparison to the straight-forward tax-farming system, [life-term tax-farming] represented an important shift towards long-term borrowing by the state" (Pamuk 2004, 17).[12] Investors collected the proceeds generated by these revenue sources for the rest of their lives and frequently bequeathed them to their heirs.

Recent studies emphasize the transformative character of life-term tax-farming in social, economic, and political terms. Although İstanbul-based elites dominated the public auctions in which revenue sources were sold to highest bidders, from the very start, these groups governed their investments indirectly, through local agents or subfarmers, many of whom were among the provincial elite. Later, the role of the provincial elite, either as initial investors or subfarmers, increased substantially. "Over the course of eighteenth century," Pamuk notes, "some 1,000 to 2,000 İstanbul based individuals, together with some 5,000 to 10,000 individuals based in the provinces, as well as innumerable contractors, agents, financiers, accountants and managers controlled an important share of the state's revenues" (2004, 17). Thus, the system semiprivatized imperial revenue sources and allowed local elites to profit from investments in them.

It is safe to assume that short- and longer-term tax-farming also became prevalent in Kastamonu during our period. As mentioned, early in the eighteenth century the district's tax revenues were assigned on a life-term basis, and may have been subcontracted to members of the local elite as smaller tax-farms (İnalcık 1977, 35–6). These included revenues generated by local dye-houses, candle-houses, caravanserais, and many other commercial ventures. We also know that the cotton stamp tax, customs revenues, copper extraction, and timber production were also auctioned as tax-farms. Determining the full extent of tax-farming in other sectors,

[12] Farmed-out public revenue sources included agricultural taxes and taxes associated with manufacturing, customs, mining, and specific services. Individuals who won the right to tax these sources in public auctions paid the state a lump sum followed by fixed installments for the duration of their contract. Between the fifteenth and seventeenth centuries, tax-farm contracts did not extend beyond five years. Life-term tax-farming was introduced at the end of the seventeenth century, as a result of increasing government demand for funds due to frequent wars and financial crises during this period.

including agriculture, and how tax-farming contracts may have changed over time, however, requires further research.

Historians disagree over the general state of the Ottoman economy in the eighteenth century. Until recently, most viewed that period as one of general economic decline, due to financial problems associated with protracted warfare, powerful inflationary pressures, superior European competition, and an increasing tax burden on the population. They perceived global trade patterns as shifting from the Mediterranean to the Atlantic, with adverse consequences for Ottoman traders. Historians also observed a general sense of restlessness and insecurity in the countryside that forced peasants to migrate to urban centers and adversely affected agricultural production (Lewis 1958; Issawi 1966; Özkaya 1985, chapter 8; Tabakoğlu 1985, 205–41).

Recently, however, Ottomanists have begun to challenge this negative characterization. For example, Karen Barkey (2008, 236–7) has suggested that the empire became "more permeable to all kinds of trade with many European nations, and the empire-wide trade routes and commodity markets flourished, bringing more and more people into contact with one another. The result was a vast increase in the raw numbers of economic transactions." Whereas imports of luxury items (spices, drugs, and gems) declined over the course of the century, exports of raw materials (grains, cotton, animal fibers, and dyestuffs) and interregional exchange of manufactured goods produced for domestic markets expanded (McGowan 1981, chapter 1). Meanwhile, trade in new consumption goods such as coffee, sugar, and tobacco brought many regions in the empire into greater contact with the global economy. In manufacturing, commercial expansion translated, if sporadically, into protoindustrial activities in rural areas (Salzmann 1995, 331 and 2004, 60–71; Kasaba 1988, 14; Faroqhi 2006, 362; Genç 1994, 69–70).

It is not clear to what extent these changes affected Kastamonu because, as is the case with many smaller urban centers in Anatolia and the Balkans, we do not possess detailed information on the socioeconomic characteristics of the town in the seventeenth and eighteenth centuries. If anything, Kastamonu, like hundreds of remote, similar-sized locations, appears to have remained cut off from major commercial developments in the eighteenth century, although the region did have some economic connections with the outside world. The fact that the town received almost no attention from foreign travelers before the nineteenth century is one indication of this likelihood (Heywood 1978). Another one is that only two or three new covered bazaars (*bedestens*), inns (*han*), or caravanserais (*kervansaray*) were built in Kastamonu during the eighteenth century, compared to perhaps four or five in the fifteenth, five to seven in the sixteenth, and nine to eleven in the seventeenth century (Kankal 2004, 203–19).

Despite the relative lack of direct information on how socioeconomic conditions changed in eighteenth-century Kastamonu, we can learn more about the topic by analyzing probate estate inventories. This is what we do in the next subsection.

Economic Change in the Eighteenth Century

In what follows, we use probate estate inventories (sing. *tereke*; pl. *terekat*, also in pl. *muhallefat*) to understand the socioeconomic dynamics and nature of change in Kastamonu during the eighteenth century. The analysis is based on a sample of estate inventories which contain about 2,200 documents covering, with lapses, the 90-year period from 1713 to 1802.[13] Prepared by court officials at the request of heirs, estate inventories provide information about the wealth of an individual at the time of death, including a monetary appraisal of the cash, property, and debt left behind (Establet and Pascual 1994, 2011). They list the full name of the deceased, including the name of his or her father, honorific title if the deceased was male (which signified membership in the military or religious establishments), indicate where the deceased was from, and give details of legal heirs. Typically, this information is followed by itemized lists and appraised values of all inherited (movable and immovable) property of the deceased, cash holdings, and outstanding loans to and from others at the time of death.

It is well known that *tereke*s have limitations as a historical source (Gradeva 2005, 152–63; Establet et al. 1994, 171–82; Ergene and Berker 2008, 26). Tax-farms and prebendal land grants are not included in these documents because they technically belonged to the state. Income and salaries generated by charitable endowments (*evkaf*), in which individuals frequently held hereditary positions, are also not reported. Moreover, *tereke*s underrepresent women, rural populations, and the poor, and overrepresent the elderly. Non-Muslim *tereke*s are particularly

[13] To prepare this data set, we consulted the microfilm copies of Kastamonu court records stored in the National Library of Turkey, in Ankara. The entire collection of Kastamonu court records begins in 1684 and encompasses the time period between the late seventeenth and early nineteenth centuries. The earliest registers contain *tereke*s only sporadically. Thus, we chose to start coverage at a later date, when the quality of documentation improves.

rare (although they exist) because the court was obliged to divide estates according to Islamic rules of inheritance. Also, many families likely tried to avoid the involvement of the court in the appraisal and division of estates since court officials charged fees for this service as well as registration.[14] The appraisal and division of estates by the court were not legally required unless the heirs included orphans who had not yet attained their majority, but disagreements over inheritance shares often necessitated intervention by court officials. We also cannot be sure that the inventories accurately reflect the actual wealth of the deceased at the time of his or her death. Heirs often tried to conceal portions of their estates from court officials in order to reduce the "inheritance tax." There is also the issue of the reliability of estate appraisals since we cannot be sure of the motivations of the court officials preparing them – they may have inflated appraisals to increase their fees. Nevertheless, such problems are not unique to Ottoman estate inventories and they have not impeded the development of rich economic historiographies based on similar documents for Western contexts.

Kastamonu court records contain a negligible number of infant and children *terekes* and we excluded those that we determined to belong to these groups. We calculated the net value of individual estates by deducting the debts and outstanding obligations of the deceased from the monetary value of their properties and cash holdings. We divided our sample of inventories into two subsamples composed of male and female *terekes* and analyzed them separately. This is because inventories belonging to women are relatively few in number and may suffer from a selection bias, in which case our sample would not be properly random and, thus, insufficiently representative of the population of women in Kastamonu. They are also likely to under-appraise the real value of wealth owned by testators since Muslim women tended to transfer their property to relatives long before death.[15] Finally, to remove price effects from the data, we deflated the nominal values in estate inventories by using the consumer price index calculated by Özmucur and Pamuk (2002) for İstanbul.[16]

It is difficult to predict exactly what percentage of the deaths in Kastamonu is represented by the estate inventories. However, we can

[14] The court of Kastamonu charged about 3.4 percent of the gross values of estates for assessing their values, dividing them among heirs, and registration (Ergene 2002, 29).

[15] See Moors (1995, chapter 3) for the prevalence of this practice in modern Palestine.

[16] We compared the consumer price index of Özmucur and Pamuk with the price of select food and consumer products from the lists of official prices (*narh*) in Kastamonu court registers, which are consistent.

propose the following rough estimate, if we assume (a) the annual crude death rate in our context to be around 0.0437,[17] and (b) that the population of the town remained around 12,000 during the eighteenth century. Under these assumptions, the total number of deaths in the town over 90 years should be about 47,000 (= 0.0437 × 12,000 × 90). Assuming that 15 percent of these were non-Muslim (Heywood 1978, 738), the total number of Muslim deaths must have been about 40,000. Considering that adult mortality was usually about half of all mortality in pre-industrial societies, we can assume that there were about 20,000 adult deaths in the town during our period. Since about 90 percent of the estate inventories belonged to urban residents, roughly 1,440 (= 0.90 × 1,600) male *tereke*s and 540 (= 0.90 × 600) female *tereke*s must have belonged to those who lived within the boundaries of the town. These figures would indicate that our subsample of male *tereke*s represents about 14.4 (= 1,440/(20,000 × 0.5)) percent of adult male deaths and our subsample of female *tereke*s represents about 5.4 (= 540/(20,000 × 0.5)) percent of adult female deaths. The rates of representation improve toward the end of our period since court records contain more *tereke*s in later years.

In Table 2.2 we provide the mean and median values of real wealth levels in three subperiods that closely approximate the periods studied in this book.[18]

The information presented in Table 2.2 suggests that real wealth levels declined in the eighteenth century. Furthermore, our data also suggests that the economic circumstances of the poorer segments of the society became disproportionately worse compared to wealthier groups (see Table 2.3).

Whereas the average wealth of the richest quartile of men declined by only about 15 percent between 1713 and 1802, the average wealth of the

17 Justin McCarthy (McCarthy 1997, 281) gives the death rate for the "Turkish population" in the eighteenth-century Ottoman Empire as 43.7 per 1,000 individuals. Wrigley and Schofield (2002, 181–2) give a lower rate (0.035) for preindustrial Italy and France. They also suggest that this rate was 0.025 to 0.03 for preindustrial England and Wales.

18 Possible indicators of the minimum requirements for survival in early to mid-eighteenth-century Kastamonu are the *nafaka*s reported in court records. The term *nafaka* refers to the monetary allowance allocated by the court to divorced or widowed women from the assets of or inheritances from their ex- or late husbands to cover daily household expenses for food, clothing, and shelter, including those for their children and slaves. Based on fifteen separate observations between 1739 and 1748, *nafaka* rates for single adult women ranged from 9 to 21 *akçe*s, depending on their social and economic background. These amounts suggest a range of 3,184 to 7,434 *akçe*s, or 26–62 *guruş* per (lunar) year. Based on these figures, we suggest 30 *guruş* per year as the poverty line for a single adult female in mid-eighteenth-century Kastamonu. Assuming that a single adult male required more food, he would have needed 40–50 *guruş* per year for survival.

TABLE 2.2: *Real Wealth Indicators for Three Subperiods (All Values in* guruş*)*

		1713–31	1732–67	1768–1802
Men	Mean	705.1 (949.7)	838.5 (2,181.1)	537.7 (1,474.3)
	Median	426.9	298.1	185.8
	N	158	607	844
Women	Mean	298.0 (615.9)	195.3 (275.7)	183.1 (285.7)
	Median	151.6	119	96.9
	N	40	227	346

Note: Standard deviations are given in parentheses. 1713 = 1.

poorest quartile dropped by about 75 percent. Also, although the richest male and female groups (the top quartiles) became wealthier in the middle of the eighteenth century, before they experienced major economic losses, three-quarters of the population became impoverished quite consistently as time passed. These findings also indicate that the richest groups' share of total wealth increased during the eighteenth century. In other words, wealth distribution in Kastamonu became more unequal (see Table 2.4).[19]

These findings support the more pessimistic depictions of economic conditions in the empire during the eighteenth century.[20] It is not immediately clear how the rich managed to better protect their wealth compared with the rest of society, although the fiscal history of the period provides clues in this regard. According to Mehmet Genç (1973), the *malikane* system provided an opportunity to accumulate wealth for those who were rich enough to invest in lucrative revenue sources for most of the eighteenth century. The calculations made by Genç indicate that between 1720 and 1750 the yearly average profit generated by *malikane*s was as high as 35 to 40 percent of the lump-sum payments made at the time of contract. Between 1751 and 1771 that rate varied between 25 and 35 percent (Genç 1973, 252). Svetla Ianeva (2009) has observed that tax-farming was potentially a more profitable investment opportunity than regional and long-distance trade in mid-nineteenth-century Rumelia, a milieu

[19] Earlier studies (Coşgel and Ergene 2012; Ergene, Kaygun, and Coşgel 2013) have demonstrated that inequality levels in Kastamonu worsened steadily from the 1720s to 1780s, before they slightly improved.

[20] Other researchers of Ottoman Kastamonu have made observations consistent with our own for this period. According to Ahmet Kankal (2004, 244), "the purchasing power of the inhabitants of Kastamonu declined in the seventeenth and eighteenth centuries. During this period, they sent petitions to the imperial center requesting reductions in the numbers of their *avarız* households," implying tax relief (also see Maden 2012, 39).

TABLE 2.3: *Quartile-based Mean and Median Wealth Levels as Reflected in Estate Inventories (all values in guruş)*

			1713–31	1732–67	1768–1802
Men	Top 25%	Mean	1793.6 (765.9)	3356.2 (3342.5)	1528.2 (844.6)
		Median	1516.70	2074.10	1309.80
	2nd 25%	Mean	640.2 (119.9)	558.6 (288.3)	338.8 (135.9)
		Median	601.9	515.9	321.2
	3rd 25%	Mean	323.9 (96.0)	250.6 (154.1)	132.2 (37.8)
		Median	308.5	213	126.1
	Bottom 25%	Mean	177.3 (126.2)	88.2 (43.4)	44.8 (9.8)
		Median	166.9	87.5	45.1
Women	Top 25%	Mean	942.8 (1,468.8)	506.5 (195.7)	447.6 (207.7)
		Median	317.2	453.8	391.6
	2nd 25%	Mean	316.9 (202.9)	187.3 (78.6)	145.3 (41.7)
		Median	233.1	163.9	141.3
	3rd 25%	Mean	200.2 (223.8)	104.2 (35.1)	78.5 (20.4)
		Median	127.7	93.8	71.9
	Bottom 25%	Mean	89.3 (78.9)	47.8 (28.3)	38.6 (10.3)
		Median	57.8	42.9	37.3

Note: Standard deviations are given in parentheses. 1713 = 1.

TABLE 2.4: *Inequality in Eighteenth-century Kastamonu*

		1713–31	1732–67	1768–1802
Men	Gini	0.45	0.63	0.63
	Coefficient of Variation	0.99	1.77	1.79
	Share of wealthiest 25%	0.60	0.75	0.76
Women	Gini	0.32	0.41	0.48
	Coefficient of Variation	0.90	0.99	1.16
	Share of wealthiest 25%	0.50	0.58	0.64

that was certainly much more commercialized and better connected to international markets than eighteenth-century Kastamonu.[21] Since it is reasonable to assume that the wealthiest inhabitants of Kastamonu, more so than the rest of the community, invested in or became associated with the expanding tax-farming system as contractors, subcontractors, or local financiers, it would make sense that they benefited more from this profitable endeavor than others.[22] It is also possible that it was these groups who benefited most from the opportunities associated with the expansion of credit networks, a possible consequence of the emergence of investment opportunities associated with spread of tax-farming, if such a development did indeed take place in Kastamonu.[23]

In addition, we should remember that provincial officials who had tax collection privileges tended to be wealthier than the rest of the society and thus it is more likely that they are included in the first quartile in our sample. These individuals had some ability to unload their economic burdens onto taxpayers. Indeed, the literature indicates that duplicitous, excessive, and extralegal taxation was common in the eighteenth century (İnalcık 1977). If the same also took place in Kastamonu, our findings may indicate that the relative ability of the wealthiest groups to maintain their wealth came, at least to some undeterminable extent, at the expense of the lower classes. The fact that the court records of Kastamonu contain a large number of complaints about illegal or excessive taxation by local military and administrative authorities (Ergene 2003, 50–1; Maden 2012, 31–4) makes this possibility likely.

21 For a similar observation in the context of seventeenth-century Greece, see Fodor (2009).

22 Establet and Pascual (2011, chapter 5) have demonstrated that the richest groups in Damascus became heavily involved in tax-farming and money-lending in the early eighteenth century.

23 According to Pamuk (2000, 80), "the greatest fortunes in the larger cities of Bursa and Edirne during the seventeenth century belonged to people who lent a large part of their assets."

How, then, can we explain the downturn in the economic conditions of the wealthiest inhabitants of Kastamonu by the end of the eighteenth century? There are several possible explanations. First, Ergene et al. (2013) have demonstrated that the financial crisis experienced in the empire after 1767 affected the wealthiest groups in Kastamonu severely, while its impact on the poorest segments of the society was less significant.[24] This finding is consistent with what historians have said about how the imperial government attempted to cope with crisis.[25] Second, according to Genç (1973, 252), the revenues generated by the *malikanes* fell significantly after the 1770s, which must have hurt the economic conditions of the wealthy even more.

Although economic inequality increased during our period, our calculations also suggest that the inequality levels in Kastamonu were generally lower than those calculated for larger urban centers in the Ottoman Empire. By using probate estate inventories, Colette Establet, Jean-Paul Pascual, and André Raymond (1994, 177–80) calculated the Gini coefficients for early eighteenth-century Damascus and Cairo, respectively, as 0.74 and 0.81. Similarly, Hülya Canbakal (2012, 8) estimated the Gini coefficient for eighteenth-century Bursa in the high 0.80s. According to the information found in Canbakal and Filiztekin (2013), inequality levels in eighteenth-century Kastamonu were closer to those in Manisa, located in western Anatolia, and Kayseri, an important commercial hub in central Anatolia.

HONORIFIC TITLES, RELIGIOUS MARKERS, AND OTHER CATEGORIES OF ANALYSIS

Socioeconomic Categories of Analysis

The previous section has demonstrated that major economic disparities existed in Kastamonu. Assuming parallel disparities among court clients,

[24] Fiscal circumstances in the empire first deteriorated with the Ottoman–Russian wars of 1768–1774 and became even worse when the Ottomans entered another war in 1787 against both Russia and Austria. In order to close the budget gap that emerged during the last three decades of the eighteenth century, the government increased revenues by imposing a variety of new taxes. See Cezar (1986, 68–74) and Tabakoğlu (1985, 295–300).

[25] Although the lower classes were also pressured by tax demands, historians make special mention of the ways in which the wealthy were financially squeezed by the government. Not only were life-term tax-farmers required to pay additional taxes such as *cebelü bedeliyesi* (equivalent to 15 percent of the initial lump sum that they paid for their tax-farms) and make frequent non-voluntary contributions to the treasury (Cezar 1986, 74, 135; Tabakoğlu 1985, 295–300), but the confiscation (*müsadere*) of the property of affluent government officials also became common in the 1780s (Cezar 1986, 110).

we intend to explore in this book how court clients who belonged to different segments of the society used the court and interacted with their counterparts within that venue. One problem in this regard is the fact that the court records do not directly identify those who used the court's services according to their class status. Thus, to accomplish our task we need to develop a methodology to distinguish court clients based on their socioeconomic differences. There are both theoretical and practical difficulties in tackling this issue. On the theoretical side, the challenge is to propose a system of social hierarchy that is historically informed and capable of representing real socioeconomic divisions. On the practical side, the problem is to empirically identify these divisions in our source base, the court records.

Until recently, it was common practice to assign social rank on the basis of tax status, which led historians to simply distinguish tax-exempt government functionaries (*askeri*) from tax-paying common men and women (*reaya*). However, the binary classification of *askeri* versus *reaya*, while simple and convenient for empirical research, does not adequately represent the complex patterns of segmentation observed in many provincial contexts. Particularly relevant to this discussion is the social and economic variation among the subgroups that constituted the *askeri* and *reaya*. For example, with respect to the provincial elite included in the *askeri* class, Albert Hourani described a three-way division in early modern Arab provinces: religious scholars (*ulema*), military leaders of the local garrisons, and those individuals he identified as "secular notables" (1981, 44–5). Meanwhile, Linda Schilcher provided possibly the most comprehensive list of socioeconomic groups in her work on eighteenth- and early-nineteenth-century Damascus. According to Schilcher, Damascene society consisted of seven "estates": military and paramilitary groups; the *ulema*; the *eşraf* (those who claimed descent from the Prophet); local *sufi*s (mystics); the *tüccar* (members of the trading community); artisans; and the residual category composed of migrant and semi-urbanized bedouin, mountaineers, peasants, and villagers (1985, 108–11). Tax-exempt or not, these groups had distinct social, cultural, and organizational identities as well as economic and vocational characteristics that cannot be accounted for in any binary classification. More recently, Colette Establet and Jean-Paul Pascual (2011) have divided the *askeri* in late seventeenth-century Damascus into four subgroups: "civil agents of the state" (*agents civils de l'état*), who included government functionaries with bureaucratic and administrative responsibilities; provincial cavalrymen (*sipahi*), many of whom lived and collected state taxes in the countryside; imperial janissaries settled in the Damascus citadel; and local janissaries.

The challenge for us is to devise a nuanced model of social segmentation that (1) adequately reflects socioeconomic divisions in eighteenth-century Kastamonu, while (2) accommodating the logic and inherent limitations of our historical sources.[26] In theory, a version of Schilcher's schema of "estates" could help us to identify all the groups in the provincial hierarchy. The problem with adopting this model, however, is that only few of the "estates" identified by Schilcher are visible in the court records. In fact, Schilcher herself acknowledges that her sources permitted a detailed consideration of only three of the seven "estates" (1985, 111; also Reilly 1992, 11). Given the nature and extent of the information presented in court records, we need categories better suited to our empirical concerns.[27] We begin this subsection by proposing a methodology that aims to draw socioeconomic distinctions among individuals represented in court records.

Discerning such distinctions in court records is not a straightforward task because these documents do not often offer any personal information about court clients beyond their name, where they were from, and the nature of the issue that brought them to court. Thus, any attempt to determine the socioeconomic characteristics of these individuals must be based on indirect indicators. The gender and religious identities of court clients can often be reliably inferred from their names. In addition, we differentiate male court clients by using three types of indirect referents, also derived from their names: honorific titles, markers of religious status, and family affiliations. In the rest of this chapter, we explain these indicators and justify our use of them.

Honorific Titles

Honorific titles indicate individuals who, at least in theory, possessed specific types of professional training or education (military-administrative or religious-judicial), who served (or were capable of serving) various sorts of military-administrative or judicial-religious functions, and who enjoyed the socioeconomic privileges associated therewith. In addition to exemption from certain forms of taxation, these benefits included

[26] See Chapter 1.

[27] On social stratification and relative class positions for our period, see Marcus (1989, 66–76), Schilcher (1985, 108–10), Barbir (1992), and Roded (1986, 147–52).

economic compensation for specific services as well as varying degrees of communal respect, influence, and/or authority derived from their involvement in the provincial administration. These markers appear in our documents as components of individuals' names and, in the absence of surnames and along with other markers of identification (such as birthplace, family nicknames, personal traits, and religious markers, which we discuss below in more detail), they distinguish individuals with reference to their affiliation with and relative position in the provincial administrative hierarchy. For example, the epithet *Efendi* in the name Ahmed Efendi ibn/bin Mehmed (Ahmed Efendi, son of Mehmed) indicates that the individual named Ahmed was a member of the religious establishment – that is, he had been educated in the religious-judicial sciences and probably held an important religious or judicial position at some point in his life, which influenced his social prominence and economic status. Similarly, the epithet *Ağa* in the name Topal Hüseyin Ağa ibn/bin Tosyalı Süleyman Efendi (Hüseyin Ağa "the lame," son of Süleyman Efendi of Tosya) suggests that Hüseyin was not only a ranked member of the military-administrative establishment, he was also a son of an *Efendi* from Tosya.

In the absence of more direct indicators of socioeconomic status, Ottoman historians have used honorific titles to distinguish individuals (Barkan 1968; Gerber 1988; Gradeva 2005; Pascual and Establet 1994; Roded 1984). We follow the same approach in this study by adopting the following title-based categories:

- Religious-judicial titleholders: members of the *ilmiyye*, or religious/judicial establishment (men designated by the titles *Efendi, Molla, Halife, Çelebi*, and *Dede*).[28]

[28] Other designations that indicate affiliation with the religious establishment almost always accompanied these titles. *Efendi* was a title used for the most respected and higher-ranking members. The names of virtually all kadıs, *müderrises* (college professors), *müftis* (jurisconsults), and other important members of the religious establishment were accompanied by this title. *Molla* was a title officially given to high-ranking judges and *medrese* teachers. In Kastamonu, however, this title frequently referred to *medrese* students and dropouts as well as individuals who had low-ranking religious and scribal positions in local charitable foundations. *Halife* is a *tarikat* (mystical order) designation, yet in Kastamonu this title was frequently used for the lower-ranked members of the religious establishment, most notably prayer leaders (*imams*) in neighborhood mosques. *Çelebi* was a generic title used for individuals who possessed some religious education or who were affiliated with influential *ulema* families; for the other ways in which this title was used in different contexts, see Tülüveli (2005). The title *Dede* was specifically used for senior dervishes; cf. Bayerle (1997).

- Military-administrative titleholders: members of the *seyfiyye*, or military/administrative establishment (men designated by the titles *Ağa, Beğ*, and *Beşe*).[29]
- Men without titles: men not affiliated with either the military/administrative or the religious/judicial establishment.

Admittedly, any effort to identify social or economic stratification in the Ottoman context using honorific titles must proceed cautiously. In the context of our discussion, it is important not to conflate membership in the military or religious establishments with occupational status. This is because members of the *seyfiyye* and *ilmiyye* could hold multiple and varied offices during their lifetime. The religious establishment, for example, included court clerks, magistrates, teachers, neighborhood preachers, and prayer leaders. Some *ilmiyye* members actually held several of these positions over the course of their lives. Others, who possessed *ilmiyye* or *seyfiyye* titles because of their training, education, or family background, may never have worked at all. Our sources also indicate that many titleholders were involved in regional and long-distance trade and artisanal activities. For example, there were many *Beşe*s, if not *Ağa*s or *Beğ*s, among the ranks of Kastamonu's artisans during our period, a situation not unique to Kastamonu (Yi 2004, 132–43; Raymond 2000, 219; Bayerle 1997, 32).

Nevertheless, a careful and nuanced use of title-based categories and some strategic assumptions in our attempts to interpret them can enable an acceptable way to distinguish court clients according to their socio-economic status. First, however, it should be emphasized that when we refer to military or religious titleholders, we mean precisely that: Individuals who held military or religious titles, rather than "real" soldiers or "real" religious functionaries. It is the same when we use phrases such as "members of the military establishment" or "religious groups" in our discussion. Respectively, these refer to men with military and religious titles. As discussed, it is likely, for example, that, not all *Beşe*s were trained soldiers. Those who carried this title could in fact include artisans or shop-owners with organic connections with local janissary corps because of

[29] Other military designations, when used, accompanied these three titles. According to Barkan (1968, 15–17), the titles *Ağa, Beğ*, and *Beşe* do not reveal an individual's exact military status. That is, these terms do not indicate whether he belonged to the janissary corps, was a *tımar*-holder, or was identified with any other military subgroup. It is difficult to make an intra-group distinction based on military titles. It is likely that an *Ağa* had a higher ranking than a *Beşe*, but it is problematic to make the same kind of distinction between a *Beşe* and a *Beğ*, given that these titles were sometimes used interchangeably in the court records; see Tülüveli (2005, 21–3).

their need for physical protection from dangerous elements in the urban environment or financial privileges associated with military status. Rather than attributing to title groups a common vocational characteristic, we refer to them as relatively coherent and identifiable socioeconomic entities. The empirical analysis that follows is meant to justify this assumption. This being said, we also assume that military and religious titleholders had disproportionately more military and religious functionaries, respectively, compared to other title groups.

Second, we can modify the title-based categorizations to better reflect wealth differentials within individual title groups. Previous research on Kastamonu has demonstrated that some titleholders, *Ağa*s and *Efendi*s in particular, were significantly wealthier than others (Ergene and Berker 2008). This finding, accompanied by the fact that individuals who carried these two titles occupied the highest provincial positions in Kastamonu, justified the division of military and religious titleholders into "elite" and "non-elite" subcategories. Thus, we divide title-based categories into subdivisions in the present study as well: While the elite military and religious titleholder group refers to the *Ağa*s and *Efendi*s, respectively, the labels non-elite military and religious titleholders indicate, again respectively, all other military and religious titleholders.

Finally, we also adopt other categories to identify those aspects of socioeconomic division that might not be fully captured by titles. These categories are religious markers and family status.

Religious Markers

Specifically, we differentiate court clients who claimed descent from Muhammad (*Seyyid* for men, *Şerife* for women) and those who had made the pilgrimage to Mecca (*Elhac* or *Hacı* for men, *Hace* or *Hacıye* for women) from the rest of our sample.[30] There are reasons to suspect that both groups occupied a unique socioeconomic position in the society. The descendants of Muhammad constituted the social entity closest to blood nobility in the Ottoman context, with their own semi-independent social hierarchy, patterns of social conduct, networks of socialization, and marriage preferences (cf. Canbakal 2005, 2009). Making the pilgrimage to Mecca, on the

[30] Such religious markers did not qualify these individuals as members of the religious establishment. In fact, the epithets *Elhac*, *Seyyid*, and *Şerife* were frequently used by people from all title groups, including the military establishment and people with no other title attached to their names.

other hand, not only contributed to one's moral and religious standing but was also indicative of considerable wealth (Ergene and Berker 2008; Faroqhi 1992). In the following analysis, we utilize the marker "pilgrim" as a signifier of social and economic status, independent of title affiliation.

Family Status

Finally, we distinguish court clients based on whether or not their names included family affiliations followed by the *zade* suffix, which technically means "descendant of." The court records identify the members of many prominent families as "descendants of," or, more accurately, "associated with" these families. For example, "Kıbrısizade" Ahmed Efendi was an elite religious titleholder affiliated with the very influential "Kıbrısi" extended family. Thus, based on our impressions in Kastamonu court records, we use the *zade* suffix as a marker of social and economic privilege, independent of title affiliations and religious markers.[31]

Justification of the Categories of Analysis

The main objective of this section is to demonstrate (a) how the various groups mentioned in the preceding discussion differed in terms of their economic characteristics, and (b) if these differences changed over the course of the eighteenth century. The following analysis is based on the same collections of estate inventories explored in the first half of the present chapter.

According to Table 2.5, elite military and religious titleholders, pilgrims, and members of prominent (*zade*s) families constituted the wealthiest groups throughout the eighteenth century. The real mean and median values of the estates that women left behind, on the other hand, were considerably smaller than those left behind by men. The table also indicates that titleless men may have included many well-off individuals in the second period. The same is also true for the descendants of Muhammad in the first period. However, since titles, religious markers, and family status were not exclusive categories, the findings may be misleading in regard to their economic import. Thus, to identify the true wealth indicators, we regressed real wealth levels on the categories of analysis identified above. The results, presented in Table 2.6, reveal the

[31] In the rest of this chapter and subsequent sections we often use the labels "Prominent" and "Non-prominent" to refer to *zade*s and non-*zade*s, respectively.

TABLE 2.5: *Period-based Real Wealth Indicators for Gender, Title, Religious Status, and Family Groups Based on Estate Inventories (mean and median values in guruş)*

Period	Wealth Measures	Women	Elite Military	Elite Religious	Non-elite Military	Non-elite Religious	No Title	Pilgrim	Desc. of Muh.	No Relig. Status	Prominent	Non-prominent
1713–31	Mean	298	2217.1	1339.5	460.8	647.9	521.0	1098.3	1009.2	433.8	1946.0	552.5
		(615.9)	(2001.8)	(1521.8)	(378.9)	(940.2)	(454.0)	(1225.9)	(746.5)	(688.4)	(2,385.6)	(701.5)
	Median	151.6	2041.80	847.9	387	350.4	365	734	672.3	229.5	487.6	316.1
	N	40	11	10	34	33	70	53	8	138	10	188
1732–67	Mean	195.3	2419.7	1313.9	419.7	400.1	730.2	1634.8	520.2	395.1	2151.9	576.6
		(275.7)	(4789.5)	(3009.1)	(608.0)	(442.3)	(1703.8)	(3323.4)	(554.8)	(1126.3)	(3768.9)	(1680.1)
	Median	119	809.2	647.7	200.4	252.6	266.3	677.3	305.2	166.5	890.3	201.3
	N	227	58	47	102	86	314	179	50	614	46	788
1768–1802	Mean	183.1	1059.4	1114.7	305.6	451.7	466.6	1318.5	478.9	272.9	1561.6	355.5
		(285.7)	(1425.6)	(2108.7)	(615.2)	(1,375.1)	(1,559.1)	(2,734.0)	(1,136.8)	(658.2)	(3777.9)	(786.0)
	Median	97	576.2	382.5	147.9	177.8	155.2	527.8	200.8	118.5	600.8	136.4
	N	346	78	61	148	82	475	175	144	893	78	1112

Note: Standard deviations are given in parentheses. 1713 = 1.

TABLE 2.6: *True Wealth Indicators: A Regression Analysis*

	(1)	(2)	(3)
VARIABLES	**1713–31**	**1732–67**	**1768–1802**
Women	–0.44**	–0.31***	–0.07
	(0.037)	(0.004)	(0.440)
Elite, religious title	0.95***	0.82***	0.80***
	(0.005)	<.001	<.001
Elite, military title	1.22***	1.30***	1.01***
	<.001	<.001	<.001
Non-elite, religious title	0.003	0.30**	0.35**
	(0.990)	(0.038)	(0.014)
Non-elite, military title	0.20	0.15	0.31***
	(0.336)	(0.253)	(0.006)
Descendant of Muhammad	0.73**	0.14	0.17
	(0.043)	(0.403)	(0.116)
Pilgrim	0.91***	1.23***	1.25***
	<.001	<.001	<.001
Prominent	0.45	0.46**	0.77***
	(0.193)	(0.014)	<.001
Constant	5.48***	5.47***	5.75***
	<.001	<.001	<.001
Observations	198	834	1190
R-squared	0.35	0.3	0.23

Note: Dependent variable is natural log of real wealth. *P*-values in parentheses.
* $p < 0.1$; ** $p < 0.05$; *** $p < 0.01$

economic significance of each category in a specific subperiod, while holding everything else constant.

In Table 2.6, the coefficients estimated for gender and honorific titles are relative to men without titles. The reference category for religious markers is individuals without religious markers. The reference category for individuals affiliated with prominent families is individuals with no such affiliations ("Non-prominent" individuals, or non-*zade*s). Overall, the regressions confirm the economic importance of elite titles and pilgrim status in all subperiods in the eighteenth century. Interestingly, while the wealth levels of women were significantly smaller than those of titleless men in the first two periods, that difference became negligible by the end of the century. On the other hand, the economic importance of affiliation with prominent families appears to have increased during the eighteenth century. Also, the wealth difference between the descendants of Muhammad and individuals with no religious markers declined over time. Finally, Table 2.6 also suggests that non-elite titles became an indicator of relative wealth in the religious establishment by the middle of the eighteenth century and in both establishments by the end of the century. In this sense the regression results, which provide indicators of the economic importance of gender identities, titles, religious markers, and family affiliations, all other factors being constant, should be seen as corrective of the means and medians given in Table 2.5, which create the impression that the economic circumstances of men without titles were better than non-elite titleholders, at least in the second subperiod.

It is likely that our findings are not unique to eighteenth-century northern Anatolia. Establet and Pascual (2011, 83) have recently argued that *Ağas* in eighteenth-century Damascus were also quite wealthy, relative to other segments of *seyfiyye*. They have also suggested that (2011, 84) at a time when general economic circumstances were worsening in Damascus, higher-level government functionaries were able to maintain or even improve their economic privilege, which is also consistent with our observations in Kastamonu.[32]

Finally, previous research on eighteenth-century Kastamonu provides important clues about how social and economic status perpetuated itself across successive generations. For example, based on ninety-seven father–son *tereke* pairs, Coşgel and Ergene (2011) demonstrated that the size of the father's wealth significantly influenced the size of his son's wealth.[33] Also, Ergene and Kaygun (2011) found that fathers and sons tended to hold identical military and religious titles.

[32] One major accomplishment of Establet and Pascual's detailed study is that it demonstrates the sources of wealth for many groups (2011, chapter 5). Their findings indicate that while high-level military and judicial government officials invested in the rural economy, the lower echelons of the military and religious establishments were active in the urban marketplace. They also suggest that the affluent members of the religious establishment managed charitable foundations. Tax-farming and money-lending were also lucrative economic endeavors, as we suspect to be the case in Kastamonu. Unfortunately, we lack comparable information for Kastamonu.

[33] The authors have estimated the elasticity of sons' wealth with respect to fathers' wealth (both in natural logarithmic scale) to be about 0.45. An elasticity measure of 1 with respect to fathers' wealth would indicate that economic status is completely immobile and sons inherit the same relative economic positions as their fathers, while a measure of 0 would conversely mean perfect mobility where the father's wealth has no influence on the son's economic position whatsoever. Clark and Cummins (2009) found this rate for eighteenth-century England as 0.66. On the other hand, the elasticity measure calculated for eighteenth-century Kastamonu is strikingly close to those estimated for some of the

How, then, should we characterize the relative position of title, religious status, and family group in the social hierarchy? In this regard, Abraham Marcus' depiction of class differences in eighteenth-century Aleppo provides help. In his work on eighteenth-century Aleppo, Marcus identified three distinct classes: The "lower class" comprised about two-thirds to three-quarters of the city's population and contained the unspecialized, poorly compensated occupations. This group included poor artisans, small shopkeepers, unskilled laborers, and street peddlers, who barely managed to make ends meet when they were lucky, and who owned little or no property (1989, 66). The "middle class," which comprised approximately one-quarter to one-third of the population, included "merchants, businessmen, master craftsmen, skilled professionals, *ulama*, officials, and tax-farmers. Most members of the city's high status groups fell into this category" (1989, 66). With respect to wealth, those who constituted this group were comfortable to affluent, as members of the middle class often owned their homes and shops and sometimes invested in real estates, tax-farms, public offices, money-lending, and trade. According to Marcus, many of these individuals were often tax-exempt and possessed "titles of honor" (1989, 66–7). Finally, the upper class in eighteenth-century Aleppo was small – consisting of four to five dozen families – but exercised, according to Marcus, major influence on the political, administrative, military, religious, and judicial affairs of the city. Unfortunately, Marcus does not provide more detail about the economic, military, and religious status of those who constituted this group (1989, 76).

If Marcus's depiction of class differences in eighteenth-century Aleppo is also valid for our context, we may suppose that that men with elite military and religious titles, pilgrims, and individuals affiliated with prominent families in eighteenth-century Kastamonu were members of what Marcus called the "middle" and "upper classes." Our findings indicate that the wealth levels of non-elite titleholders (both military and religious) and men without titles were closer to one another, particularly in the early eighteenth century. However, since one's relative position in the communal hierarchy was probably not determined solely by economic factors, we surmise that titles, even non-elite ones, indicate a relatively elevated social and/or professional status. For example, members of the court personnel, the local police force, prayer leaders of neighborhood mosques, and pious endowment

more modern societies. Using a sample from nineteenth- and early twentieth-century France, Arrondel and Grange (2006) estimated the elasticity of children's wealth levels relative to parental wealth to be between 0.44 and 0.45 for different samples.

functionaries were among those who carried lower-level military and religious titles. The same logic must have also applied to the communal position of the descendants of Muhammad. Although not demonstrably wealthier than individuals with religious markers, their claims of lineage from the Prophet may have enhanced their status in the social hierarchy. Indeed, according to Ergene and Kaygun's (2012) observations, in the otherwise endogamic marital market of eighteenth-century Kastamonu, marriages between the children of titleless descendants of Muhammad and wealthy elite titleholders were common, which the authors interpreted as evidence of the desirability of *Seyyid* and *Şerife* status.

In light of this discussion, we can perhaps represent the correspondence between Marcus' class categorizations and our categories of analysis as in Figure 2.1.

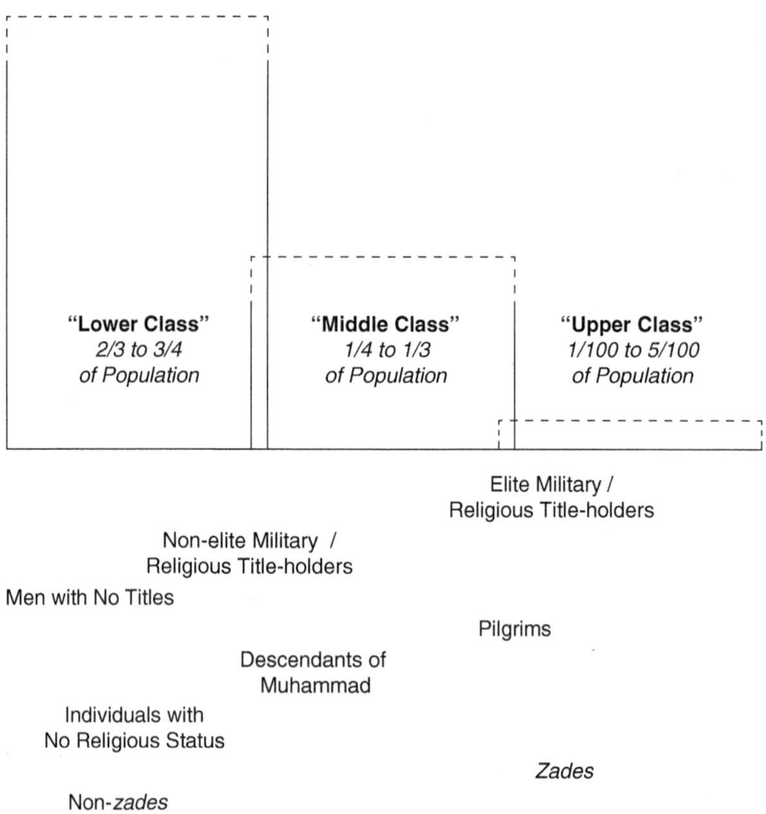

FIGURE 2.1: Socioeconomic Stratification in Eighteenth-century Kastamonu
Note: Very rough juxtaposition. Relative positions of groups based on a number considerations discussed in the text and not solely on wealth.

CONCLUSION

This chapter has served two purposes. First, it has provided detailed information about Kastamonu in the eighteenth century. Based on the court records, we have demonstrated that the town remained a modest-sized urban center and was probably not a major commercial or manufacturing hub during the eighteenth century. Moreover, our analysis of the probate estate inventories has suggested that the economic conditions of the town's population deteriorated during our period. Interestingly, the poorest segments of the population may have suffered during this period more so than the wealthy, which we attribute to the latter group's ability to take advantage of widening tax-farming and money-lending opportunities, among other possible factors. Consequently, wealth distribution in Kastamonu deteriorated in the course of the century.

The chapter has also introduced and justified the categories of analysis that we use in the legal investigations presented in subsequent chapters. These are based on markers associated with court clients' gender and religious identities, military and religious establishment affiliations, claims to religious status, and family backgrounds. In addition to being indicators of distinct positions in the social, cultural, and political hierarchy, we demonstrated that these markers can be used to make economic differentiations among court clients. In very general terms, our examination of the estate records has revealed that *Ağa*s, *Efendi*s, pilgrims, and members of prominent families constituted the socioeconomic elite in eighteenth-century Kastamonu.

PART TWO

THE COURT AND COURT CLIENTS

3

The Court, Its Actors, and Its Archive

INTRODUCTION

This chapter launches our exploration of the court of Kastamonu, its documents, and its activities. We begin by introducing the main actors of the court, based on the secondary literature on the topic and our observations in the court records. In addition to providing clues about the functions and identities of various court personalities, our discussion aims to demonstrate how local actors assumed official and unofficial roles in the court's operations, which is why we pay significant attention to a particular group of court actors: "witnesses to proceedings" (*şuhudülhal*).

We then examine the contents of the court's archive for three subperiods (1684–96, 1735–43, and 1781–90) during the late seventeenth and eighteenth centuries, revealing some of the court's primary legal and judicial responsibilities and also demonstrating how these evolved over relatively short periods of time. The latter point is critical to appreciate the dynamic nature of the court's functions and the ways in which its work was influenced by changing circumstances. Finally, the chapter demonstrates, in a preliminary manner, how specific client groups employed the court's services and temporal variations in their patterns of court use.

THE COURT AND COURT FUNCTIONARIES

The kadı presided over the court. In his absence, which was often in the eighteenth century, the *naib* assumed this role. The kadı was appointed to the position by sultanic warrants (*berat*s) from outside of the region and usually served a twelve- to twenty-month term.[1] The frequent rotation of kadıs was meant to prevent them from establishing strong connections with local interests and power-holders that could threaten their impartiality (İnalcık 1986, 1988b; Jennings 1978a). Secondary sources do not provide information about the rank of Kastamonu's kadı-ship in the judicial hierarchy for our period,[2] though the position was not a *mevleviyet*, or high-ranking judgeship.[3] As the highest judicial authority

[1] While appointments to high-ranking kadı-ships (*mevleviyets*) were usually for twelve months, ones to low-ranking posts ranged between eighteen and twenty months during our period (Tak 2009, 29; Yurkadul 2008, 143).

[2] According to two documents published by Turan Gökçe (1994a, 1994b), the kadı-ship of Kastamonu had a daily salary (*yevmiye*) of 55 *akçes* in 1513 and 60 *akçes* in 1528, which puts it below the kadı-ships of Bursa (300 *akçes* in 1513 and 1528), Amasya (150/200 *akçes* in 1513/1528), Ankara (130/150 *akçes*), Tokat (130 *akçes* in 1513), Tire (100/200 *akçes*), Antalya (100/100 *akçes*), Kütahya (90/150 *akçes*), İzmir (80/150 *akçes*), Konya (80/130 *akçes*), Manisa (80/120 *akçes*), Beçin (80/100 *akçes*), Larende (60/100 *akçes*), and Beğşehri (55/100 *akçes*) in the provincial judicial hierarchy of early sixteenth-century Anatolia. The salary level of the kadı-ship was identical or comparable to those of Çankırı (55/60 *akçes*), Bolu (55/60 *akçes*), Niğde (40/60 *akçes*), Mud (40/60 *akçes*), and Birgi (50/80 *akçes*) kadı-ships. From among those listed above Bursa, İzmir, Ankara, Tire, Birgi, and Tokat were among the highest-ranking kadı-ships (*mevleviyets*) in seventeenth- and eighteenth-century Anatolia (Uzunçarşılı 1965, 292).

[3] Uzunçarşılı (1965, 292) lists the *mevleviyets* in the seventeenth and eighteenth centuries in a rough descending order of rank as follows: Rumelia and Anatolia military-kadı-ships (*kazaskerlikler*), the kadı-ships of İstanbul, Mecca, Medina, Edirne, Bursa, Damascus, Egypt, Plovdiv, Jerusalem, Aleppo, Eyüp, Salonika, Yenişehir, Fener, Galata, İzmir, Üsküdar, Baghdad, Diyarbakır, Antep, Sofia, Belgrade, Bosnia, Erzurum, Maraş, Tripoli, Ankara, Gallipoli, Mihaliç, Chios, Kayseri, Tire, Birgi, Balıkesir, Menemen, Tokat, Mudurnu, Boyabat, Nicosia, Heraklion, and Kamyanets. *Sicill-i Osmani* does not mention any person of importance who served as the kadı of Kastamonu, which may indicate that the position was not a particularly prominent one. Interestingly, however, Kastamonu in the eighteenth century was a location where some high-ranking kadıs were sent (perhaps exiled) to after they were dismissed from prominent positions. For example, Sadreddinzade Abdurrahman *Efendi* (d. 1747) was sent to Kastamonu in 1738, after he served as the kadı of Damascus, Mecca, and İstanbul. *Sicill-i Osmani* (Mehmed Süreyya 1996, vol. 1, 93) indicates that he was dismissed (*azl*) from the last position but it does not reveal under what circumstances. It is also not clear what Abdurrahman *Efendi* did while he was in Kastamonu, although the source points out that he would receive the rank of Anatolia military-kadı-ship or *kazasker* (*Anadolu payesi*) after his return from Kastamonu. A similar pattern is also clear in the case of Reiszade Aşir Mustafa *Efendi* (d. 1804). Aşir Mustafa *Efendi* was a judge of the highest rank, who would eventually be promoted to the position of *şeyhülislam*. Earlier in his career he served as the kadı of Bursa, Mecca, and İstanbul, and *kazasker* of Anatolia and Rumelia. It was during his tenure as the *kazasker* of Rumelia that he was dismissed and ordered to move to Kastamonu (in 1790). A modern source implies that his dismissal and exile were related to his falling into disfavor with the *şeyhülislam* of the period, Hamidizade Mustafa *Efendi*. After Mustafa *Efendi* left the position, however, Aşir Mustafa *Efendi* was reappointed as the *kazasker* of Rumelia in 1793 (İpşirli 1991, 8). Finally, Köstendilli Tahir *Efendi* (d. 1812?) was sent to

in the subprovince, the kadı was responsible for applying Hanafi jurisprudence (*fiqh*) and Ottoman state laws (sing. *kanun*) in his jurisdiction. İnalcık (1986, 2–3) indicates that the kadı "had the power to administer *ta'zir* [discretionary] punishments and to imprison debtors," but he must have relied on the assistance of the local military authorities, such as governors, subgovernors, and their representatives, in so doing. According to İnalcık (1986, 2), provincial kadıs had to refer to İstanbul "all cases concerning the military class, state interests and public security, as well as those involving more than a certain amount of money."

In addition to his judicial functions, the kadı was also responsible for administering the municipal affairs of his jurisdiction, such as maintaining public roads, supervising the financial affairs of the mosques and pious endowments, overseeing guild activities, and regulating local prices. It is for this reason that Kaldy-Nagy (1978, 375) hesitates to translate the term kadı as "judge." Those who held the position were also responsible, in principle, for keeping an eye on local military-administrative authorities and protecting subjects from potential abuse. Finally, we know that the kadı played a role in the collection and transfer of local taxes and the mobilization of troops during military expeditions.

The kadı, as a judicial and administrative authority, was charged with administering Islamic law and enforcing imperial orders and regulations. However, the legitimacy of his actions was also based on local expectations of propriety and fairness. In this sense, we can presume that he was inclined to act in ways that met the social, cultural, and political expectations of the communities he served. According to Lawrence Rosen (2000), a distinctive feature of Islamic law is its ability to appropriate local perceptions and worldviews. But Ottoman judges also had other reasons for being sensitive to communal expectations: The number of disputes brought to court by local people, and the kadı's income from court fees, which likely constituted the bulk of his earnings, depended on local perceptions of his fairness. Potential court clients might avoid court altogether as a venue of dispute resolution or choose a court in one locale over another in a neighboring region, depending on the reputation of the judge or other considerations, although this was not always legal.

Other court functionaries, including deputy judges (*naib*s) and scribes (*katib*s), were often recruited from the local community. When they

Kastamonu in 1792/3 after he served as the kadı of İzmir. Following his return from Kastamonu he would be granted the rank (*paye*) of the kadı of Mecca (Mehmed Süreyya 1996, vol. 5, 1613).

worked with the kadıs these individuals must have influenced the kadı's interpretation of the events that he was asked to consider, his opinions of specific persons and their actions, and his verdicts. Generally, these were experienced court functionaries who served the court for a long time. Thus, they almost certainly played a role in shaping the kadı's actions so that they conformed to local beliefs, customs, and interests.

In Kastamonu court records, *naib*s and *katib*s are sometimes identified as teachers (singular, *müderris*), indicating that they were knowledgeable in the religious and legal sciences. It was the *naib*'s responsibility to assist the kadı in the functioning of the court and represent him either in his absence or when it was necessary for judicial authorities to travel outside of the town to hear and decide cases. Like the kadıs, the *naib*s charged fees for the cases they heard, although it is not always clear how much. According to Halil İnalcık (1986), kadıs often farmed out their positions to local *naib*s in the eighteenth century and preferred not to travel to and serve in their jurisdictions.[4] Indeed, there were periods during which the judgeship of Kastamonu was held by local *naib*s. It is not clear in our sources how much it cost to acquire the position, but this is the way one source describes the financial benefits associated with it:

> The position was sometimes acquired though trust-based delegation (*emaneten*) or on the basis of tax-farming (*iltizam suretiyle*). In the first case, the *naib* would claim one-fourth or one-fifth of the revenues. In the second case, he would pay, based on the revenues produced by the judgeship, 200, 300, even 600 *guruş* to the person whom he substituted, and claim the rest of the earnings minus court expenses for himself. (Uzunçarşılı n.d., 51; cf. Uzunçarşılı 1965, 117)

The source does not indicate which period these observations are based on, but the references in the text to the *History of Cevdet Paşa* and the *Koçi Bey Treatise* suggest the seventeenth and eighteenth centuries. The article suggests the spread of this form of tax-farming as one reason for increasing corruption in the judicial system and identifies this practice as one of the mechanisms through which the position was acquired by uneducated and corrupt power-holders at the local level (ibid.; Uzunçarşılı 1965, 117–18).

[4] After 1591–2 the imperial government allowed the kadıs to remain in their residences after appointments and send *naib*s as their representatives to assume their judicial responsibilities in their jurisdictions. Many, perhaps most, did so (Tak 2009, 12). In the late eighteenth century, the government was issuing directives that urged the kadıs to choose their representatives only from qualified and honest individuals, which gives an idea about the types of complaints that İstanbul frequently received at that time. In 1799 the government required the kadıs to travel to their jurisdictions and personally assume their responsibilities (ibid.; Yurdakul 2008, 140 and 301–2).

It was the *katib*'s responsibility to record the court's operations, keep and maintain the court's ledgers, and prepare legal-administrative documentation for the private use of court clients. Scribes may have also traveled outside of Kastamonu to hear disputes, sometimes on their own, independent of *naib*s, which might be a sign of their importance in local legal processes and/or legal training. İnalcık (1986) suggests that scribes occasionally served as *naib*s. Other court functionaries included individuals who held designations such as *çukadar* (messenger), *muhzır* (who summoned individuals to court), and *mübaşir* (bailiff) (cf. Jennings 1978a). Beyond what their official designations might indicate, however, there is little information in the court records about their specific duties.

Probate estate inventories provide a few clues about the economic circumstances of select court personnel. For example, they indicate that the one kadı who passed away while serving in Kastamonu was quite wealthy according to contemporary standards: The net value of the estate left behind by Esseyyid İbrahim Efendi from İstanbul, who died in 1776, was about 6,020 *guruş* in 1713 prices.[5] Presumably, this amount does not take into consideration the property of the deceased in İstanbul or elsewhere (Kastamonu Court Records [KCR], register/volume 60 – *tereke* in the volume 34 [or 60–34]). The estate inventories also identify ten deceased as "kadı" or use terms that can be interpreted in this way (for example, *kudatdan*, meaning "from among kadıs," or *fahrülkudat*, meaning "the pride of the kadıs").[6] The net values of the estates of these individuals range from approximately 400 to 8,900 *guruş* in 1713 prices, the average being about 2,970 *guruş* (std. dev.: 3,270 *guruş*) (KCR, 17–11, 22–52, 33–5, 52–5, 55–45, 56–37, 59–29, 63–61, 70–12, 75–3). The inventories indicate that the wealth of other court personnel was more modest. We found individuals identified as "bailiff," or *muhzır* (Mustafa, deceased in 1782); "court scribe," or *mahkeme katibi* (Elhac Ali Efendi, deceased in 1787); and "messenger," or *çukadar* (Esseyyid Ömer Ağa, deceased in 1801), and the net values of theirs estates were, respectively, about 130, 200, and 100 *guruş* in 1713 prices (KCR, 62–38, 65–31, 75–25). Our collection includes the inventories of two more

[5] The estate values are given in 1713 prices in this chapter in order to make comparisons to our calculations in Chapter 2 possible.

[6] What these signifiers meant is not exactly clear. Perhaps these individuals were retired kadıs, residing in Kastamonu at the time of their death, or they served as *naib*s in or outside of Kastamonu.

scribes, with substantially larger values, but it is not clear if these scribes worked in the court.[7]

One group of court actors about whom we know especially little is the "witnesses to proceedings" (*şuhudülhal*). These individuals, whose names appear at the end of judicial entries in the court records, functioned primarily to authenticate the transactions documented in the court records for future reference. Given the precarious position of written documentation in Islamic law and legal practice (see Chapter 8), it was their act of witnessing that ensured the binding authority of the court's actions, decisions, and contractual agreements. In principle, witnessing was open to all Muslims and it is well known that many individuals who came to court for different reasons often acted as witnesses in cases that did not directly concern them, simply because they happened to be at the court when these cases were heard. This being said, it is also likely that other factors played a role in determining who served as witnesses. In other words, "witnessing to proceedings" may not have been completely arbitrary.

For one thing, a careful examination of the court records reveals that the names of a select group of individuals appear among witnesses repeatedly. For example, in the period between 1735 and 1743, about one hundred individuals appeared as members of *şuhudülhal* at least four times. About thirty of these were cited as witnesses at least sixteen times, and five of them, more than fifty times. One particular individual, Kıbrısizade Elhac Ahmed Efendi, who was not an "official" court functionary as far as we can tell, was named as a witness in 127 separate entries. Who were these individuals? Of forty-three frequent witnesses cited more than ten times, seven were identified as the "pride of the kadıs" (*fahrülkudat*), indicating that they were elite members of the religious-judicial establishment, who may have served as kadıs or *naib*s in the past. The group also included two individuals identified as *şehir kethüdası*, who were responsible for representing the town population to imperial authorities, hosting official guests and travelers to town, and managing town expenses incurred on such occasions (Maden 2012, 28); two *serdar*s, or commanders of the local janissary units in town; one *nakıbüleşraf kaimakamı*, or the local head and representative of the descendants of Muhammad in Kastamonu; two *imams*; one *müderris* or teacher in a religious college; five *müezzin*s or individuals who called Muslims to

[7] Both died in 1801; Mehmed Efendi and Sadık Mahmud left behind estates of about 800 and 1800 *guruş* in value respectively, in 1713 prices. See KCR 75–3 and 75–9.

prayer; a son of the sheikh of the local Sufi lodge; and a son or grandson of the local *müfti*. Also included in this group are two *muhzırs*, or court bailiffs. Between 1684 and 1696, the two most frequently cited witnesses are two *muhzırs* of the court.

Some families are well represented among *şuhudülhal*. For example, there are two Kıbrısizades (Elhac Ahmed Efendi and his brother, Hafız Mehmed Efendi) among the most frequently cited witnesses in the second subperiod (1735–43). The same group also contains two Şalkımcızades and two Rıftarizades. Members of some extended families appear as frequent witnesses in more than one subperiod. For example, Kıbrısizade Hafız Ahmed Efendi, presumably the nephew of Kıbrısizade Elhac Ahmed Efendi and a son of the aforementioned Kıbrısizade Hafız Mehmed Efendi, is among frequent witnesses in the third subperiod (1781–90). The members of the Gazibeşezade, Şatırzade, Makberzade, Vildanzade, and Cennetzade extended families also appear among frequent witnesses in the second and third subperiods. Çetinzades, Ayna/İnehanzades, and Rıftarizades are cited among frequent witnesses in the first and second subperiods. There are Bereketzades among frequent witnesses in the first and third subperiods, which are about nine decades apart. Amazingly, it is possible to find a Muharremzade among frequent witnesses in every subperiod, indicating that the family continued to be represented in court for almost the entire eighteenth century.

In terms of the economic characteristics of frequent witnesses, we have been fortunate enough to identify the estate inventories of eight of the forty-three individuals cited in more than ten *sicil* entries, including that of Kıbrısizade Elhac Ahmed Efendi. The estate of Ahmed Efendi, who died in 1776, was worth about 1,640 *guruş* in 1713 prices. The values of the eight estates ranged between approximately 220 and 16,400 *guruş*, the average being about 2,900 *guruş* in 1713 prices (std. dev.: 5,460 *guruş*), which is significant by eighteenth-century standards. This finding is not surprising given the distribution of honorific titles, religious markers, and family statuses among frequent witnesses in the second period. Table 3.1 indicates that titleholders in general, and elite titleholders in particular, are disproportionately well represented among frequent witnesses. The same is also true for the members of prominent families, i.e., *zades*.[8] Our

[8] This finding may be somewhat misleading because it is easier to identify individuals with distinctive family names followed by the *zade* suffix among frequent witnesses, compared to individuals who had no such designation attached to their names.

TABLE 3.1: *Honorific Title, Religious Marker, and Family Status of Frequent Witnesses between 1735 and 1743*

	Frequency of Appearance as *şuhudülhal*								
	2–3	4–5	6 –10	11–15	16–20	21–30	31–50	51+	Total
Elite Religious	9	2	11	3	6	6	4	3	44
Non-elite Religious	15	5	2	3	1	2	3	0	31
Elite Military	15	6	7	3	1	2	3	0	37
Non-elite Military	7	4	9	1	0	0	0	1	22
No Title	8	7	5	0	1	0	0	0	21
Pilgrim	9	7	4	2	6	2	2	1	33
Descendant of Muhammad	4	1	2	1	1	1	1	0	11
No Religious Status	41	16	28	7	2	7	7	3	111
Prominent	31	9	14	6	6	4	6	3	79
Non-prominent	23	15	20	4	3	6	4	1	76
Total witnesses	54	24	34	10	9	10	10	4	155

Note: Since witnesses belonged to specific title, religious status, and family groups simultaneously, the figures in the final row do not correspond to the sum of figures in corresponding columns.

observations based on the first and third subperiods draw a similar picture.

Broadly, then, frequent witnesses were among the upper crust of the local community. They included prominent inhabitants of the town, who often occupied positions of influence and authority. There may be a number of reasons for this tendency. Legally, witnesses to proceedings served the function of validating the details and/or the overall legality of the processes and transactions recorded in the court registers, in case they later came under scrutiny. But what made the testimony of a witness credible? As we explain in Chapter 8, it was his stature within the community and his general reputation. For example, kadıs routinely inquired about the honesty and reliability of witnesses in evidentiary processes (not to be confused with witnesses to proceedings or *şuhudülhal*) during litigation before accepting their testimony, a procedure called *tezkiye*. For this reason, it made legal sense to repeatedly employ as witnesses to proceedings, who could subsequently act as witnesses in evidentiary processes, individuals whose reputations were considered to be beyond reproach.

In fact, the frequent reliance on a small number of prominent individuals in eighteenth-century Kastamonu resembles what Rudolph Peters has documented for eighth-century Egypt, where the need to ensure the credibility of witnesses in important transactions led to the emergence of a small group of legally trained, highly reputable "professional witnesses" (called *shuhūd ʿadl* in Arabic), not unlike notary-publics (Peters 1997, 298). This is not to suggest that the frequent witnesses in eighteenth-century Kastamonu were professionals in any sense of word, nor is it necessarily the case that they were hired or fired by the kadı. But they may have served a very similar function: Their prominence, good reputation, and, in some cases, religious-legal training made the proceedings they witnessed relatively secure from future challenge.[9]

The distinction we make between "official" and "unofficial" court actors may be moot, even anachronistic in the context of eighteenth-century Kastamonu, at least to an extent. Consider the following incident: Late one night in June or July of 1735, İbrahim son of Ahmed from the İkirciler (?) village of Kastamonu caught Mustafa Beşe son of Mehmed having intercourse (*zina*) with İbrahim's wife, Cennet daughter of Hasan. According to the court registry in which this incident was recorded, İbrahim seized Mustafa Beşe and immediately presented him to an assembly (*cemiyyet*) of local Muslims where Mustafa Beşe admitted (*ikrar*) his crime, alleging that Cennet had invited him in the house (*zevcen gel deyü beni davet itmeğle*). Although Mustafa Beşe denied the accusation later in court, the testimony of the Muslims who constituted the assembly secured a decision against him, based on his earlier confession (KCR, vol. 34, entry of? Safer 1148 /? June or July 1735). Given the difficulty of proving *zina* according to Islamic law and the severe legal repercussions associated with false allegations of *zina*,[10] the testimony of those in the assembly was

[9] It is important to remember that the law even allowed the kadı to keep some frequent witnesses immune from the *tezkiye* requirement, which may have generated an incentive for involving such individuals in legal acts and/or transactions. The article 1723 of the *Mecelle* states that if the credibility of a witness is demonstrated in one case, the judge does not need to inquire into his credibility for a different case within a period of six months (Berki 1986, 386). Thus, using as witnesses those individuals who appear in court often may have made future legal processes easier to handle.

[10] *Zina* is a *hadd* offence or "crime against God." Although the punishment for *zina* could be severe (100 lashes, banishment, or stoning to death, depending on whether the offender is single or married, free or slave, and Muslim or non-Muslim), *zina* punishment requires almost impossible evidentiary substantiation: Four male, Muslim eye-witnesses to the actual act of intercourse (Peters 2005, 59–62). False accusation of *zina* is also a *hadd* crime, which requires a punishment of "eighty lashes and the removal of the right to testify until one repents, or, according to the Hanafi doctrine, forever" (ibid., 63).

absolutely critical in securing a decision against Mustafa Beşe. Without a credible report of confession, İbrahim would have not only lost the case, but may have been punished himself for making an unsubstantiated *zina* allegation. For the concerns of our discussion, what is remarkable is that Kıbrısizade Elhac Ahmed Efendi, the most frequent name among witnesses to proceedings in the second subperiod, was among the individuals in the assembly. The fact that İbrahim specifically called on him along with a few other "trustworthy" Muslims in the middle of the night to witness Mustafa Beşe's confession suggests that Kıbrısizade possessed a special status, unique qualities, and/or influence over the court. Even if he was not among the "official" court personnel, he occupied the blurred space that separated the court from the community, and provided much-needed communication between the two entities (or their individual constituents). In an instance of emergency, as in the present example, he could act as the court's trusted informer.

There may also be other, not necessarily judicial, factors that explain why members of the local elite often and repeatedly appeared as witnesses to proceedings. Mustafa Akdağ (1974, 404) has argued that the *şuhudülhal* acted as an "advisory council" and functioned, to some extent, to influence the opinions of the kadı in keeping with the values and traditions of the community. Similarly, Farhat Ziadeh (1990, 78) has suggested that prominent members of the community often made their views known to the court about matters brought before it. Witnesses also had the authority to confirm the integrity and reliability of individuals who came to the court, and this constituted a significant source of power for the members of the *şuhudülhal*, and a means for discrimination against "undesirable" elements within the community (Ziadeh 1990, 91). İnalcık (1986, 2–3) has even suggested that one important function of the *şuhudülhal* was "to check the kadı" and to ensure that "a decision was reached in the presence of on unbiased body." If the *şuhudülhal* were expected to serve all these functions, it makes sense that it included prominent and powerful representatives of the community.

This discussion about the role of the elite, prominent members of the community in the *şuhudülhal* should not cloud the fact that a vast majority of the witnesses did not belong to this group, which is why it makes sense to search for other factors that may have influenced its composition. One possibility is that the identity of litigants or parties to contractual arrangements also affected the identity of witnesses. It is likely that relatives, friends, neighbors, and colleagues of court clients occasionally acted as witnesses to their legal transactions, although a systematic analysis of the topic is difficult because, in most cases, court records do not provide detailed information about the identity, occupation, or the location of residence for individual witnesses, or their relationship to clients.

It is, however, possible to conduct a comparable analysis by using honorific titles, religious markers, and family identities of court clients and witnesses. In the following table, we provide as a demonstration the title distribution of witnesses according to the titles of court clients in whose cases they participated. Our sample includes all litigations, amicable settlements, and contractual arrangements in the second period. The table distinguishes the cases based on (a) the title group of the court clients, and (b) whether their counterparts belonged to the same title group. For example, the table distinguishes cases which involved only elite religious titleholders (the column labeled as "With ER") from cases which involved elite religious titleholders and other title groups (the column labeled as "With others").[11]

The table reveals the relationship between court client and witness titles. This relationship is most obvious in cases that involved court clients with identical titles. For example, in cases that involved elite military (EM) titleholders only ("Cases that involved EM clients with EM clients"), the average number of witnesses with EM titles (2.2) is higher than the average numbers of EM witnesses in other cases (that is, higher than the figures in the same row). The relationship between witness and client titles is generally evident even in cases that involved clients with non-identical titles. For example, the average number of witnesses with non-elite religious (NER) titles is both higher than the averages observed for witnesses with other titles in cases that involved NER clients with other titleholders (compare 2.13 with the figures in the same column) and the averages observed for NER witnesses in cases that did not involve any NER clients (compare 2.13 with figures given for "Cases that involved ER clients with ER clients" [2], "Cases that involved EM clients with EM clients" [0.6], "Cases that involved NEM clients with NEM clients" [0.92], and "Cases that involved NT clients with NT clients" [1.53], in the same row).[12]

In considering the reason for this finding, a number of possibilities come to mind. First, the title association between clients and witnesses

[11] Some cases included multiple parties on one or both sides. We did not exclude these cases from our sample but, unless all parties in both sides belonged to the same title group, these cases are counted separately according to the title identities of each client. Cases that involved women are categorized according to the title identities of the male clients.

[12] "With others" might include NER clients.

TABLE 3.2: *Title Distribution of Witnesses according to Titles of Court Clients between 1735 and 1743*

	Cases That Involved ER Clients				Cases That Involved NER Clients				Cases That Involved EM Clients				Cases That Involved NEM Clients				Cases That Involved NT Clients			
	With ER Clients		With Others		With NER Clients		With Others		With EM Clients		With Others		With NEM Clients		With Others		With NT Clients		With Others	
Şuhudülhal	Total	Per Case	Total	Per Case	Total	Per Case	Total	Per Case	Total	Per Case	Total	Per Case	Total	Per Case	Total	Per Case	Total	Per Case	Total	Per Case
Elite Religious	25	6.25	138	2.26	12	1.33	241	1.65	13	2.6	147	1.6	33	1.27	263	1.14	95	1.02	379	1.09
Non-elite Religious	8	2	115	1.89	22	2.44	311	2.13	3	0.6	109	1.19	24	0.92	306	1.32	142	1.53	582	1.68
Elite Military	2	0.5	72	1.18	10	1.11	122	0.84	11	2.2	127	1.38	35	1.35	245	1.06	61	0.66	263	0.76
Non-elite Military	0	0	70	1.15	5	0.56	165	1.13	4	0.8	132	1.43	78	3	405	1.75	153	1.65	491	1.41
No Title	2	0.5	80	1.31	12	1.33	289	1.98	4	0.8	123	1.34	35	1.35	375	1.62	194	2.09	620	1.79
Total # of Cases	4		61		9		146		5		92		26		231		93		347	
Witnesses per Case	9.25		7.79		6.78		7.73		7		6.93		7.88		6.9		6.95		6.73	

ER: Elite Religious; NER: Non-elite Religious; EM: Elite Military; NEM: Non-elite Military; NT: No title.

may be an indication of preexisting relationships between court clients and witnesses founded on establishment-based affiliations. Assuming that the choice of *şuhudülhal* was potentially a strategic decision given the functional expectations from witnesses, i.e., to participate in possible future evidentiary proceedings, such affiliations may have allowed clients to better assess the reputations of those whom they could ask to witness their legal proceedings, and, as critical, enhanced their ability to locate and bring them to court later again if or when necessary. Another possible factor is the inclination on the part of the establishment-based communities to support their members in the legal arena by participating in their cases. Witnessing may have been a way to oversee the affairs of colleagues and associates and ensure they received the legal assistance they needed.

Thus, the title association between court clients and witnesses might be indicative of the various ways that communal relationships and mechanisms influenced witness choices. If this was indeed the case, it is likely that other relationships also played a role in determining witness composition. Indeed, our examination of clients' and witnesses' religious markers and family status in the second period also revealed a strong client–witness association for the descendants of Muhammad (though not for pilgrims or members of prominent families). Accordingly, we should expect that court clients also relied on neighbors, relatives, and friends as witnesses.

Finally, the nature of the legal case might have also influenced witness composition. In order to examine this possibility, we classified the court records in the second period in two different ways. First, we separated litigations, contractual agreements, and amicable settlements. Second, we distinguished cases (litigations, contracts, amicable settlements) based on whether they involved (a) private matters and civil disputes (1st type), (b) public matters such as taxation, communal responsibility, and supervision of charitable endowments (2nd type), or (c) criminal affairs (3rd type). Table 3.3 demonstrates the title distribution of witnesses in cases classified in this fashion.

Table 3.3 provides some support for a relationship between the distribution of witness titles and case-types. Unfortunately, we cannot explain every variation in the table. Nevertheless, it is clear that the proportion of elite titleholding witnesses is higher in cases that concerned public affairs in Kastamonu (2nd type). Also noteworthy is the fact that military titleholders are well represented as witnesses in crime-related legal processes, which might be due to the fact that the military establishment played a role in the litigation and punishment of criminals, and/or that court clients in crime-related cases tended to be the members of the

TABLE 3.3: *Title Distribution of Witnesses according to Case-type*

	Litigations		Contracts		Settlements		1st Type (Private Matters and Civil Disputes)		2nd Type (Public Matters)		3rd Type (Criminal Affairs)	
Şuhudülhal	**Total**	**Per Case**	**Total**	**Per Case**	**Total**	**Per Case**	**Total**	**Per Case**	**Total**	**Per Case**	**Total**	**Per Case**
Elite Religious	361	1.245	553	1.298	175	1.496	846	1.25	158	2	83	1.122
Non-elite Religious	359	1.238	805	1.89	180	1.538	1160	1.713	91	1.152	88	1.189
Elite Military	290	1	307	0.721	129	1.103	526	0.777	102	1.291	97	1.311
Non-elite Military	441	1.521	605	1.42	207	1.769	959	1.417	125	1.582	163	2.203
No Title	375	1.293	848	1.991	198	1.692	1204	1.778	103	1.304	110	1.486
Total # of Cases	290		426		117		677		79		74	
Witnesses per Case	6.297		7.319		7.598		6.129		7.329		7.311	

military establishment. When we conducted a similar type of analysis based on the religious marker and family affiliation of witnesses, we observed that members of prominent families are overrepresented in legal processes concerning public/communal matters. The same analysis did not reveal any significant variation in the representation of pilgrims and descendants of Muhammad in different types of cases.

Given the extent of literature on Ottoman courts of law, it is remarkable how little information exists about the compensation of the kadıs and other court personnel. We know that before the Tanzimat era (1839–76) the income of court personnel was based largely on court fees (Uzunçarşılı 1965, 84); however, the court's archives do not provide any clues about the fees it charged for a given service. In an earlier study, Ergene (2003, 77) compiled the fees prescribed in sultanic law books (*kanunnames*) and other sources from different periods. We reproduce this table here with additional information.

The figures presented in Table 3.4 indicate, perhaps unrealistically, that court fees did not change much between the fifteenth and nineteenth centuries although, according to Özmucur and Pamuk, prices in İstanbul increased about seven- to eight-fold in the same period (2002, 301). It is likely that after the sixteenth century court personnel adjusted their fees in response to inflation and to compensate for increasingly shorter tenures in a particular jurisdiction and longer wait times between appointments (İnalcık 1986; Zarinebaf 2010, 143–4).

However, we are quite uninformed about how much the court functionaries *actually* charged for their services, beyond a few observations. The estate inventories in the court records constitute a rare form of documentation that reveals explicitly how much the court charged for its services – in this particular case, dividing the estates of the deceased among their heirs. Ergene (2003, 89) has demonstrated that the courts in Çankırı and Kastamonu charged about 3.4 percent of the gross value of the estates in the late seventeenth and eighteenth centuries. This value is substantially higher than what was dictated in official prescriptions (1.5 percent, see Table 3.4). Furthermore, the rate varied substantially among individual inventories and reached up to 7 percent in Kastamonu and 7.5 percent in Çankırı records. Based on these observations it seems clear that the official guidelines were not observed in the courts of Çankırı and Kastamonu.

Other researchers have also made a few relevant observations. For example, Abraham Marcus (1989, 106) informs us that kadıs claimed 10 percent of the sum awarded in litigations in late-eighteenth-century

TABLE 3.4: *Court Fees Prescribed for Different Services (in* akçes*)*[13]

Services	15th Century	Late 16th Century	Late 16th–early 17th Century	1644–5	1676–77	Early 18th Century	Dec. 1780
Manumission of slaves		–	62	66	–	62	–
Registration of marriage (*nikah*)	32 for virgins; 12/15 for previously married	–	25 for virgins	25	25 for virgins	25 for virgins	–
Inheritance (*miras*)	20 for every 1,000 *akçes* of estate's value	25 for every 1,000 *akçes* of estate's value	15 for every 1,000 *akçes* of estate's value	15 for every 1,000 *akçes* of estate's value	15 for every 1,000 *akçes* of estate's value	15 for every 1,000 *akçes* of estate's value	–
Notary service (*hüccet*)	32	26	25	25	25	25	25
Signature (*imza*)	12	–	12	12	12	12	12
Registration fee	7	8	8	12	8	8	8
Letters to authorities (*mürasele*)		8	6	8	6	6	6

Note: The fees presented in the table include the share for kadıs and other members of the court.
Sources: Table 5.1 in Ergene (2003, 77). Additional information is from Uzunçarşılı (1965, 84–5).

[13] In addition to the services identified in the table, the court also charged fees for tax-farm registrations (*mukataa resmi*), divorces (a hefty 66 *akçes* in the late sixteenth century), and the supervision of local taxes (Uzunçarşılı 1965, 85–6).

Aleppo, to be paid by winning parties. Not included in this amount were the fees owed to other court personnel such as scribes or bailiffs. On the other hand, Kuran and Lustig (2012, 635) have suggested that "judges might collect, for instance, 2 percent of the amount at stake" in commercial disputes in seventeenth-century İstanbul. It is important to remember that, according to contemporary Ottoman sources and Western travelers' accounts, gifts and bribes came to be associated with court use in the early modern period (Ergene 2003, 99–124). Nevertheless, it is impossible to know the extent to which the cost of court use kept pace with inflation.

Finally, let us conclude with a brief note on where legal proceedings were conducted. We know that not every judgeship had a courthouse. In many cases the kadı heard and decided cases in a designated room or section of his residence, or in a public location such as the market or mosque (İnalcık 1986). For example, Ankara, a bigger urban center than Kastamonu, and presumably a more important judgeship, did not have a courthouse in the early seventeenth century (Kankal 2004, 46). However, our sources indicate that Kastamonu had one in the early eighteenth century, although it is not clear when it was built (ibid., 46–7). Apparently, this building burned down in 1719 and needed to be rebuilt at substantial expense (ibid.). Eyüpgiller suggests that the building burned again in 1790 and was rebuilt in 1791 (1999, 165; Maden 2012, 24–5).

COURT RECORDS: BASIC CLASSIFICATIONS AND CHANGE OVER TIME

For the analyses presented in this book, we examined nineteen court registers of Kastamonu. These registers contain a variety of documents, either composed by court functionaries or received from outside sources, such as the imperial center or other provincial authorities. The documents that originated in Kastamonu include summary accounts of disputes decided in the court, amicable settlements, copies of contracts, probate estate inventories, divorce cases, and cases related to suretyship (*kefalet*), support after divorce (*nafaka*), and guardianship (*vesayet*). The documents that originated elsewhere include imperial orders and correspondence regarding matters concerning taxation, troop and material deployment during war, and internal security. These documents are almost always recoded in a separate section in court ledgers, apart from the entries that originated in Kastamonu. The variety of documents found in the court records reflects the multifaceted nature of the kadı's responsibilities.

The collection of Kastamonu court records begins in 1095 H. /1684 C. E. and contains a total of seventy-eight registers covering the period between the late seventeenth and early nineteenth centuries.[14] For this study we examined the registers from three subperiods comparable in length. These subperiods are as follows: (1) 1095 H. / 1684 C. E. – 1107 H. / 1696 C. E.; (2) 1148 H. / 1735 C. E. – 1156 H. / 1743 C. E.; and (3) 1195 H. / 1781 C. E. – 1204 H. / 1790 C. E.[15] We kept the first period slightly longer than the other two because it lacks documentation for some years.[16]

Here, we should clarify that our data set is not composed of three *samples* of legal documentation for each subperiod, but contains *all* available documentation of interest (see below) for these periods. In other words, we kept our data set as large as possible, constrained only by our choices of temporal coverage. Although we could have increased the available data by expanding the subperiodic coverages from roughly decade-long spans to longer (say, fifteen- or twenty-year) periods, this would have reduced our ability to capture temporal variations in court use, one of our main focal areas of exploration. The decade-long span allows for a better snapshot examination of the court's activities. In choosing the number and length of the subperiods, we were also constrained by the overall temporal coverage of the Kastamonu *sicil*s and by our ability to identify in them multiple, similar-length eras with mostly unbroken documentation. Given these considerations, some types of documents may appear relatively infrequently in specific subperiods. Instead of being a cause for concern about the representativeness of our records for broader functions of the court, we should regard such an instance as a valuable historical finding about legal practice: A type of documentation poorly represented in the court records for about a decade tells us something about how the court was *not* used by the people of Kastamonu.

[14] The microfilm copy of the earliest register in the catalogue – register number 412/2, dated 1084–6/1673–5 – is missing

[15] For the first subperiod we examined seven court registers (volumes 1, 3, 4, 5, 6, 7, and 55), for the second subperiod, seven registers (volumes 34, 35, 36, 37, 38, 39, and 40), and for the third subperiod, five registers (volumes 62, 63, 64, 65, and 66). We also occasionally consulted case entries from other registers for the purposes of comparison and identifying representative examples to be used in subsequent chapters.

[16] Otherwise, the overall coverage of our documentation appears to be complete. We should note also that since our analysis is largely based on the *proportions* of various types of documents (rather than their absolute numbers), any missing documentation for the subperiods should not affect our findings.

TABLE 3.5: *Types of Documents in Kastamonu Court Records*

	1684–96	1735–43	1781–90	Total # of Documents for Each Type
Litigations	233 (56%)	272 (44%)	354 (33%)	859 (41%)
Contracts	137 (33%)	224 (36%)	437 (41%)	798 (38%)
Settlements	44 (11%)	118 (19%)	272 (26%)	434 (21%)
Total # of Judicial Entries	414 (100%)	614 (100%)	1063 (100%)	2091 (100%)

Note: Percentages represent shares per period.

Our study is based on a detailed analysis of the documents originating in Kastamonu. This includes three types of records: Summary accounts of litigations; contracts and agreements recorded in court registers; and records of amicable settlements. The contracts in the sample include commercial and property-related agreements (including loans, partnerships, transactions of movable and immovable assets) and exclude records documenting other forms of interactions such as arrangements involving representation (*vekalet*), guardianship (*vesayet*), and payments based on previous debts or contractual obligations. Technically, amicable settlements are also contractual arrangements, so they could justifiably be included in the contracts. However, we have chosen to treat them separately since, as a form of dispute resolution, they are more similar to litigations. Table 3.5 shows the number of each type of document for each subperiod.

Table 3.5 reveals a number of important insights into the operations of the court. First, it is striking how different the total number of documents is for each period. The fact that they increased about two-and-a-half times over the course of the century, without an accompanying demographic change or change in the jurisdictional boundaries that we are aware of, suggests that court use became more popular over time. Reasons for the shift in court-use patterns this variation indicates are not immediately clear. One possibility is premised on the assumption that the court in Kastamonu, whose archives do not go back beyond the 1680s, was established in the late seventeenth century. If this was indeed the case, it may have taken time for the local population to accept the court as a legitimate venue for dispute resolution and other legal and judicial activities. Another possibility is that the cost of court use became relatively cheaper over time. Remember that the official rates for court fees did not change during our period, although according to Özmucur and Pamuk (2002, 301), the prices in İstanbul increased about four times during the eighteenth century alone. Even though court functionaries may have managed to adjust their actual incomes in a variety of (legitimate or illegitimate) ways, it is not certain that the real cost of court use remained unaffected by inflationary pressures.

Also, economic changes over the course of the eighteenth century may be related to the increase in the numbers of court-produced documents. As noted earlier, historians now consider the eighteenth century as a period of growing commercialization and intensified economic activity, developments associated with "de facto" privatization of public revenue sources, emerging local credit markets, and flourishing regional and inter-regional trade relations.[17] We have significant doubts that Kastamonu experienced these trends to the extent that many other locations did, but it is not inconceivable that it had a modest economic surge of its own. Thus, the trends that we observe in the volume of documentation in the court's archive could be indicative of a greater demand for the court's notarial and litigious functions due to the upsurge in economic and commercial transactions.

If there existed a connection between economic change and court-use patterns in eighteenth-century Kastamonu, it would mean that the economic trends of the era played a role in the court's better, if gradual, integration into local affairs. Ariel Salzmann (1993) famously suggested that the spread of short- and long-term tax-farming arrangements in the seventeenth and eighteenth centuries led to the "Ottomanization" of provincial power-holders as these groups invested heavily in regional revenue sources and, consequently, came to represent the state in their locales as low- and mid-level administrators of state assets. If the connection that we have proposed between economic change and court-use patterns is valid, it might represent a different form of "Ottomanization," defined as a greater degree of reliance by the local population on an imperial institution to manage their day-to-day affairs.

Whatever the reason(s) for the increase in court documentation, the locally generated legal workload of the court does not seem to have been excessive.[18] Even during the late eighteenth century, for which we find the largest number of court-produced records, the number of documents in

[17] See Chapter 2.

[18] For an analysis of the non-locally generated documentation in the court records of Kastamonu, see Ergene (2003, 32–43).

the sample averages less than nine per month. This number does not change significantly even when we count all types of court-produced documentation that we excluded from our sample. Thus, even in the busiest times, the court does not appear to have played a major role in the daily lives of the people of Kastamonu, at least as a judicial institution. A disproportionally large number of disputes must have been resolved outside of court, and most contracts must have been arranged independently of the court's notarial supervision.

In an earlier study, Ergene (2003, chapter 3) demonstrated that one court's judicial-administrative functions might differ significantly from another's in a given time period, even in a neighboring region. Table 3.5 reveals that a single court's functions could also vary over a relatively short period of time. While the court of Kastamonu was primarily an arena of litigation in the late seventeenth century, its notarial responsibilities, such as document registration and record-keeping, expanded in the course of the eighteenth century. During this period, the number of contracts in the court's archives increased more than three times and the number of settlements increased about six times. The number of litigation entries, meanwhile, increased about one-and-a-half times (see Figure 3.1). It is possible that the relative growth of the court's notarial responsibilities is somehow reflective of the general changes in the economy, as discussed above. But before we make any assumptions about what purposes the

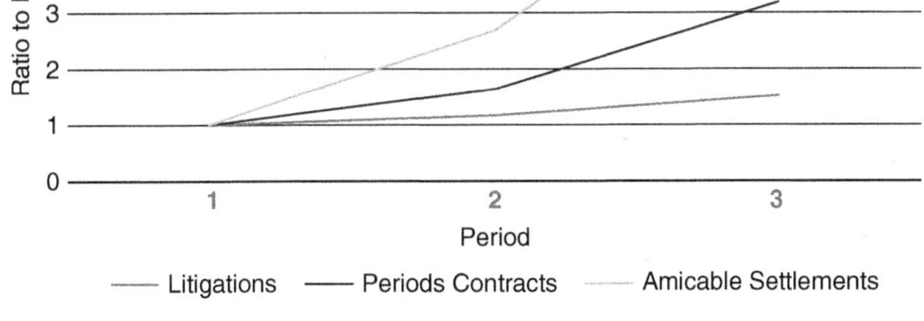

FIGURE 3.1: Temporal Change in the Proportions of Different Types of Documents
Note: The figures on the *y*-axis indicate the ratios of the numbers of different types of documentation in three subperiods to the numbers in the first period.

court-produced or -authorized documentation served in or outside of the court, we need to grasp the legal status of written records as evidence in Islamic and Ottoman jurisprudence, a topic we return to in Chapter 8.

In addition to distinguishing three major document types, we also adopt in this study two supplementary forms of differentiation in our treatment of the material in the court records. First, we distinguish legal interactions among unrelated parties from those that involved family members and extended kin, including, but not limited to, parents, siblings, spouses, cousins, in-laws, nieces, and nephews.[19] This is because litigations and legal interactions that involved relatives tended to have different dynamics and concern different issues than those that involved unrelated parties. For example, criminal disputes among family members and kin rarely came to court. It is also likely that a separate set of considerations, such as the desire to shield family relationships from tensions generated by the conflict, influenced adversarial relationships and interactions among related disputants.

Second, we divide disputes into civil contentions and crimes against individuals and property. While civil disputes included disagreements over property ownership, usufruct rights over land, debt, contractual obligations, revenues generated by charitable foundations, and taxation, criminal disputes included murder and assault cases (sexual and otherwise), crimes against property (theft, robbery), banditry, usurpation, insults and swearing, complaints of administrative abuse, and a few other categories. Obviously, no jurisprudential categories analogous to Western concepts of civil, criminal, or penal law exist in classical Islamic legal theory (cf. Gerber 1994, 32–3). Nevertheless, this fact matters little for the purposes of this study since our analysis is not exclusively a jurisprudential one. While our differentiation among documents pertaining to litigations, contracts, and settlements is more consistent with the logic of Islamic jurisprudence, the intent to understand the general attitudes toward various types of conflicts justifies our choice to adopt this classification as well, based on the assumption that "criminal" disputes generate socio-communal (if not jurisprudential) consequences different from "civil" ones. Representing a socio-legal approach, the analysis presented in this book follows the examples set by earlier researchers including Uriel Heyd (1973), Eyal Ginio (1998), Rudolph Peters (2005), and

[19] The court records meticulously identify family relationships and kin-connections among court clients.

Fariba Zarinebaf (2010), whose work focused on the criminal aspects of Islamic and Ottoman law.

In the following analysis we recategorize litigations, amicable settlements, and contracts according to case-types in three subperiods. Table 3.6 does this for litigations.

As discussed earlier, litigations increased about 50 percent from the late seventeenth to the late eighteenth century. This finding may suggest that the tendency to resolve disputes through formal litigation increased over time, assuming that the population of the district remained stable. Again, however, the fact that the court decided about 23 to 35 litigations per year in a judgeship of about 30,000 or more people strongly suggests that it was not the primary arena of dispute resolution at any time during our period.[20] This finding (a) forces us to reconsider the place of the provincial court and the formal processes of litigation based on Islamic jurisprudence in the lives of local people[21] and (b) makes us wonder about the types of disputes that were brought to court and how representative they were of the kinds of problems, contentions, and conflicts that shaped daily life in Kastamonu. We return to these questions in the second and third parts of the book.

Table 3.6 reveals that the types of litigation brought to court significantly varied over time. Whereas litigations among related adversaries increased, significantly fewer crime-related disputes appear in the registers by the end of the eighteenth century compared to the late seventeenth century. Apparently, Kastamonians became less hesitant over time to air family squabbles in the public arena of the court, although it is not clear why. What is more certain is that, unless Kastamonu suddenly became a more peaceful society by the end of the century, crime-related disputes

[20] It is very likely that the kadıs did not decide every litigation they heard. If such cases were never recorded in the court records, the number of litigations found in the court records cannot precisely represent the court's adjudicative workloads.

[21] It is impossible to know how disputes were settled outside of the court. While communal and/or official mediation must have been common (see Chapter 5), there might have also existed unofficial arenas for litigation or litigation-like processes. Relevant in this regard is James Baldwin's recent characterization of the ways in which influential and powerful individuals in eighteenth-century Cairo (*beys*) frequently administered justice independent of local courts, a phenomenon that he calls "privatized justice" (forthcoming, chapter 3). According to Baldwin, many Egyptians preferred "privatized justice" over the courts of law as they were critical of many aspects of the courts' operations, including their corruption and "pedantic proceduralism." Egyptians also appreciated the "aggressive and sometimes violent approach" of the "*beys*" in their efforts to administer justice (ibid.). We are grateful to Baldwin for allowing us to see his book manuscript before its publication.

TABLE 3.6: *Litigations Classified according to Type and Period*

	1684–96	1735–43	1781–90	Total # of Litigations According to Type
Civil litigations among unrelated parties	160 (69%)	156 (57%)	208 (59%)	524 (61%)
Civil litigations among related parties	46 (20%)	66 (24%)	126 (36%)	238 (28%)
Criminal litigations among unrelated parties	27 (12%)	48 (18%)	19 (5%)	94 (11%)
Criminal litigations among related parties	0 (0%)	2 (1%)	1 (0%)	3 (0%)
Total # of litigations according to period	233 (100%)	272 (100%)	354 (100%)	859 (100%)

Note: Percentages represent shares in a given subperiod.

became increasingly resolved by mechanisms other than litigation in court. One possibility in this regard is the increasing use of the office of the governor, subgovernor, or their representatives. We know that the system required their involvement in criminal disputes (Uzunçarşılı 1965, 110), which is why many crime-related hearings were held in the mansions of governors and subgovernors – often, if not always, in the presence of executive and judicial officers (Ergene 2003, 172; Aykan 2012; Ginio 1998; Ursinus 2004; Gradeva 2006). Thus, a decline in criminal litigations in court records may suggest that executive authorities became more involved in the management of criminal disputes, possibly independent of the court. It is also possible that such cases were forwarded to the imperial center more frequently in the second half of the eighteenth century.[22]

[22] Ekrem Tak (2009, 152–3) argued that after 1741–2, the Üsküdar court referred cases that involved crimes against persons and property (including theft, sexual and non-sexual assault, murder, kidnapping) and matters that concerned "public law" (*kamu hukuku*) to the imperial council (*divan-ı hümayun*) for resolution, instead of deciding them on its own, like it used to before. Although Tak does not explain the reasons for this change, the reduction in the numbers of crime-related disputes in the Üsküdar court's workload is consistent with our findings in Kastamonu. According to Tak, the Ottoman judicial system experienced a "reform" in mid-eighteenth century, which enhanced the central

TABLE 3.7: *Amicable Settlements Classified according to Type and Subperiod*

	1684–96	1735–43	1781–90	Total # of Settlements According to Type
Civil settlements among unrelated parties	16 (36%)	34 (29%)	76 (28%)	126 (29%)
Civil settlements among related parties	23 (52%)	66 (56%)	140 (51%)	229 (53%)
Criminal settlements among unrelated parties	5 (11%)	17 (14%)	54 (20%)	76 (18%)
Criminal settlements among related parties	0	1 (1%)	2 (1%)	3 (1%)
Total # of settlements according to period	44 (100%)	118 (100%)	272 (100%)	434 (100%)

Note: Percentages represent shares in a given subperiod.

The cases resolved through litigation are not the only disputes documented in the court ledgers. Our sources also contain amicable settlement (*sulh*) registrations, which represent a type of negotiated settlement process. Table 3.7 provides the number of different types of settlements observed in three periods.

Settlement registrations in court records are even rarer than adjudications, ranging from about four to twenty-seven per year. Given the population of the town and district of Kastamonu, this finding indicates that a great majority of settlements did not come to court for registration, which was not a legal requirement. It is, however, striking that they increased about six-fold over the course of the century, much faster than litigations.

In Chapter 7, we discuss in detail what types of disputes were resolved through litigation and which ones through settlement (and why), but a comparative reading of Tables 3.6 and 3.7 provides some preliminary

government's (and, presumably, the provincial military-administrative authorities') direct involvement in the administration of justice and limited the judicial autonomy of the local kadıs.

observations. For example, while litigations usually involved unrelated adversaries, settlements were often among family members and extended kin. Even though the proportion of litigations involving related parties increased over time, they were still in the minority by the end of the eighteenth century. It is not difficult to guess why *sulh* was a popular form of dispute resolution among related parties. Since the process involved a negotiated resolution of conflict, and not a third party's (kadı's) judgment that might generate a zero-sum result for the litigants, it had greater potential to protect preexisting relationships from potentially disruptive tensions. The likelihood of maintaining amiable relations after one party was declared a winner and the other a loser was undoubtedly slimmer. Another interesting difference between litigations and settlements is noticeable in criminal conflicts. While criminal litigations declined sharply in the third period, settlements that involved crime-related disputes appear to have increased significantly. These contrasting tendencies make sense, since there is no reason to expect that the increasing role of executive authorities in the resolution of criminal disputes influenced the recording of settlements. In both litigations and settlements, however, crime-related disputes that involved family members and kin are underrepresented.

Table 3.8 demonstrates what an analogous classification of the contracts would look like. The contracts in our sample include agreements involving property ownership (predominantly immovable property, including homes, shops, gardens), sales and transfers, and, to a lesser extent, land use, debts, rental arrangements, commercial dealings, the affairs of charitable endowments, and salary or compensation. Obviously, no crime-related matters are represented in them.

TABLE 3.8: *Contracts Classified according to Type and Subperiod*

	1684–96	1735–43	1781–90	Total # of Contracts According to Type
Contracts among unrelated parties	110 (80%)	125 (56%)	290 (66%)	525 (66%)
Contracts among related parties	27 (20%)	99 (44%)	147 (34%)	273 (34%)
Total # of contracts according to period	137 (100%)	224 (100%)	437 (100%)	798 (100%)

Note: Percentages represent shares in a given subperiod.

Contracting parties were not obligated to report their agreement to court or have it registered in the court's archive. Registration of contracts was also not free of charge although their cost is unclear, notwithstanding the official, unrealistic rates mentioned earlier. Thus, it is not clear why we find contracts in the court records. It is possible that the people of Kastamonu had their contractual arrangements recorded in the court's ledgers and obtained copies of these entries for evidentiary purposes, a topic to which we return in Chapter 8. It might also be the case that by bringing their agreements to court for inspection and registration, contracting parties ensured that they were legally sound and protected from future challenges.

As Table 3.8 indicates, the average number of contracts in court records ranges between fourteen and forty-four per year in different subperiods, the higher average being observed in the late eighteenth century. Also, and as in litigations, contract registration by related parties increased noticeably between the late seventeenth and mid-eighteenth century, although a mildly opposite tendency exists between the mid- and late eighteenth century. Overall then, our findings suggest that the court's involvement in intra-family affairs, whether collaborative or contentious, increased over time, a finding that supports our impression that, over time, court became better integrated into the affairs of the local people. Figure 3.2 demonstrates this trend.

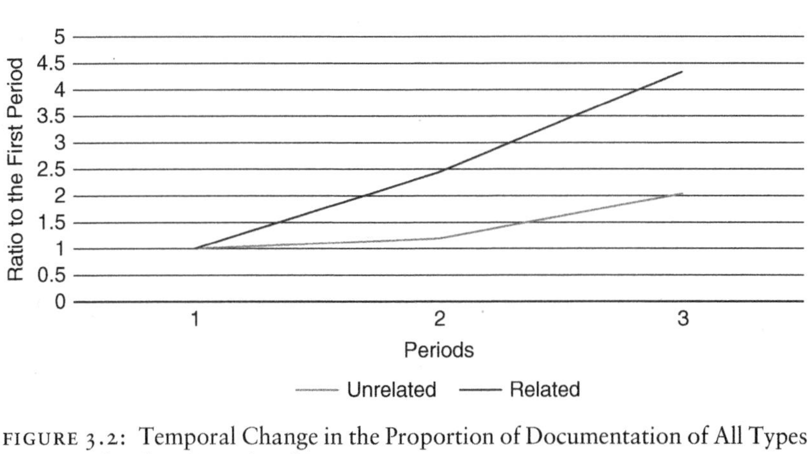

FIGURE 3.2: Temporal Change in the Proportion of Documentation of All Types among Related and Unrelated Parties
Note: The figures on the *y*-axis indicate the ratios of the numbers of different types of documentation in three subperiods to the numbers in the first period.

Issues and Problems Handled in Court

Table 3.9 shows the number and proportion of the most common types of litigation in three subperiods.

Some of the categories included in Table 3.9 are self-explanatory. Others require clarification. "Immovable property and land use" refers to litigations regarding the ownership of houses, shops, gardens, and orchards, and very rarely, the usufruct and tax-farming rights over agricultural lands and other revenue sources. "Taxation" refers to litigations over tax collection, which arose, for example, when an individual failed to pay his tax share or when groups objected to the processes of tax division or assignment. "Marital" litigations include disputes over marriage, divorce, or spousal separation, as well as financial disagreements over *nafaka* (maintenance) or *mehr* (dowry) payments. It was not always easy to categorize a particular litigation according to a predetermined criterion. In fact, some litigations involved disputes over multiple issues, including, for example, property ownership, contractual obligations, or previous debts. Such cases could be classified in different ways and our choice to include them in a specific category was based on what we considered to be the primary issue in a particular case.

The figures presented in Table 3.9 and subsequent tables are also based on other arbitrary decisions on our part. For example, every murder or rape case involved a physical assault, and litigations related to inheritance were in essence disputes over property (in most instances, immovable property). We have separated murder and rape cases from physical assault cases to provide more detailed information about the nature and consequences of various sorts of crime, and specifically identified adjudications concerning inheritance to demonstrate how disputes involving related parties differed from disputes among unrelated ones. For all these reasons the figures presented in Table 3.9 and subsequent tables should be considered rough characterizations of the variety of disputes that were brought to court.

Table 3.9 reveals that the proportions of inheritance-, property-, and land-related litigations increased over time. The trend is most noticeable in litigations among related parties: Overall, litigations among related parties that involved inheritance division, immovable property ownership, and land use increased from 12 percent to 28 percent of all litigations. We also observe a similar, albeit less dramatic, trend in litigations over immovable property and land use among unrelated litigants during the same period: While these types of litigations constituted about 42 percent of all litigations among unrelated parties in the first

TABLE 3.9: *Most Common Types of Litigations*

		1684–96	1735–43	1781–90	Total per Type
Civil litigation –unrelated parties	Immovable property and land use	59 (25%)	66 (24%)	87 (25%)	212 (25%)
	Debt and contractual disputes	59 (25%)	43 (16%)	61 (17%)	163 (19%)
	Taxation	20 (9%)	8 (3%)	10 (3%)	38 (4%)
Civil litigation –related parties	Estate division and appropriation of inheritance shares	21(9%)	35 (13%)	62 (18%)	118 (14%)
	Marital (including disputes over *mehr* and *nafaka* payments)	14 (6%)	22 (8%)	36 (10%)	72 (8%)
	Immovable property and land use	6 (3%)	11 (4%)	37 (10%)	54 (6%)
Criminal litigation –unrelated parties	Murder	10 (4%)	6 (2%)	10 (3%)	26 (3%)
	Sexual crimes (kidnapping, rape, prostitution)	9 (4%)	2 (1%)	3 (1%)	14 (2%)
	Assault (physical, verbal)	8 (3%)	28 (10%)	2 (1%)	38 (4%)
	Theft, robbery	8 (3%)	16 (6%)	10 (3%)	34 (4%)
Total number of litigations per period		233 (100%)	272 (100%)	354 (100%)	859 (100%)

Note: Values in parentheses give percentage proportions in a given time period. The sum of individual categories and percentages do not add up to the totals given in the last row because litigations in less frequent categories are not included in the table.

subperiod, they constituted about 46 percent in the same group of cases in the third subperiod. Taken as a whole, by the 1790s, the court of Kastamonu litigated proportionally more immovable property- and land-use-related cases (including disputes over inheritance shares) than it did in the 1690s and the 1740s (37 percent in the first subperiod, 41 percent in the second subperiod, 53 percent in the third subperiod). Given the significant reduction in crime-related adjudications during this period, these observations suggest that the court of Kastamonu increasingly adopted as its primary adjudicative responsibility the hearing and deciding of disputes over immovable property and land use.

Table 3.10 demonstrates the most frequent types of disputes resolved by amicable settlement, which generally overlapped with common types of litigation, although, and as noted earlier, conflicts among related parties tended be resolved through settlement rather than litigation. The total proportion of settled disputes over immovable property, land use, and inheritance division (55 percent) appears to be larger than the share of litigations involving similar types of conflict (45 percent), though in settlements as well we observe a rising trend over time (if a gradual one): 51 percent in the first subperiod, 54 percent in the second subperiod, and 57 percent in the third subperiod. Thus, litigations and settlements collectively generate an impression that disputes over immovable property and land use became more frequent during the eighteenth century, indicating perhaps an increasing degree of anxiety about property ownership, usufruct rights, or revenue collection, which could all be perceived as consequences of changing economic circumstances.

As we saw before, contracts also increased during the eighteenth century, and a vast majority of these concerned the sales and exchange of houses (often including adjacent structures and gardens), orchards, or shares of ownership in these properties. The proportion of these types of contracts in our sample of all contractual entries is 82 percent in the first subperiod, 95 percent in the second subperiod, and 72 percent in the third subperiod. Although we do not observe a general trend of increase in these proportions, as we did for the shares of disputes over immovable property and land use, the facts that their overall number increased over time and that they constituted such a high volume are remarkable. Thus, it seems that the practice of registering contracts in the court's archive was considered critical for these types of transactions and possibly nonessential for other types of agreements. The contracts related to debt–credit transactions and the affairs of charitable foundations, the second and third most common types of contract in the sample, collectively range from 7 to

TABLE 3.10: *Most Common Types of Settlements*

		1684–96	1735–43	1781–90	Total Settlements per Type
Civil settlements – unrelated parties	Immovable property and land use	3 (7%)	16 (14%)	29 (11%)	48 (11%)
	Debt and contractual disputes	6 (14%)	14 (12%)	31 (11%)	51 (12%)
	Taxation	1 (2%)	3 (3%)	4 (1%)	8 (2%)
Civil settlements – related parties	Estate division and appropriation of inheritance shares	17 (39%)	40 (34%)	113 (42%)	170 (39%)
	Marital (including disputes over *mehr* and *nafaka* payments)	4 (9%)	7 (6%)	6 (2%)	17 (4%)
	Immovable property and land use	2 (5%)	7 (6%)	12 (4%)	21 (5%)
Criminal settlements – unrelated parties	Murder	1 (2%)	8 (7%)	30 (11%)	39 (9%)
	Sexual crimes (kidnapping, rape, prostitution)	1 (2%)	0 (0%)	0 (0%)	1 (0%)
	Assault (physical, verbal)	1 (2%)	7 (6%)	17 (6%)	25 (6%)
	Theft, robbery	1 (2%)	0	2 (1%)	3 (1%)
Total number of settlements per period		44 (100%)	118 (100%)	272 (100%)	434 (100%)

Note: Values in parentheses give percentage proportions in a given time period. The sum of individual categories and percentages do not add up to the totals given in the last row because litigations in less frequent categories are not included in the table.

13 percent in different subperiods. In fact, contractual arrangements among related parties almost exclusively involved real estate transactions in the mid- and late eighteenth century: The share of such agreements among contracts among family and kin members hovers around 90 and 93 percent in the second and third subperiods, respectively.

In regard to conflicts based on criminal matters, we should note the high rate of settlements in murder cases in the second and third subperiods and assault cases in the third subperiod compared to murder and assault litigations. Most of these settlements involved the payment of compensation to those who were hurt in physical confrontations and, in cases of murder, relatives of victims. As discussed, the limited number of criminal litigations in the court records could be related to the executive authorities' involvement in crime-related disputes. Thus, one might consider the proportion of such disputes among settlements as being arguably closer to the actual share of these types of conflicts in eighteenth-century Kastamonu. On the other hand, the tables also reveal a discrepancy between litigations and settlements over sexual crimes: Unlike in murder and assault cases, conflicts involving sexual offenses appear to be significantly underrepresented in settlements. It is possible that cases of abduction and rape remained outside the purview of legal and administrative authorities. Possibly because of the public shame associated with these crimes, victims (or their relatives) may have been more inclined to handle them privately. It is not clear what recourses were available to those who felt wronged in such circumstances. The subsequent marriage of victims (raped women or abductees) to the perpetrators (rapists/abductors) was probably one way that such conflicts were resolved, as is the case in many modern Middle Eastern contexts. Or the wronged side may have sought vengeance by committing similar crimes against those related to the perpetrators.

COURT CLIENTS AND COURT USE: PRELIMINARY OBSERVATIONS

Following the general discussion of the court's functions, we can now turn to how specific client groups used the court's services and how these patterns changed over time. More detailed analyses in subsequent chapters will complicate this picture, but the next two tables reveal some broad trends.

In Table 3.11, we observe the variations in the proportions of client groups across case-types and periods. The upper part of the table separates

TABLE 3.11: *Percentages of Court Clients in Specific Case-types and Periods*

	Types of Legal Interactions			Periods		
	Litigations	Settlements	Contracts	1684–96	1735–43	1781–90
Single	82	77	92	85	81	81
Multiple	16	21	18	13	18	19
Corporate Bodies	2	2	0	2	1	1
Women	24	34	27	21	26	29
Elite Religious	5	4	9	10	4	6
Non-elite Religious	9	4	10	8	12	7
Elite Military	8	7	9	10	6	9
Non-elite Military	17	16	11	12	17	14
No Title	37	35	34	39	35	34
Pilgrim	8	6	12	11	8	9
Desc. of Muh.	9	9	11	3	5	15
No Status	81	84	76	86	83	75
Non-Muslim	3	1	1	1	3	1
Prominent	3	3	5	3	5	4
Non-prominent	96	97	95	97	95	96

court clients according to whether they participated in legal processes as individuals, multiple parties (for example, as multiple plaintiffs or defendants on the same side in a litigation), or corporate bodies (such as guilds, artisanal groups, villages, or neighborhoods). The lower part, based only on legal interactions that involved single client pairs (for example, a litigation with single plaintiff vs. single defendant), provides gender, honorific title, religious marker, and family status information for individual court clients.

The upper segment of Table 3.11 indicates that although a majority of legal encounters in court involved single parties, multiple parties are better represented in settlements, for reasons that we explore in Chapter 7. The table also indicates that the proportions of legal interactions that involved multiple parties and corporate bodies increased, if slightly, in the middle of the eighteenth century. The lower portion of the table reveals that women are underrepresented in all case-types and periods. However, they appear relatively frequently in settlements, which may be due to the fact that women were often party to legal arrangements with members of their immediate or extended family, and that disputes in such arrangements tended to be more often settled than litigated. Also, women's representation in legal interactions consistently increased over time. Non-Muslims, who constituted up to 15 percent of the population, are also severely underrepresented in legal processes.

In regard to various title, religious status, and family groups, it is impossible to determine whether they are under- or overrepresented in the court records. This is because it is impossible to know the exact proportions of these groups in the population, not only for Kastamonu, but for any location in Ottoman Anatolia. It makes sense, however, to assume that the upper classes (elite titleholders, pilgrims, member of prominent families), those who were familiar with the operations of the court and could afford its services, are well-represented in the court records. In Table 3.11, the upper classes (elite titleholders, pilgrims, members of prominent families) appear to be especially prominent in contractual interactions compared to litigations or settlements, perhaps due to the nature and frequency of their economic activities, relative literacy levels, the value they attributed to court-approved documentation, and ability to resolve disputes outside the court.

In general, we observe no clear temporal pattern of court use in most title, religious marker, and family status categories. Earlier, we suggested that court use became more frequent among the people of Kastamonu during the eighteenth century. However, according to Table 3.11, there is little evidence that it also became more democratized as time passed, except for the fact that female representation among court clients increased somewhat. Finally, we suspect that the remarkable increase in the descendants of Muhammad at the end of the eighteenth century reflects artificial inflation in the use of this label, rather than changes in the attitudes of these individuals toward the court.

One factor that influenced variations in court use is the extent to which different groups involved the court in family and kin affairs. Table 3.12 reveals the percentages of parties in each court client group who were related to their counterparts in legal interactions.

In line with what we observed earlier, the proportions of related parties were higher in settlements than in other types of legal engagements (except for non-Muslims, for whom we observe higher proportions in contracts), which is not surprising since it must have been easier to settle disputes when disputants were related, and contracts among related parties must have been less likely to be registered in court compared to contracts that involved unrelated parties. The table also reveals that the share of related parties was higher among contracts than litigations for all gender, title, religious status, and family groups. Although the overall representation of related parties among court clients increased between the late seventeenth and late eighteenth centuries, there appears to be no common temporal pattern of change among individual client groups.

The proportions of related court clients were higher among women compared to men (represented in title groups). As suggested, this may be because women became part of legal arrangements and disputes with relatives more often than did men. On the other hand, the proportions of related parties were lower among upper classes (i.e., elite titleholders and members of prominent families) in all types of legal interactions, which may be due to either their relative tendency to interact with individuals from outside their family and kin circle or their disinclination to involve the court in family matters. The latter possibility would explain why it seems especially rare for the upper classes to have litigated disputes with relatives. The hesitancy to air conflicts with relatives in the public venue of the court may have been especially significant for those who possessed elevated social status in the community. We substantiate these observations in subsequent chapters.

TABLE 3.12: *Related Court Clients according to Case-type and Period (Given as Percentage of Overall Figures in Individual Cells)*

	Types of Legal Interactions			Periods		
	Litigations	Settlements	Contracts	1684–96	1735–43	1781–90
Single	28	55	36	24	39	40
Multiple	28	48	23	23	36	34
Corporate Bodies	0	0	0	0	0	0
Women	53	75	60	55	63	62
Elite Religious	13	43	21	16	3	32
Non-elite Religious	23	50	33	20	39	27
Elite Military	9	26	17	4	23	17
Non-elite Military	16	42	27	8	25	30
No –Title	26	55	34	21	37	39
Pilgrim	20	43	21	11	31	25
Desc. of Muh.	29	57	34	26	21	40
No Status	30	59	40	26	42	44
Non-Muslim	19	33	58	0	46	19
Prominent	13	29	17	27	8	21
Non-prominent	29	58	39	25	42	42

CONCLUSION

This chapter introduced the court of Kastamonu, its functionaries, and the contents of its archive at different points in the seventeenth and eighteenth centuries. In addition to providing information on better-studied court functionaries such as the kadı, *naib*, and the *katib*, our discussion focused on one underexplored group of legal actors: the witnesses to proceedings. Our analysis demonstrated that a group of prominent individuals frequently appeared as witnesses in court, and also that some families were represented among witnesses over long periods of time. The involvement of prominent individuals as frequent witnesses in court proceedings not only protected the court's decisions and legal transactions from future challenges but also facilitated communal supervision over the court's activities. Finally, our analysis suggested a relationship between the identities of court clients and witnesses on one the hand, and case-types and witness identities on the other.

The second part of the chapter explored the contents of the court's archive, in particular records pertaining to litigations, amicable settlements, and commercial and property-related contractual arrangements. Our analysis revealed that the overall number of entries in the court records increased during the eighteenth century, which may mean, given the stable demographic environment, that the people of Kastamonu utilized court services more frequently at the end of the eighteenth century compared to the late seventeenth century. Also important is the fact that the notarial functions of the court, compared to its adjudicative ones, became more pronounced. Aside from these changes, we also observed that in litigations and (to a lesser extent) amicable settlements, the shares of conflicts over immovable property and land use increased. The proportions of property transactions as represented in contracts were never less than 70 percent during the entire period.

It is not entirely clear how these changes in the court's operations reflect wider socioeconomic developments in the region. However, increasing court use might be a sign that the court became more accepted as a venue of social, economic, and legal interaction, assuming that it first appeared in the late seventeenth century. It is also possible, as we argue, that the real cost of court use decreased over time given the inflationary pressures of the eighteenth century and stagnant official rates for court fees, although it is almost certain that court functionaries tried to adjust their actual intake. In addition, we might interpret the growing emphasis on the court's notarial functions in general, and its increasing preoccupation with disputes over immovable property and land use in particular, as related to the growing frequency of property transactions in an era of "de facto" privatization in the economy, a development historians have associated with the spread of long-term tax-farming in the eighteenth century. This is a hypothesis that merits further research.

All of the temporal variations in general court-use patterns observed here should not overshadow the most striking empirical finding of the chapter: Given the likely population of the town and district of Kastamonu, the court remained, at best, an underutilized legal venue. Based on the overall number of litigations, settlements, and contractual arrangements in the court records, one cannot help but wonder how the majority of disputes, which never came to court, were resolved and what the many contractual agreements not represented in the *sicil*s involved. Unfortunately we lack the sources to answer these questions.

In the final section of the chapter we provided glimpses of the ways in which different client groups utilized the court's services. This preliminary analysis revealed gender- and status-based variations in court use. While court use might have become more popular over time, we have found little evidence that the underprivileged groups, except for females, became better represented among court clients. In general, women were better represented in settlements than in litigations and contracts, and men of the upper classes were underrepresented in legal engagements that involved related parties. Our analysis also demonstrated that the preference for court use among specific client groups varied considerably during the eighteenth century. The rest of this book is dedicated to a more detailed exploration of court-use patterns among different groups of court clients.

4

Court Use: Disputes versus Agreements

In this chapter we use the information from the *sicil*s for a quantitative analysis of the difference between types of legal matters handled by the court. This is the first step in a multilayered set of questions that we will explore in the remainder of this book. More specifically, in this chapter we focus on the questions of who came to court, against whom, and for what purpose, and examine the differences between disputes and agreements. In subsequent chapters, we will narrow the focus on disputes and ask which cases went to trial. Finally, in Part IV we will examine litigations in more detail and address the question of how the characteristics of parties, procedural rules, and trial strategies affected trial outcomes.

Although we have already offered a description of the caseload and clients of the court in the preceding chapter, here we offer a more sophisticated analysis that examines the socioeconomic characteristics of legal actors in relation to those with whom they interacted in court, instead of studying these parties in isolation. As mentioned earlier, Ottoman courts performed a variety of functions and served all segments of society in some capacity. To simplify this complexity, we propose a broad categorization among legal matters of record into two groups based on whether they were disputes or agreements. For each legal matter, we identify the two sides of the matter and determine the characteristics of parties in size-composition (single, multiple, or corporate body), gender, honorific title, religion and religious marker, and family affiliation. We then examine whether the parties participated in legal matters differently based on with whom they interacted. The basic question here is whether the characteristics of parties affected the likelihood of a legal matter being an agreement rather than a dispute. To determine whether the patterns varied across case-types, we calculate results separately for criminal matters, civil interactions between individuals who were related to each other through family and kinship ties, and civil interactions between unrelated individuals. In the same vein, we examine each time period separately to see how the relationship between the characteristics of parties and the proportion of agreements varied over time.

AGREEMENTS VERSUS DISPUTES IN COURT RECORDS IN THE AGGREGATE

In the previous chapter, we discussed differences between contracts, amicable settlements,[1] and litigations. Leaving a systematic analysis of the difference between settlements and litigations to Part III, here we lump them together into the same group as matters of dispute. Put differently, we classify the documents in our possession according to whether they represent potential (contracts) or actual (settlements and litigations) instances of conflict/dispute. The objective of this grouping is to contrast actual disputes collectively with contracts, which we view as matters of agreement at the time they were filed in court. Although the parties may obviously have a dispute in the future over the terms or enforcement of a contract, the important thing for our distinction is that they recorded the contract in court as an agreement in an attempt to pre empt future conflict. In the same vein, although a settlement is a contractual arrangement between the disputants, we group them together with litigations because litigations and settlements were commonly brought to court as matters of dispute.[2] So the basic distinction of interest in this chapter is between agreements that were recorded in court as contracts and disputes that were resolved through settlement or formal litigation.

For a quantitative analysis of the characteristics of parties that affected the likelihood of their legal interaction to be a matter of dispute or agreement, we first consider all matters in the aggregate and focus on the proportion of those recorded as agreements. Table 4.1 shows how the proportion of agreements varied across types and over time. For each combination of type and period, the entries show the total number of legal

[1] In the forthcoming discussion, we use the terms "*sulh*," "amicable settlements," and "settlements" interchangeably.

[2] It is true that a certain "contract" could in reality represent a settlement, even if this is not acknowledged in the record. Nevertheless, we adopt the court's terminology in categorizing all contracts as agreements for lack of further information to make the distinction.

TABLE 4.1: *Proportion of Agreements over Time and across Types*

	Number of Cases				Proportion of Agreements			
TYPE	**1684–96**	**1735–43**	**1781–90**	**All**	**1684–96**	**1735–43**	**1781–90**	**All**
Criminal	32	68	76	176	0	0	0	0
Civil between related	96	231	413	740	0.28	0.43	0.36	0.37
Civil between unrelated	286	315	574	1175	0.38	0.40	0.51	0.45
All	414	614	1063	2091	0.33	0.36	0.41	0.38

matters brought to court in this combination and the proportion of those that were agreements.

The numbers of criminal matters were generally small in each period, and all of these matters were disputes by definition. The total number of civil matters between unrelated parties was significantly higher (about one-third) than those between parties related by family ties, though the discrepancy diminished over time, as noted in the previous chapter. The proportion of all matters recorded as agreements was also significantly higher between unrelated (45 percent) than between related (37 percent) parties, indicating that for family members and kin the court functioned more as a venue for dispute resolution than as a venue akin to a notary. We discuss below how this observation was nuanced based on gender and socioeconomic status.

The overall proportion of agreements rose over time from 33 percent to 41 percent, possibly related to the structural changes in the local economy and property relationships in an age of major economic transformation, as discussed earlier. The rise in the proportion of agreements, however, was not uniform among types. Whereas in civil matters between related parties the proportion of agreements rose significantly between the first and second periods and fell in the third period, it stayed about the same between the first and second periods and rose sharply thereafter in civil matters between unrelated parties.

THE SIZE-COMPOSITION OF THE PARTIES AND THE PROPORTION OF AGREEMENTS

For a more detailed analysis of how the proportions of agreements varied by the characteristics of parties, we first consider size-composition – more specifically, whether the parties were single individuals, multiple individuals, or corporate bodies. In this distinction, corporate bodies refer to groups and communities (such as guilds, artisanal groups, or the inhabitants of villages or quarters) represented in court by affiliated individuals in positions of power and influence, such as village elders and guild officials. In contrast, multiple individuals consist of two or more court clients who collectively acted as parties to contractual arrangements, settlements, and trials. The latter group represented not the interests of corporate bodies, but those of their own and other individuals for whom they might act as proxies. These parties could meet each other in court in various combinations. We group these combinations into six categories, with three corresponding to cases where the parties are of the same composition (i.e., both single individuals, both multiple individuals, and both corporate bodies) and the other three corresponding to cases of different compositions, namely single versus multiple individuals, single individual versus a corporate body, and multiple individuals versus a corporate body.

Here we do not further differentiate within each combination depending on the specific roles of parties, though such differences will be important in later chapters. There is obviously a big difference between being a plaintiff or a defendant in a trial, so a litigation that involved a single person in the position of plaintiff against multiple defendants might have a different dynamic than a litigation that pitted multiple plaintiffs against a single defendant, and one would need to further differentiate within each of our six combinations to capture these differences. In agreements, however, parties have no specific roles to require such a distinction. Hence, for the simple purpose of differentiating between agreements and disputes, we ignore further distinctions regarding the specific status of parties in disputes.

In the next two tables we examine how the proportion of agreements varied by the size-combinations of parties. Table 4.2 shows the variation across case-types – more specifically, how for each size-combination the proportion of agreements differed between criminal disputes, civil matters between related parties, and civil matters between unrelated parties. As noted, all criminal matters are disputes by definition. Nevertheless, we include them in the table to show their distribution among combinations.

As seen in the table, a high proportion (about two-thirds) of all legal matters recorded in court was between two single individuals, followed by those between single and multiple individuals. There were only eighty-eight matters that did not involve a single individual.

Although the proportion of agreements was uniformly higher in civil matters between unrelated parties than between related parties, the discrepancy varied among combinations. The difference was narrower in matters between two individuals – the biggest category – than in other combinations, the highest difference being that between two parties consisting of multiple individuals. This is an interesting discrepancy because it implies that the higher proportion of disputes between related parties compared to unrelated parties was more pronounced in larger groups, namely in families compared to other court clients with multiple individuals. Here, we provisionally suggest that this discrepancy could be a consequence of the ability of the extended family to serve as an informal "registry" for intra-family agreements, lessening the need for formal involvement of the court, which was a more appropriate option available

TABLE 4.2: *Size-combinations of Parties and Agreements across Types of Legal Matters*

	Number of Cases				Proportion of Agreements			
SIZE	Criminal	Civil Related	Civil Unrelated	All	Criminal	Civil Related	Civil Unrelated	All
Single vs. Single	104	526	776	1406	0	0.40	0.45	0.40
Single vs. Multiple	53	194	330	577	0	0.30	0.48	0.38
Single vs. Corporate	6		18	24	0		0	0
Multiple vs. Multiple	9	20	35	64	0	0.25	0.49	0.34
Multiple vs. Corporate	4		10	14	0		0.1	0.07
Corporate vs. Corporate			6	6			0	0
All	176	740	1175	2091	0	0.37	0.45	0.38

to unrelated parties. We qualify this proposition below in our discussion of gender and socioeconomic characteristics. Note, finally, that all of the eighteen civil matters involving single individuals against corporate bodies were disputes, as were all but one of the nineteen civil matters between multiple individuals against corporate bodies and all of the six civil matters between corporate bodies.

In Table 4.3, we shift attention to variations over time and show in more detail how the rise in the proportions of agreements, first observed in Table 4.1, varied among the size-combinations of parties. The most noteworthy difference is between the first two categories. In matters between two single individuals the proportion of agreements was about the same between the first two periods and rose significantly in the third period. In matters between single and multiple individuals, by contrast, the proportions first rose significantly and remained about the same in the third period.

INDIVIDUAL CHARACTERISTICS AND THE PROPORTION OF AGREEMENTS

To examine how the tendency toward agreement varied by individual characteristics, we now narrow our attention to legal matters between two single individuals and drop from analysis those observations that involved multiple parties or corporate bodies. As seen in Table 4.4, the proportion of matters in each type–period combination is about the same as those observed in Table 4.1 for the aggregate population. More specifically, the number of legal matters between single individuals that were recorded in court rose over time, and the majority of these matters were between unrelated individuals, followed by those between related individuals. Criminal matters were a small fraction of the total.

The proportion of legal matters recorded as agreements between individuals followed an interesting pattern over time. Overall, the proportion was about the same in the first two periods, unlike the gradual rise over time observed in the aggregate sample (Table 4.1). The pattern was quite different, however, between types of legal matters. Whereas in matters between related individuals the proportion of agreements rose sharply from the first period to the second and fell somewhat in the third period, in matters between unrelated individuals the pattern was reversed, as the proportion of agreements first fell and then rose sharply. Overall, the proportion of agreements was

TABLE 4.3: *Size-combinations and Agreements over Time*

	Number of Cases				Proportion of Agreements			
SIZE	1684–96	1735–43	1781–90	All	1684–96	1735–43	1781–90	All
Single vs. Single	299	406	701	1406	0.36	0.36	0.43	0.40
Single vs. Multiple	92	177	308	577	0.28	0.40	0.39	0.38
Single vs. Corporate	11	8	5	24	0	0	0	0
Multiple vs. Multiple	7	16	41	64	0.29	0.31	0.37	0.34
Multiple vs. Corporate	4	6	4	14	0	0.17	0	0.07
Corporate vs. Corporate	1	1	4	6	0	0	0	0
All	414	614	1063	2091	0.33	0.36	0.41	0.38

TABLE 4.4: *Legal Matters and Agreements between Single Individuals: Variation across Types and over Time*

	Number of Cases				Proportion of Agreements			
TYPE	**1684–96**	**1735–43**	**1781–90**	**All**	**1684–96**	**1735–43**	**1781–90**	**All**
Criminal	22	43	39	104	0	0	0	0
Civil between related	74	162	290	526	0.30	0.46	0.39	0.40
Civil between unrelated	203	201	372	776	0.43	0.36	0.51	0.45
All	299	406	701	1406	0.36	0.36	0.43	0.40

higher in interactions between unrelated parties than between unrelated ones, as was the case in Table 4.1.

Going beyond differential patterns in the aggregate, we need to examine how the number of legal matters and the proportion of agreements further varied among the subcategories of individuals. In what follows, we detail the breakdown by the individual characteristics observed in our sample, separately for gender, honorific titles, religion, religious markers, and family status.

Gender

Consider first the relationship between gender and agreements, reported in Table 4.5. The majority of legal matters recorded in court were between two men, followed by those between a man and a woman. Only a small fraction (6 percent) of these matters were between two women. Interestingly, the legal interactions of women in court were almost exclusively with the other sex, a majority of such interactions being civil matters with related men. Note also that a very small proportion of the legal interactions of women involved criminal matters. These observations provide an insight into the gendered nature of legal relationships in early modern Kastamonu.

The proportion of legal matters recorded as agreements varied systematically among the gender combinations and across types. Among men, family relation did not affect the likelihood of agreement, as the proportion was about the same between related and unrelated parties. Although the same was true in matters between two women, the proportion of agreements was lower when the parties were both women than when they were both men, indicating that it was more disputes than agreements that caused women to come to court as compared to men. Our sources do not include sufficient information to determine to what extent this tendency was the outcome of a differential tendency between men and women in their legal interactions with the same gender, or whether it resulted from a selection effect based on differential attitudes toward court use. The latter could be the case if women expected to incur higher (monetary, emotional, and/or social) costs than men in pursuing legal matters in court and attributed greater urgency to resolving disputes than registering contracts.

Interestingly, when the matter involved a man and a woman the proportion of agreements varied between related and unrelated parties. When parties were of different genders, the proportion of agreements was

TABLE 4.5: *Gender and Agreements*

	Number of Cases			Proportion of Agreements			Number of Cases			Proportion of Agreements			N	%
GENDER	Criminal	Civil Related	Civil Unrelated	Criminal	Civil Related	Civil Unrelated	1684–96	1735–43	1781–90	1684–96	1735–43	1781–90	All Cases	
Male vs. Male	70	131	537	0	0.43	0.44	187	217	334	0.37	0.28	0.49	738	0.40
Male vs. Female	30	329	221	0	0.39	0.48	96	163	321	0.34	0.46	0.39	580	0.40
Female vs. Female	4	66	18	0	0.38	0.39	16	26	46	0.38	0.42	0.33	88	0.36

39 percent if they were related by family ties and it rose to 48 percent if they had no family relation, indicating that in cases of gender difference parties brought proportionally more agreements to court if they were unrelated to each other than if they had a family relation. Since the proportion of agreements was about the same in legal interactions between two women as it was in those between a woman and a related man, the implication is that gender difference was more likely to affect women's behavior against unrelated men. Whereas in their interactions with related men, women seem to have resorted to the court to resolve disputes, against unrelated men they were more likely to use the court as a registry of agreements to preempt future disputes. Membership in the same extended family or kinship network must have provided some security to women in their contractual arrangements with related men. In this sense, the court and the family might have served similar purposes for women by facilitating the enforcement of contractual obligations. Note also that women could have felt pressure to refrain from officially registering agreements with their husbands, brothers, or fathers because doing so might signal distrust to close family members, a potentially shameful, embarrassing, or simply unsavory scenario. Regardless of the underlying reason, the lower tendency of women to register agreements with related than with unrelated men, observed in Table 4.5, explains why in Table 4.1 the rate of agreement in the overall sample was lower in matters between related parties than between unrelated ones.

Table 4.5 also shows systematic gender differences in the way the proportion of agreements changed over time. As noted, the proportion of agreements in the aggregate remained about the same between the first and second periods and rose somewhat to 43 percent in the third period (Table 4.4). When we look at the subcategories of gender combinations, however, we see vastly different patterns. Whereas in matters between men the proportion of agreements fell between the first and the second periods and rose sharply in the third period, the pattern was reversed in matters involving women, as the proportion rose in the second period and then fell in the third. This discrepancy could be attributable to various factors that differentially influenced how men and women accessed and used the courts over time. In addition to various socioeconomic trends that may have affected the court's role in society, men and women may have faced different obstacles in accessing the court as time passed, court personnel may have had changing proclivities in their treatment of legal matters, or the availability of alternative venues of dispute resolution may have varied.

Honorific Titles and Elite Status

Although court records do not include systematic information on the incomes, occupations, or educational backgrounds of individuals, we can use their honorific titles and family affiliation as indicators of socioeconomic status. As noted in Chapter 2, honorific titles allow us to determine whether a man belonged to the military/administrative establishment (*seyfiyye*, in Ottoman Turkish) or the judicial/religious one (*ilmiyye*). *Seyfiyye* included those men with military/administrative responsibilities or affiliations, such as governors, members of the police force, and officers as well as the rank-and-file of the provincial militia. These individuals carried the following titles: *Ağa, Beşe*, and *Beğ*. *İlmiyye*, on the other hand, was composed of individuals with religious and judiciary responsibilities or affiliations, such as local magistrates, jurisconsults (*müftis*), and mosque imams. Such individuals carried the following titles: *Efendi, Molla, Halife, Çelebi*, and *Dede*.

Using these differences, we divide individuals into four groups. Since titles were recorded exclusively for men, we separate women into the first category. Men are divided into three groups based on whether they belonged to the judicial/religious establishment, the military/administrative establishment, or those without a title. For all combinations of these categories, Table 4.6 shows the number of individuals in each combination and the proportions of the legal matters between them recorded as agreements. As seen in the table, in civil matters involving women a higher number of these matters were between related individuals, particularly in those with other women and men with no titles. In matters involving men, by contrast, most of the legal matters were between unrelated individuals.

The average proportions of agreements reported in the table allow us to look one step further into the distinct pattern observed above (Table 4.5) in matters involving parties of different gender. First, it is interesting that the proportions of agreements are generally higher in legal interactions between women and religious titleholders, an issue we return to below. Second, whereas the proportion of agreements is slightly higher between related individuals than between unrelated ones in civil matters between women and men with religious titles, the opposite is true in civil matters between women and men with military titles and between women and men with no titles.

In legal interactions between men, the proportion of agreements is higher in matters involving religious titleholders. This could be an indication that this group was less involved in disputes than agreements, or that

TABLE 4.6: *Gender, Honorific Titles, and Agreements*

	Number of Cases			Proportion of Agreements			Number of Cases			Proportion of Agreements			N	%
GENDER AND TITLE	Criminal	Civil Related	Civil Unrelated	Criminal	Civil Related	Civil Unrelated	1684–96	1735–43	1781–90	1684–96	1735–43	1781–90	All Cases	
Woman vs. Woman	4	66	18	0	0.38	0.39	16	26	46	0.38	0.42	0.33	88	0.36
Woman vs. Men with religious title	4	69	54	0	0.59	0.56	24	45	58	0.42	0.60	0.59	127	0.56
Woman vs. Men with military title	11	85	72	0	0.35	0.44	19	43	106	0.26	0.40	0.38	168	0.37
Woman vs. Men with no title	15	175	95	0	0.33	0.45	53	75	157	0.34	0.41	0.32	285	0.35
Man, religious title vs. Man, religious title		9	39		0.22	0.49	14	16	18	0.43	0.44	0.44	48	0.44
Man, religious title vs. Man, military title	3	6	67	0	0.83	0.46	16	17	43	0.50	0.24	0.56	76	0.47
Man, religious title vs. Man, no title	6	19	97	0	0.42	0.55	38	35	49	0.58	0.37	0.53	122	0.50
Man, military title vs. Man, military title	12	6	83	0	0.33	0.33	26	34	41	0.31	0.06	0.46	101	0.29
Man, military title vs. Man, no title	23	31	138	0	0.39	0.42	42	57	93	0.31	0.25	0.46	192	0.36
Man, no title vs. Man, no title	26	60	113	0	0.45	0.43	51	58	90	0.25	0.36	0.47	199	0.38

they were more inclined to have their contracts registered in court. According to the latter interpretation, religious titleholders may have been more legalistic in their daily affairs and mindful of potential problems in their dealings with others, compared to other segments of the society, because of their presumably higher literacy rates and better access to legal information. Interestingly, we do not observe such variations between military titleholders and men with no titles.

Over time, the proportions of agreements between gender combinations followed a similar pattern in the aggregate (Table 4.5) as they did in title subcategories. Whereas the average proportion rose between the first and second periods and fell after the second period in all matters involving women, the opposite pattern was observed in all but two (religious title vs. religious title; no title vs. no title) subcategories of matters involving men.

Beyond using honorific titles to differentiate between affiliations with the religious and military establishment, we can also use them to determine whether a man belonged to the elite group within each category. As detailed in Chapter 2, elite groups included individuals who assumed leadership roles, collectively managed the legal and administrative affairs of the town and its environs, and took advantage of economic opportunities associated with their responsibilities. In the following analysis we reclassify title groups into three new categories based on whether a man had an elite title (*Efendi* or *Ağa*), a non-elite title (comprised of all other religious and military titles), or no title. Once again, since these titles applied to men, we include women as a fourth category in the analysis to observe how their involvement in legal matters with men varied by the men's elite status. Table 4.7 shows how the proportion of agreements varied between various gender–elite combinations and among the types of legal matters and time periods.

Small numbers of observations in specific cases notwithstanding,[3] Table 4.7 indicates generally higher proportions of agreements for men with elite titles. This is not surprising because these men typically had higher levels of wealth, literacy, legal knowledge, involvement in mercantile and commercial affairs, and ability to anticipate future legal problems.

[3] As explained in Chapter 3, such instances are not consequences of limited sampling on our part since our dataset is comprised of *all* relevant documentation available in the *sicil*s for each subperiod. So they should be perceived not as causes for lament for statistical purposes but as historically informative findings, indicative of the fact that certain types of legal interactions never (for example, criminal disputes among elite titleholders) or rarely (for example, criminal disputes among women and elite titleholders) appeared in the court of Kastamonu.

TABLE 4.7: *Gender, Elite Status, and Agreements*

	Number of Cases			Proportion of Agreements			Number of Cases			Proportion of Agreements			N	%
GENDER AND ELITE STATUS	Criminal	Civil Related	Civil Unrelated	Criminal	Civil Related	Civil Unrelated	1684–96	1735–43	1781–90	1684–96	1735–43	1781–90	All Cases	
Woman vs. Woman	4	66	18	0	0.38	0.39	16	26	46	0.38	0.42	0.33	88	0.36
Woman vs. Elite Man	2	40	59	0	0.55	0.56	24	13	64	0.50	0.62	0.55	101	0.54
Woman vs. Non-Elite Man	13	114	67	0	0.43	0.43	19	75	100	0.16	0.48	0.39	194	0.40
Woman vs. Men with No Title	15	175	95	0	0.33	0.45	53	75	157	0.34	0.41	0.32	285	0.35
Elite Man vs. Elite Man		7	46		0.43	0.43	18	8	27	0.33	0.38	0.52	53	0.43
Elite Man vs. Non-Elite Man	3	6	80	0	0.50	0.50	23	26	40	0.61	0.08	0.68	89	0.48
Elite Man vs. Man with No Title	4	11	92	0	0.55	0.51	31	26	50	0.39	0.46	0.58	107	0.50
Non-Elite Man vs. Non-Elite Man	12	8	63	0	0.38	0.27	15	33	35	0.13	0.24	0.29	83	0.24
Non-Elite Man vs. Man with No Title	25	39	143	0	0.36	0.45	49	66	92	0.47	0.23	0.43	207	0.38
Man with No Title vs. Man with No Title	26	60	113	0	0.45	0.43	51	58	90	0.25	0.36	0.47	199	0.38

This is also consistent with what we have observed for the members of the religious establishment in Table 4.6.

Whereas the proportion of agreements was about 38 percent in legal matters between two women, the proportion was higher in women's matters against men with non-elite titles (43 percent) and even higher against men with elite titles (about 55 percent). This is consistent with what we have observed in the previous paragraph about differences in agreement proportions across different title groups. Note also that these proportions were about the same between related and unrelated individuals. In legal matters between women and men with no titles, by contrast, family relation made a big difference, as the proportion of agreements fell significantly if the parties were related to each other by family ties (33 percent) rather than unrelated (45 percent). Because the majority of cases between men and women were in this category, this difference also goes to explain why in Table 4.5 the proportions of agreements varied significantly between related and unrelated parties in legal matters between men and women but remained about the same for those between two men or between two women.

Turning attention to changes over time periods, we see that in all combinations of parties that included women the proportions of agreements in Table 4.7 rose in the second period and fell back in the third, consistent with the aggregate results observed in Table 4.5 and with different title combinations in Table 4.6. Among men, the proportion of agreements rose steadily over time in matters between parties of the same elite status. When both parties were elite men, for example, the proportion rose from 33 to 37 percent in the second period and to 52 percent in the last period. There are no other clear patterns in the way proportion of agreements varied over time in matters between the remaining combinations involving men of different status. By and large, however, the proportions of agreements among both male parties were greater by the end of the eighteenth century compared to the late seventeenth century, indicating that over time men used the court more for its notarial services than to resolve disputes.

Religion and Religious Markers

As Table 4.8 shows, most of the legal matters recorded in the Kastamonu court were brought by Muslims, presumably because non-Muslims had alternative mechanisms to resolve disputes and record legal agreements. There were a total of thirty-four matters that involved non-Muslims. Sixteen of these were civil matters against unrelated non-Muslims, about

TABLE 4.8: *Religion, Religious Markers, and Agreements*

	Number of Cases			Proportion of Agreements			Number of Cases			Proportion of Agreements			N	%
RELIGION AND RELIGIOUS MARKER	Criminal	Civil Related	Civil Unrelated	Criminal	Civil Related	Civil Unrelated	1684–96	1735–43	1781–90	1684–96	1735–43	1781–90	All Cases	
Muslim vs. Muslim	98	518	756	0	0.40	0.46	295	390	687	0.37	0.37	0.43	1372	0.40
Muslim vs. Non-Muslim	2	1	16	0	1	0.31	4	8	7	0.25	0.38	0.29	19	0.32
Non-Muslim vs. Non-Muslim	4	7	4	0	0.43	0		8	7		0.13	0.29	15	0.2
Pilgrim vs. Pilgrim		3	16		0.33	0.5	2	9	8	0	0.22	0.88	19	0.47
Pilgrim vs. Desc. of Muh.	2	6	10	0	1	0.7	1	2	15	0	0.5	0.8	18	0.72
Pilgrim vs. No Religious Marker	9	42	134	0	0.40	0.56	57	47	81	0.49	0.38	0.57	185	0.50
Desc. of Muh. vs. Desc. of Muh.		20	11		0.4	0.64	3	2	26	0.33	0	0.54	31	0.48
Desc. of Muh. vs. No Religious Marker	9	52	130	0	0.35	0.45	12	36	143	0.17	0.33	0.43	191	0.40
No Marker vs. No Marker	84	403	475	0	0.39	0.41	224	310	428	0.35	0.37	0.38	962	0.37

a third of which were agreements. There were also a very small number of civil matters among non-Muslims, more specifically seven matters between related and four between unrelated non-Muslims, only three of which were agreements.

Turning to various combinations of religious markers, we see that the proportions of agreements followed more or less the same pattern in most combinations. With the exception of matters between pilgrims and descendants of Muhammad (for which we have a very limited number of observations),[4] the proportion of agreements was higher in civil cases between unrelated individuals than between related individuals. In most cases, the proportion of agreements rose over time.

Family Status

Finally, we look at how court use varied by family status. As seen in Table 4.9, there were seven legal matters recorded in court in which both parties were members of prominent families, and in all of these cases the matter at hand was a dispute. It appears that members of these families had alternative mechanisms or social institutions to "register" their agreements; they must have felt safe enough to lack the need to have their agreements registered in court records.

The situation was quite different, however, in their legal interactions with members of non-prominent families. The proportion of such interactions that were recorded as agreements was about two-thirds in civil matters, sharply higher than that observed between members of non-prominent families. It is also noteworthy that the number of legal matters between members of prominent and non-prominent families and the proportion of these matters recorded as agreements both grew steadily and significantly over time.

[4] Limited numbers of legal interactions between pilgrims and descendants of Muhammad may be related to the relatively small populations of these groups in Kastamonu or indicative of their preferences of court use (or both). As noted in Chapter 3, court records identify family relationships and kin-connections among clients meticulously. Given the variety of historical factors that influenced specific groups' representation in the *sicil*s, some of our more nuanced breakdowns of data might provide relatively uncertain results for some client groups compared to others. This is why we conduct here and in subsequent chapters a series of parallel analyses by using multiple, overlapping socioeconomic classifications. Often, what may be missed in analyses based on, say, religious status markers could be captured in those based on honorific titles or family statuses.

TABLE 4.9: *Family Status and Agreements*

	Number of Cases			Proportion of Agreements			Number of Cases			Proportion of Agreements			N	%
FAMILY AFFILIATION	Criminal	Civil Related	Civil Unrelated	Criminal	Civil Related	Civil Unrelated	1684–96	1735–43	1781–90	1684–96	1735–43	1781–90	All Cases	
Prominent vs. Prominent	1	2	4	0	0	0	2	3	2	0	0	0	7	0
Prominent vs. Non-prominent	4	15	77	0	0.67	0.62	11	33	52	0.27	0.52	0.73	96	0.60
Non-prominent vs. Non-prominent	99	509	695	0	0.39	0.43	286	370	647	0.37	0.35	0.41	1303	0.38

CONCLUSION

To examine how different segments of society used the court, we divided legal matters of record into two broad categories as disputes (litigations and settlements) or agreements. We then identified the parties on the two sides of the matter and analyzed quantitatively the characteristics that raised the likelihood of using the court to register an agreement. More specifically, we used the information in court archives to determine the characteristics of parties in size-composition (single, multiple, or corporate body), gender, honorific title, religion and religious marker, and family affiliation. Taking each category separately, we examined how different combinations of parties within this category affected the likelihood of their legal interaction being an agreement rather than a dispute. To determine how the results varied over time and by the type of legal matter, we calculated averages separately for civil disputes involving related and unrelated individuals and for the three time periods of our analysis.

For gender, our results show that in matters involving a man and a woman the proportion of agreements varied between related and unrelated parties such that women tended to use the court to resolve disputes in interactions with related men and to register agreements against unrelated men. Incorporating the honorific titles of men into the analysis, we see the nuanced interaction of women against men, based on their establishment affiliations. In their interactions against men with religious titles, women tended to have a higher proportion of agreements with related individuals than with unrelated ones. The opposite was true in matters against men with military titles and no titles. We see similarly interesting patterns when we redefine title categories based on whether they designated elite status. For example, the proportion of agreements was about the same in matters between related and unrelated individuals in women's legal interactions with men with elite and non-elite titles. In matters between women and men with no titles, however, the proportion of agreements differed significantly depending on whether the parties were related to each other by family ties.

In legal interactions between men, there were systematic differences in the way the proportions of agreements varied across types and over time. The proportion was generally higher in interactions involving men with elite titles than in those with non-elite titles or no titles. The proportion was similarly higher in interactions involving men with religious titles. Interestingly, in combinations of parties according to elite status, the proportions of agreements did not vary significantly between related and unrelated parties. In combinations according to religious markers, in contrast, the proportion of agreements was higher in civil cases between unrelated individuals than between related individuals. In most combinations between men, the proportion of agreements rose over time.

Although the proportion of agreements rose steadily over time in the aggregate for all legal matters regardless of the size-composition of parties, those between individuals remained about the same between the first and second periods and rose thereafter. Examining subcategories of characteristics, we see even more interesting patterns behind the overall change. For example, whereas in matters between related individuals the proportion of agreements rose between the first and second periods and fell afterwards, the opposite trend was observed in matters between unrelated individuals, as the proportion of agreements first fell and then rose sharply in the third period. Note similarly the way the patterns were systematically different between genders. Whereas in matters between men the proportion of agreements fell between the first and the second periods and rose sharply in the third period, the pattern was reversed in matters involving women. In the previous chapter, we speculated how various socioeconomic trends and institutional changes might have affected the general functions of the court in Kastamonu. Our sources, however, do not provide clues to explain how gender and family networks differed in their legal interactions with others over time. The same is also true for the temporal variations in the interactions involving various title, status, and religious groups.

In closing, we should re-emphasize a distinctive aspect of the analytical framework introduced in this chapter. For each legal matter brought to court, we identified the parties on both sides of the matter and examined them with respect to each other, rather than in isolation or lumped together. This aspect of our analysis acknowledges the relational nature of the court experience, the fact that decisions made by legal actors are sensitive to the identities of their counterparts. In the next two parts of the book, we will continue to use this framework to examine more sophisticated questions, namely the likelihood that parties will settle a dispute without trial and the likelihood that the plaintiff will win among cases that wound up at trial. In answering both questions we will discuss theoretically and analyze empirically the factors affecting the likelihood.

PART THREE

TO SETTLE OR NOT TO SETTLE

5

Dispute Resolution in Ottoman Courts of Law

In this chapter we provide a general introduction to alternative methods of dispute resolution in the Ottoman context. For this purpose, we examine litigations and amicable settlements and the specific socio-legal purposes they served. In addition to offering background information for our analysis in subsequent chapters, we begin building here a comprehensive approach to dispute-resolution processes that captures the complexity and interrelated nature of trial-settlement decisions. The latter theme will be our main focus in Chapter 6.

In our discussion, we make a special effort to employ insights gleaned from the growing anthropological literature on dispute resolution and reconciliation practices in modern Muslim contexts. This is largely because our historical sources provide little direct information on legal practice and especially on mediative processes. Thus, our treatment of the topic is deliberately interpolative, as we import findings from anthropological research that arguably have relevance for the Ottoman context. This literature also provides conceptual tools that can help us explain the functional differences among alternative methods of dispute resolution.

We realize that a multidisciplinary approach to Ottoman legal practice may not be particularly popular among Ottoman historians. According to Haim Gerber (1994, 14), it would be a mistake to apply anthropological insights on legal practice to Ottoman society since the latter differs significantly from those in which anthropologists have studied dispute-resolution processes:

> Culturally we have here [in Ottoman lands] a literate society, based mainly on the religious output of classical Islam, with large doses of Central Asian and Iranian influence. The cultural world featured formal institutions of learning, formal law

codes and institutionalized law courts of one form or another, and an intellectual elite fluent in three languages – Arabic, Persian and Turkish. I would add that another important feature of the society studied here is its distinctly nonritualistic nature. It is difficult to think of any modes of thinking that could alert us to the possibility that seventeenth-century west Anatolian Turkish culture was similar to, say, Bali in being deeply different from modern Western societies in ways observed by Geertz.

Elsewhere, Gerber further emphasizes the bureaucratic aspect of the Ottoman administrative structure as the primary factor for its rational legal system, in Weberian terms:

> If, in the anthropological cases examined, resonance existed between the legal system and the society, this book argues that such resonance existed in the Ottoman Empire, as well. In other words, my argument is that the most fundamental feature of the Ottoman society in its core area was the existence within it of a bureaucratic state, and that this fact apparently had much to do with the bureaucratic structure of the law. (1994, 18)

And later, "(a)n important question that remains to be broached at this point is why the bureaucratic Ottoman state gave rise to the particular form of legal system that it did. It is natural for a bureaucratic state to strive for the creation of a relatively unified court system where all sorts of legal business is dealt with" (1994, 21).

Gerber is of course right about the importance of historical and contextual factors in molding the ways in which a legal system is structured and how the law is practiced. It is not clear, however, that his characterization of the Ottoman state and society as developed, rational, "non-ritualistic" entities is applicable to all Ottoman settings, at all times. Nor is it certain that the Ottoman state, as a premodern imperial structure, could or would even desire to impose (just like a modern nation-state does) a legal system and influence legal practices, without any attempt to accommodate local needs and requirements (cf. Meshal 2010, 2014). In this regard, Gerber does not consider how provincial actors' involvement in legal processes and their expectations of the legal system might have shaped legal practice. As we point out in this chapter, most anthropological treatments of Islamic legal practice in a wide variety of settings, and not only in various "underdeveloped" African contexts, underline the considerable flexibility of the legal system(s) and its actors in accommodating regional customs, practices, and definitions of justice. The fact that we have not yet seen this in Ottoman scholarship may be less a reflection of the unique characteristics of the Ottoman state or society than of the inherent limits of our sources.

LITIGATION AND SETTLEMENT IN OTTOMAN COURTS OF LAW

In the anthropological scholarship on dispute resolution we find two hypothetical models of conflict management, with dissimilar socio-legal objectives. These are the "court" and "bargain" models, and Table 5.1 summarizes their differences (cf. Ergene 2003, 191).

Generally, the court model represents legal processes in which the consequences of a proposed resolution do not aim to accommodate the interests of disputants. Since preserving relationships between disputants is not a concern for adjudicators, resolutions usually involve zero-sum results for disputing parties. The bargain model, on the other hand, is "utilitarian" as its goal is to maximize the combined interests of the disputants. Negotiation and mutual compromise are assumed to be intrinsic to resolution and reconciliation is the main objective of the process, which often requires the parties involved to address the real causes of the conflict as well as its judicial consequences. In this sense, the bargain model aims to clean up the "social mess" at the heart of the dispute in order to resolve the conflict, rather than focusing strictly on its judicial aspects (Ergene 2003, 192).

TABLE 5.1: *Hypothetical Models of Conflict Management*

Court Model	Bargain Model
1. Triadic in nature (adjudication)	1. Dyadic in nature (mediation)
2. Coercive power part of the resolution process	2. Absence of coercive power in the resolution process
3. Application of highly regarded norms and values in the resolution process	3. Pursuit of the interests of the opposing parties
4. Establishment of past facts (guilt)	4. Not necessary to establish past facts
5. Retroactively oriented reasoning	5. Prospectively oriented reasoning
6. Legal experts participate in the resolution process	6. No legal experts in the resolution process
7. Conclusion is a verdict	7. Conclusion is an agreement
8. Purely distributive decisions	8. Distributive/generative decision
9. Either/or decision (zero-sum game: win or lose)	9. Compromise (give a little, get a little)
10. Reaffirmation of previous legal cases	10. No necessary implication concerning validity
11. Affinity to legal scholarship	11. Affinity to utilitarian thinking

Source: Nader (1969).

It is not our objective here to recap the anthropological discussions surroundings these categorizations, which Ergene (2003, chapter 10) does to some extent. Rather, we will focus on how the models may help us better understand different dispute-resolution methods utilized in the Ottoman context. As Ergene has observed, Ottomanists generally describe something closer to the court model in their characterizations of dispute resolution in Ottoman courts. Not surprisingly, perhaps the best example in this regard is Haim Gerber, who emphasized the legalistic and norm-driven orientation of Ottoman judicial authorities, in particular the kadı, who, he insisted, enforced a uniform set of adjudicative procedures and sought primarily to apply the letter of the law rather than seeking social harmony or conciliation (Gerber 1994, 15–18).[1] Few have been as explicit as Gerber in emphasizing the formal and rational aspects of the Ottoman legal system,[2] although many Ottomanists have tended to characterize the courts' operations as formal, rational, and not particularly sensitive to extralegal contextual factors (for clear examples of this tendency, see Bayındır 1986 and Akgündüz 1988, volume 1).

[1] Gerber's dispute is primarily with the Weberian characterizations of Islamic legal practices as *kadijustiz*, which portrays Islamic legal practice as a process that lacks a formal structure and procedural consistency, and with those researchers whom he considers to be the contemporary representatives of this tendency, in particular Lawrence Rosen (1984, 1989). Ironically, Gerber's critique of *kadijustiz* in the Ottoman setting itself is very much based on Weberian categories of analysis. In the context of this discussion, we should also mention that Rosen's approach to Islamic legal practice is somewhat different from Weber's. Unlike Weber (1968, 976–81), whose interpretation of Islamic legal practice is based on a framework of differences in the form and degree of rationality inherent to Western and non-Western legal systems, Rosen aims to reveal the cultural logic of Islamic law in action. On Rosen's work, also see Powers (1994 and 2002, chapter 1) and Peletz (2002, 118–122).

[2] Gerber's claim for the overall rationality, consistency, and predictability of the Ottoman legal system is based on his impression that legal practices remained consistent with Islamic jurisprudential principles as depicted in major Hanafi doctrinal works, and also that they did not vary contextually. As evidence for this position, he cites court records from seventeenth-century Bursa, in western Anatolia, and examples of court-produced documentation as found in contemporary pedagogical manuals (*sukuk* treatises) (1994, 22). It is, however, not clear if his sample from the Bursa court records is limited to a specific subperiod or spans the entire century. Furthermore, the pedagogical manuals were compiled by contemporary jurists not to demonstrate how a specific court interpreted or enforced the law in a particular context, but to instruct and exemplify legal and scribal standards that courts were expected to observe in documentation. Gerber does not explain how these manuals were produced and where their compilers found the documents they chose to include in their works. We emphasize this point because a systematic demonstration of the claim that Ottoman courts of law functioned in a consistent and predictable fashion requires a *random* exploration of comparable collections of the court records in multiple periods and locations.

It is true that the litigations represented in Ottoman court records generally evoke the court model. These appear to be triadic processes, presided over by the kadı,[3] in which decisions appear to be made according to the well-established prescriptions of Islamic jurisprudential traditions and state-produced law codes (*kanunnames*). Litigation entries make no obvious reference to the extralegal considerations as variables that may have influenced decision-making processes, and the court's verdicts often identify clear winners and losers. Consider the following example:

Şahin bin [son of] Allahverdi, an adolescent (or "smooth-faced youth"; *şâbb-ı emred*) of average height, black eyes, and black eyebrows sued Hüseyin Beğ bin Hüseyin, known as "Kara Keloğlu," of Boğaz village, who owns him as his slave, claiming: "When I was in Iran, I was free and never a slave. Yet, Hüseyin Beğ possesses me as a slave, claiming that I am of Armenian origin and that I previously confessed of my slave status. I want him to be questioned and my lineage be confirmed."

Hüseyin Beğ denied Şahin's claim, claiming that "my father, from whom I inherited the aforementioned Şahin, had brought him from Iran. He [the father] told me that Şahin is Armenian in origin and that he had acknowledged his slave status. It is for this reason that I keep him as a slave."

When Şahin was invited to establish his claim, he presented to court two trustworthy individuals, Mehmed Beşe bin Osman and Ali Beşe bin Ali, who testified as follows: "Indeed, the plaintiff Şahin is the son of a free Muslim named Allahverdi from the Karadağ region in Iran. No one among his relatives was a slave and he was born a free man. We are witnesses to this situation and testify as such." After their testimonies were accepted Hüseyin Beğ was instructed to release Şahin. [This entry was] recorded as requested.

Entry of 24 Cemaziyelevvel 1155/27 July 1742 (Kastamonu Court Records vol. 39)

Witnesses . . .

According to Islamic law, free-born Muslims cannot be enslaved, which is why Şahin sought to demonstrate his family and religious history in order to challenge Hüseyin Beğ's claims over him. He did this by presenting witnesses who confirmed his Muslim lineage and testified to his free status at birth. The document creates the impression that this was enough to decide the case in his favor. The entry provides no information on the circumstances surrounding Şahin's enslavement or how he found witnesses who could support his claims so far from home. Nor is there any

[3] The court records of Kastamonu do not explicitly indicate whether a kadı or a *naib* presided over legal proceedings. In our discussion of the material found in these documents, we use the terms "kadı" and "judge" inclusively to refer to the judicial authority in charge of the process for the sake of simplicity, whether this person was an actual kadı or *naib*.

indication that the court assessed the accuracy of the defendant's response, which was not technically necessary. Legally, such information was superfluous and had no bearing on the court's decision (see Chapter 8 for a discussion of litigious and evidentiary procedures).

Before concluding that the court model accurately represents the Ottoman courts' role in dispute resolution, however, we should consider a number of factors. First, there is a danger in attempting to decipher the logic of legal practice from court documents, whose main function is to "translate" court proceedings into a language that highlights legal details and deliberately omits extralegal aspects of the dispute. The discursive representation of the events surrounding a particular dispute is designed primarily to justify the legal outcome of the court proceedings, rather than to report its ethnographic content. For this reason, it is difficult to glean from the court records the social reality that surrounded a particular case, the motivations of the parties involved, or, most important for the purposes of this discussion, the ways in which court functionaries may have negotiated a path between socio-communal realities and legal expectations.

Legal historians often lack the ability to observe the processes that generated legal documents (cf. Agmon 1996, 2006; Messick 1993, 2008). In this regard, legal anthropologists are fortunate since they possess the ability to juxtapose "court room ethnography with court-produced documents" (Stiles 2009, 34). Erin Stiles' work on Zanzibari courts is useful here as she was able to document how disputes were "entextualized" by kadıs and court clerks, based on their understanding of Islamic law, court procedure, and local custom. According to Stiles (2009, 35, 62–3), entextualization, or the production of "extractable" texts by legal functionaries from litigant narratives, involves a "strategic framing" of disputes in order to make them "sensible," "logical," and "coherent" from legal perspective. Consequently, it may be impossible to decipher the extrajudicial concerns or intentions of the court in a particular case solely from court documentation. The result of entextualization could be drastic. In one particularly interesting case, court functionaries reframed the case of a woman who had asked the court to force her former husband to take custody of their children by devising a litigation in which the father appeared as the claimant, suing the woman for custody of the children. The court-produced document reflected this formulation (Stiles 2009, 33, 60–3).

Given the problems associated with relying exclusively on the court records for a sophisticated understanding of the court's operations, the historian requires other sources of insight. We find one such source in anthropological studies, which often provide strikingly dissimilar depictions of legal practice in different settings. According to anthropologist Lawrence Rosen, Islamic law recognizes cultural conceptualizations and local information (Rosen 1990, 2000) as bases for legal action, which can generate context-based variations. In jurisprudential terms, local customs are legitimate, if secondary, sources of law, provided that they do not explicitly contradict canonical principles. In actual legal practice, the relationship between jurisprudential tradition and local custom could be even more complicated. For example, Aharon Layish (1991, 186–7) has demonstrated that modern Libyan courts recognized custom-based practices, even when they explicitly contradicted jurisprudential principles. In anthropological literature, such observations are common to the extent that an increasing number of researchers refuse to represent legal practice as "instance(s) of some general model of 'Islamic Law'" (Dupret 2006, 167). Instead of using Islamic legal doctrine as a "framing device" and perceiving customary practices as a complementary source of law, these researchers represent legal practice as an independent ontological entity in its own terms (Stiles 2009, 3). Judith Scheele's recent work (2010) on communities in the Touat region of the Algerian Sahara reveals, for example, that while local expectations and customary definitions of fairness regulated property rights in ways that often undermined some of the most basic jurisprudential prescriptions, frequent references to Islamic law served other, not necessarily legal, functions: "The real importance of the *shari'a* ... lies in its capacity to inscribe the local and all its internal complexities and contradictions into the universal framework of Islam, thereby making it part and parcel of an ordered world that is valid and recognizable beyond the vicissitudes of Saharan life and the irrigated perimeter of local oases" (372).

Similar research on legal practice and comparable conceptualizations is rare but not completely absent in historical literature. For example, in his work on late nineteenth- and early twentieth-century Tashkent, Paolo Sartori has demonstrated that evidentiary procedures in litigations that involved animal theft reflected not well-defined Hanafi standards, but nomadic customs and practices (2011a). Even in the Ottoman context, and despite the smoothening effects of the scribal practices that produced the *sicil*s, Jun Akiba (2013) has recently observed in a preliminary study that the courts in eighteenth-century Ankara, Tokat, and Ayntab decided marriage annulment cases in dissimilar fashions. Remarkably, two of these courts, those in Ankara and Tokat, were presided over by the same kadı, one Şemdanizade Fındıklılı Süleyman Efendi, which led Akiba to explain the variations in court practice with reference to differences in regional customs.[4] Akiba's findings make it easier to suppose that context- and custom-based variations colored the court's actions in Ottoman lands as well.[5]

Finally, the question of whether the court or bargain model better describes the Ottoman court should take into consideration the possibility that courts' involvement in dispute resolution processes was not limited to litigation. As we know, the court records contain a large number of amicable settlements (*sulh*). And yet, until recently many Ottomanists seem to have assumed that these settlements were arranged outside of the court, without the involvement of court functionaries, and were recorded in the *sicil*s merely for notarial purposes (Ergene 2010).[6] This is largely because

[4] For one study that emphasizes the extensive role that local customs played in court decisions, see Gerber (1981: 139–42). Note that in this earlier study, Gerber's treatment of the kadı's actions is radically different from his later characterizations. He suggests (1981: 145), for example, that "[o]ne of the most important characteristics of the Ottoman legal system ... was the process of reaching a decision in the kadi court. This process was informal and arbitrary. By 'arbitrary' we do not in the least mean 'unjust' but, rather, that it could never be clear to the disputants just what had led to the kadi's decision ... It is this point which is the crux of Max Weber's concept of 'kadi justice,' and judging from the case of Bursa, Weber's analysis is precise to a surprising degree."

[5] In this regard it is important to remember that most court functionaries, if not the kadı, were local individuals and that their income, including that of the kadı, was generated by court fees. Thus, for both cultural and economic reasons, these individuals must have been sensitive to and accommodative of local expectations and practices. Anthropologists have demonstrated in multiple contexts how local court personnel translate local expectations into legal practice. For example, in describing court clerks' contributions to legal processes, Stiles (2009, 41) uses the phrase "culture brokers," which is appropriate for Hirsch's (1998, 123–4) description of clerks' function in Kenyan courts: "In their roles as record keepers, mediators, and kadhis' consultants, clerks wield considerable power to negotiate relations among the court, the state, and the local community." For a consistent interpretation in a late Ottoman context, see Agmon (2006, 116).

[6] Jennings (1978a, 148) suggests, for example, that "[s]ulh might occur in any *mahalle* [neighborhood] or village and the negotiation of sulh was a neighborly process, not a formal legal procedure. The *muslihun* (mediators) must have been friends, relatives, neighbors or other Muslims who helped litigants or potential litigants settle their disputes out of court or before the court brought forth its own judgment anyway." Similarly, Gerber (1981, 132) characterizes *sulh* as a process that "took place outside the *kadi* courts." According to Eyal Ginio (1998, 204–5), "[m]ost criminal cases in Ottoman Salonika were resolved through compromise reached with the help of mediations. The kadı's role was confined to validating the compromise through registration." Likewise, Rossitsa Gradeva (1997, 52–9) identifies *sulh* exclusively with mediation outside the court. Leslie Peirce (2003, 120, 186) also describes *sulh* as "communal mediation" and a "service performed by community members." In the Egyptian context, Galal el-Nahal (1979, 20) states, after emphasizing the difficulty of determining the identities of the mediators, that "[t]he [court] documents occasionally mention that litigants brought to

the records of settlements do not explicitly acknowledge the participation of court officials in settlement processes.[7] Here is a typical example:

> Mehmed bin Derviş of (?) village of Kastamonu made the following statement in the presence of his maternal uncles, Hüseyin and İbrahim of the same village: "Previously, when I demanded from Hüseyin and İbrahim my share of inheritance from my late mother, Fatma bint Mehmed Hatun, a severe quarrel emerged among us. Subsequently, mediators (*muslihun*) intervened and convinced us to settle the dispute amicably, in return for three and one third of a *guruş* cash payment and a sword worth four *guruş* to be transferred to me. I collected the sum and the sword from Hüseyin and İbrahim. From this day onwards I release the two from any demand associated with my late mother's estate." Hüseyin and İbrahim confirmed the statement and this record was prepared as requested.
>
> Entry of 25 Rebiyülevvel 1104 / 4 December 1692 (KCR vol. 5)
>
> Witnesses . . .

This entry, like most others in the *sicil*s, reveals very little about the role of court officials in the settlement process. In court documents, an amicable settlement is almost always reported as the result of the intervention of "mediators," a label that does not explicitly identify the kadı or other court officials as the parties responsible for settlements. Although it is possible to read this rubric as a formulaic, short-hand expression that is not intended to exclude any actor from the mediation process, until recently, Ottomanists have generally interpreted it to refer exclusively to members of the community unaffiliated with the court. And yet, authoritative works on Islamic jurisprudence identify mediation as one of the ways in which the kadı is allowed to settle conflicts.[8]

the court people (possibly neighbors or associates) as *Muslims*, who attended the trial. Since the trials were usually open to the public, the *muslihun* [mediators] may have come from among those who attended, whether out of curiosity or personal interest in a particular case." This is a limited exposition; Ergene (2010) provides examples from the works of other researchers.

[7] Only recently have some Ottoman historians come to recognize the possibility that court officials played a role in the arrangement of amicable settlements. See Mutaf (2004), Tamdoğan (2008), and Ergene (2010). For a relevant discussion based on a non-Ottoman historical setting, see Sartori (2011b).

[8] Although jurisprudential sources generally recognize arbitration (*tahkim*) as another technique of dispute resolution in addition to amicable settlement and litigation, we have seen no records of arbitration in Kastamonu court records. Based on a *fetva* by *şeyhülislam* Ebussuud Efendi (d. 1575), Abdullah Demir (2010, 199–200) has argued that the Ottomans disallowed *tahkim* before the nineteenth century because they were concerned that the practice might undercut the court's business and also lead to resolutions not consistent with Islamic legal prescriptions. Even if such a ban existed, *tahkim* may have been unofficially practiced. It is also possible that some arbitration based resolutions were recorded in the *sicil*s as if they were mediated settlements. Nevertheless, in what follows,

According to Aida Othman (2007), who surveyed the premodern jurisprudential literature on the topic, there is little question that jurists considered the kadı's direct involvement in mediative/arbitrative processes and indirect participation in communal conciliatory initiatives as among his judicial responsibilities. Most legal treatises insist that the kadı is obligated to push the disputants toward settlement before initiating adjudication. In disputes that involved relatives and neighbors, jurists emphasized, it was especially critical to insist on settling disputes in order "to maintain the ties of family, brotherhood, and community" (Othman 2007, 69).

We should also note that anthropologists and legal scholars studying modern contexts have highlighted the commitment of modern Islamic courts to mediation and conciliation. The earliest examples of such observations are found in the works of Richard Antoun (1980, 1990), Aharon Layish (1975), and Enid Hill (1979), who respectively studied Jordanian, Palestinian, and Egyptian courts in the 1970s and 1980s. Their observations are in line with more recent findings relating to Indonesia, Zanzibar, Kenya, Morocco, Iran, Malaysia, Libya, Israel, and Egypt (Stiles 2006, 2009; Bowen 2003; Hirsch 1998; Layish 1991; Rosen 1984, 1989; Mir-Hosseini 2000; Shahar 2006; Welchman 2000; Peletz 2002; Shaham 1994, 1997). Although the degree to which these courts are inclined to push disputants toward settlement varies, mediation, in particular, appears to be a popular method of resolution. In fact, Rosen (1990, 2000) has gone so far as to claim that the main function of the Islamic court in modern Morocco is to help people negotiate their differences.[9] Consistent with the premises of the bargain model, the resolutions produced by Moroccan courts depend on the type of dispute, the characters of those involved in the case, the nature of the relationships between the disputants, and local values and traditions. In this sense, justice is nothing more than a regulation of reciprocity among freely contracting members of the community.

our discussion of non-adjudicative methods of dispute resolution is limited to amicable settlements.

9 Cf. Peletz (2002, 120), where he also states, "[A]s is also true elsewhere in the Muslim world, the central goals of the *kadi* and his staff are to get people back into a situation where they can successfully (re)negotiate their relationships. Hence the importance of providing a forum, such as the kadi's chambers or the office of the [court] counselor, in which people can ideally thrash out and resolve their differences."

Admittedly, our discussion presumes the existence of a practice (court-facilitated settlements) in our setting that we do not clearly detect in our sources. True, the observations in the classical jurisprudential sources and relevant anthropological research may in fact reflect concerns and processes that are embedded in different realities, which may or may not resemble the circumstances in the Ottoman context. At the same time, given the facts that the Ottomans shared the roots of their jurisprudential traditions with many other societies and that these traditions often generated uniformly consistent practices in most settings, we are inclined to discount the possibility that the Ottomans constituted an exception. Furthermore, and as we have indicated, the court records do not reject the possibility of court-facilitated settlements. They just fail to recognize court-facilitated settlements in a manner that modern historians would like them to be identified, which is hardly evidence for their absence. In any case, the accounts of the contemporary observers of Ottoman administration of justice provide hints about the ways in which court functionaries became involved in settlement processes (Ergene 2003, chapters 6 and 10). For all these reasons, we take our cues from the jurisprudential and anthropological literature on the topic and imagine a complex, multifaceted approach by the court to dispute resolution that included both litigation and settlement.

SETTLEMENT AS A METHOD OF DISPUTE RESOLUTION ACCORDING TO ISLAMIC LAW

Assuming that amicable settlements were an alternative method of dispute resolution used by Ottoman courts, one wonders how they were arranged and to what extent they conformed to the bargain model. Due to the nature of the court records, which reveal little regarding the details of settlement processes, we know little about this topic. A brief examination of the legal prescriptions for binding settlements, however, may provide some help in this regard.

Jurisprudential texts and legal manuals define settlement as a contract that resolves a dispute. According to law, parties to settlements should be sound in mind. A minor is allowed to participate in a settlement if the agreement does not generate a loss for him or her. The settlement should involve a formal invitation to and acceptance by disputing parties (Berki 1986, 321) and often requires monetary or in-kind compensation to be transferred by the accused (*müdde'a aleyh*) to the claimant (*müddei*), in return for the latter's agreement to drop his or her claim(s) against the former. Most types of disputes can be resolved through settlement, except for disputes that involve *hadd* offenses,[10] which require litigation.

As contracts, settlements represent a set of legal conditions for and expectations from settling parties. For example, a previously agreed-upon debt payment cancelled by a subsequent settlement cannot later be claimed.[11] Likewise, a settlement that resolves a dispute over physical harm or injury protects the accused from future claims. Also, jurisprudential prescriptions require settlements to meet the standards for legitimate agreements.[12] They determine how various types of disputes over property ownership, debt, legal rights, and entitlements should be negotiated,[13] what conditions settlement compensation should satisfy, and how compensation should be treated legally.[14] These prescriptions also specify the legal rights and responsibilities of settling parties.[15] Thus, it would be wrong to assume that settlements, at least those that meet

[10] Peters (2005, 53) defines *hadd* crimes as "offences with fixed, mandatory punishments that are based on the Koran or Sunna. This definition encompasses not only the specific offences mentioned in the Koran, but intentional homicide and wounding. Hanafite and Shiite authors, however, add another element to the definition, i.e. that a *hadd* crime must be entirely or predominantly a violation of a claim of God, i.e. violation of a public interest, which excludes homicide and wounding, since retaliation is a claim of men. The distinguishing feature is that claims of God, unlike claims of men, cannot be waived by men." According to Hanafis, *hadd* crimes include theft, banditry, illicit sexual intercourse, a false accusation of illicit sexual intercourse, and apostasy.

[11] Here is a relevant entry from the court records:

> Elhac Mazhar sued Yusuf, claiming the following: "Yusuf owed me 9 *guruş* from a previous transaction between us. Now, when I demand this sum, he refuses to pay it. I would like him to be questioned and the sum to be transferred to me." Yusuf rebutted (*def'*) this claim, claiming that they had settled (*sulh*) the dispute in return for a caftan that Elhac Mazhar received from him. When Yusuf was asked to prove his rebuttal he brought to court İbrahim bin Veli and Elhac Receb, who testified that that Elhac Mazhar and Yusuf settled the dispute over 9 *guruş* in return for a caftan Elhac Mazhar received from Yusuf. Their testimonies were accepted and Elhac Mazhar was instructed not to pursue the issue.
>
> Entry of 14 Şevval 1104 / 18 July 1693 (KCR vol. 5)
>
> Witnesses . . .

[12] For example, settlements that resemble arrangements involving interest payments are unacceptable. A settlement of the debt dispute that involves a deferred payment that is larger than the original loan amount is an example for this situation.

[13] For example, settlements of disputes over inheritance shares are not valid until the debts of the deceased are paid.

[14] The item(s) comprising compensation should belong to the accused and be well-specified (*malum*) at the time of the settlement. Also, if it consists of specific objects transferred from the accused to the accuser, it is treated like sold property (*mebi'*). If it is a debt payment, then it is treated as a price (*semen*) due to the accuser.

[15] Once settlements are arranged, they cannot be unilaterally revoked. And while settlements that involve property and monetary exchange can be revoked with the agreement

jurisprudential expectations, as a means for communal reconciliation and harmony are be completely free from formal, judicial rationale. In this sense, there is some truth to Aida Othman's (2007, 86) claim that settlements were not necessarily extra-judicial mechanisms for dispute resolution.[16] The problem with this assertion from the perspective of the researcher interested in legal practice, however, is our uncertainty about the relationship between theory and practice, a topic to which we return below.

For the time being, let us emphasize that even the most jurisprudence-compliant settlement represents a radically different method of dispute resolution compared to litigation; it much more closely resembles the bargain model (see Table 5.1). This is because:

1) The validity of the settlement, at least according to the Hanafi school, the official *mezheb* in the Ottoman Empire, is not based on the truth of the claims or counter-claims that frame the dispute in question or on identifying which party is in the right. Hanafi sources recognize three types of settlement: "settlement based on admission" – that is, admission by the accused of the truth of the claim(s) against him or her (*sulh an-ikrar*); "settlement based on denial" – that is, denial by the accused of the claim (*sulh an-inkar*); and "settlement based on silence" – that is, the accused party's decision not to respond to or take a position in relation to the claim (*sulh an-sükût*) (Berki 1986, 322; Othman 2007; Heyd 1973).[17] In the latter two cases, the parties fail to reach an agreement on the nature and/or details of the dispute and yet decide to bring the conflict to an end, often in return for symbolic or substantial compensation to the claimant. Since the primary objective of settlement is to establish peace and reconciliation, any attempt to determine whose claims are accurate and whose are based on falsehood could be counterproductive. Because the desire to establish past facts that underlie a dispute is at best irrelevant, and potentially harmful for the primary concerns of a settlement, the Hanafi perspective permits it to be ignored.

of both parties, settlements that involve the termination of legal rights and entitlements cannot later be revoked even if both parties agree to it.

16 *Sulh* settlements are also recognized in Ottoman state laws (*kanunnames*) (Heyd 1973, 137). For example, and as Tamdoğan (2008, 64–5) has observed, according to the *kanunname* of Selim I (r. 1512–20), settlements involving criminal offenses cause a reduction in the fines owed to military authorities.

17 The Shafi'is disagree with the Hanafis on this issue. They reject the validity of settlements based on the accused party's denial and silence (Othman 2007, 82–3).

2) Settlements are compromise-based arrangements that generate consequences that are, at least in theory, acceptable to both parties. They aim to uphold the interests of both parties by offering what they both consider to be acceptable resolutions. Obviously, what counted as an acceptable resolution might vary significantly, and must have been determined by many factors. The claimant's (in)ability to prove a claim; the type and severity of the claim against the alleged offender; the nature of the prior relationships between the disputants; their relative social position, prominence, and influence in the community; and their inclination to reconcile, among other factors, must have determined the specifics of resolutions, including the size of compensation. Tamdoğan (2008, 69) suggests that in mid-eighteenth-century Üsküdar, *sulh* payments made in cases that involved wrongful death varied significantly (between 16.5 and 250 *guruş*).[18] Nevertheless, concessions were expected from both parties. Again, Tamdoğan (2008, 71) observes that the payment determined in debt settlements amounted to about 50 percent of the disputed debts.[19]

We should note here that Ibrahim Halebi's influential *Mülteka el-Ebhur* (n.d., vol. 3, 325) defines settlement precisely in terms of compromise: "A settlement of a debt dispute involves the transfer of a portion of what had been originally borrowed from the claimant back to him or her, and a release of the rest." In fact, the law is suspicious of any settlement that might benefit one party at the expense of the other. For example, a settlement of a dispute over an unpaid loan by a promise of a future, larger payment is not acceptable, presumably because it might constitute usury. Likewise, according to *Mecelle* (Berki 1986, 323) a settlement in which one of the parties is a minor is unacceptable if it generates a loss for the latter, whether the agreement is reached by the minor him- or herself or by a legal guardian (*veli*). Because settlements should involve compromise, they are capable of serving future-oriented objectives such as preserving existing social and/or familial relationships.

[18] In other locations in seventeenth- and eighteenth-century Anatolia, payments also included objects with monetary and symbolic value, such as Qur'ans, swords, and horses (Tamdoğan 2008, 75; Mutaf 2004, 134; Ergene 2003, 184).

[19] Zeynep Dörtok Abacı (2006, 111–15) has identified settlements in eighteenth-century Bursa *sicil*s in which no payments were made for damages caused in incidents that later generated disputes. In these settlements, victims simply released (*ibra*) their opponents from future claims and demands for compensation. We have not encountered such settlements in Kastamonu *sicil*s.

3) The kadı, or his legal deputy, is central to litigations. Other court functionaries also play important roles in litigations and/or in processes that lead to or follow them. Consequently, the law clearly defines what qualities a kadı needs to possess and meticulously describes his role in adjudicative processes. On the other hand, legal prescriptions on settlement do not specify who may participate in mediative processes. In this sense, the law is more flexible and open to accommodating local traditions and practices, which may have encouraged the involvement of specific individuals or groups in mediative processes.

As indicated, the wording of settlement entries almost always refers to third parties (*muslihun* [mediators]), although records do not clearly specify who they were. Historians have suggested that local notables, community leaders, and high-ranking members of the military and religious establishments must have been among those who became involved in mediations (Tamdoğan 2008, 70–1; Jennings 1978a, 148; Mutaf 2004, 133). The anthropological literature generates a consistent impression: tribal chiefs, religious dignitaries, and elders are necessary to push for conciliation and negotiate settlement terms (Welchman 2000; Scheele 2010; Abu Nimer 1996). According to Abu Nimer (1996, 47–8), the tendency for mediators to be communal leaders serves two functions in the settlement process. First, in their capacity as communal leaders, mediators "bring a considerable knowledge of events, the character of the dispute, and the disputants, and they are involved in the day-to-day life of the disputants." Second, the elevated status of the mediators is critical because they represent the "the values and norms of the society (honor, shame, dignity, religious and patriarchal identity)" and embody the communal pressure upon disputants to settle the conflict and abide by the settlement. In fact, according to Abu Nimer, there is a strong relationship between the status of the mediators and the durability of the settlement because an attempt to renege on the settlement or alter its terms might be interpreted as a challenge to the influence and/or authority of the mediators *cum* communal leaders.[20]

In addition to these considerations, the fact that mediators could act as witnesses in subsequent litigations or legal processes between the settling

[20] *Pace* what the bargain model proposes, there is nothing *dyadic* about the settlement process as described above. In fact, according to Abu Nimer, direct, face-to-face negotiations between the disputants are avoided in many Middle Eastern settings. It is the mediators' responsibility to propose settlement terms and convince the disputants to agree to them (1996, 47–8).

parties must have made the mediative services of men with unassailable public reputations, a requirement for legal witnessing (see Chapter 3), valuable. Thus, it is conceivable that local elites were considered ideal *muslihun*, not only because they could use their communal influence to pressure disputing parties to settle, but also because they were better able to protect existing settlements from potential future challenges.

As stated, the literature based on Ottoman court records has by and large ignored the possibility of the kadı's involvement in mediative processes, at least until very recently. However, given the jurisprudential expectations of the kadı to encourage mediated settlement and also the legal technicalities that binding settlements are expected to satisfy, it is likely that they, alongside other court functionaries, played an important role in the arrangement of settlements. What is less certain is how the court functionaries, including the kadı, became involved in mediative processes. Did they participate in them primarily as respected and influential members of the community, or merely as legal experts with advisory responsibilities, or both? In what ways did they collaborate with local actors? How flexible were they in conforming to or tolerating communal and/or regional mechanisms of conflict management? According to the bargain model, mediation requires an affinity to utilitarian thinking. To what extent were legal functionaries, when they participated in mediative processes, able to balance their affinity with the law with this utilitarian orientation? Unfortunately, there is no easy way to answer these questions.

Another important question that we cannot answer here for the lack of documentation is how settlements found in the court records differed from those that were never brought to court. We should, however, expect disparities with respect to the type of dispute involved, identity of the parties, and the degree to which they were consistent with jurisprudential prescriptions. It may be the case that settlements on more trivial matters or those that involved family members were rarely recorded in the *sicil*s. Also likely is that settlements that involved parties who could afford the court's registration fees are overrepresented. The identities of mediators may have also played a role in the decision to have the settlements recorded or not. For example, settlements that were arranged by particularly prominent and/or influential individuals may not have been taken to court for registration.

It is clear from the above discussion that the court or bargain models cannot individually account for all the ways that Ottoman courts of law pursued dispute resolution. It would be more accurate to see them as

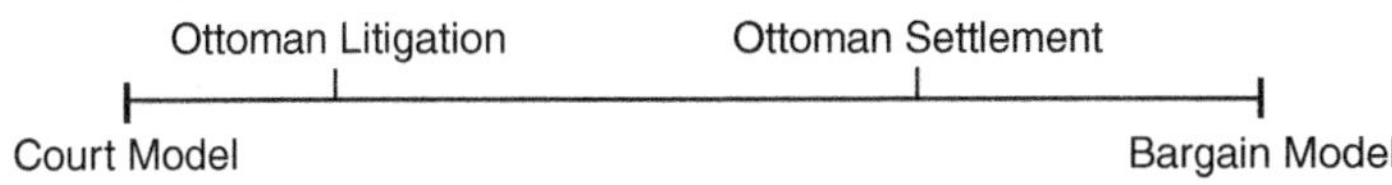

FIGURE 5.1: Ottoman Litigations and Settlements in Relation to Court and Bargain Models

corresponding to specific resolution techniques the courts employed with contrasting socio-legal objectives. In other words, the court's attempts at dispute resolution likely occurred on a spectrum that ranged between very different dispositions, depending on the circumstances surrounding each case. We have also argued that Ottoman litigations and settlements had qualities not entirely consistent with the processes evoked in the court and bargain models. Although adjudicative processes in the court records may appear to have been legalistic, uniformly formal, and consistent over time and space, there are reasons to suspect that context-based variations influenced them to a degree. On the other hand, while mediative processes sought reconciliation among disputing parties, they were also shaped by jurisprudential rules and expectations to a significant extent. We can perhaps represent the two modes of dispute resolution in the arena of the court with reference to the court and bargain models as shown in Figure 5.1. In the figure, the distance between the court model and Ottoman litigations is shorter than the distance between the bargain model and Ottoman settlements, based on our very subjective readings of the material in the court records. And although the distance between Ottoman litigations and settlements may not be as great as that between the court and the bargain models, the figure still identifies them as separate, alternative approaches to dispute resolution.

AN ASSESSMENT OF DISPUTE RESOLUTION PROCESSES IN OTTOMAN COURTS OF LAW

Assuming that litigations and settlements were both employed in Ottoman courts as methods of dispute resolution, we can infer the following with respect to dispute resolution processes in Ottoman courts of law:

1) It must have been difficult to predict the nature and outcome of a court proceeding beforehand. Seemingly similar claims may have been resolved by different methods, depending on the circumstances, the nature of the relationship between the litigants, communal expectations of fairness and propriety, and other factors. In other words,

the courts may have had dissimilar inclinations about how to resolve comparable disputes and the decision to employ a particular resolution technique was case-dependent. It is also likely that separate courts exhibited different tendencies in treating disputes.[21]

2) The availability of different methods of dispute resolution must have both enhanced the discretionary power of legal authorities and limited their options to a degree, due to communal scrutiny of their actions. For example, whereas a kadı presumably had the ability to push for mediation or litigation in a case involving a husband and a wife or siblings, he probably felt the need to begin the process with mediation since this technique would have been least likely to generate socially adverse consequences.
3) Related to the first two points, courts must have possessed the ability to adopt contradictory socio-judicial strategies in their operations. Whereas litigations likely sought primarily to establish the "facts" and "truth" in disputes brought to court, in mediative proceedings concern for "what really occurred" must have taken a back seat to reconciliation and compromise, not only in the court officials' interaction with the disputants but also in their subsequent allocation of responsibility and the ultimate disposition of the case. Likewise, evidentiary procedures and finer points of Islamic law may have received less attention when court officials were predisposed to resolving disputes amicably (Peletz 2002, 86).
4) From the disputants' point of view, the availability of separate methods of dispute resolution in the court may have enhanced its attractiveness as a venue for conflict management, encouraging them to approach the court for a (mediated) resolution even when litigation was undesirable or likely to generate adverse consequences.[22]
5) At the same time, the availability of different resolution techniques and the contextual character of the resolution process must have complicated the task of anticipating the court's operations

[21] Erin Stiles discusses (2009, 153–7) how various Zanzibari judges resolved disputes in divergent fashions. Some of these judges were more prone to litigating disputes while others were more willing to resolve them through mediation.

[22] Ergene (2010) explains in this way why some women in eighteenth-century Kastamonu appear to have gone to court with unsubstantiated rape claims against specific men, which put them at risk of being charged with the crime of false accusation of unlawful intercourse (*kazf*), a *hadd* offense with potentially severe repercussions. According to Ergene, women may have approached the court not necessarily to pursue litigation, but, rather, mediation.

beforehand and, thus, predicting outcomes. For disputants who were not familiar with the court or uninformed about the predilections of the court personnel it must have been especially difficult to assess how their cases would be treated, which made legal knowledge, familiarity with local legal practices, and connections to court functionaries invaluable in deciding whether to take disputes to court. We return to this topic in the next chapter.

6) The court's employment of mediative techniques must have significantly enhanced the local character of court processes, as they (possibly more so than litigation), tend to accommodate regional perceptions of fairness and propriety. In modern Libya, according to Aharon Layish (1991, 188), custom-based practices, if likely to generate conciliation, are taken very seriously by the kadıs. For the Libyan kadıs, Layish suggests, "the mutual agreement anchored by the nature of things in customary practice, is stronger than any other, even a *shar'i* legal norm. Indeed, their principal concern when about to confirm agreements is that these agreements shall have been achieved voluntarily. A fitting expression of this concept is given by Israeli *qadi*s in the context of customary *khul'* [or wife's purchase of her freedom from her husband and the consequent end to marriage]: 'The mutual agreement prevails over the *qadi*'."[23] In her work on the Touat in the Algerian Sahara, Scheele (2010) cites instances in which kadıs recognized settlements that, although very much based on local customs and communal practices, conflicted with jurisprudential principles.[24]

   We are not aware of such remarkable examples in Ottoman court records, although their absence may reflect (a) the standardizing effect of the records themselves, rather than actual practice, or (b) the possibility that such settlements were not brought to court for recording. However, since mediation often requires the involvement of local actors (whether associated with courts or not), the utilization of communal mechanisms of peace-making, and the satisfaction of indigenous standards of justice, we should expect that the courts engaged in a continuous and mutually accommodating negotiation with regional culture and local expectations in their efforts to reconcile disputes.

[23] According to Layish (1991, 194–5), the inclination to reject custom in favor of juristic doctrine is strong when there is "no agreement between the parties, in which case the qadis apply the shari'a strictly and uncompromisingly, although perhaps without much enthusiasm."

[24] In one case, the agreement endorsed by the kadı was enforced by local notables against disputants' will, which is a clear violation of the law (Scheele 2010, 368).

7) Finally, the availability of alternative methods of dispute resolution in the venue of the court raises the possibility of simultaneity in their utilization, adding another layer of complexity to the processes of dispute resolution. Depending on the perspective, the system appears to have allowed disputants to bargain in the shadow of the law or to litigate while they negotiated. In this sense, it is justifiable to characterize mediation and litigation as related components of a larger process. For experienced players of the legal game, they must have been complementary tools, useful in various phases of the same game, and ones that could be deployed strategically. Thus, treating litigation and mediation as separate and distinct processes, a consequence of the ways in which they are depicted in the court records, may lead to a major misunderstanding of the nature and scope of dispute resolution in the arena of the court. We return to this topic in the next chapter.

This chapter has studied alternative dispute resolution techniques in the Ottoman context and provided background information on amicable settlements, an understudied topic in the literature. Litigations will receive further consideration in the final part of the book. In particular, we discussed Islamic jurisprudential dispositions toward litigation-settlement questions, considered the roles that Ottoman courts might have played in dispute resolution, and identified source-based difficulties in deciphering related processes in court and outside. Given the nature and primary functions of the court records, we contend, a sound understanding of various conflict management mechanisms in the Ottoman context requires comparative and multidisciplinary approaches to the issue.

Overall, our discussion has suggested that the conflict management processes that involved these techniques were complex, multilayered, and, in all likelihood, served a plurality of legal and communal functions. This characterization makes sense if we remember that the court, in addition to being a judicial and administrative body, was also embedded in a specific social, economic, and political environment. Our depiction of its operations indicates that it was responsive to multiple and possibly conflicting judicial expectations.

In the next chapter we shift our focus from broader jurisprudential considerations and the institutional setting of the court to disputants' preferences concerning the two methods of conflict resolution. In particular, we address the factors and/or considerations that may have led them to choose one method over the other and how they utilized these methods in specific circumstances.

6

Trial versus Settlement: An Economic Approach

INTRODUCTION

Chapter 5 provided background information on the jurisprudential and institutional aspects of the settlement process in the Ottoman Empire. In the present chapter we shift attention to factors that influenced trial-settlement decisions by complementing the preceding chapter's legal, historical, and anthropological discussion with an economic analysis that aims to identify the variables affecting the likelihood of a dispute winding up at trial in Ottoman courts of law.

Although the economic approach to law has been slow to impact Islamic legal studies, the broader academic field of Law and Economics has recently grown into a mature area of specialization, thanks to contributions from both legal scholars and social scientists, including economists. Despite having its origins in the economics discipline and its first applications in Western (particularly American) systems, the field has made significant progress in incorporating insights from other disciplines and in expanding applications to non-Western legal traditions.[1] Several new journals devoted exclusively to this field have been established, and courses in Law and Economics are now being regularly offered in most law schools and economics

[1] The Law and Economics literature based on non-Western settings is still relatively rare. See, for example, Ma and Van Zanden (2011) and Mattei (1997). For a discussion of how this approach is represented in various modern and historical settings, see Bouckaert and De Geest (2000). For recent applications of Law and Economy methodology in the Ottoman context, see Kuran and Lustig (2012) and Coşgel and Ergene (2014a; 2014b; 2014c).

departments.[2] Applying standard economic concepts such as incentives and efficiency, researchers have made significant contributions to the analysis and evaluation of legal behavior and institutions, including models of legal disputes and their resolution by courts or alternative mechanisms.[3]

In this chapter we first provide a brief background to the Law and Economics approach for readers who are not familiar with this field and then propose a simple model of trial-settlement decisions based on insights found in the economic analysis of dispute resolution. In the next chapter we will use these insights and information from court records for a quantitative analysis of dispute resolution in Kastamonu.

LAW AND ECONOMICS RESEARCH: BACKGROUND

Although scholars have long been interested in the relationship between economics, politics, and the law, until the second half of the twentieth century there was no well-established methodology to explore this relationship systematically. As early examples of this interest, the Scottish Enlightenment thinkers wrote on the relationship between monopoly grants and public goods, the likelihood of collective action under scarcity and limited foresight, and various other questions that became major topics of investigation in the modern Law and Economics literature. MacKaay (2000) identifies the late nineteenth and early twentieth centuries as the period that saw the first wave of the Law and Economics movement, including works by European and North American economists on property rights and the consequences of anti-trust laws after the Great Depression. As Duxbury (1995, 318–19) notes, however, studies that constituted the literature before World War II did not share common methods, core theses, or grand themes.

In the 1960s, led by the Chicago School, neoclassical economists developed the building foundations for an economic approach to law and applied it to various sub-fields, such as criminal law, corporate law, externalities, public utility regulation, and accident law. This was part of a wider movement that broke from tradition by extending economic reasoning to behaviors outside of the traditional market

2 Examples of leading journals in this field include *American Law and Economics Review*, *European Journal of Law and Economics*, *Journal of Competition Law and Economics*, *Journal of Empirical Legal Studies*, *Journal of Law and Economics*, *Journal of Law Economics & Organization*, *Journal of Legal Studies*, and *Review of Law and Economics*.

3 For reviews of this literature, see Kerkmeester (2000), Mackaay (2000), and Mercuro and Medema (2006).

setting – a controversial approach at the time. Gary Becker, a Nobel laureate and leading proponent of this movement, used basic economic concepts such as cost and incentives to study such non-traditional topics as love, marriage, divorce, drug-use, crime, and racial discrimination. Extending this movement to law, Guido Calabresi, Ronald Coase, and Richard Posner pioneered the application of economic models to study legal behavior and institutions – also a controversial approach at the beginning. Over time, as the expansion of economic reasoning to non-market settings gained wider interdisciplinary acceptance and as economics became increasingly defined not by its subject matter but by its methodology, controversies ultimately subsided and the economic analysis of law became a mainstream approach, a major field of inquiry in both Law and Economics.

Essential to understanding the economic approach to law is a set of fundamental methodological principles (Miceli 2014). The most important is the postulate that human beings are rational decision-makers in a world of scarce resources and unlimited wants.[4] By rationality we mean that human behavior is mostly goal-directed such that – whatever aims individuals might have and however these aims may be measured – they would choose the best course of action available for achieving their aims within the various constraints that they face. Whereas in the market setting the constraints typically consist of prices and incomes, in the legal arena they may include legal sanctions (e.g., fines and punishment) and the reactions of other parties. Just as in the market they would choose as guided by prices and incomes, so too in law they would behave as guided by legal sanctions and the expected cost and benefits of their actions. For example, as we detail below, faced with a choice between settling a dispute and going to litigation, they would reach a decision by considering the probability of success at trial and the relative cost and benefits of the two options. Individuals respond to incentives the same way in both the market and legal settings by altering choices in reaction to changing circumstances, such that they would normally buy more of a good if its price falls and they would settle a lawsuit if the cost of litigation rises sufficiently.

Another fundamental principle of the economic approach to law concerns the nature of costs. In studying choice, economists consider not the

[4] Other neoclassical assumptions include methodological individualism of decision-makers, which implies that "complex social phenomena can be explained in terms of the elementary individual actions of which they are composed" (Scott 2000, 127) and efficiency associated with the unimpeded operation of market forces.

sunk (already incurred) costs of a decision, but its "opportunity cost," defined as the value of the best alternative forgone. Sunk costs should be irrelevant with respect to current decisions because they were incurred in the past and cannot be recovered by these decisions. By contrast, opportunity costs are essential because their impact on the outcome is immediate, incurred with the decision of not taking the next-best alternative. Since the economic costs thus include an imputed component, the cost of a decision involves not just explicit costs in the form of direct monetary payments, but also implicit costs in the form of forgone opportunities that are not reflected in cash outflow but implied in the allocation of resources. In deciding whether to litigate a lawsuit, therefore, parties would be better off focusing on the opportunity cost of going to trial and ignoring any costs of the dispute resolution process that cannot be recovered through litigation.

Opportunity costs are not restricted to monetary expenditures or material concerns. They include the value of the lost pleasures of foregone alternatives and the mental or emotional benefits of passed-up opportunities. Hence, the cost of litigation includes not just the monetary court fees and travel costs to and from court, but also the lost satisfactions of being in the more peaceful alternative environment of settlement and the value of time that could be spent doing other things instead of being engaged in litigation, even though no monetary exchange may take place regarding these alternatives.

The economic approach to law does not restrict the researcher to a limited set of assumptions regarding the aims of individuals, the availability of information about their opportunities, or the bounds of their ability to choose among alternatives. Although some of the earlier applications of the economic approach were based on simple neoclassical assumptions, later studies have developed more sophisticated models that incorporate explicit limitations on the abilities of humans and broader motivations for their behavior. A well-known example of human limitations is the notion of "bounded rationality," developed by Herbert Simon (1957). According to Simon, human rationality is "bounded" in the sense that it is limited by the lack of full information about opportunities or complete ability to process the information about these opportunities. It is also limited by uncertainty about what the future holds.[5] In another path-breaking work of behavioral economics, Kahneman, Slovic, and Tversky (1982) have emphasized the use of

[5] See Duxbury (1995, 370) for a summary.

shortcuts and rules of thumb, such as the "familiarity heuristic," which are generally predictable and useful in decision-making, but may also lead to erroneous conclusions in certain circumstances.[6]

Relaxing some of the assumptions made by the pioneering contributions to the Law and Economics literature, researchers have broadened the applicability of the economic approach to law by incorporating developments from behavioral, social, and historical disciplines since the 1970s. For example, behavioral economists have explored the limits to means–end calculations and proposed models of legal behavior that do not require strict postulates of rational choice (Jolls, Sunstein, and Thaler 2000). Public-choice theorists have similarly examined how legal and administrative authorities (such as judges) have influenced outcomes and institutions in their pursuit of self-interest. While game theorists have developed more sophisticated models of legal interactions, sociologists have called for closer cooperation with the sociology of law literature, urging Law and Economics researchers to consider social norms and expectations as legitimate constraints for decisions (MacKaay 2000).

The Law and Economics movement currently draws inspiration from various sources and welcomes systematic analysis of legal behavior and institutions in all social and historical settings. Given this brief overview of the economic approach to law, it should be clear that in applying this approach to dispute resolution in the Ottoman Empire we do not mean to postulate strict rationality for Ottoman subjects in eighteenth-century Kastamonu or to imply that they had the same objectives or legal means as those who lived in contemporary London or in twenty-first-century New York City. Whatever their objectives, our postulate is simply that they chose among available alternatives in a way that allowed them to achieve these objectives in the best possible manner. If we accept the view that individuals make decisions to maximize utility in the market place, it is methodologically consistent to accept the view that they continue doing their best within non-market constraints, otherwise we would have to assume that they undergo some sort of character transformation when they switch from exchanging goods in markets to negotiating disputes in the legal process or participating in other social settings. In this chapter, we simply propose a historical extension of this logic by viewing the participants in eighteenth-century Kastamonu court proceedings as individuals with aims who wished to achieve these aims in the best way possible.

[6] See Jolls, Sunstein, and Thaler (2000) for a review of contributions to Law and Economics literature from a behavioral approach.

RESOLVING A DISPUTE: A LAW AND ECONOMICS APPROACH

The literature on dispute resolution is enormous, so our objective in this section is not to engage in an exhaustive review of this literature or to offer a comprehensive economic analysis of the problem. Instead, combining selective insights from various approaches in the Law and Economics literature, we seek to introduce a coherent framework that can be used to study dispute resolution in the Ottoman Empire.[7] Systematic thinking about the trial and settlement process in a combined fashion is novel in the literature on Ottoman law. We contribute to this literature a fresh framework of analysis that is inspired by the economic approach to law and informed by the realities of Ottoman courts.[8] For a more formal discussion of these ideas, we have also developed a standard economic model of dispute resolution as included in an appendix to this chapter.

In 1984, George L. Priest and Benjamin Klein published a seminal article in *The Journal of Legal Studies* which became a landmark of legal scholarship for its demonstration of how cases are selected for trial. Formally developing the idea that litigations are a non-random sample of filed cases, they identified the factors affecting the likelihood of trial, an approach that has attracted much interest from social scientists and legal scholars. Although the approach was originally developed to examine dispute resolution in modern Western (particularly American) courts, with critical modifications reflective of specific cultural and institutional variations, it is sufficiently general to be applied to historical and non-Western legal environments. This is what we demonstrate in the rest of our book.

The Priest and Klein model set the stage for economic models of dispute resolution that share certain basic characteristics. For example, these models generally view the choice between trial and settlement as part of a larger process of dispute resolution. They also formally identify the basic parameters of this process, such as trial and settlement costs, and clarify how these factors would be expected to affect the likelihood of trial.

[7] The model presented here has been adopted from Priest and Klein (1984) and Miceli (2009, chapter 8). For other pioneering works in this literature, see Bebchuk (1984), Grossman and Katz (1983), Landes (1971), Posner (1973), and Shavell (1982). See also Cooter and Rubinfeld (1989), Kessler and Rubinfeld (2007), and Spier (2007) for reviews of the literature.

[8] In this sense, this chapter differs from an earlier article (Coşgel and Ergene 2014a) in which we offered a variety of factors that likely influenced trial and settlement decisions in the Ottoman Empire. This chapter aims to treat trial-settlement decisions in a more systematic manner.

Finally, they articulate the steps of the process and how the parties decide jointly whether to settle the dispute or go to trial. Although the plaintiff initiates the litigation, the defendant can avoid it either by accepting the charges leveled against him or her or by offering the plaintiff terms of settlement. Since parties would likely settle disputes in which one side is expected to be a clear winner, we would expect the litigations that wind up in court to be only a small fraction of all disputes, consisting of only the difficult and uncertain cases for which there is greater disagreement.[9]

In the standard treatment of dispute resolution in the Law and Economics literature, the basic structure of a lawsuit is a multi-stage process, progressing chronologically from the emergence of a legal dispute to its resolution through settlement or trial. The first stage consists of an event that causes a dispute between two parties. This may be an accident or crime in which one party (the injured) claims to have suffered harm at the hands of another party (the injurer). In the second stage the injured party decides whether or not to file a legal claim. In the economic analysis of dispute resolution, this decision depends on whether the expected benefits, such as the settlement amount or court judgment, outweigh the cost of filing a claim. Since lawsuits are costly in monetary and non-monetary terms,[10] parties to the conflict would avoid these costs unless they expect greater benefits, so the proportion of injured parties who file a claim is typically very small.

According to the theory, once a lawsuit is filed, parties engage in pretrial bargaining in the third stage by exchanging information about the dispute and discussing whether and how to compensate the alleged damages in an effort to settle the dispute without formal trial. As we discuss in detail below, since settlement is a joint decision of the parties, the possibility of resolving the dispute at this stage depends on whether they can agree to terms that benefit them both. Studies generally show that parties are ultimately able to settle in a vast majority of cases filed in modern courts (Spier 2007, 268; Kessler and Rubinfeld 2007, 381–3).[11]

9 Studies in modern Western settings show that only a fraction of disputes go to trial (Eisenberg and Lanvers 2009), which is consistent with the relatively low number of litigations in Ottoman Kastamonu (see Chapter 3).

10 Although monetary expenses associated with court use might have been considerably different in modern Western and Ottoman settings, Ergene (2002 and 2003, chapter 5) has demonstrated that the latter was still significant. See also Chapter 3, this volume.

11 See Eisenberg and Lanvers (2009) for a summary and critique of the literature on settlement rates. Although the authors suggest that settlement rates may vary depending on how one defines a range of formal outcomes, and also across different types of cases, they still agree that settlement is the primary outcome in civil cases (ibid., 112).

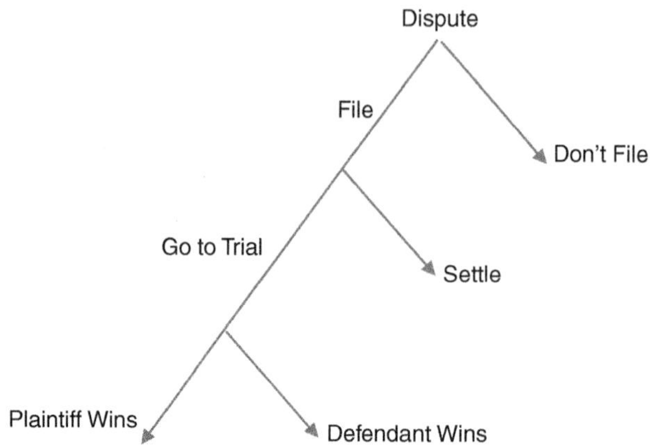

FIGURE 6.1: Settlement–Litigation Decision

In a small proportion of cases, however, the parties fail to settle and the case goes to trial in the fourth and final stage of the process. Whereas the resolution in the third stage is consensual through bargaining, the outcome in the fourth stage is dictated by the court. Reaching the final stage is puzzling because trial is costly and settlement can generate a positive surplus for the parties to share through bargaining. An important question of the Law and Economics literature that has attracted significant attention is why some cases go to trial. See Figure 6.1 for a schematic illustration of the four stages of the dispute-resolution process.

To examine the selection of litigated cases in more detail, consider the trial-settlement decision as a simple bargaining problem. When a lawsuit is filed, parties may resolve the dispute without litigation if they can agree on a payment to be made by the defendant to the plaintiff as settlement. Since an agreement can be reached if the defendant offers an amount or concession that exceeds the plaintiff's settlement demand, it is easy to see in this framework why most disputes are settled before trial. Since trial is costly and uncertain, settlement would clearly be the preferred choice if parties share the same assessment of the expected outcome of trial (such as when both parties know that the evidence is overwhelmingly in favor of the plaintiff) and face the same costs and expected payoffs of going to trial, because in that case they can implement the same outcome in a settlement without incurring the costs and uncertainty of trial.

To illustrate this, suppose that an individual caused damages worth 100 *akçe*s to another individual in front of several witnesses in Kastamonu. Suppose also that if the case went to trial each party would incur litigation costs of 10 *akçe*s (for court fees, travel expenses, lost income for time spent in court, etc.). In this case, the injurer would pay any amount less than 110 *akçe*s to settle out of court, and the victim would accept any amount greater than 90 *akçe*s. Since any settlement amount between these figures would make the parties better off than going to trial, we should expect them to settle the case without litigation as long as they could agree on how to share the surplus of 20 *akçe*s thus created (= 110 – 90). Moreover, if the parties were risk-averse, the likelihood of settlement would rise even further because they would prefer the certainty of settlement to the uncertain outcome of trial.

Although this simple argument explains why a vast majority of disputes typically settle out of court, by carefully re-examining some of the underlying assumptions of the above example we can also see why some cases wind up at trial. An important implicit assumption that we made above was that the parties had the same assessment of the likelihood of the victim's chances in court, as implied by the information regarding the presence of several witnesses to the case. Suppose instead that the parties differed significantly in their beliefs regarding the outcome of trial, such as would be the case if, for example, there were questions regarding the credibility of the witnesses or the non-negligence of the victim. Since this would alter the *expected* value of the trial for the two parties, they could find themselves in a situation in which settlement is no longer possible. Consider, for example, the extreme case of each party believing with total certainty that they would win the case at trial. In this scenario, the victim would still demand an amount greater than 90 *akçe*s to settle out of court, but the injurer would pay no more than 10 *akçe*s, the cost of trial. Settlement is clearly not feasible anymore.

The likelihood of trial thus originates from differences between the parties in their assessments of trial outcome and expected net payoffs from trial. Since the net payoff depends on the cost and benefits of trial, we should also reconsider how parties may differ along these dimensions, which we implicitly assumed away in the above example for simplicity. The opportunity costs of going to trial may vary systematically among the types of cases and litigants, and the parties may receive systematically different *indirect* (negative or positive) subjective payoffs from going to trial, such as reputational stakes and personal cost or benefits.[12] These

12 See Priest and Klein (1984, 24–9) and Siegelman and Waldfogel (1999, 109) for examples of stake asymmetry.

differences can cause the likelihood of trial to vary systematically among types of disputes.

To recap, the likelihood of trial would depend on three basic characteristics of the litigation environment, namely the parties' subjective assessments of the probability of plaintiff victory at trial, their cost of pursuing a trial, and the benefits they expect from the trial outcome. These factors consequently indicate three sets of conditions that could affect the likelihood of trial.[13] As we detail below, the likelihood of trial would tend to rise under the following conditions, all else being the same:[14]

1) divergent expectations about the trial outcome such that the plaintiff is more optimistic than the defendant about his or her chance of success at trial,
2) asymmetric stakes from the trial outcome such that the plaintiff expects higher indirect payoffs than the defendant in the case of plaintiff victory at trial, and
3) lower trial costs.

Differential Sophistication and Divergent Expectations

Consider first the possibility of divergent expectations regarding the outcome of trial. The literature on dispute resolution has identified two general reasons why the parties might not share the same expectations.[15] The first is that they might have different opinions about the trial outcome, possibly originating from the difference in the parties' legal sophistication and the consequent divergence in their probabilistic assessments of the quality of their cases. In general, parties may differ in their opinions about trial outcome if they have different knowledge or experience concerning the law governing a case or how it will be applied. This could be the case if, for example, one of the parties was previously involved in a similar legal dispute in court.

[13] For a different approach to identifying these conditions, see Siegelman and Waldfogel (1999).

[14] We have identified elsewhere more specific factors that likely affected the likelihood of trial in Ottoman courts, such as the availability of alternative mechanisms of dispute resolution, predictability of the court's decisions, speed of litigation, and fictitious litigations (Coşgel and Ergene 2014a). For information on fictitious litigations also see Chapter 10.

[15] These approaches are known as the "Divergent Expectations" and the "Asymmetric Information" theories of litigation. See Waldfogel (1998) for an attempt at reconciling these approaches.

Disputes in which differential sophistication leads both parties to be optimistic about the outcome would likely wind up at trial. Note that this requires the plaintiff to expect victory at a high probability and the defendant to expect plaintiff victory at a low probability. In general, the likelihood of trial would rise as the difference between the parties' assessment of plaintiff success rises.

The second reason for divergent expectations is the case of asymmetric information. In an accident, for example, one or both parties may have private information about the facts of the case, information that would be costly to obtain by the other party prior to trial. The plaintiff may know how his or her own negligence contributed to the accident and the defendant may have first-hand information about his or her actual liability, but it would not be in either party's interest to share this information with the other party. Similarly, although the plaintiff may know the true cost of the injury or the reliability of witnesses, this information might not be available to the defendant before trial. The resulting asymmetry of information explains why the parties in such cases would have divergent expectations about the trial outcome and fail to reach a settlement.

In the Ottoman context, divergent expectations could exist between groups and individuals, between individuals with honorific titles and others, between those with religious markers and others, and between individuals who belonged to prominent families and others. The former parties in these comparisons were more likely to have legal experience, religious training, and/or better access to legal information compared to their counterparts and, consequently, greater ability to estimate the strength of their cases. Since in such situations the parties would likely have different assessments of trial outcome, we would expect these disputes to be more likely than others to go to formal trial. In the next chapter we will have the opportunity to test this hypothesis.

Asymmetric Stakes

The second general condition in the litigation environment that affects the likelihood of trial is the degree of stake asymmetry across parties (Siegelman and Waldfogel 1999). Stakes are symmetric in the baseline case because all that matters is the amount of trial award to be paid by the defendant to the plaintiff. But if one party derives some private cost or benefit from the outcome that is not captured entirely by the amount of the damages to be paid by the defendant, the stakes become asymmetric. This can be the case if, for example, the plaintiff expects to derive a reputational benefit (such as public recognition as a tough legal player) from the trial award that could be useful in future trials. Well-known examples of stake asymmetry include disputes between manufacturers and consumers, employers and employees, and corporate bodies and individuals. The first party in each of these pairings is likely to have greater stakes than the opposing party because they are more likely to be repeat players in litigation and thus expect to have higher long-term costs or benefits in future litigation. Stakes may be asymmetric even in one-shot trials if one of the parties is more interested in the law or reputation than the other or faces additional personal or social stigma attached to losing at trial.

When stakes are asymmetric, a dispute may wind up in litigation even though the parties may have the same assessment of plaintiff success. If there is a positive reputational benefit, the differential stake would reduce the range of settlement offers that the plaintiff would be willing to accept, thereby raising the likelihood of trial, even though the litigants may have the same assessment of trial outcome. Similarly, the defendant might expect to suffer a loss beyond the judgment amount paid to the plaintiff, such as enduring the publicity of a trial. If it is important to avoid this cost, he or she might make a settlement offer even if the chance of losing at trial is low. Empirical studies of settlement behavior have shown various ways in which differential stakes or external benefits can affect the proportion of tried cases (Kessler and Rubinfeld 2007, 381–3).

In the Ottoman context, the stakes of losing at trial could be different between men and women, individuals with honorific titles and others, individuals with religious markers and others, and members of prominent families and others.[16] For example, a man with an elite title (e.g., *Efendi* or *Ağa*), presumably a prominent and respected person, likely faced higher stakes from losing in the public arena of the court than a titleless peasant. In a dispute between a titleless peasant and a man with a title, therefore, we would expect the latter to seek settlement if he was concerned about the reputational consequences of losing because of its implications for future trials. We would expect similar stake differentials in trials between individuals and corporate bodies and in other combinations of size differentials, if corporate bodies or multiple individuals were more likely to be repeat players in litigation and thus had more to lose in reputation than a single individual.

[16] The possibility of losing at trial sometimes accomplished other, possibly non-legal, objectives such as announcing an offence or declaring one's innocence in the public forum of the court (cf. Peirce 2003; Agmon 2006).

Trial Costs

Litigations would be more likely in suits with lower trial costs, all else being the same, simply because this would reduce the surplus available to settling. The basic difference between the cost and stakes of trial in this context is that litigants have to incur the cost regardless of the outcome. To see how the trial costs could vary across disputes, recall that the total cost includes both monetary payments and non-monetary items such as the stress caused by the uncertainty of trial outcome, the social stigma associated with choosing litigation over settlement, and the personal scars and strains that accompany litigation. Trial costs could thus vary systematically from one type of trial to another because of differences in monetary or non-monetary components.

Consider first the variation in monetary costs. This could be the case if, for instance, the litigation costs varied systematically across case-types or over time periods. Across case-types, the standard of decision at trial could vary such that the cost of trial could be lower in some cases than in others. Such variations have been observed in modern courts between criminal and civil litigations. Whereas the decision in the former category concerns determining whether the accused has committed a crime, the decision in civil cases is to determine whether the defendant is liable for the plaintiff's alleged injuries. Typically the latter category further consists of a variety of subcategories, such as contracts, real property, worker injury, and product liability. If the trial cost varies systematically among case-types, one would expect the differential to be reflected in the likelihood of trial because it would affect the range of acceptable settlement offers. This expectation is generally confirmed by empirical studies of adjudication. Using data from suits initiated in the Southern District of New York after 1979 and resolved by 1989, Siegelman and Waldfogel (1999) studied differences in trial rates across six case-types. Their results show systematic differences in trial rates, ranging from being generally low for tort cases (varying between 9 and 25 percent) to significantly higher for prisoner cases (67–79 percent) and in mid-range within contract (29 percent), civil rights (37–49 percent), labor (33 percent), and intellectual property (32–44 percent) cases.

The procedures and standards that applied to criminal and civil cases in the Ottoman legal system were often different as well. For example, the standards of proof in criminal litigations against individuals of poor reputation were generally low (Heyd 1973; Peters 2005; Ginio 1998). This is because in criminal cases the court's legitimacy was not based on its neutrality, as in civil litigations, but on its ability to protect communal interests and earn communal approval (Fadel 1995), which led the courts to relax evidentiary standards in cases pertaining to general security (such as banditry) or when the accused in criminal litigations were people of ill repute. This is largely why in crime-related trials, circumstantial evidence (such as hearsay, otherwise inadmissible in civil litigations) was accepted and confessions could be extracted through torture. We would thus expect the trial ratios in Ottoman courts to vary systematically between criminal and civil cases, as they do in modern US courts.[17]

Consider next the variation in non-monetary costs, which likely depended on the characteristics of parties and their relationship to each other. In Ottoman courts, the social stigma of litigation could vary, for example, by the gender of the parties and their family connection to each other. If the stigma was higher for women than men, we would expect disputes between two women to be less likely to go to trial than those between two men. In the same vein, if the stigma was higher for litigations between parties related through family ties, we would expect the trial ratio to be lower in civil cases between related individuals than those between unrelated parties. This is also consistent with the effect of the scars and strains that accompany litigation, another non-monetary cost. Litigations among family members would be more likely than others to have lasting consequences, regardless of the outcome, indicating higher trial costs and lower trial rates in disputes among family members and kin. We examine the empirical implications of these expectations in the next chapter.

CONCLUSION

We have discussed the evolution and basic tenets of the Law and Economics approach to law and developed a formal model of dispute resolution to examine trial-settlement decisions in the Ottoman Empire. We view the basic structure of a legal dispute as a multi-stage process that progresses chronologically from the emergence of a conflict to its resolution through settlement or litigation. What happens in one stage determines the options

[17] This does not mean that trial-settlement decisions in criminal and civil disputes varied only because of cost differentials in these cases. Rather, cost differentials were likely to be just one factor that influenced the variations in trial-settlement decisions in civil and criminal contentions. For a discussion of other reasons that trial and settlement decisions could be different in criminal and civil cases in the Ottoman context, see Coşgel and Ergene (2014a).

available in the next. Since trial is costly, the parties generally tend to avoid these costs by settling their disputes.

By identifying the stages of dispute resolution, we bring insights from the Law and Economics literature that have been largely overlooked in Ottoman legal studies. First, litigation is not an isolated event that can be studied on its own. It is part of a larger, more complex process that begins long before the trial and sometimes continues long after. To understand litigation, we must thus view it in relation to settlement and compare their consequences. Second, since litigation is generally costlier than settlement, only a small percentage of legal conflicts wind up in litigation. Moreover, since disputants choose whether to take their disputes to court for trial, litigations constitute neither a random nor a representative sample of all disputes.

Although only a minority of disputes go to trial, scholarly interest in these cases has heightened as researchers have sought to determine the reasons for the failure of parties to settle. We argued in this chapter that from an economic perspective, the likelihood of trial depends on factors that cause the plaintiff to have a more optimistic assessment of trial outcome than the defendant, that make the plaintiff receive higher indirect benefits from trial outcome than the defendant, and that reduce the cost of going to trial. In the next chapter we use these general insights to examine how the characteristics of cases affected the likelihood of trial in the court of Kastamonu.

APPENDIX TO CHAPTER 6: A SIMPLE ECONOMIC MODEL OF DISPUTE RESOLUTION

To examine the litigation puzzle in a simple setting, consider the following bargaining model of the trial-settlement decision. Once a lawsuit is filed, parties engage in bargaining in an effort to reach a settlement prior to trial, which involves a payment made by the defendant to the plaintiff to resolve the dispute. An agreement is reached if the defendant's offer exceeds the plaintiff's settlement demand. The likelihood of settlement in this simplified setup depends on three basic characteristic of the litigation environment, namely the parties' subjective assessments of the probability of plaintiff victory at trial, their cost of pursuing a trial, and the benefits they expect from the trial outcome. Formally, let $\boldsymbol{P_p}$ denote the plaintiff's assessment of his or her chances of success at trial, and $\boldsymbol{P_d}$ be the defendant's assessment of the same probability (that is, his or her chance of losing at trial). Let $\boldsymbol{C_p}$ and $\boldsymbol{C_d}$ be the plaintiff's and the defendant's costs of going to trial, including court fees and the value of time and expenditures spent in preparing and attending the trial. Assume, for simplicity, that settlement costs are zero (alternatively, assume they are less than trial costs for the same results to hold).

If the plaintiff wins, he or she will recover a monetary judgment denoted by J. Suppose also that the trial outcome may confer various other *indirect* (negative or positive) subjective payoffs to the parties, including reputation, future stakes, and personal cost or benefits. Let I_p and I_d denote the values of these payoffs to the parties corresponding to the case of plaintiff victory at trial.

Settlement is possible if there is a positive surplus to settling, the difference between the defendant's maximum offer and the plaintiff's minimum demand. To see the minimum settlement offer acceptable to the plaintiff, note that the expected value of trial for him or her is $P_p(J + I_p) - Cp$, the difference between the expected benefits from trial outcome and trial costs. He or she would accept any settlement offer S such that

$$P_P(J + I_P) - C_P \leq S. \tag{1}$$

Similarly, the expected total cost of trial to the defendant is $P_d(J + I_d) + C_d$, the sum of expected losses and trial costs. Since this is the maximum amount that the defendant would offer to settle the lawsuit out of court, he or she would settle for any amount S such that

$$S \leq P_d(J + I_d) + C_d. \tag{2}$$

A settlement would thus be feasible if (1) and (2) hold simultaneously.

$$P_P(J+I_P) - C_P \leq P_d(J+I_d) + C_d. \tag{3}$$

Note that settlement would clearly be the preferred choice if parties agreed on their assessments of the expected outcome of trial $(P_p = P_d)$ and did not expect any indirect payoffs from trial outcome $(I_p = I_d = 0)$, because under these conditions (3) always holds $[- C_p \leq C_d]$. In that case the parties can implement the same outcome in a settlement without incurring the cost of trial and by sharing the surplus thus created $(C_p + C_d)$.

The likelihood of trial thus originates from differences between the parties in their assessments of trial outcome and expected payoffs from trial. To identify the factors affecting this likelihood, we reverse the inequality in (3) and rearrange terms so that the trial condition becomes:

$$P_P(J + I_P) - P_d(J + I_d) + C_d + C_P. \tag{4}$$

It is easy to see from this inequality the three general sources of the likelihood of trial. More specifically, the likelihood of trial would tend to rise under the following conditions, all else being the same:

4) divergent expectations about the trial outcome such that the plaintiff is more optimistic than the defendant about his or her chance of success at trial ($P_p > P_d$),
5) differential stakes from the trial outcome such that the plaintiff expects higher indirect payoffs than the defendant ($I_p > I_d$) in the case of plaintiff victory at trial, and
6) lower trial costs ($C_p + C_d$).

7

Which Disputes Went to Trial? Case-type- and Period-based Analyses

We now turn to an empirical analysis of the theoretical insights developed in the previous chapter. In Chapters 3 and 4 we studied the types of legal matters brought to court and the relationship between the characteristics of parties and the proportions of their matters that were filed as agreements as opposed to disputes. In this chapter we shift attention from agreements to disputes and examine the factors that affected the likelihood of parties taking their dispute to trial rather than settling it.

In most legal systems, parties are encouraged to settle their disputes before trial. Since it typically costs significantly more to go through a formal trial than to negotiate a settlement, one would expect most disputes to be settled out of court, and only a small fraction to wind up at trial. Empirical studies of settlement behavior in modern courts generally support this expectation because most states have developed various formal and informal institutions, such as mediation and arbitration, as alternative mechanisms of dispute resolution and, consequently, achieved very low ratios of litigation (Spier 2007, 268; Kessler and Rubinfeld 2007, 381–3). In the United States, for example, about 2 percent of civil cases filed in federal courts go to trial, and less than 4 percent of those filed in state courts go to trial (Spier 2007, 268). Although we possess little direct information about the availability and relative cost of alternative mechanisms of dispute resolution in the Ottoman Empire, our findings indicate that a significant proportion of disputes in Ottoman lands were resolved through settlements.

For a quantitative analysis of the factors affecting the likelihood of litigation, we use information from the Kastamonu court records to compare the case characteristics of disputes that were settled with those that wound up at trial. Although we obviously know nothing about the disputes that were never brought to court, the records nevertheless include those that were registered as settlements, allowing us to differentiate between them and formal litigations. Using the information about the characteristics of all disputes and the parties involved in them, we examine the patterns in which settled and litigated disputes differed systematically.

In this chapter, we present the results of our empirical investigation in two stages. In Tables 7.1–7.8, we list simple descriptive statistics (mean, standard deviation, and the number of observations) of the trial ratio corresponding to different categories of court clients, and we engage in selective comparisons of these statistics to arrive at some preliminary conclusions. Although these comparisons provide interesting information regarding the relationship between court clients and the likelihood of trial, we have to be careful to recognize the tentative nature of any conclusions based on these tables because we cannot draw ceteris paribus conclusions based on singleton comparisons. Since a multitude of variables probably affected the likelihood of trial simultaneously, in the second stage of our investigation (Tables 7.9–7.12) we use multiple regression analysis to identify the individual effect of each variable by controlling for others explicitly. To ensure smooth transition between the two stages of our investigation, for readers who may not be familiar with regression analysis we include a brief discussion of why this technique is necessary and which estimation model is most appropriate.

We saw in Chapter 4 that the characteristics of parties differed significantly among types of cases and over time periods. This raises the possibility that the effect of these characteristics on the likelihood of trial also varied significantly across types and over time. To consider this possibility, we differentiated across the three case-types (i.e., criminal disputes and civil disputes among related and unrelated parties) by examining how the size-composition, gender, honorific title, and religious and socioeconomic status of the parties affected the likelihood of trial in each category. To see how these influences varied over time, we similarly examined the effects of these variables on the likelihood of trial separately for each time period.

Our analysis of settlement behavior in Ottoman courts is related to the broader literature on dispute resolution, specifically the empirical analysis of selection effect in the Law and Economics literature. Since Priest and Klein's (1984) pioneering analysis of the selection effect in settlement-trial decisions, an enormous empirical literature has developed to identify the factors affecting the likelihood of trial.[1] Using data from modern courts, researchers have shown how the selection of cases for trial has depended on the characteristics of the parties and the nature of case-types (Kessler and Rubinfeld 2007, 381–6). Selection bias is a serious, yet overlooked, problem in Ottoman historiography because numerous scholars have relied exclusively on litigations for information on disputes, despite the vulnerability of documents on litigation to selection bias (Coşgel and Ergene 2014b; Klerman 2012). By investigating the way settlement–litigation decisions depended on the characteristics of parties and varied systematically across case-types and over time, we provide in this chapter the first empirical analysis of disputant behavior in the Ottoman context and one of the very few for anywhere before the nineteenth century.

TRIAL AND SETTLEMENT IN KASTAMONU COURT

Consistent with general practice in the Ottoman legal system, the primary responsibility of the Kastamonu judge was to resolve disputes by facilitating settlements or by presiding over formal trials. When a dispute was brought to court, he could initiate a settlement personally or by assigning intermediaries to hear the case and find a mutually agreed-upon resolution, possibly resulting in the case being dropped without further action or in one disputant agreeing to a transfer payment or non-monetary action requested by the opponent. It is more than likely that settlements were also arranged outside of the court. If settlement could not be reached, the judge would hear the case formally in court and decide.

Ottoman court registers typically provide the same type of information about settled and tried disputes. This information includes the identities of disputants, the evidence presented in court, and the resolution. Consisting of abbreviated descriptions of the disputes brought to court, the records typically begin by identifying the parties through their full names, honorific titles and other distinguishing markers attached to their names,

[1] As mentioned earlier, central to Priest and Klein's analysis is that the decision to litigate or settle a dispute is a joint decision by the disputants. Even though plaintiffs initiate the litigation, defendants can avoid it either by accepting the charges leveled against them or by offering plaintiffs attractive settlement terms. According to Priest and Klein, particularly strong (or weak) cases from any party's point of view are likely to be settled because in such cases the results of possible litigation are not in doubt. Thus, only those cases about which both parties feel reasonably strong are litigated and they do not resemble disputes resolved in other ways. Consequently, litigations constitute a non-random and unrepresentative sample of all disputes.

religious identities, and their places of origin. If the disputants were related to each other, this information is also provided. The records then describe the nature of the dispute, often in the form of direct quotations from the individuals who approached the court, followed by their opponents' responses to the accusations directed at them. Next, the entries disclose the evidence and/or other supporting material submitted to court by the litigants, such as the full names and testimonies of the witnesses. If the case was tried in court, the records show how the judge decided on the dispute.

Note also that settlement and litigation entries resemble each other in style and organization. Just as the party identified first in a settlement registry is often the one who made the accusation, the same was true for the plaintiff in a litigation entry. This similarity underlines the parallels between the case entries in the *sicil*s documenting the two forms of dispute resolution, as both processes required the court to determine the specific roles of the disputants (as plaintiffs or defendants; see Chapter 8). For a court-recognized settlement to thwart future litigation, the court needed to specify the parties and the dispute in exactly the same way as they would have been specified in a litigation.

The fact that *sicil*s contain settlement entries as well as litigations makes them a suitable medium to study the selection principle. Unlike litigations, however, settlements did not have to be registered in court for them to be legally binding. This raises the question of whether the settlements that we find in court records were representative of those that were never filed in court, a question that we obviously cannot answer without external evidence. The analysis presented in this chapter, therefore, captures only one aspect of the selection bias in court records. We can only surmise that our results, which are based on the differences between litigations and settlements found in court records, are indicative of those that likely existed between litigations and unrecorded settlements.

DISPUTANTS AND TRIAL RATIO

We use the information from court records to examine the relationship between the trial ratio and the characteristics of parties. We have information on 1,293 disputes filed in court. Table 7.1 shows the distribution of these disputes across case-types and over time periods. Overall, 434 of these disputes were settled and 859 (66 percent) were tried. As seen in the table, the proportion of disputes that were tried varied by case-type. Whereas about 80 percent of civil disputes among unrelated parties

TABLE 7.1: *Distribution of Disputes across Case-types and over Time*

	Number of Cases				Trial Ratio			
TYPE	1684–96	1735–43	1781–90	All	1684–96	1735–43	1781–90	All
Criminal	32	68	76	176	0.84	0.74	0.26	0.55
Civil between related	69	132	266	467	0.67	0.50	0.47	0.51
Civil between unrelated	176	190	284	650	0.91	0.82	0.73	0.81
All	277	390	626	1293	0.84	0.70	0.57	0.66

went to trial, the proportion was significantly lower for criminal disputes (55 percent) and civil disputes among related parties (51 percent). The latter difference is not surprising because, for reasons discussed earlier, we would expect settlement to be more likely among related parties than among unrelated ones. Over time, the trial ratio fell significantly, from 84 percent in the first period to 57 percent in the final period, though the magnitude of the decline varied among case-types. Whereas in criminal cases the trial ratio plummeted to 26 percent, the decline was less pronounced in civil cases.

The observed decline in the trial ratio is consistent with the arguments we made in Chapters 3 and 4 about the rising prominence of the notarial services of the court over time. We saw this clearly in the rising proportion of agreements in Table 4.1, an indication of the court's greater engagement with the approval and registration of contracts. Interpreting settlements as contractual agreements, we can regard the findings of Table 7.1 as a reflection of the same trend, an indication of a parallel transformation in the mechanisms of dispute resolution over time. While the court played a less pronounced role in adjudication over time, its role in facilitating settlements increased.

Entries in Table 7.2 show the distribution of disputes according to the size-composition of parties on each side. Note that the specific roles of the parties in a dispute are important in the tables of this chapter and afterwards. This was not the case in Chapter 4 because in differentiating between agreements and disputes it did not matter whether a legal interaction was between parties "X and Y" or between "Y and X." In differentiating between settlements and trials, in contrast, it is important to know whether X is the actual or potential plaintiff or the defendant. Table 7.2 thus includes all possible combinations of parties, distinguishing between, for example, disputes in which single plaintiffs are positioned against multiple defendants ("single vs. multiple") and those that pitted multiple plaintiffs against a single defendant ("multiple vs. single").

Whereas most of these disputes pitted one individual against another, about a third of all cases involved multiple individuals or corporate bodies. Even then, a majority of such cases involved a single individual as one of the parties. Only a small proportion of cases (about 4 percent) involved multiple individuals or a corporate body on both sides.

Because the single vs. single combination constituted about two-thirds of all disputes, it is not surprising that the average trial ratio of this combination followed the same pattern as the whole sample across case-types and over time. More specifically, the trial ratio was highest for civil

TABLE 7.2: *Disputes according to Size-composition*

	Number of Cases			Trial Ratio			Number of Cases			Trial Ratio			N	%
SIZE	Criminal	Civil Related	Civil Unrelated	Criminal	Civil Related	Civil Unrelated	1684–96	1735–43	1781–90	1684–96	1735–43	1781–90	All Cases	
Single vs. Single	104	317	427	0.64	0.53	0.83	190	259	399	0.85	0.73	0.60	848	0.70
Single vs. Multiple	28	72	96	0.50	0.44	0.82	37	56	103	0.78	0.59	0.61	196	0.64
Single vs. Corporate	3		5	0.67	0.46	0.40		4	4		0.50	0.50	8	0.50
Multiple vs. Single	25	63	76	0.32	0.53	0.71	29	50	85	0.79	0.66	0.41	164	0.55
Multiple vs. Multiple	9	15	18	0.44		0.61	5	11	26	1.00	0.73	0.38	42	0.55
Multiple vs. Corporate	2		3	0.00		1.00	2		3	1.00		0.33	5	0.60
Corporate vs. Single	3		13	0.33		0.92	11	4	1	0.82	1.00	0.00	16	0.81
Corporate vs. Multiple	2		6	0.50		1.00	2	5	1	1.00	0.80	1.00	8	0.88
Corporate vs. Corporate			6			0.50	1	1	4	1.00	0.00	0.50	6	0.50
All	176	467	650	0.55	0.51	0.81	277	390	626	0.84	0.70	0.57	1293	0.66

cases among unrelated parties, followed by criminal cases and civil cases among related parties, and the trial ratio declined steadily over time periods. Some of the other size-combinations, however, followed a different pattern. In cases involving multiple versus single individuals, for example, the trial ratio was lower in criminal cases than in civil cases between related parties. Similarly, whereas the trial ratio steadily declined over time for most size-combinations, it fell sharply from the first to the second period in single versus multiple cases and stayed about the same in the third period. Note also that the disputes involving multiple parties were generally more likely than "single vs. single" cases to be settled. We return to these interesting results later in this chapter and discuss how they could be outcomes of divergent beliefs, asymmetric stakes, and trial costs.

To observe how the likelihood of trial varied by the characteristics of individuals, Table 7.3 shows only the distribution of disputes between single individuals by excluding from analysis those observations that involved multiple individuals or corporate bodies. We see in the table that the proportions of different types of disputes that went to trial in single vs. single cases followed an identical pattern over time periods.

In Table 7.4 we examine the distribution of disputes that involved single parties by combinations of men and women across case-types and over time. As seen in the table, about half of all cases were between two men, though this ratio varied significantly across case-types. Whereas in criminal cases and in civil disputes among unrelated parties the disputes between two men constituted about 70 percent of all cases, about two-thirds of all cases involved parties of opposite gender in civil disputes among related parties – an observation consistent with our findings in earlier chapters. The number of cases in which the parties were both female was generally small across the three categories, indicating that women rarely brought their disputes with other women to court.

The trial ratio varied significantly among gender combinations, with disputes between two men being more likely to go to trial than those between two women. Overall, 75 percent of all cases in which the plaintiff was a man wound up at trial, and the proportion fell to 48 percent when both parties were female. In civil cases between men and women, trial was more likely when the man was the plaintiff rather than the defendant. The cases brought by women were thus more likely to be settled than litigated. This could be either because women brought to court a higher proportion of disputes against related parties, which were more likely to be settled than litigated as argued in Chapter 3, or because women were more likely than men to compromise toward settlement under social pressure, or for

TABLE 7.3: *Disputes between Individuals*

	Number of Cases				Trial Ratio			
TYPE	1684–96	1735–43	1781–90	All	1684–96	1735–43	1781–90	All
Criminal	22	43	39	104	0.86	0.84	0.31	0.64
Civil between related	52	87	178	317	0.67	0.54	0.49	0.53
Civil between unrelated	116	129	182	427	0.93	0.81	0.77	0.83
All	190	259	399	848	0.85	0.73	0.6	0.7

TABLE 7.4: *Gender and Trial Ratio*

	Number of Cases			Trial Ratio			Number of Cases			Trial Ratio			N	%
GENDER	Criminal	Civil Related	Civil Unrelated	Criminal	Civil Related	Civil Unrelated	1684–96	1735–43	1781–90	1684–96	1735–43	1781–90	All Cases	
Male vs. Male	70	75	300	0.66	0.48	0.84	117	156	172	0.89	0.78	0.64	445	0.75
Male vs. Female	2	56	42	0.50	0.63	0.93	13	30	57	0.92	0.83	0.67	100	0.75
Female vs. Male	28	145	74	0.68	0.56	0.72	50	58	139	0.80	0.59	0.57	247	0.62
Female vs. Female	4	41	11	0.25	0.41	0.82	10	15	31	0.60	0.53	0.42	56	0.48

other reasons that caused a gender differential in beliefs, stakes, and trial costs. Over time, however, gender combinations did not differ significantly in the way the trial ratio declined between the three periods.

Consider next the variation between individuals in their honorific titles, proxies for socioeconomic status. Following a similar procedure as in Chapter 4, we created two different sets of categories from titles: one that differentiates between religious and military titles and another that differentiates between elite and non-elite titles. In both sets, we included additional categories for women and men with no titles as the remaining segments of the population. Tables 7.5 and 7.6 show the number of disputes and the proportions of agreements in the two sets of combinations.

As common entries in the two tables, disputes involving just women and men with no titles constituted a significant proportion of all disputes. More specifically, the disputes between two women (56), women vs. men with no titles (141), men with no titles vs. women (44), and two men with no titles (123) altogether constituted 43 percent of all disputes between single individuals (848). In the remaining disputes between single individuals (364), at least one party was a man with a title.

To examine how trial-settlement decisions varied by honorific title, consider first the combinations with religious and military titles as reported in Table 7.5. These entries allow us to look behind the general gender combinations in Table 7.5 to see how women's legal interactions varied among men with religious, military, and no titles across case-types. In civil disputes against men, for example, women initiated a slightly lower number of disputes against related than against unrelated men with religious titles, but the situation was reversed and the gap was widened in disputes against other men, as women were (actual or potential) plaintiffs in a significantly higher number of disputes against related than against unrelated men with military or no titles. There was a similar discrepancy among these combinations in the proportion of civil cases that went to trial. Whereas a higher proportion of disputes against related than against unrelated men with religious titles wound up at trial, the inequality was reversed and the difference widened in disputes against men with military or no titles. There was no clear pattern in criminal cases involving these combinations, possibly because of the small number of such cases.

Examining disputes between men, we see that in almost all title combinations there were more cases between unrelated than between related men, the opposite of what we observed in cases between two women. The proportion of these cases that wound up at trial, however, still followed a

TABLE 7.5: *Religious/Military Titles and Trial Ratio*

	Number of Cases			Trial Ratio			Number of Cases			Trial Ratio			N	%
GENDER AND TITLE	Criminal	Civil Related	Civil Unrelated	Criminal	Civil Related	Civil Unrelated	1684–96	1735–43	1781–90	1684–96	1735–43	1781–90	All Cases	
Woman vs. Woman	4	41	11	0.25	0.41	0.82	10	15	31	0.60	0.53	0.42	56	0.48
Woman vs. Man, religious title	4	16	19	0.75	0.81	0.74	10	14	15	0.90	0.79	0.67	39	0.77
Woman vs. Man, military title	10	34	23	0.50	0.44	0.70	10	13	44	0.60	0.46	0.55	67	0.54
Woman vs. Man, no title	14	95	32	0.79	0.56	0.72	30	31	80	0.83	0.55	0.56	141	0.62
Men, religious title vs. Woman		12	5		0.67	1.00	4	4	9	1.00	1.00	0.56	17	0.76
Man, religious title vs. Man, religious title		7	20		0.29	0.80	8	9	10	0.88	0.67	0.50	27	0.67
Man, religious title vs. Man, military title	2	1	28	1.00	1.00	0.86	6	11	14	1.00	1.00	0.71	31	0.87
Man, religious title vs. Man, no title	2	2	18	1.00	0.50	0.94	10	5	7	0.90	1.00	0.86	22	0.91
Man, military title vs. Woman	1	21	17	0.00	0.62	0.82	4	13	22	1.00	0.77	0.59	39	0.69
Man, military title vs. Man, religious title	1		8	0.00		1.00	2	2	5	1.00	1.00	0.80	9	0.89

(continued)

TABLE 7.5: *(continued)*

	Number of Cases			Trial Ratio			Number of Cases			Trial Ratio			N	%
GENDER AND TITLE	Criminal	Civil Related	Civil Unrelated	Criminal	Civil Related	Civil Unrelated	1684–96	1735–43	1781–90	1684–96	1735–43	1781–90	All Cases	
Man, military title vs. Man, military title	12	4	56	0.42	0.00	0.86	18	32	22	0.94	0.75	0.55	72	0.74
Man, military title vs. Man, no title	6	10	38	0.67	0.50	0.84	16	15	23	0.88	0.73	0.70	54	0.76
Man, no title vs. Woman	1	23	20	1.00	0.61	1.00	5	13	26	0.80	0.85	0.77	44	0.80
Man, no title vs. Man, religious title	4	9	26	1.00	0.67	0.85	6	17	16	0.83	0.76	0.88	39	0.82
Man, no title vs. Man, military title	17	9	42	0.71	0.67	0.81	13	28	27	0.92	0.89	0.56	68	0.76
Man, no title vs. Man, no title	26	33	64	0.65	0.45	0.81	38	37	48	0.84	0.65	0.58	123	0.68

similar pattern as that of women, meaning that in almost all combinations the trial ratio was higher in cases between unrelated than between related parties.

Although we saw in Table 7.4 that the proportions of agreements fell steadily over time in all gender combinations, this pattern did not hold generally for all title subcategories of men. According to Table 7.5, whereas the proportion of settlements fell steadily in women's disputes against men with religious titles, the proportion actually rose after the second period in disputes against men with military titles and stayed about the same after a sharp fall in disputes against men with no title. There were different trends in other title combinations too, but the number of observations is too low to generalize in all cases. It is worth mentioning, however, that, overall, religious titleholders appear to be the most litigious group: Whereas the average trial rate was over 0.80 in disputes involving men with religious titles, it was about 0.72 for military titleholders and men without titles, and the average fell to the about 0.63 for women, the lowest rate among the title–gender combinations (not shown in the table). Also, the trial rates among men were the lowest in disputes that involved individuals who had identical title characteristics within specific groups, implying that establishment affiliations made settlements easier.

We now turn to results for the combinations of titles according to elite status, reported in Table 7.6. Looking behind the aggregate gender combinations, we see interesting variations across gender and elite combinations in the numbers of disputes and the proportions that went to trial. Across case-types, the disputes brought to court by women and men with no titles differed significantly from those in which the plaintiff was a man with (elite or non-elite) title. As stated earlier, a high number of the cases that women brought to court were civil disputes against family members. The number of criminal cases filed by women was also considerable, as was the number brought by men with no titles, especially against men with non-elite titles or no titles. In contrast, men with elite and non-elite titles brought to court primarily civil disputes against unrelated individuals (as did religious titleholders, according to Table 7.5). It is particularly noteworthy that the elites filed only five criminal disputes, none against women or other elites, and only eleven civil disputes against related individuals. Elite titleholders either did not get involved in criminal disputes or had such disputes resolved outside of the court, possibly with the involvement of local military-administrative authorities (or both). Also, over time, whereas the number of disputes rose steadily in most gender and title combinations, those filed by elites followed no clear pattern.

TABLE 7.6: *Elite Status and Likelihood of Trial*

GENDER AND ELITE STATUS	Number of Cases			Trial Ratio			Number of Cases			Trial Ratio			N	%
	Criminal	Civil Related	Civil Unrelated	Criminal	Civil Related	Civil Unrelated	1684–96	1735–43	1781–90	1684–96	1735–43	1781–90	All Cases	
Woman vs. Woman	4	41	11	0.25	0.41	0.82	10	15	31	0.60	0.53	0.42	56	0.48
Woman vs. Man, elite title	2	13	15	0.50	0.54	0.60	8	2	20	0.63	0.00	0.60	30	0.57
Woman vs. Man, non-elite title	12	37	27	0.58	0.57	0.78	12	25	39	0.83	0.68	0.56	76	0.64
Woman vs. Man, no title	14	95	32	0.79	0.56	0.72	30	31	80	0.83	0.55	0.56	141	0.62
Elite vs. Woman		5	11		1.00	0.82	4	3	9	1.00	1.00	0.78	16	0.88
Elite vs. Elite		4	26		0.00	0.65	12	5	13	1.00	0.60	0.15	30	0.57
Elite vs. Non-elite	3		20	1.00		0.95	6	10	7	1.00	0.90	1.00	23	0.96
Elite vs. No title	2	2	21	1.00	0.50	0.95	14	7	4	0.93	0.86	1.00	25	0.92
Non-elite vs. Woman	1	28	11	0.00	0.57	0.91	4	14	22	1.00	0.79	0.50	40	0.65
Non-elite vs. Elite		3	20		0.33	0.90	3	14	6	1.00	0.79	0.83	23	0.83
Non-elite vs. Non-elite	12	5	46	0.33	0.40	0.91	13	25	25	0.85	0.80	0.68	63	0.76
Non-elite vs. No title	6	10	35	0.67	0.50	0.83	12	13	26	0.83	0.77	0.69	51	0.75
No title vs. Woman	1	23	20	1.00	0.61	1.00	5	13	26	0.80	0.85	0.77	44	0.80
No title vs. Elite	2	3	24	0.50	0.33	0.75	5	7	17	0.60	0.86	0.65	29	0.69
No title vs. Non-elite	19	15	44	0.79	0.73	0.86	14	38	26	1.00	0.84	0.69	78	0.82
No title vs. No title	26	33	64	0.65	0.45	0.81	38	37	48	0.84	0.65	0.58	123	0.68

The proportion of cases that went to trial showed interesting variations among gender and elite combinations of parties. Among criminal disputes, the trial ratio was generally higher if the defendant was a titleless man rather than a woman or a titleholder, regardless of the plaintiff, except when the plaintiff was also a titleless man. Although the trial ratio was generally higher in civil disputes against unrelated individuals than in those against related individuals, the gap between the two ratios varied across title and gender combinations. In cases filed by women, the gap was considerably higher in disputes against other women than against other defendants. In cases filed by men, the gap remained also high in most combinations, other than in civil disputes between titleless men against those with non-elite titles. Over time, the trial ratio fell steadily in almost all gender and elite combinations.

Trial rates appear to reflect status and economic differentials between elites and others. Disputes initiated by men with elite titles against others had significantly higher trial rates (ranging between 88 and 96 percent) than those initiated by others against elite titleholders (ranging between 57 and 83 percent). Whereas men with elite titles likely took to trial their disputes against others, other gender and title groups tended to settle their claims against elite titleholders. Note also that the trial rates among men were lowest in disputes between men with elite titles. On the other hand, disputes initiated by women against others had low trial rates. Such patterns among gender and title groups have clear implications for how differential beliefs, stakes, and trial costs may have affected the likelihood of trial, as discussed hypothetically in the previous chapter and further explored in more detail below.

Based on the names of the disputants, we can also distinguish in court records between Muslims and non-Muslims, and further differentiate among Muslims according to their religious markers. As noted earlier, these markers, which were included in individuals' names, signified that he or she claimed descent from Muhammad or had made the pilgrimage to Mecca. Table 7.7 shows the distribution of the number of disputes and the trial ratio in combinations of religion and religious markers. The proportion of disputes involving non-Muslims was small (3 percent), presumably because non-Muslims (up to 15 percent of the population) had access to various other mechanisms (possibly their own denominational courts) of dispute resolution. In cases involving Muslims, less than a third of all cases involved an individual with a religious marker, and a high proportion of those were against opponents who did not carry such a title. It is also worth noting that the proportion of cases involving individuals with a

TABLE 7.7: *Religion, Religious Markers, and Trial Ratio*

	Number of Cases			Trial Ratio			Number of Cases			Trial Ratio			N	%
RELIGION AND RELIGIOUS MARKER	Criminal	Civil Related	Civil Unrelated	Criminal	Civil Related	Civil Unrelated	1684–96	1735–43	1781–90	1684–96	1735–43	1781–90	All Cases	
Muslim vs. Muslim	98	313	412	0.64	0.53	0.83	187	247	389	0.85	0.72	0.60	823	0.69
Muslim vs. Non-Muslim	1		3	0.00		0.67	1		3	1.00		0.33	4	0.50
Non-Muslim vs. Muslim	1		8	1.00		1.00	2	5	2	1.00	1.00	1.00	9	1.00
Non-Muslim vs. Non-Muslim	4	4	4	0.75	0.75	1.00		7	5		0.71	1.00	12	0.83
Pilgrim vs. Pilgrim		2	8		1.00	0.88	2	7	1	1.00	0.86	1.00	10	0.9
Pilgrim vs. Desc. of Muh.	1		1	1.00		1.00	1	1		1.00	1.00		2	1
Pilgrim vs. No marker	3	7	27	1.00	0.86	0.85	11	16	10	0.91	0.81	0.90	37	0.86
Desc. of Muh. vs. Pilgrim	1		2	0.00		0.50			3			0.33	3	0.33
Desc. of Muh. vs. Desc. of Muh.		12	4		0.42	0.75	2	2	12	0.50	0.50	0.50	16	0.50
Desc. of Muh. vs. No marker	4	16	32	0.75	0.50	0.81	4	11	37	1.00	0.91	0.62	52	0.71
No marker vs. Pilgrim	6	18	32	0.67	0.44	0.78	18	13	25	0.83	0.54	0.60	56	0.66
No marker vs. Desc. of Muh.	5	18	40	0.60	0.67	0.80	6	13	44	1.00	0.85	0.68	63	0.75
No marker vs. No marker	84	244	281	0.63	0.52	0.84	146	196	267	0.84	0.71	0.58	609	0.68

TABLE 7.8: *Family Prominence*

	Number of Cases			Trial Ratio			Number of Cases			Trial Ratio			N	%
FAMILY AFFILIATION	Criminal	Civil Related	Civil Unrelated	Criminal	Civil Related	Civil Unrelated	1684–96	1735–43	1781–90	1684–96	1735–43	1781–90	All Cases	
Prominent vs. Prominent	1	2	4	1.00	0.50	0.50	2	3	2	1.00	0.67	0.00	7	0.57
Prominent vs. Non-prominent	1	1	12	1.00	1.00	0.83	3	8	3	1.00	0.75	1.00	14	0.86
Non-prominent vs. Prominent	3	4	17	0.67	0.50	0.82	5	8	11	0.80	0.75	0.73	24	0.75
Non-prominent vs. Non-prominent	99	310	394	0.64	0.53	0.83	180	240	383	0.85	0.73	0.60	803	0.69

religious marker was lowest for criminal cases, followed by civil cases among related parties.

Since the number of cases involving religious minorities is small, it would not be wise to generalize based on the trial ratios observed in Table 7.7. We should still note, however, that the trial ratio in the small number of such cases is considerably higher than in cases between Muslims, underscoring the last-resort nature of the Muslim court for members of other religious communities. Note, in particular, that the ratio was higher when non-Muslims initiated the dispute than the other way around. The number of cases filed by pilgrims is similarly small, with a high trial ratio. Just like elite titleholders (with whom pilgrims shared similar socioeconomic status), pilgrims had higher trial rates when they were the plaintiffs. No distinct patterns emerge from the trial ratios of disputes filed by descendants of Muhammad.

Finally, we examine the number of disputes and the trial ratio in combinations of parties according to family prominence as noted in court records by the suffix *zade*. As seen in Table 7.8, a small number (about 5 percent) of all disputes filed in court involved members of prominent families, and in only seven of these disputes were both parties members of prominent families. Overall, the entries in Table 7.8 are nevertheless consistent with our earlier findings. More specifically, the trial rate in disputes initiated by *zade*s against non-*zade*s was significantly higher than the rate in disputes initiated by non-*zade*s against *zade*s.

REGRESSION ANALYSIS

The information presented in Tables 7.1–7.8 provides interesting insights into the legal disputes handled by the Kastamonu court. They show the numbers of disputes brought to court by various combinations of parties, how the disputes varied among case-types and over time, and what proportion of them went to formal trial in court. By comparing the average trial ratios between the combinations of parties, one can begin to see whether the observed patterns seem consistent with the theoretical arguments developed in the previous chapter and to reach some preliminary conclusions regarding the effect of variations in the characteristics of parties.

For a more systematic investigation of influences on the likelihood of trial, however, we need regression analysis, the most widely used tool of quantitative research. Regression analysis is an indispensable tool for the quantitatively oriented historian because it allows us to specify the nature of the relationship between variables, use the data to estimate the parameters of this relationship, and refer to the signs, magnitudes, and standard errors of the coefficients of variables to assess the direction, strength, and significance of their effects. Suppose we are interested in investigating the relationship between x and y. Regression analysis will make our investigation more rigorous because in specifying a model we will be forced to think carefully about the hypothesized direction of causality between these variables and the functional form (e.g., logarithmic, quadratic) of their relationship. The basis for our reasoning may range from simple intuition to sophisticated social-scientific theorizing, depending on the complexity of the phenomena studied. Once we estimate the regression equation, we will be able to use the coefficient of the explanatory variable – say, x – to describe the direction and strength of its influence of y, the dependent variable, and make inferences regarding how y varies with changes in x.

If there are several variables affecting the dependent variable simultaneously, we need multiple regression analysis. This technique is necessary for ceteris paribus (other things being equal or held constant) analysis because it allows us to explicitly control for other variables that influence the dependent variable. If, for example, influences on y also include z, we will not be able to easily make ceteris paribus inferences regarding how x affects y based on a simple regression analysis between these two variables because changes in x in our data may correspond to changes in z and we will not be able to identify those changes in y that can be attributed to x alone. Instead of running separate simple regressions for x and z to estimate their individual effects on y, we would be better off including them in the same equation. In general, multiple regression allows us to estimate the combined influence of all explanatory values on y as well as the individual influence of each variable while controlling for others. Although the data are typically not collected in a ceteris paribus fashion, multiple regression analysis effectively allows us to get the same interpretation through technical simulation. Since our investigation involves multiple variables affecting the likelihood of trial simultaneously, we use multiple regression analysis to estimate their influence.

The dependent variable in our analysis is a binary variable that takes on the value of 1 if the dispute goes to trial, 0 otherwise. Commonly used in quantitative research, such binary variables have been effective in quantitative analysis of qualitative information. Many important questions of interest can be described by a binary variable, such as one's gender (=1 if male), literacy (=1 if literate), and whether one is married, employed, or belongs to a certain religious or social group. By formulating these phenomena through a binary dependent variable, researchers can use multiple regression models to identify the factors affecting the probability of their occurrence.

Econometricians have developed several sophisticated models for the estimation of binary response models. Since the dependent variable in such models is restricted to two values, it may be problematic to treat it as a continuous variable that can be less than 0 and more than 1, as required by linear probability models such as the well-known Ordinary Least Squares (OLS). Although in many applications the results from an OLS estimation may turn out to be consistent with those developed specifically for binary response models, it is still advisable to use one of the more sophisticated alternatives to avoid the potential drawbacks of the OLS model.

In this analysis, we use the probit model (the name derived from "probability unit"), one of the most widely used methods. As its unique technical feature, this model assumes that the cumulative probability function, used to transform the values of explanatory values to a probability that ranges between 0 and 1, is normal. The primary goal of the model is to estimate the probability that the dependent variable will take on the value of 1 for various values of explanatory variables. In our case, it will be used to identify the effects of the various characteristics of the parties and disputes on the probability that the case will go to trial. Although from a practical perspective the probit model has some disadvantages in the presentation and interpretation of results, it is preferred in this case because it overcomes the limitations of the linear probability model and produces reliable estimates.

In the tables that follow, we present the coefficient estimates and the *p*-values (a statistic used to test the significance of results – the lower the *p*-value, the higher the significance) of the effects of each variable. Since the usual OLS R-squared cannot be used as a measure of goodness-of-fit in the binary response models, we report a pseudo R-squared measure computed for the probit model. As usual, each coefficient gives the sign of the individual effect of the explanatory variable on the likelihood of trial, and we include asterisks next to coefficients to emphasize the statistical significance of each variable as determined by whether we can reject the hypothesis that the estimated coefficient equals zero at the 0.01, 0.05, and 0.10 levels of significance. To interpret the signs and significance of these coefficients, we use the theoretical arguments discussed in the previous chapter.

WHICH CASES WENT TO TRIAL?

We present the results of our regression analysis of influences on the likelihood of trial in Tables 7.9–7.12. These tables show the results separately for the size-composition of parties in all disputes (Tables 7.9 and 7.10) and for the individual characteristics of parties in single vs. single cases (Tables 7.11 and 7.12). Ideally, these analyses would include variables on the substance of disputes and more direct measures of the relative strength of the evidence presented by the parties and differences in their stakes from trial outcome. However, our records do not include sufficient detail on all disputes to measure these variables consistently. Instead, we use the same variables as presented in Tables 7.1–7.8 to examine their effects simultaneously.

To see how the influences on the likelihood of trial varied across case-types and over time periods, we ran separate regressions for each type and period. Tables 7.9 and 7.11 show the regression results for the size-composition (7.9) and individual characteristics (7.11) of parties, separately for criminal disputes, civil disputes between related parties, and civil disputes between unrelated parties. We also included two temporal variables (based on the three periods of our data) in these regressions to control for the effect of possible unobserved changes in the decision standard over time. Using period 1 as the base, we included periods 2 and 3 as dummy variables in the regression equation. Finally, we ran the same regression for all observations, controlling for differences in case-types and time periods through dummy variables, and reported the results in the last column.

To see how influences on the likelihood of trial changed over time, we ran the same regressions separately for the three time periods, as reported in Tables 7.10 and 7.12. The only difference between Tables 7.9 and 7.11 is that we replaced the temporal variables that were included to control for the effect of variations over time with those that control for difference in case-types. More specifically, using "Civil Disputes between unrelated parties" as the base, we included "Criminal disputes" and "Civil disputes between related parties" as dummy variables. As before, we ran the same regression for all observations to see how the results differed between the whole sample and subperiods.

Differences among case-types and time periods suggest the possibility of correlation of the observations within each type or period. To correct for this possibility, in each column we divided observations into clusters and used clustered robust standard errors in regression analysis. The clusters are based on the three time periods or the three case-types in the first three columns of the tables and on the nine combinations of case-types and time periods in the last column.

Although the probit model would normally drop the variables that perfectly predict success or failure in the dependent variable along with their associated observations, we have decided to retain them to be able to incorporate this information in the analysis. We have already observed in some of the preceding tables in this chapter that the trial ratio for some combinations of parties was a perfect 100 percent. For example, all disputes were litigated in the following combinations: all four "corporate vs. single" disputes during the 1735–43 period, all four "Non-Muslim vs. Non-Muslim" civil disputes between unrelated parties, and all three "Prominent vs. Non-prominent" disputes during the 1781–90 period. Conversely, none of the disputes in the following combinations of parties were litigated: the two "Multiple vs. Corporate" criminal disputes, the criminal dispute between a man with a military title and a man with a religious title, and the two civil disputes between two unrelated prominent members of the town. Despite the uniqueness of such cases, it is possible to incorporate this information into the analysis. Stata, the statistical package we have used for probit estimation, allows their inclusion through the "asis" option, and we felt it appropriate to choose this option because doing so had no effect on our estimates of any of the other coefficients. Rather than drop these observations for greater statistical precision, we have decided to use the information in the estimation process for a more comprehensive historical analysis of our data and more explicit and meaningful presentation of our findings.

To interpret the results presented in the following tables, recall the theoretical insights from the Law and Economics literature on dispute resolution that were discussed in the previous chapter. To recap, we have argued that most disputes are settled before trial, depending on trial costs and various asymmetries between the litigants that affect their assessments of trial outcome and expected benefits. Since trial is costly and uncertain, settlement would clearly be the preferred choice if parties share the same assessment of the expected outcome of trial (such as when both parties know that the evidence is overwhelmingly in favor of the plaintiff) and face the same payoffs of going to trial, because in that case they can implement the same outcome in a settlement without incurring the cost and uncertainty of trial. When their expectations and stakes differ significantly, however, they may fail to agree on the terms of settlement and may have to go to formal trial for resolution. Trial is also more likely in types of cases that have lower cost of going to trial.

SIZE-COMPOSITION OF PARTIES AND THE LIKELIHOOD OF TRIAL

In Table 7.9, we examine how the size-composition of parties affected the likelihood of trial and how this relationship varied across case-types. Since the specific position of parties (defendant or plaintiff) would affect the direction of the divergent expectations (relative optimism) and differential stakes (relative payoffs), we include the plaintiff and defendant roles separately to identify the exact source of the influence on settlement decisions. Each explanatory variable listed in the table is a dummy variable that takes on the value of 1 if the parties differ along the specified characteristic, 0 otherwise. For example, the variable "single vs. multiple" takes the value of 1 if the plaintiff is a single individual and the defendant is a set of multiple individuals. Using the combinations of size-compositions discussed in Chapter 4, we thus constructed nine variables that make up all possibilities.

We excluded one of the size-combinations from the regression equation because including all nine variables would have caused perfect multicollinearity. This is simply because the value of the ninth variable would be determined once the other eight are specified (since only one of these combinations is possible in each case). The standard procedure in this case is to exclude the most frequently observed combination from the equation so that it serves as the "reference" category with which we compare the other combinations. The coefficient estimates of all other combinations thus need to be interpreted in comparison with the omitted category. Following this procedure, in Table 7.9 we omitted the "single vs. single" combination, the largest category, so the coefficients of size-composition variables show the difference from disputants being "single vs. single," controlling for the other independent variables.

When we compare the results across case-types, we see that the signs of significant coefficients are generally consistent between equations, with the exception of the coefficient of "Multiple vs. Corporate" that remains significant but changes signs between criminal disputes and civil disputes between unrelated parties. The magnitude and significance of the coefficients are much lower, however, for civil cases between related parties than for criminal cases or civil cases between unrelated parties. The fact that the significant coefficients in the overall regression (last column) are all negative indicates that the variations in size-combinations generally increased the likelihood of settlements compared to single vs. single cases.

TABLE 7.9: *The Influence of Size-composition on the Likelihood of Trial across Case-types*

	(1)	(2)	(3)	(4)
VARIABLES	Criminal	Civil Related	Civil Unrelated	All Cases
Single vs. Multiple	-0.31	-0.19	-0.03	-0.18
	(0.153)	(0.422)	(0.884)	(0.273)
Single vs. Corporate	-0.40***		-1.03***	-0.25
	<.001		(0.008)	(0.181)
Multiple vs. Single	-0.72***	-0.16	-0.39*	-0.51***
	(0.003)	(0.181)	(0.093)	(0.001)
Multiple vs. Multiple	0.00	-0.02	-0.53	0.13
	(0.978)	(0.945)	(0.191)	(0.429)
Multiple vs. Corporate	-4.56***		4.06***	-5.63***
	<.001		<.001	<.001
Corporate vs. Single	-1.33***		0.16	-0.76***
	<.001		(0.733)	(0.001)
Corporate vs. Multiple	-1.05		4.08***	-0.19
	(0.324)		<.001	(0.855)
Corporate vs. Corporate			-0.87***	-5.77***
			(0.005)	<.001
Criminal				-12.56***
				<.001
Civil Related				-5.71***
				<.001
Period 2	-0.42***	-0.42***	-0.40***	-0.20
	<.001	<.001	<.001	(0.835)
Period 3	-1.69***	-0.48***	-0.65***	-1.29
	<.001	<.001	<.001	(0.138)
Constant	1.26***	0.47***	1.38***	12.85***
	<.001	<.001	<.001	<.001
Observations	176	467	650	1,293
Pseudo R^2	0.240	0.0159	0.0620	0.808

Notes:

a. See the text for definitions of variables. The dependent variable takes the value of 1 if the case was litigated.

b. Standard errors have been adjusted for clustering on case-type and time period.

c. Robust *p*-values in parentheses.

d. The omitted variables are "Single vs. Single" in the litigant characteristics category; "Civil Dispute among Unrelated Parties" in the case-type category; and "1684–96" in the time-period category.

e. *** indicates significance at 1%, ** at 5%, and * at 10% for a two-tailed test.

The signs of significant coefficients displayed in Table 7.10 are also mostly consistent over time periods. The only exception here is the coefficient of "Corporate vs. Multiple," which remains significant but becomes negative after the first period, perhaps related to the lower trial likelihood of disputes brought by corporate parties against all size-combinations.

The results in Tables 7.9 and 7.10 confirm the preliminary observations made earlier (Table 7.2) on how the trial ratio varied across case-

TABLE 7.10: *The Influence of Size-composition on the Likelihood of Trial over Time*

	(1)	(2)	(3)	(4)
VARIABLES	1684–96	1735–43	1781–90	All Cases
Single vs. Multiple	–0.77***	–0.18	0.16	–0.18
	<.001	(0.489)	(0.140)	(0.273)
Single vs. Corporate		–0.09	–4.90***	–0.25
		(0.714)	<.001	(0.181)
Multiple vs. Single	–0.34	–0.60*	–0.46***	–0.51***
	(0.269)	(0.068)	<.001	(0.001)
Multiple vs. Multiple	5.41***	4.95***	–0.03	0.13
	<.001	<.001	(0.171)	(0.429)
Multiple vs. Corporate	–5.95***		–4.95***	–5.63***
	<.001		<.001	<.001
Corporate vs. Single	–0.77***	–9.64***	–5.08***	–0.76***
	(0.002)	<.001	<.001	(0.001)
Corporate vs. Multiple	5.58***	–8.32***	–4.74***	–0.19
	<.001	<.001	<.001	(0.855)
Corporate vs. Corporate	–5.95***	–6.31***	–4.90***	–5.77***
	<.001	<.001	<.001	<.001
Criminal	–11.75***	–16.40***	–11.88***	–12.56***
	<.001	<.001	<.001	<.001
Civil Related	–5.98***	–10.28***	–4.84***	–5.71***
	<.001	<.001	<.001	<.001
Period 2				–0.20
				(0.835)
Period 3				–1.29
				(0.138)
Constant	12.09***	16.50***	10.85***	12.85***
	<.001	<.001	<.001	<.001
Observations	277	390	626	1,293
Pseudo R^2	0.752	0.718	0.867	0.808

See notes to Table 7.9.

types and over time periods. The coefficients of "Period 2" and "Period 3" are all negative and significant, consistent with the decline in the trial ratio over time. The negative and significant coefficients of criminal disputes and civil disputes between related parties similarly confirm the lower trial ratio in these type of disputes compared to those between unrelated parties.

Examining variables individually, we see that the signs of significant coefficients are generally consistent with our argument about the way we would expect divergent expectations and asymmetric stakes to affect the likelihood of trial. Note, once again, that these coefficients show the difference from disputants being "single vs. single." The coefficient of "single vs. corporate body" was negative and significant, indicating that individuals were less optimistic than corporate bodies about their chances of success at trial, or that corporate bodies had higher stakes than individuals, or both, relative to symmetric "single vs. single" combinations, all else being equal. As yet another possibility, even if one of these factors could have actually raised the likelihood of trial, this was offset by the negative effect of the other factor so that the net effect was negative and significant. In the same vein, the negative and significant coefficient of "multiple vs. single" can be explained by the divergent expectations or asymmetric stakes between such combinations of parties as compared to cases between two individuals. Although we do not have evidence to determine which of these possibilities was more likely than others, the theoretical concepts developed in the previous chapter allow us to identify these possibilities as topics of future investigation.

INDIVIDUAL CHARACTERISTICS AND THE LIKELIHOOD OF TRIAL

Going beyond differences in size-compositions, we now shift attention to disputes between two individuals and drop from analysis all observations involving multiple individuals and corporate bodies. The advantage of focusing on individuals is that we have information on gender, honorific titles, family status, religion, and religious (pilgrimage) markers, which we can include in the regression analysis of factors affecting the likelihood of trial. Although court records do not include direct information on the expectations, stakes, or trial costs of individuals, we can infer this information indirectly from their observable characteristics.

Table 7.11 shows probit estimates of the way influences on the likelihood of trial varied across case-types in disputes between single

TABLE 7.11: *Individual Characteristics and the Likelihood of Trial across Case-types*

	(1)	(2)	(3)	(4)
VARIABLES	Criminal	Civil Related	Civil Unrelated	All Cases
Woman vs. Woman	-1.21***	0.01	0.25*	-0.77***
	<.001	(0.944)	(0.060)	(0.004)
Woman vs. Man, title	0.05	0.39***	-0.12	0.02
	(0.935)	<.001	(0.674)	(0.951)
Woman vs. Man, no title	0.80***	0.39	-0.08	0.66**
	<.001	(0.195)	(0.903)	(0.017)
Man, title vs. Woman	-6.38***	0.60***	0.48	-5.35***
	<.001	<.001	(0.538)	<.001
Man, title vs. Man, title	-0.19	-0.51	0.41	-0.38**
	(0.650)	(0.361)	(0.334)	(0.013)
Man, title vs. Man, no title	0.23	0.24	0.37**	-0.09
	(0.752)	(0.421)	(0.033)	(0.735)
Man, no title vs. Woman	4.28***	0.53***	4.81***	4.96***
	<.001	(0.002)	<.001	<.001
Man, no title vs. Man, title	0.03	0.54***	0.14	0.05
	(0.945)	<.001	(0.488)	(0.749)
Muslim vs. Non-Muslim	-4.71***		-0.42	-10.99***
	<.001		(0.195)	<.001
Non-Muslim vs. Muslim	4.45***		4.78***	5.74***
	<.001		<.001	<.001
Non-Muslim vs. Non-Muslim	0.43	0.86***	4.78***	1.09
	(0.747)	<.001	<.001	(0.338)
Pilgrim vs. Pilgrim		5.11***	0.33**	-6.19***
		<.001	(0.049)	<.001
Pilgrim vs. Non-pilgrim	4.84***	0.66	0.06	-0.16
	(0.002)	(0.364)	(0.779)	(0.619)
Non-pilgrim vs. Pilgrim	-0.13	-0.05	-0.21	-0.22
	(0.387)	(0.651)	(0.155)	(0.256)
Prominent vs. Prominent	4.22***	0.31	-1.39*	-0.13
	<.001	(0.763)	(0.056)	(0.819)
Prominent vs. Non-prominent	4.05***	4.16***	-0.09	-0.48***
	<.001	<.001	(0.865)	(0.003)
Non-prominent vs. Prominent	-0.85	-0.30	0.15	-0.20
	(0.583)	(0.281)	(0.121)	(0.634)
Criminal				-22.42***
				<.001

(continued)

TABLE 7.11: *(continued)*

VARIABLES	(1) Criminal	(2) Civil Related	(3) Civil Unrelated	(4) All Cases
Civil Related				−10.47***
				<.001
Period 2	0.20	−0.49***	−0.73***	−0.09
	(0.215)	<.001	<.001	(0.925)
Period 3	−1.47***	−0.55***	−0.80***	−1.39*
	<.001	<.001	<.001	(0.066)
Constant	0.88***	0.20	1.35***	22.73***
	<.001	(0.237)	<.001	<.001
Observations	104	317	427	848
Pseudo R^2	0.343	0.0552	0.103	0.827

Notes:

a. See the text for definitions of variables. The dependent variable takes the value of 1 if the case was litigated.
b. Standard errors have been adjusted for clustering on case-type and time period.
c. Robust *p*-values in parentheses.
d. The omitted variables are "Man with No Title vs. Man with No Title" in the Gender–Title category; "Muslim vs. Muslim" in the Religious Affiliation category; "Non-pilgrim vs. Non-pilgrim" in the Religious Marker category; "Non-prominent vs. Non-prominent" in the Family Affiliation category; "Civil Dispute among Unrelated Parties," in the Case-type category; and "1684–96" in the Time Period category.
e. *** indicates significance at 1%, ** at 5%, and * at 10% for a two-tailed test.
f. For simplicity, the Religious Marker category includes only the pilgrim status.

individuals. For an appropriate interpretation of the coefficients, recall again that they show the differential effect from the omitted category. In the set of variables on gender and title combinations, for example, the omitted category is "Man, no title vs. Man, no title," so the coefficients of all other variables in this set show how the likelihood of trial differed for stated combinations of parties as compared to disputes between two men with no titles. Whereas for some variables the signs and significance of estimated coefficients are consistent across case-types, others vary considerably. We try to identify and explain these variations in more detail below.

Our estimates of influences on trial-likelihood over time show a few remarkable changes, as seen in Table 7.12. The signs of significant coefficients among the gender and title categories are mostly consistent over time periods in this table, with the exception of disputes that men with no

TABLE 7.12: *Individual Characteristics and the Likelihood of Trial over Time*

	(1)	(2)	(3)	(4)
VARIABLES	**1684–96**	**1735–43**	**1781–90**	**All Cases**
Woman vs. Woman	−3.90***	−0.55	−5.05***	−0.77***
	<.001	(0.108)	<.001	(0.004)
Woman vs. Man, title	−5.80***	-0.24	0.30	0.02
	<.001	(0.410)	(0.402)	(0.951)
Woman vs. Man, no title	5.75***	5.30***	0.06	0.66**
	<.001	<.001	(0.867)	(0.017)
Man, title vs. Woman	−5.17***	−5.27***	−5.03***	−5.35***
	<.001	<.001	<.001	<.001
Man, title vs. Man, title	−5.87***	−0.26	−0.69***	−0.38**
	<.001	(0.194)	<.001	(0.013)
Man, title vs. Man, no title	0.58	0.25	−5.18***	−0.09
	(0.123)	(0.276)	<.001	(0.735)
Man, no title vs. Woman	−5.18***	5.35***	−4.44***	4.96***
	<.001	<.001	<.001	<.001
Man, no title vs. Man, title	0.31	0.40***	−5.16***	0.05
	(0.313)	<.001	<.001	(0.749)
Muslim vs. Non-Muslim	−15.01***		−5.36***	−10.99***
	<.001		<.001	<.001
Non-Muslim vs. Muslim	5.82***	−16.44***	−4.75***	5.74***
	<.001	<.001	<.001	<.001
Non-Muslim vs. Non-Muslim		−0.12	7.04***	1.09
		(0.889)	<.001	(0.338)
Pilgrim vs. Pilgrim	−15.01***	−5.63***	−8.98***	−6.19***
	<.001	<.001	<.001	<.001
Non-pilgrim vs. Pilgrim	−0.90***	0.47	−0.26**	−0.22
	<.001	(0.488)	(0.017)	(0.256)
Pilgrim vs. Non-pilgrim	0.57**	−0.75***	0.11***	−0.16
	(0.022)	<.001	<.001	(0.619)
Prominent vs. Prominent	−10.65***	0.13	−4.54***	−0.13
	<.001	(0.882)	<.001	(0.819)
Prominent vs. Non-prominent	−0.05***	−0.56***	−4.89***	−0.48***
	<.001	<.001	<.001	(0.003)
Non-prominent vs. Prominent	11.58***	−0.41***	−5.37***	−0.20
	<.001	(0.001)	<.001	(0.634)
Criminal	−23.30***	−22.08***	−17.45***	−22.42***
	<.001	<.001	<.001	<.001
Civil Related	−11.63***	−11.07***	−5.47***	−10.47***
	<.001	<.001	<.001	<.001

(continued)

TABLE 7.12: *(continued)*

	(1)	(2)	(3)	(4)
VARIABLES	**1684–96**	**1735–43**	**1781–90**	**All Cases**
Period 2				–0.09
				(0.925)
Period 3				–1.39*
				(0.066)
Constant	23.34***	22.19***	16.63***	22.73***
	<.001	<.001	<.001	<.001
Observations	190	259	399	848
Pseudo R^2	0.842	0.739	0.909	0.827

See notes to Table 7.11.

titles had against women and against men with titles. Similarly, the significant coefficients of "Non-Muslim vs. Muslim," "Pilgrim vs. Non-pilgrim," and "Non-prominent vs. Prominent" changed from positive to negative between the first and second periods.

In the last columns of both tables, we included variables to control for the effects of variations in the average trial ratio across case-types and time periods. The coefficients of the second and third periods are negative, indicating that our previous findings of a declining trial ratio over time among all disputes, as displayed in Tables 7.1, 7.9, and 7.10, held true for the subset of disputes between single individuals when we control for other factors. The coefficients of criminal disputes and civil disputes between related parties are negative and significant in the last columns of Tables 7.11 and 7.12, again consistent with earlier findings (Tables 7.1, 7.9, and 7.10) based on all observations that the trial ratio was lower in these type of disputes compared to those between unrelated parties. The negative and significant coefficient of civil cases among related individuals indicates that in the socio-legal environment of eighteenth-century Kastamonu, the overall (including non-monetary) cost of going to trial in civil cases was likely higher on average for related parties than if they were unrelated, all else being the same, probably the outcome of a negotiation process that involved other family members and social customs and sanctions.

The negative coefficient of criminal cases between individuals could be the outcome of various factors. The evidentiary standards, for example, could be more onerous in criminal than civil disputes, raising the costs of trial in the former category and thus reducing the likelihood of litigation. Moreover, since many criminal disputes were handled by military and administrative officials instead of the court, many disputes that might have escalated to trial never came to court for litigation. A similar tendency for settlements may be less pronounced because many of these, if not all, were brought to court not for resolution but for official registration. The overrepresentation of settlements among criminal disputes seems particularly high in the third period of our analysis.

Going beyond the variables that control for case-types and time periods in Tables 7.11 and 7.12, we now discuss some of the systematic patterns regarding the characteristics of parties within regression equations. As one would expect, the signs and significance of coefficients could vary in numerous ways in an equation. The question here is whether the variations in our results displayed systematic patterns that can be explained by applying our economic approach to disputes along with known facts about the socio-legal circumstances of Kastamonu in the eighteenth century. Deferring for a moment the discussion of differences across case-types and over time periods, we first focus on the aggregate results listed in the "all cases" column of Tables 7.11 and 7.12 to keep things simple. For a systematic analysis of these results, we differentiate between two types of patterns: among those involving parties with the same characteristics (e.g., "Woman vs. Woman," and "Prominent vs. Prominent"), and among those involving reversed roles (e.g., "Man, title vs. Woman" and "Woman vs. Man, title") in disputes.

A pattern that clearly stands out among the coefficients that correspond to parties with the same characteristics is that they are all negative and mostly significant. This is true for disputes between two women, between two men with titles, and between two pilgrims. Though insignificant, the coefficient of "Prominent vs. Prominent" is also negative. To make sense of this interesting pattern, recall once again that the coefficients of these variables show the difference from the omitted category. The coefficient of "Woman vs. Woman," for example, shows the difference from "Man, no title vs. Man, no title," the base category. The pattern that needs to be explained is thus why symmetric variations of parties from the baseline categories had a negative effect on the likelihood of trial.

This pattern cannot be related to the expectations or stakes of the parties because there is no reason to expect them to vary systematically. Since the parties on both sides of these disputes have the same characteristics, we would expect the stakes and expectations to be parallel across these combinations, all else being the same. If there was a certain difference in stakes or expectations in the base category, we would anticipate the same difference to carry over to other symmetric combinations, with no significant effect on the likelihood of trial.

For a more satisfactory economic explanation of the negative coefficients of most symmetric party combinations, we turn to trial costs. Although the monetary cost of going to trial might be the same for all individuals, the non-monetary costs could differ systematically. Consider the gender difference. If women faced higher social stigma attached to participating in trials and exposing their affairs to the public, we would expect two women to face higher trial costs than two men with no titles (the omitted category). The negative coefficient of the "Woman vs. Woman" variable is consistent with this expectation. In the same way, if men with titles and members of prominent families faced greater shame than others from public discussion of their disputes, the social cost of attending trial would be higher for them than for men with no titles, again indicating a negative effect on the likelihood of trial, as seen in our results. Finally, since pilgrims, representing clients with high religious status, were presumably pious and respected individuals, two pilgrims could face higher non-monetary costs of attending trial than two non-pilgrims.

Consider next an interesting pattern concerning the effects of positional reversals between plaintiffs and defendants. In some of these reversals, as seen in the last columns of Tables 7.11 and 7.12, the coefficients of variables corresponding to reversed characteristics switch signs. This is true for gender–title combinations that involve an economic or socio-legal hierarchy, such as in disputes between women and men with titles, wherein the sign changes from positive for "Woman vs. Men, title" to negative and significant for "Men, title vs. Woman." We see a similar reversal of signs in disputes between men with titles and those without titles. The underlying pattern in both comparisons is that the sign is positive when the men with titles (the more privileged party) are defendants, and negative when they become plaintiffs. Moreover, we observe the same reversal of signs from negative to positive in the reversal from "Muslim vs. Non-Muslim" disputes to "Non-Muslim vs. Muslim" disputes, within a parallel legal hierarchy. While we do not observe a sign reversal from "Prominent vs. Non-prominent" disputes to "Non-prominent vs. Prominent" ones, here too the results are consistent with the increased likelihood of settlement when the less-privileged party assumes the position of defendant.

Among other possibilities, this pattern might be related to systematic changes in the abilities and stakes of individuals that correspond to reversals of positional status in disputes. More specifically, the greater likelihood of settlement in pairings in which the defendant was the less-privileged party could have been caused by a greater uncertainty of trial to the defendant or a greater asymmetry of stakes between the parties in such cases as compared to those in which the privileged party was the defendant.

To illustrate this, consider the obvious implication of these pairings for the resources available to the parties for trial – more specifically, the greater resources of the more privileged individuals than of others. Given the constraints on their resources, the less-privileged individuals would thus be disadvantaged in terms of education level and legal experience. Gender differences, for example, could affect the parties' ability to estimate their chances of success because men typically received more formal education than women and participated in legal disputes more frequently (Table 7.4). By the same token, men with no honorific titles would be expected to have lower levels of education than men with titles, especially those in elite positions that presumably required higher training and experience in law and administration.

Educational differences between the privileged parties and others could have a differential effect on their ability to estimate their chances for success in court, and consequently on the uncertainty of trial to the defendant if education and experience were more binding constraints to less-privileged individuals as defendants than as plaintiffs. Although all plaintiffs, privileged and others alike, may have sufficient knowledge about the facts of their dispute to feel comfortable bringing it to court, the less-privileged may be at a greater disadvantage as defendants if they have no or little previous familiarity with facts, legal standards, and trial procedures. Consequently, they may be more likely to settle as defendants than as plaintiffs, all else being the same. If true, this asymmetry could be one of the causes of the switch in the signs of coefficients corresponding to variables with reversed positions.

Resource differential could also affect the stakes of parties if they valued the trial award differently as plaintiffs than as defendants. In the event of a lost trial, the loss may not be too important to a privileged defendant for whom the trial award may be a small amount relative to total wealth. But the same trial award could be a bigger deal to a less-privileged defendant for whom resource constraints were binding on his or her ability to make the payment. Moreover, individuals might value the same trial award differently as defendants facing the chance of a loss than as plaintiffs hoping for a gain, due to a phenomenon known in economics and decision theory as "loss aversion" (Kahneman and Tversky 1984).

Yet another (perhaps complementary) possibility is directly related to our findings in Chapter 10, where we examine how Islamic evidentiary processes affected trial results. Although we do not consider in the present chapter how trials were conducted or resolved, we should mention for the concerns of the present discussion that, due to certain procedural aspects of litigations, it was uncommon for less-privileged groups to win trials as defendants against more privileged plaintiffs. Thus, if underprivileged parties were aware of this general pattern, they might have considered it prudent to settle their disputes with actual/potential plaintiffs who belonged to privileged groups. Given the fact that privileged parties won more often as defendants (Chapter 10), it makes sense that they were more likely to force trials against less-privileged opponents. We explore how differences in court clients' stakes, variations in their legal expectations, and litigation costs influenced trial results in the following chapters.

Finally, we discuss the question of how the results from the subsamples of case-types and time periods, displayed in the first three columns of Tables 7.11 and 7.12, differ from those obtained from the full sample, last column. Interestingly, even though some variables have consistent results across case-types or time periods, none of the variables have coefficients that are fully consistent in sign and statistically significant across all types and all periods. For example, the coefficient of "Man, no title vs. Woman" is consistently positive and significant across case-types, but it is negative and significant in periods 1 and 3. Likewise, although the coefficient of "Man, title vs. Woman" is consistently negative and significant across all time periods, it is positive and significant in civil disputes between related parties. This clearly reflects the great diversity of influences on the trial-settlement decision in their varying historical contexts, as shaped by the specific socioeconomic circumstances of each type and period.

Some of the differences in results between subsamples and all cases may be puzzling. For example, the coefficient of "Pilgrim vs. Pilgrim" is positive and significant in both types of civil cases, yet it is negative and significant for all cases combined. Likewise, the coefficient of "Man, title vs. Man, title" was insignificant in all case-types, yet it became significant for the full sample. Econometric novelties to be sure, these cases are nevertheless quite possible because the effects of these variables on the likelihood of trial may vary across samples depending on how their local effects in a type fit into the global effect in the whole sample.

Careful examination of some of the seemingly contradictory results yields interesting insights into the subtleties of factors influencing trial-settlement decisions. Consider, for example, the variation in the sign and significance of the coefficient of "Woman vs. Woman." This variable's effect on the likelihood of trial is negative and significant in all cases, but positive and significant in civil disputes between unrelated parties. Previously we explained the negative coefficient of this variable in all cases by emphasizing the higher cost of litigation for women in comparison to men with no titles (the reference combination). To explain the positive coefficient of "Woman vs. Woman" in civil cases between unrelated parties, we thus need to identify the benefits of litigation to women that more than offset their cost in this setting.

One possible explanation rests on the importance of the court for the resolution of disputes among unrelated women. If the court was the only venue for dispute resolution for women who had no family connection to each other, we would expect this to raise the expected benefits of litigation to the plaintiff, hence raising the likelihood of her desire for trial, in such cases compared to others. The seemingly inconsistent coefficient of this variable across case-types may thus simply be an indication that women had more limited alternatives to the court in resolving disputes against unrelated women. This result may have further implications concerning the availability to women of non-litigious mechanisms for resolving disputes against other women, but the number of observations in this category is too low to generalize with any certainty.

Another interesting comparison with subtle implications concerns the changing sign of the coefficient of "Man, title vs. Woman" across case-types. Whereas this combination of parties had a negative and significant effect on the likelihood of trial in all cases, the effect was positive and significant in the category of civil disputes between related individuals. This result too may seem contradictory to our previous argument about the litigation decisions of women as defendants against men with titles, because we attributed the negative coefficient in the full sample to the differential privilege between these parties.

To explain the positive and significant coefficient of "Men, title vs. Woman" in civil disputes between related parties, therefore, we need to identify factors peculiar to this type of dispute that may have helped to offset the greater uncertainty, the higher stakes, or lower chances of women in such cases in comparison to others. One possibility is that women related to titleholding men were likely to be more privileged than other women in court. As members of prominent and well-off families, these individuals might have been better educated than their counterparts and had access to crucial resources, legal information, and support from influential and knowledgeable family members. Thus, their dispositions toward trial-settlement decisions were conceivably different from those common among other female court clients.

Returning to the methodological objective of our analysis, we note that our results clearly establish the presence of a selection bias in the court records of Kastamonu during this period. Although some of our coefficients are insignificant and some of our regression equations fit poorly, the results nevertheless identify a systematic bias in the selection of cases for trial. If there were no such bias, the entire process would be random and none of our variables on the differential characteristics of parties would be able to explain why disputes went to trial. Since our coefficients are significant with signs that are generally consistent with the theoretical discussion, we conclude that parties followed definite and reasonable patterns in choosing between trial and settlement. The methodological implication of the selection bias for the literature using Ottoman court records is simple. Instead of the conventional method of treating dispute-related material in court documents as the starting point of our analysis, we need to adopt a novel approach that considers them as end-products of a series of decisions that collectively shaped the dispute-resolution process.

On a final note, for readers interested in more detailed analysis of honorific titles, we report in the Appendix to this chapter the breakdown of titles by elite status and religious and military affiliation. Using the subcategories of titles described in Tables 7.5 and 7.6, Appendices 7.A and 7.B show regression analysis of how title combinations of parties affected the outcome, controlling for other factors. The results show some of the subtle ways in which the socioeconomic status of the parties affected the likelihood of trial. For example, as seen in the "All Cases" column of Appendix 7.A, the negative effect of "Man, title vs. Man, title" observed in Tables 7.11 and 7.12 applied more to men with elite titles than non-elite titles. Appendix 7.B similarly shows how variations in religious and military affiliation affected the likelihood of trial. For example, consistent with the theoretical arguments made in the previous chapter, disputes between men with religious titles against those with military titles had a higher likelihood of winding up at trial. Some of the results in the Appendix, however, contradict the argument offered in this chapter regarding the differential likelihood of trial between advantaged and disadvantaged parties. For example, in disputes between men with elite and non-elite titles, the direction of influence switches from positive to negative when the position of elite titleholders is reversed from plaintiff to defendant. Contrary to the outcome of parallel reversals in Tables 7.11 and 7.12, this shift indicates that while elite titleholders, a privileged group, were more inclined to settle as defendants against non-elite titleholding plaintiffs, trial was more likely when the roles were reversed. Unfortunately, our sources do not allow us to explain this variation.

CONCLUSION

In this chapter we used information from court records to identify influences on the likelihood of disputes winding up at trial. Categorizing disputes according to case-type and time period, we explored how observable characteristics of parties affected the likelihood of trial in each category. More specifically, we examined the effects of size-composition, gender, honorific titles, family prominence, religion, and religious markers of the parties. To interpret the results, we studied the socio-legal circumstances of disputes in Kastamonu in light of the theoretical insights developed in the previous chapter as to how divergent expectations, asymmetric stakes, and trial costs between the parties could affect the likelihood of trial.

Our preliminary observations identified major variations in trial-settlement decisions across case-types and time periods. In general, the likelihood of trial was lower in disputes among related parties and the overall trial rate declined during the eighteenth century. We also observed noticeable disparities among client groups: While elite and religious titleholders were more litigious compared to other title groups, women were more prone to settle compared to men. Subsequently, we used regression analysis to identify systematic patterns in factors affecting the likelihood of disputes winding up at trial in Kastamonu court. The results for size-composition varied by case-type such that although some of the coefficients were significant and mostly in expected directions in criminal cases and civil disputes among unrelated individuals, none of the coefficients were significant in civil cases among related individuals. This indicates that in disputes involving family members, this relationship dominated the differential effect of size-composition and associated differences in beliefs and stakes between the parties on the likelihood of trial. The rising cost of trial associated with larger parties also reduced the likelihood of trial.

In disputes between individuals, trial was less likely between two women, between two men with titles, and between two pilgrims in comparison to their respective reference categories. To explain this interesting pattern, we considered how the non-monetary costs of going to trial, including personal stress and social stigma, could differ systematically across these combinations of parties. Specific roles in a dispute were also important, such that influences on the likelihood of trial switched direction corresponding to positional reversals between plaintiffs and defendants. For example, the direction of influence changed from positive to negative when the combinations of parties was reversed from women against men with titles to men with titles against women. Since this pattern holds true for some gender–title combinations that involve an economic or socio-legal hierarchy, we explored how the decision to litigate could depend on the varying uncertainty of trial, stakes from the outcome, and positional advantages across these combinations.

The methodological implication of our results is that the disputes that went to trial were not a random sample of all disputes, but went through a systematic selection process. This is contrary to the presumption sometimes made in the literature that Ottoman trial records are representative of all disputes in the society. Since these records were filtered systematically through a selection process, scholars would be well advised to identify this process before using these records for historical research.

APPENDIX 7.A: *Individual Characteristics (Including Breakdown by Elite Status) and the Likelihood of Trial across Case-types and over Time*

	(1)	(2)	(3)	(4)	(5)	(6)	(7)
VARIABLES	**Criminal**	**Civil Related**	**Civil Unrelated**	**1684–96**	**1735–43**	**1781–90**	**All Cases**
Woman vs. Woman	−1.23***	0.03	0.27	−0.08	0.22	−0.15**	−0.77***
	<.001	(0.867)	(0.104)	(0.811)	(0.567)	(0.017)	(0.002)
Woman vs. Man, elite title	5.84***	0.31	−0.55***	−0.38	−10.44***	0.11	−0.55
	<.001	(0.103)	<.001	(0.304)	<.001	(0.830)	(0.431)
Woman vs. Man, non-elite title	−0.01	0.43***	0.14	0.42	0.36	0.12	0.11
	(0.989)	<.001	(0.701)	(0.456)	(0.354)	(0.711)	(0.732)
Woman vs. Man, no title	0.80***	0.40	−0.10	0.58*	0.21	0.22	0.59**
	(0.001)	(0.183)	(0.885)	(0.058)	(0.709)	(0.661)	(0.037)
Man, elite title vs. Woman		5.67***	0.29	5.31***	4.89***	0.45	−4.43***
		<.001	(0.743)	<.001	<.001	(0.761)	<.001
Man, elite title vs. Man, elite title		−9.48***	−0.38	4.63***	0.07	−1.69***	−11.96***
		<.001	(0.693)	<.001	(0.946)	(0.009)	<.001
Man, elite title vs. Man, non-elite title	17.06***		1.06***	4.51***	0.99***	4.97***	1.09***
	<.001		<.001	<.001	(0.004)	<.001	<.001
Man, elite title vs. Man, no title	4.96***	0.30***	0.67	0.38*	0.98*	5.03***	0.59
	<.001	<.001	(0.142)	(0.062)	(0.089)	<.001	(0.410)
Man, non-elite title vs. Woman	−6.75***	0.39	0.73	5.28***	0.96	0.07	−4.90***
	<.001	(0.113)	(0.260)	<.001	(0.184)	(0.638)	<.001

(continued)

	(1)	(2)	(3)	(4)	(5)	(6)	(7)
VARIABLES	Criminal	Civil Related	Civil Unrelated	1684–96	1735–43	1781–90	All Cases
Man, non-elite title vs. Man, elite title		-0.09	0.65***	4.55***	0.13	0.80***	-5.16***
		(0.892)	<.001	<.001	(0.784)	(0.010)	<.001
Man, non-elite title vs. Man, non-elite title	-0.44	-0.13	0.74***	0.05	0.44	0.19	-0.31
	(0.236)	(0.859)	<.001	(0.934)	(0.250)	(0.664)	(0.128)
Man, non-elite title vs. Man, no title	0.12	0.21	0.26**	-0.04	0.42***	0.37***	-0.27
	(0.856)	(0.554)	(0.012)	(0.919)	<.001	(0.001)	(0.300)
Man, no title vs. Woman	4.57***	0.55***	4.74***	0.21	1.07**	0.72***	4.37***
	<.001	(0.003)	<.001	(0.696)	(0.039)	<.001	<.001
Man, no title vs. Man, elite title	-0.39	-0.08	-0.26	-1.38***	0.11	0.06	-0.99**
	(0.464)	(0.349)	(0.401)	<.001	(0.367)	(0.742)	(0.010)
Man, no title vs. Man, non-elite title	0.07	0.64***	0.43**	4.51***	0.65***	0.18	0.36*
	(0.842)	<.001	(0.030)	<.001	<.001	(0.323)	(0.058)
Muslim vs. Non-Muslim	-5.02***		-0.40	4.55***		-0.94***	-11.93***
	<.001		(0.155)	<.001		<.001	<.001
Non-Muslim vs. Muslim	4.89***		5.05***	5.11***	4.71***	4.89***	5.11***
	<.001		<.001	<.001	<.001	<.001	<.001
Non-Muslim vs. Non-Muslim	0.43	0.88***	4.71***		0.45	4.97***	1.06
	(0.744)	<.001	<.001		(0.502)	<.001	(0.343)

Pilgrim vs. Pilgrim		5.54***	0.38	4.55***	0.57	5.03***	–5.72***
		<.001	(0.118)	<.001	(0.212)	<.001	<.001
Non-pilgrim vs. Pilgrim	0.29	0.02	–0.08	–0.30*	0.03	0.01	–0.03
	(0.356)	(0.916)	(0.645)	(0.077)	(0.958)	(0.855)	(0.909)
Pilgrim vs. Non-pilgrim	16.53***	0.85	0.17	0.10	0.28	1.33	–0.33
	<.001	(0.210)	(0.662)	(0.821)	(0.498)	(0.218)	(0.423)
Prominent vs. Prominent	4.58***	4.87***	–0.72	–0.21***	–0.23	–3.76***	5.62***
	<.001	<.001	(0.318)	<.001	(0.847)	<.001	<.001
Prominent vs. Non-prominent	–0.39	4.81***	–0.25	4.38***	–0.69***	4.46***	–1.21***
	(0.195)	<.001	(0.640)	<.001	<.001	<.001	<.001
Non-prominent vs. Prominent	–12.45***	–0.24	0.23	0.63	4.63***	0.10	–0.30
	<.001	(0.107)	(0.438)	(0.516)	<.001	(0.580)	(0.473)
Criminal							–20.39***
							<.001
Civil Related				–1.03***	–0.86***	–0.50*	–9.40***
				(0.005)	<.001	(0.055)	<.001
Period 2	0.39***	–0.47***	–0.90***				–0.10
	<.001	<.001	<.001				(0.915)
Period 3	–1.34***	–0.52***	–0.81***				–1.30**
	<.001	<.001	<.001				(0.046)
Constant	0.72***	0.16	1.37***	1.20***	0.50*	0.30	20.68***
	<.001	(0.381)	<.001	<.001	(0.083)	(0.545)	<.001

(continued)

APPENDIX 7.A: *(continued)*

	(1)	(2)	(3)	(4)	(5)	(6)	(7)
VARIABLES	**Criminal**	**Civil Related**	**Civil Unrelated**	**1684–96**	**1735–43**	**1781–90**	**All Cases**
Observations	104	317	427	190	259	399	848
Pseudo R^2	0.402	0.0788	0.144	0.231	0.158	0.120	0.841

Notes:

a. See the text for definitions of variables. The dependent variable takes the value of 1 if the case was litigated.

b. Standard errors have been adjusted for clustering on case-type and time-period.

c. Robust *p*-values in parentheses.

d. The omitted variables are "Man with No Title vs. Man with No Title" in the Gender–Title category; "Muslim vs. Muslim" in the Religious Affiliation category; "Non-pilgrim vs. Non-pilgrim" in the Religious Marker category; "Non-prominent vs. Non-prominent" in the Family Affiliation category; "Civil Dispute among Unrelated Parties," in the Case-type category; and "1684–96" in the Time Period category".

e. *** indicates significance at 1%, ** at 5%, and * at 10% for a two-tailed test.

f. For simplicity, the Religious Marker category includes only the pilgrim status.

APPENDIX 7.B: *Individual Characteristics (Including Breakdown by Religious and Military Titles) and the Likelihood of Trial across Case-types and over Time*

	(1)	(2)	(3)	(4)	(5)	(6)	(7)
VARIABLES	Criminal	Civil Related	Civil Unrelated	1684–96	1735–43	1781–90	All Cases
Woman vs. Woman	–1.34***	–0.03	0.19*	–3.08***	–0.44	–4.94***	–0.68**
	<.001	(0.849)	(0.099)	<.001	(0.176)	<.001	(0.019)
Woman vs. Man, religious title	6.30***	1.05*	–0.17	–5.75***	–1.14	1.25	0.26
	<.001	(0.084)	(0.403)	<.001	(0.362)	(0.123)	(0.698)
Woman vs. Man, military title	–0.26	0.07	–0.22	–5.80***	0.24	0.02	0.13
	(0.519)	(0.849)	(0.586)	<.001	(0.444)	(0.871)	(0.554)
Woman vs. Man, no title	0.85***	0.35	–0.14	5.93***	5.62***	0.15	0.77***
	(0.001)	(0.159)	(0.837)	<.001	<.001	(0.620)	(0.009)
Man, religious title vs. Woman		0.65	4.67***	–3.19***	–4.39***	–3.99***	–4.42***
		(0.155)	<.001	<.001	<.001	<.001	<.001
Man, religious title vs. Man, religious title		–9.38***	–0.61	–12.57***	–13.92***	0.74	–11.74***
		<.001	(0.271)	<.001	<.001	(0.364)	<.001
Man, religious title vs. Man, military title	17.09***	15.03***	0.86	1.79***	6.21***	–5.76***	7.00***
	<.001	<.001	(0.127)	<.001	<.001	<.001	<.001
Man, religious title vs. Man, no title	4.99***	0.03	0.83	5.91***	15.69***	–5.50***	1.27
	<.001	(0.978)	(0.122)	<.001	<.001	(0.001)	(0.108)
Man, military title vs. Woman	–6.94***	0.44***	0.26	–11.16***	–5.44***	–4.90***	–5.12***
	<.001	<.001	(0.749)	<.001	<.001	<.001	<.001
Man, military title vs. Man, religious title	–5.13***		4.71***	–12.62***	–14.30***	–10.01***	–13.06***
	<.001		<.001	<.001	<.001	<.001	<.001

(continued)

	(1)	(2)	(3)	(4)	(5)	(6)	(7)
VARIABLES	Criminal	Civil Related	Civil Unrelated	1684–96	1735–43	1781–90	All Cases
Man, military title vs. Man, military title	−0.38	−5.09***	0.29	−12.62***	−0.09	−0.39*	−0.20
	(0.350)	<.001	(0.480)	<.001	(0.712)	(0.052)	(0.350)
Man, military title vs. Man, no title	0.20	0.21	0.14	0.33	−0.01	−4.72***	−0.24
	(0.782)	(0.225)	(0.443)	(0.393)	(0.959)	<.001	(0.315)
Man, no title vs. Woman	4.51***	0.49***	4.72***	−3.27***	5.69***	−4.72***	4.84***
	<.001	(0.001)	<.001	<.001	<.001	<.001	<.001
Man, no title vs. Man, religious title	4.79***	0.30***	0.21	0.25	−0.48	−4.70***	−0.13
	<.001	<.001	(0.454)	(0.277)	(0.459)	<.001	(0.647)
Man, no title vs. Man, military title	−0.19	0.51*	−0.01	0.42	1.26	−4.76***	0.32
	(0.678)	(0.087)	(0.970)	(0.222)	(0.106)	<.001	(0.370)
Muslim vs. Non-Muslim	−5.13***		−0.60**	−12.62***		−5.13***	−5.63***
	<.001		(0.035)	<.001		<.001	<.001
Non-Muslim vs. Muslim	5.17***		4.76***	5.68***	−14.95***	−5.63***	5.62***
	<.001		<.001	<.001	<.001	<.001	<.001
Non-Muslim vs. Non-Muslim	0.35	0.83***	4.68***		−0.01	6.96***	1.20
	(0.789)	<.001	<.001		(0.990)	<.001	(0.281)
Pilgrim vs. Pilgrim		5.51***	0.27*	−12.62***	−5.88***	−10.27***	−5.89***
		<.001	(0.065)	<.001	<.001	<.001	<.001
Non-pilgrim vs. Pilgrim	−0.49	−0.03	−0.19	−0.68***	1.08*	−0.78**	−0.09
	(0.381)	(0.754)	(0.266)	<.001	(0.069)	(0.023)	(0.757)
Pilgrim vs. Non-pilgrim	16.50***	0.95	−0.03	0.61**	−1.36*	−0.15***	0.04
	<.001	(0.154)	(0.814)	(0.014)	(0.075)	<.001	(0.931)

Prominent vs. Prominent	–1.79***	4.76***	–1.31	–1.18***	0.61	–0.11	–0.17
	(0.001)	<.001	(0.125)	<.001	(0.413)	(0.431)	(0.744)
Prominent vs. Non-prominent	–0.48	4.73***	0.08	8.11***	–8.96***	–5.55***	–1.20***
	(0.142)	<.001	(0.860)	<.001	<.001	<.001	<.001
Non-prominent vs. Prominent	–12.32***	–0.27	0.25*	4.46***	–0.10	–5.03***	–0.91**
	<.001	(0.435)	(0.070)	<.001	(0.826)	<.001	(0.013)
Criminal				–23.60***	–23.74***	–17.39***	–21.89***
				<.001	<.001	<.001	<.001
Civil Related				–11.85***	–11.53***	–5.72***	–10.18***
				<.001	<.001	<.001	<.001
Period 2	0.48***	–0.43***	–0.73***				–0.00
	(0.003)	<.001	<.001				(0.996)
Period 3	–1.33***	–0.48***	–0.84***				–1.35*
	<.001	<.001	<.001				(0.083)
Constant	0.76***	0.18*	1.44***	23.61***	23.75***	16.53***	22.03***
	(0.001)	(0.051)	<.001	<.001	<.001	<.001	<.001
Observations	104	317	427	190	259	399	848
Pseudo R^2	0.431	0.0912	0.124	0.847	0.780	0.914	0.835

See notes to Appendix 7.A.

PART FOUR

LITIGATIONS

8

Rules and Tools of Litigation

INTRODUCTION

After exploring trial-settlement decisions in the preceding chapters, we now turn our attention to litigations. The present chapter explains the rules and processes of litigation. We review how trials were conducted, litigants' responsibilities, rules of evidence, and the ways in which litigants employed various tools of litigation.[1] In the light this information, Chapter 9 will provide an economic model designed for Ottoman litigation processes. Chapter 10 will offer an empirical analysis of the relevant information in the *sicil*s of Kastamonu according to this model.

The information provided in the present chapter is largely based on legal texts and jurisprudential commentaries known to have influenced and represented Ottoman legal practices in different periods. These include Burhaneddin Merginani's influential twelfth-century commentary *Hidaye*,[2] Molla Hüsrev's fifteenth-century commentary *Dürer el-Hükkam Şerh Gürer*

[1] One could devote many pages to the treatment of these topics. Our objective in this chapter is not to explain every detail in the litigation process but to provide a solid background to help the readers to make sense of the analysis we offer in Chapter 10. For more comprehensive discussions of the material presented in this chapter, please consult the jurisprudential sources cited in the text. For a recent study in Turkish, see Demir (2010).

[2] The work is also available in English: *The Hedaya or Guide: A Commentary on the Mussulman Laws*. Trans. Charles Hamilton. Delhi: Islamic Book Trust, 1982. In this study we use the following translation of this work: *İslam Fıkhında Tahkikli ve Tahriçli el-Hidaye Tercemesi*. Trans. Ahmet Meylani. 3 volumes. İstanbul: Kahraman Yayınları, 1986. All our references to this work in the text are identified as "*Hidaye*."

el-Ahkam,[3] and Ibrahim el-Halebi's popular sixteenth-century manual *Mülteka el-Ebhur*.[4] We also rely extensively on the Ottoman Civil Code, *Mecelle-i Ahkam-ı Adliye*,[5] and provide examples from Kastamonu court records.

Before we move on, a word may be necessary to justify our use of the *Mecelle*, a product of the nineteenth-century Ottoman legal reform. The *Mecelle* represents a relatively systematic and comprehensive compilation of mainly Hanafi jurisprudential prescriptions pertaining to contracts, torts, and civil procedure, which is why it is useful for our objectives in this chapter. Although the codification of Islamic law was a stark innovation of the late nineteenth century, the *Mecelle*'s prescriptions on specific issues and the content of its individual clauses are based largely on established jurisprudential opinions of the past. Also, the *Mecelle* dates closer to our period than any other legal text or jurisprudential commentary available to us, the most recent of which is from the sixteenth century. Since possible variations between *Mecelle*-based prescriptions and those found in earlier texts may reflect shifts in legal practice and jurisprudential opinion during the seventeenth or eighteenth centuries (or even earlier) as much as they do nineteenth-century reformers' attempts at legislative interpretation, there is no a priori reason for us to overlook the *Mecelle* as a source that could inform our analysis. Nevertheless, we acknowledge here the potential dangers of drawing from a legal source produced when the legal system and ideology was undergoing a major transformation. This is why we also make a special effort in our discussion to compare the relevant prescriptions in the *Mecelle* with those found in the earlier texts listed above.[6]

The chapter is divided into three subsections. The first provides a general overview of the phases of the litigation process, in particular the evidentiary procedures. The second offers detailed information about frequent forms of evidence, documentation, and other bases of legal

[3] We use the following translation: *Gurer ve Dürer Tercümesi (İslam Fıkhı ve Hukuku)*. Trans. Arif Erkan. 4 volumes. İstanbul: Eser Neşriyat, 1980. All our references to this study are identified as "*Dürer.*"

[4] We use the following translation of this work: *İzahlı Mülteka el-Ebhur Tercümesi*. Trans. Mustafa Uysal. 4 volumes. İstanbul: Çelik Yayınlari, n.d. All references to this study are identified as "*Mülteka.*"

[5] All the references to this work, identified as "*Mecelle*," are to the following publication: *Açıklamalı Mecelle (Mecelle-i Ahkām-ı Adliyye)*. Ed. Ali Himmet Berki. İstanbul: Hikmet Yayınları, 1986. We cited this work in previous chapters as Berki (1986).

[6] On the process of legal transformation that also produced the *Mecelle*, see Miller (2005), Rubin (2007, 2008), and Agmon (2006).

judgment that are mentioned only briefly in the first subsection. In the final section we discuss the nature of and rules pertaining to *fetva* and litigant representation, which, although having no direct bearing on court decisions, nevertheless influenced trial processes and results.

LITIGATION PROCESS AND EVIDENTIARY PROCEDURES

Islamic evidentiary procedures are anything but straightforward. As a general rule, however, evidentiary expectations in Ottoman litigations depended on the nature of the claim made in court. The particular position that the litigants assumed in litigations (as plaintiffs or defendants) did not have a predetermined bearing on who should assume the responsibility of providing evidence; technically, it was the kadı who assigned the burden of proof, based on the type of dispute at the heart of the case.

The litigation begins when the plaintiff (*müddei*) makes an allegation against the defendant (*müdde'a aleyh*). Article 1816 of the *Mecelle* states that "[when] the parties approach the judge for trial, the judge first asks the plaintiff to state his or her case. . . . The judge then asks the defendant to respond." It is possible for the defendant to admit (*ikrar*) the truth of the plaintiff's claim, in which case the trial is concluded in favor of the latter. Here is an example of this type of litigation:

Example 1: Defendant admission

Mehmed bin [son of] Şaban of Medrese-i Atabeğ quarter in Kastamonu accused Meryem bint [daughter of] Elhac Mustafa of the same quarter as follows: "About 10 years ago, Meryem sold me a house of well-known boundaries in Medrese-i Atabeğ quarter for 80 *guruş*, which she collected from me in full at the time. However, she also gave the same house to her husband, İbrahim bin Ali, who took the house in his possession afterwards. Subsequently, I sued her and proved my case in court, as a result of which the court ordered her to return the sale price to me. She still has not returned my 80 *guruş*. I would like her to be questioned and ordered to return the money."

When questioned, Meryem admitted (*ikrar*) that she had not returned the money to Mehmed. The court instructed Meryem to return the money in full. This record was produced as requested.

Entry of 11 Rebiyülevvel 1105 / 10 November 1693 (KCR vol. 5)

Witnesses . . .

It is also possible for the kadı to dismiss the case immediately if he decides that it lacks legal merit or if any of the minimum conditions to initiate litigation are missing.[7] Or he can pronounce a judgment based on litigants' depositions without requesting proof, if he feels the claim does not require any. Often, however, the litigation proceeds to the phase of evidentiary corroboration, during which complex procedures are followed. In general terms, the assignment of responsibility for providing proof depends on the defendant's reaction to the plaintiff's allegation(s). In the following discussion we identify three general permutations of litigant positions that generate specific evidentiary requirements.

Permutation 1 – Defendant's Denial: If the defendant simply denies (*inkar*) the plaintiff's claim – that is, claims that no aspect of the allegation bears any truth – the latter assumes the burden of proof (*Mecelle*, 413). We discuss in the next subsection what counted as proof, but it was very often witness testimony. If the plaintiff fails to provide proof within a specific time period or if the credibility of the proof is challenged, the kadı is obligated to rule for the defendant, frequently after asking the latter to swear an oath to the truthfulness of the denial. It is the plaintiff's prerogative to request such an oath upon failing to prove his or her claim (*Mecelle*, 414; cf. *Hidaye* vol. 3, 277–9; *Dürer* vol. 4, 158–61; *Mülteka* vol. 3, 275).[8] Technically, if the defendant refuses, the kadı would decide in favor of the plaintiff – again, often after requiring the latter to take an oath (*Mecelle*, 414). If the plaintiff refuses to take an oath, the kadı is expected to rule for the defendant.

Here are examples from Kastamonu court records that represent three possibilities associated with the first permutation:

[7] For a litigation to proceed, the disputants have to be unambiguously identified. Also, they have to be adult and sane, though those who lack these qualities may be represented by their guardians. Disputants should be present at the time of the litigation or have representatives in court who can answer questions on their behalf. The nature of the dispute has to be clearly stated at the beginning of the litigation and the objects or property that constitute the source of the conflict should be unambiguously identified by the parties. For more on this topic, see Demir (2010, 67–72).

[8] In exceptional circumstances the kadı may require a party to take an oath without any appeal from his or her opponent (Demir 2010, 178–82).

Example 2: Plaintiff allegation supported by plaintiff's witnesses

Bağdadi Abdülcelil Ali, an adolescent [or "smooth-faced youth"; *şabb-ı emred*] from Halife quarter in Kastamonu made the following claim against Saliha bint Mehmed Ağa of the same quarter, the wife and heir of the late Ahmed Ağa bin Mehmed Ağa: "When my former master (*seyyidim*) late Mehmed Ağa died, and his estate was divided among his heirs, I was inherited by his wife Zülfiye (?) kadın bint Ahmed Ağa [presumably daughter of Saliha's late husband]. Subsequently, while she was in sound mind, Zülfiye (?) kadın freed me. Now Saliha claims that I was a slave of the late Ahmed Ağa and wants to include me into his estate to be apportioned among his heirs. I want her to be questioned and her response to be recorded."

When questioned, Saliha denied (*inkar*) that Ali had been Mehmed Ağa's slave and that he was subsequently inherited by Zülfiye (?) kadın. When Ali was asked to prove his claims, he brought the court two trustworthy witnesses named Abdulrahman bin Süleyman and Mustafa bin Mehmed, who testified as follows: "We testify that Ali used to be a slave of the late Mehmed Ağa. After Mehmed Ağa died, he was inherited by his wife, Zülfiye (?), who subsequently freed him. We are witnesses to these events and testify as such." After their testimonies were accepted, Saliha was instructed not to meddle with Ali's affairs. This record was prepared as requested.

Entry of 1–10 (*evail*) Rebiyülahir 1110 / 7–16 October 1698 (KCR vol. 8)

Witnesses . . .

Example 3: Plaintiff unable to prove allegation; defendant wins after taking oath

Himmet of Kübceğiz quarter made the following accusation against Ali, who is known as "Keçecioğlu": "In the day that this record was produced, Ali opened the lock of the front door of my house, secretly entered there, approached my wife from behind, cut off her hair tie, and ran away with it. I want him to be questioned and what is legally required be done."

Example 3: (cont.)

When questioned, Ali denied the accusation. When Himmet was asked to prove his claim, he could not do so and demanded Ali to take an oath [to his innocence]. When Ali was asked to take an oath by God that he did not enter Himmet's house secretly, approach Himmet's wife, cut off her hair tie, or ran away with it, he did so. Subsequently, Himmet and his wife were instructed to cease their accusations against Ali. This record was produced as requested.

Entry of 10 Şevval 1104 / 14 June 1693 (KCR vol. 5)

Witnesses . . .

Example 4: Plaintiff unable to prove allegation; plaintiff wins after defendant refuses to take oath of innocence

Receb bin Timur of the village of Sahib accused Süleyman Beşe bin İlyas, who had been brought to court by the officers of Kastamonu's deputy-governor (*mütesellim*), Ahmed Ağa, as follows: "Two days ago, while I was putting my buffalos out to pasture around my village, Süleyman Beşe hit me with a piece of black wood and injured my head and other limbs. I want him to be questioned and my injuries inspected by the court." Receb's body was inspected and his wounds were noted in the court records.

When questioned, Süleyman Beşe denied Receb's accusations. Subsequently, Receb was asked to prove his claims, but he failed to do so. When he demanded Süleyman Beşe to take an oath that he did not attack or injure Receb, Süleyman Beşe declined to take the oath. The court decided that the requirement of law should be carried out [against Süleyman Beşe]. Recorded as requested.

Entry of 29 Zilhicce 1148 / 11 May 1738 (KCR vol. 35)

Witnesses . . .

Permutation 2 – Defendant's Rebuttal: The evidentiary expectations would be different if the defendant responded to the plaintiff's allegation with a rebuttal (*def*'), rather than a denial. A rebuttal represents a "counter-claim" in that the particulars of the case are characterized by the defendant differently. Article 1631 of the *Mecelle* (354–5) provides the following examples as acceptable rebuttals (cf. *Mülteka* vol. 3, 285–6):

(1) Assume that one person sues another for a certain sum of money previously accrued through a loan. The defendant claims to have already paid the plaintiff or to have been released by the latter from the debt, or that they have come to a settlement, or that the sum in question was not a loan but was the price of some property that the defendant sold to the plaintiff, or that the defendant had transferred to the plaintiff a debt owed by a third party and got paid by the plaintiff as a result of that transfer.
(2) Assume that one person sues another, claiming that the latter became surety for the payment of a sum due to him or her from a third party. The latter claims that the third party has already paid the sum in question.
(3) Assume that one person sues another, claiming that the latter is in possession of property that in fact belongs to former. The defendant argues that previously a third party had sued him or her for the same property and that at that trial the plaintiff testified for the third party.
(4) Assume that one person sues the heirs of a deceased person, claiming a sum of the money they inherited from the estate. [Even if] the plaintiff proves the claim, the heirs allege that the deceased had paid the debt while still alive.

If the defendant "rebuts" the plaintiff's allegation, the burden of proof shifts to the defendant, assuming the plaintiff denies the defendant's rebuttal. If the defendant can submit acceptable proof to court, he or she should win the case. In the absence of proof, the defendant can demand that the plaintiff take an oath, whereupon the kadı would rule in the latter's favor. If the plaintiff refuses, the kadı would rule in favor of the defendant after forcing him or her to take the oath. If the defendant refuses, the judge would rule for the plaintiff.

The following case summary is an example of the defendant's rebuttal and the subsequent evidentiary procedures:

Example 5: Plaintiff's allegation "rebutted" by defendant

Hüseyin, Ahmed, Receb, and Hasan of Deveciler quarter of Kastamonu made the following accusation against Mehmed bin Receb of the same quarter: "Mehmed illegally occupies a house with known neighbors and boundaries located in the aforementioned

Example 5: (cont.)

quarter that used to belong to our late grandfather, Arab Elhac Mehmed, who passed away fifteen years ago, and whom we are heirs of. We want Mehmed to be questioned and the house transferred to us."

When questioned, Mehmed responded as follows: "the late Elhac Mehmed sold the said house to his daughter Fatma for 40 *guruş* before he died. Fatma was my wife. She sold the house to me for 30 *guruş* before she herself passed away." When asked for proof, Mehmed introduced to court two trustworthy witnesses, Ahmed Çelebi bin Elhac Ali and Ahmed bin Mehmed of Deveciler quarter, who testified as follows: "We testify that about fifteen years ago Arab Elhac Mehmed sold the said house to his daughter Fatma for 40 *guruş*. Fatma later sold the house to Mehmed for 30 *guruş*. We are witnesses to these events and testify thus." After their testimonies were accepted, the plaintiffs were instructed to cease their accusations. Recorded as requested.

Entry of 21 Cemaziyelahir 1104 / 27 February 1693 (KCR vol. 5)
Witnesses . . .

Permutation 3 – Plaintiff's Rebuttal of Defendant's Rebuttal: Following the rebuttal of the defendant, it is possible for the plaintiff to rebut the defendant's rebuttal. Though very rare, if this happened, the evidentiary expectations would follow the order described under permutation 1.

Again, it was the kadı's responsibility to fit litigants' interactions to one of these scenarios. In many cases, if not all, it must have been easy to differentiate a denial from a rebuttal. But we can also imagine instances in which such a differentiation was not easy. For example, how should one interpret the defendant's decision to remain silent when faced with an allegation? For such instances, the jurisprudential traditions established conventions that helped the kadı enforce a consistent precedent.[9] In other complex cases, where multiple allegations and counter-allegations were made by the litigants, each allegation–counter-allegation pair was treated independently and required a separate evidentiary process. In such cases the kadı was required to identify individual sources of contention, and

[9] Article 1822 of *Mecelle* (414) instructed the kadı to interpret the defendant's silence as denial; cf. *Hidaye* (vol. 3, 280); *Dürer* (vol. 4, 154–5); and *Mülteka* (vol. 3, 275).

assign the responsibility for proof to the parties in accordance with their relative positions in relation to specific contentions.

On "Preferred Evidence"

In some types of disputes, it is the actual substance of the contention, rather than the type (whether it is a denial or rebuttal) that determines who is expected to submit evidence. This is because in such disputes it is particularly difficult to figure out what constitutes a denial or a rebuttal. Examples of such cases are described in the "Book of Evidence" in the *Mecelle* under the subsection "On the Preference of Evidence" (*Tercih-i Beyyinat Hakkındadır*). For example, Article 1756 (396) prescribes that if two people sue each other over a piece of property, with one alleging sole ownership and the other alleging joint ownership, "the evidence [provided by the party who claims] sole ownership is superior (*evladır*)." Here are some other examples from the same subsection:

Article 1757 (396): In a trial on the absolute ownership of the property, the evidence provided by the person not in possession is preferred [to evidence provided by the party who is in possession of the property], if no date is mentioned....

Article 1758 (396–7): Trials relating to ownership arising from causes which are capable of repetition, such as purchase, are regarded as identical to trials about absolute ownership [see Article 1757], if the date is not mentioned ...

Article 1759 (397): In actions relating to ownership arising out of a cause which is incapable of repetition, as in the case of an animal giving birth to young, evidence of the person in possession is preferred ...

Article 1760 (ibid.): In a claim for ownership dependent on date, the evidence of the person giving the earliest date should be preferred ...

Article 1763 (398): Evidence for ownership [of a specific property] is preferred to evidence for loan [of that property] for use.

Article 1764 (398): Evidence for sale is preferred to evidence for gift, or pledge, or hire, and the evidence for hire is preferred to the evidence for pledge ...

Article 1766 (399): Evidence of good health is preferred to evidence of mortal sickness. For example, assume that a person makes a gift to one of his or her heirs and dies. Afterwards, another heir alleges that the gift was made during the course of a mortal sickness [and, therefore, not legally binding]. The person in whose favor the gift was made alleges that the gift was made while in good health. The evidence provided by the person who alleges good health is preferred.

Article 1767 (399): Evidence of sound mind is preferred to evidence of madness or imbecility.

Article 1771 (400): If a husband and wife quarrel about the ownership of things in a house in which they live, the nature of the things must be examined. In the case of things fit for the husband only, such as a gun or a sword, or of things suitable for both, such as kitchen utensils and furniture, the evidence provided by the wife is preferred. [...] In the case of things appropriate for women, the husband's evidence is preferred.

Similar types of prescriptions, though not mentioned in the *Mecelle*, also exist in *Hidaye*, *Dürer*, and *Mülteka*.[10] What consequences stemmed from one party's evidence being "superior" or "preferred"? The question is important for the more general problem of how contradictory evidence submitted by opposing parties was treated in court. An answer by implication is available in Articles 1769 and 1770 of the *Mecelle* (400). Article 1769 states that "in case the person whose evidence is preferred is unable to ... produc[e] evidence, evidence is asked from the person whose evidence has not been preferred." And according to Article 1770, if that party produces evidence, "judgment shall be given" in his or her favor.

Articles 1769 and 1770 make clear that the kadı is not supposed to weigh the evidence submitted by both parties but, instead, chooses the party whose evidence is considered to be technically allowable/preferred, and considers the strength and credibility of that party's evidence on its own terms, not in relation to the opposing party's evidence. This is consistent with our observations in the court records of Kastamonu. Here is an example:

Example 6: Example of "preferred evidence" I

Receb Ağa bin Derviş of Ata Beğ quarter of Kastamonu accused Elhac Mehmed bin Elhac Mustafa of the town of (?) as follows: "About five years ago a sorrel-colored mule of mine, born to a mare that I had owned, disappeared. I recently found it in Elhac Mehmed's possession. I want him be questioned and the mule returned to me."

When questioned, Elhac Mehmed made the following statement "I purchased this mule two years ago in the town of Ankara from a

[10] For example, these works instruct that in a dispute over ownership of a camel or a horse, the evidence provided by the party who rides the animal is preferred to the evidence of the individual who merely holds its bridle. In the same type of a dispute, the evidence provided by the person who sits in the front of the saddle is preferred to the person who rides in the back. The evidence of the person whose property the animal carries is preferred to the evidence of the person who merely hangs the water vessel on the animal. In a dispute on the ownership of a garment, the evidence provided by the individual who wears the garment is preferred to the person who holds on its sleeves (*Dürer* vol. 4, 196–7; *Hidaye* vol. 3, 308–9; *Mülteka* vol. 3, 289–93, 294–5).

Example 6: (cont.)

man named Bayram for 54 *guruş*. I do not recognize that it belonged to the plaintiff."

Since evidence provided by that party that lacks possession is preferred (*haricin beyyinesi evla olmağla*), Receb was asked to provide evidence. He presented to court Elhac Mehmed bin Elhac Ahmed of Ata Beğ quarter, Osman bin Ali of Türbe quarter, and Hüseyin bin Alhac Abdi of Kubbeli quarter, who testified as follows: "Indeed, the sorrel-colored mule belongs to Receb Ağa and that it disappeared five years ago."

After their testimonies were accepted, the plaintiff was invited to take an oath that he had not sold the mule to another person. After Receb took the oath, Elhac Mehmed was instructed to return the mule to him. Recorded as requested.

Entry of 24 Rebiyülevvel 1104 / 3 December 1692 (KCR vol. 5, 99–189)

Witnesses . . .

In the example above, the court gave Receb Ağa the opportunity to prove his claim, even though Elhac Mehmed may also have been able to present witnesses willing to testify on his behalf. Because of the substance of their claims, Receb Ağa's evidence was "superior" (*evla*) to whatever Elhac Mehmed could have submitted, which is clear in the document's explicit recognition of the principle that the party who lacks possession of the disputed propriety bears the burden of proof. Since the court deemed the testimonies of Receb Ağa's witnesses credible, it must have refused to consider, or even listen to, Elhac Mehmed's witnesses, if they were present at the time of the trial. This interpretation conforms to a number of *Mecelle* articles that discuss preferred evidence in which the phrase "is preferred . . ." is followed by " . . . and heard" (*tercih ve istima' kılınır*),[11] indicating that the preferred evidence is the one that is heard in court.[12]

[11] See, for example, Articles 1757, 1758, and 1765 (*Mecelle*, 396–7, 399).

[12] We have identified only one possible scenario in the *Mecelle* that required the kadı to consider the evidence provided by both the plaintiff and the defendant simultaneously: Article 1756 (396) prescribes that "(i)f two individuals claimed sole ownership of a property [that is in possession of both of them], and they both provide the court with evidence, the property should be considered to be under joint-ownership by them."

The next case entry, which differentiates between evidence of sound mind and evidence of confusion (cf. Article 1767, *Mecelle*, 299), makes this point very clear:

Example 7: Example of "preferred evidence" II

Aişe bint Musa from the village of Karaçomak of Kastamonu sued Hüseyin bin Ahmed Beğ while the tımar-holder (*sahib-i arz*) of the plots subject to the dispute was present, claiming: "at a time that I was confused (*mahlut el-akl*), I surrendered and Hüseyin accepted four pieces of land located in the aforementioned Karaçomak village. Since this land transfer should not be legally valid, I demand the court instruct the aforementioned Hüseyin to return the aforementioned lands to me."

When questioned, Hüseyin made the following statement: "At the time Aişe transferred the said lands she was rational and coherent (*akile ve kamile*). I refuse to relinquish these lands to her."

Since the "evidence of reasonable action" is preferable, Hüseyin was asked to prove his claim. He introduced Mustafa bin Hasan and Molla Mehmed bin Elhac Hasan to court, who both testified: "Indeed, at the time that the aforementioned territories were acquired by Hüseyin, Aişe was rational and coherent. We are witnesses to this fact and testify thus."

The court accepted their testimony and ordered Aişe not to interfere in Hüseyin's affairs.

Entry of 16 Muharrem 1153 / 13 April 1740 (KCR vol. 38).

Witnesses . . .

Noticeable in the above examples is the fact that the court's objective is not necessarily to establish the truth of past events or relationships with reference to complex, and possibly contradictory, traces of the past, but to enforce a hierarchy of rules and regulate the game of litigation according to preestablished criteria. As we see later, the question of who assumed the proof responsibility had a major bearing on trial results.

BASES OF DECISION IN LITIGATION

After a general treatment of Islamic adjudicative and evidentiary processes, we next discuss in detail various bases for legal decisions in trials, including admission, witness testimony, and oath, with reference to the information found in jurisprudential sources and court records. We also consider the ways in which written documentation was used in litigations.

İkrar *or Admission*

İkrar, often translated as "admission" or "acknowledgment" (see Case 1, above) represents a "recognition by the person against whom the petitioner alleges a fact, or a right, of the soundness of the request" (De Bellefonds 1971, 1078; cf. *Mecelle*, 333). According to Brunschvig (1960, 1151), *ikrar* may be a decisive legal act because it is an intervention that can immediately conclude legal proceedings without further action. "At this juncture, the procedure goes no further. The judge cannot neglect this recognition [i.e., *ikrar*] and demand a further proof" (De Bellefonds 1971, 1078). Indeed, *Dürer* (vol. 4, 216) distinguishes evidence (*beyyine*) from *ikrar* because while the former requires the kadı's recognition of its evidentiary relevance, *ikrar* does not require such an external confirmation, unless it is rejected by the party in whose favor it is made (*Beyyine, ikrarın aksinedir. Çünkü kadının hükmüyle hüccet olur ... İkrar, hükme muhtaç değildir*).[13]

The *Mecelle* (and other legal texts) provides detailed discussions of who may offer legally valid and binding admissions and how such admissions should be worded. For example, admissions made by minors and individuals who are of unsound mind are not acceptable. Nor are admissions by their parents and guardians in relation to such people (333).[14] An admission made by force is invalid (334). One who is legally prohibited from spending his or her wealth may not make a legally binding admission involving it (ibid.). Although an admission does not require the acknowledgment of the person in whose favor it is made, if the latter refuses to accept it, the admission is invalid (335). An admission dependent on any condition is unacceptable (336). Admissions are not allowed to be retracted (338). According to de Bellefonds (1971, 1081), however, if an admission involves a confession to an offense punishable by *hadd*, a retraction might be permissible.

[13] On the other hand, *Dürer* (vol. 4, 214) suggests that *ikrar* should be considered an act of informing (*haber*), but not documenting or substantiating (*isbat*), because it could be based on truth or untruth ([*İkrar*] *kendisinde olan başkasının hakkını haber vermektir. Yoksa onu isbat değildir*). Also, "*(i)krar bir ihbardır, ki doğru ve yalana ihtimali vardır*" (*Dürer* vol. 4, 215); also see *Mülteka* (vol. 3, 300).

[14] See Articles 1573 and 1574 for exceptions (ibid.).

Witness Testimony

Witness testimony represents the most important and common evidentiary tool in the Kastamonu court. The very first article of "The Book of Evidence and Administration of Oath" in Article 1676 of the Ottoman Civil Code defines evidence (*beyyine*) as "strong proof" (*Beyyine, hüccet-i kaviyye demektir*) (*Mecelle*, 373; cf. *Dürer* vol. 4, 158),[15] and the default form of evidence is orally given witness testimony, which consists of "giving of information by a person in front of a judge and in the presence of the two adversaries, about one of these parties' claims against the other" (*Mecelle*, 374).

Overall, what we see in *Hidaye, Dürer, Mülteka*, and the *Mecelle* is a high level of formalism, developed to regulate the potential uncertainties associated with orality. In theory and practice, this formalism defines who should be considered a credible witness, what counts as acceptable testimony, and the legitimate ways in which testimony can be used in litigation. Article 1705 of the *Mecelle* (376) states that "the witness must be a just/upright (*adil*) person. An upright person is one whose good deeds are more pronounced than his or her bad deeds" (cf. Tyan 1960, 209–10). Consequently, the testimony of persons who habitually "behave in a manner inconsistent with honor and dignity," such as dancers and comedians, and persons who are known to be liars, is inadmissible (*Mecelle*, 379).[16] Also, Article 1686 of the *Mecelle* (374) excludes the mute and the blind as qualified witnesses. *Hidaye, Dürer*, and *Mülteka* appear to be more discerning in their screening of potential witnesses. For example, testimony by apostates, slaves, those who consume alcohol or play backgammon (chess is okay!) or with birds, and those who appear naked in public baths should not be accepted. Also, individuals who accept interest (*riba*), urinate on public roads or eat publicly while traveling, men "who act like women," or women who cry aloud in public (such as at funerals) should not be asked to testify (*Hidaye* vol. 3, 217–18; *Dürer* vol. 4, 256–68; *Mülteka* vol. 3, 231–4). According to Hanafi principles, non-Muslims are not allowed to testify against Muslims, although they may testify against non-Muslims (*Dürer* vol. 4, 259–60; *Mülteka* vol. 3, 235).

Beyond these more general requirements, there are also specific standards based on the relationship between litigants and witnesses. For

[15] Brunschvig (1960, 1150) defines "bayyina" as "proof *per excellentiam*."

[16] Peters (1997, 297) defines acceptable witnesses as those who have not "committed great sins or persevered in small sins and not displaying unbecoming behavior."

example, Article 1700 of the *Mecelle* (378) states that testimony given by (grand)parents on behalf of their (grand)children or (grand)children on behalf of their (grand)parents, or by spouses on behalf of each other is inadmissible (cf. *Mülteka* vol. 3, 232). Testimony submitted by someone on behalf of another person who maintains or employs the former is also inadmissible (*Mecelle*, 378). Article 1702 of the *Mecelle* (379; also Peters 1997, 297) states that for a testimony to be acceptable, there should be no enmity between the witness and the person against whom he or she testifies. According to *Hidaye* (vol. 3, 217) and *Mülteka* (vol. 3, 232), the testimony of an individual on behalf of his or her business partner in a dispute related to a property owned by both is inadmissible.

The performance of witnessing has to follow a script, and most phases of the procedure are designed to eliminate any doubt about the nature and intent of the witness's statements. For example, Article 1685 of the *Mecelle* (374) requires witnesses in most instances to be comprised of two men, or one man and two women. In cases involving issues about which men cannot be expected to possess necessary information, such as menstruation, childbirth, virginity, or female sexual organs, testimony should be sought from women. Witnesses have to make it absolutely clear that their statements are meant to be testimonies and that they are aware of their legal consequences. This is why the law expects witnesses to begin their statements with the phrase, "I testify that . . . " (cf. *Dürer* vol. 4, 244; *Mülteka* vol. 3, 224 and 227–8). If they neglect to do this, it is the kadı's responsibility to ask if it is their intention to testify (*Mecelle*, 374). If the witness fails to declare that his or her statement represents a testimony and the kadı does not elicit an explicit acknowledgment to this effect, the testimony is not acceptable (ibid.). Testimony about an individual who is absent during the proceedings and not particularly well known (*meşhur ve ma'ruf*) needs to mention the name of his or her father or grandfather in order to prevent any confusion. If the individual is present, and if the name of the father or grandfather is not mentioned, the witness must explicitly point him or her out (*Mecelle*, 376). Also, "(w)hen testifying on immovable property (*akar*), its boundaries must be stated. If the witness is unable to describe its boundaries, but states that he or she could indicate them on the spot, the witness shall proceed to the spot and there show the boundaries" (ibid.).[17]

Once a testimony is given, it may be withdrawn only before the kadı. If a withdrawal happens before the end of the litigation, the kadı cannot render a judgment. If the withdrawal occurs after the verdict, the verdict cannot be

[17] See in Case 8 below how the house subject to dispute is described in the document.

changed or withdrawn but the witness who withdrew testimony is liable for half of the damage caused to his or her adversary. If the verdict involves a death sentence, the witness is liable for blood money (*diyet*) (Peters 1997, 298).

Given that testimony by two or more witnesses is the default procedure in litigations, the credibility of the witnesses is critically important. According to Article 1712 of the *Mecelle* (384), for example, testimonies that contain conflicting information in regard to the price of the property subject to a dispute may be unacceptable.[18] Also unacceptable are conflicting testimonies about the color of an animal whose ownership is disputed or whether it is male or female (*Mecelle*, 383; *Dürer* vol. 4, 269–75).[19] Remarkable in this regard is how actual court records represent witness testimonies. As is evident in the examples of registries given earlier, witnesses appear to speak in one voice, with no indication of varying accounts. As recorded, their statements are identical, and often match the claim made by the party bearing the burden of proof. In truth the situation is a consequence of the court's efforts to translate individual stories into one coherent, legally unproblematic testimony.

The system's obsession with the institution of witnessing extends beyond technicalities that aim to fix potentially unstable meanings of oral statements to include scrutiny of truth claims. Given the difficulty of distinguishing truthful statements from false ones, the court considers the public reputations of witnesses as proxies for the reliability of their statements. The *Mecelle* contains eleven articles (Articles 1716 to 1726) on determining the credibility of witnesses. If the litigant against whom testimonies are submitted challenges the credibility of the witnesses or even simply the accuracy of the testimonies against him or her, the kadı is required to investigate the reputation of the witnesses (*Mecelle*, 384).[20] This process is called *tezkiye-i şuhud*, or "purification/clearance of witnesses." Article 1717 in the *Mecelle* (384) states that "the inquiry into the credibility of witnesses is conducted either publicly or privately, by consulting the peoples or groups with whom they are affiliated."

[18] *Mülteka* (vol. 3, 238) suggests that in such cases the testimony that points to the lesser amount should be accepted.

[19] *Mülteka* (vol. 3, 239) recognizes a plurality of opinions in this regard. According to *Hidaye* (vol. 3, 225) and *Dürer* (vol. 4, 273), testimonies that conflict on the date of an event subject to a dispute (such as murder) are inadmissible.

[20] Some Hanafi authorities insisted that the kadı should investigate the reputations of all witnesses, regardless of the litigants' opinions about them (*Dürer* vol. 4, 248–50). This does not seem to be a common practice in Ottoman courts except, perhaps, in cases that could lead to serious punishments, such as *hadd* and *kısas* (retaliation) litigations (ibid.).

Private inquiries must be made in writing. If answers to these inquiries, also in writing, confirm the good reputation of the witness, the testimony is accepted. If they cast doubt on a particular witness' reputation or fail to respond to the inquiry in the fashion that they are supposed to, the kadı asks the litigant with proof responsibility to name alternative witnesses (*Mecelle*, 385). According to *Dürer* (vol. 4, 249) and *Mülteka* (vol. 3, 225), private inquiry was common at the time these works were composed (the fifteenth and sixteenth centuries, respectively) because public inquiry might generate hostility between potential witnesses and those who informed the kadı about their reputations. It might be the case that these texts simply adopted this explanation from earlier sources.

It is not clear from judicial sources exactly how investigations were supposed to proceed or what questions might have been asked those from whom information was requested about the witnesses. As stated, Article 1705 defines an acceptable witness as an upright person, "whose good deeds are more pronounced than his or her bad deeds." The witness is also expected to be someone "who habitually behaves" in a manner consistent with honor and dignity. These criteria are vague. *Hidaye* (vol. 3, 214–17), *Dürer* (vol. 4, 263–5), and *Mülteka* (vol. 3, 231–6) reflect a similar vagueness in relation to witness qualities as well. On the one hand, these sources disqualify potential witnesses who gamble, play backgammon, play with pigeons, expose themselves in public baths, or sing and play musical instruments, because these activities amount to *fisk*.[21] On the other hand, they acknowledge that *fisk* in itself does not necessarily make witness testimony inadmissible. For example *Hidaye* (vol. 3, 207–8) states that a testimony given by an immoral person (*fasık*) should be considered legitimate if it is accepted by the kadı. *Dürer* (vol. 4, 248) not only makes the same point, but also develops a legal argument explaining why *fisk* should not automatically disqualify witnessing: "Justice (*adalet*) is required for a [legal] action based on witnessing. It is not a requirement for being qualified as a witness. An immoral person (*fasık*) is qualified for guardianship, kadıship, rulership, and imamate. We believe that such a person is also qualified to be a witness."[22]

[21] Redhouse's *A Turkish and English Lexicon*, 2nd ed., defines *fisk* as "sin, immorality"; 1384. Devellioğlu's *Osmanlıca Türkçe Ansiklopedik Lugat* defines it as "1. Being separated from the way of God; rebellion against God. 2. Debauchery. 3. Treachery. 4. Separation form religion; immorality"; 265.

[22] "*Adalet, şahadet ile amelin vacib olmasında şarttır. Şahadete ehliyyet için şart değildir. Çünkü fasık velayet, kaza, saltanat, imamlık için ehldir. Bize göre şahadete de ehldir*" (*Dürer* vol. 4, 248). However, Molla Hüsrev also makes clear in the same place that

There is also little in the court records about the *tezkiye* process, and they do not contain the names of rejected witnesses. Of course, this does not mean that such disqualifications did not happen or happen often. The *Mecelle* (385) states that if the reputation of a witness was challenged in the process of examination, the kadı should simply ask the party who assumed the proof responsibility to supply an alternative one, without making any public pronunciation about the rejected witness or the reason(s) for which the latter was disqualified. This might be one reason that we do not observe in court records a *tezkiye* process that led to the rejection of a witness.

It is also likely that the litigants against whom witnesses were testifying had little say in choosing the individuals at whom the inquiries were directed. In fact, other than what is described in Article 1717 (384), our sources provide no information on how these people were to be chosen. Nevertheless, Article 1723 of the *Mecelle* (386) states that "if the justice of the witnesses has been demonstrated in relation to one particular case, the judge does not need to inquire into the credibility of the same witnesses within six months. If more than six months have passed since the first testimony, however, the judge must again conduct an inquiry."

In Kastamonu, those who participated in *tezkiye* inquiries may have been forthcoming with the court because they wanted to protect their own reputations or uphold the integrity of the legal process. However, it is also possible that the integrity of the investigation was disregarded or its procedures partially or completely overlooked, short-circuited, or manipulated. We do not know the social consequences of publicly challenging the reputation of a potential witness or of declining to confirm his or her trustworthiness, although both *Hidaye* (vol. 3, 209) and *Dürer* (vol. 4, 249) acknowledge that this might generate tensions within the community. We do not even know what, precisely, the term *'adl* (just/upright) might have meant in various local contexts when used to describe an individual.[23]

according to the prevalent opinion among jurists, testimonies given by immoral persons should not be accepted (ibid.). Peters (1997, 297) argues that "(a)ccording to the Hanafis, unbecoming behavior (such as playing backgammon, eating or urinating in public) does not affect the status of being *'adl* (that is suitable to act as a witness) but may cause the qadi to reject someone's testimony." *Mülteka* (vol. 3, 195) suggests that although the testimony of a *fasık* is admissible in principle, it is better not to accept it.

23 The official correspondence between the imperial center and the court of Kastamonu contains regular references to false witnessing (*şahid-i zur/zor*), sometimes due to the complicity of local kadıs or their deputies (*naibs*). See, for example, the entries of 11 Şevval 1155/ December 9, 1742; 27 Receb 1156/ September 16, 1743; and 8 Ramazan

According to *Hidaye* (vol. 3, 232–3) and *Mülteka* (vol. 3, 248), jurists disagreed about how to punish false witnesses. Although Hanafi jurists Abu Yusuf and Imam Muhammad Shaybani suggested that false witnesses should be publicly shamed and beaten, Abu Hanifa and Shafi'i prescribed shaming the offenders but no corporal punishment (*Hidaye*, vol. 3, 232–3). The latter course is based on the assumption that false witnessing is often revealed by the confession of the perpetrator, which is why a threat of physical punishment would discourage those who might otherwise be inclined to confess.

Written Documents as Evidence?

While the Ottoman Civil Code contains two sections on written documents and their use in legal processes, there are no comparable sections in *Hidaye, Dürer*, and *Mülteka*, which contain merely brief, passing comments on the topic, indicative of the code's modern mind-set. In the section titled "On Written Evidence," the *Mecelle* provides four articles on the use and status of written documents in court processes (390). The first one (Article 1736) states that "(n)o action may be taken on writing and seal alone. If writing and seal are free from any taint of fraud or forgery (*şüphe-i tezvir ve tasni*), however, they become valid grounds for action (*ma'mulun bih*), that is, bases for judgment (*medar-i hüküm*). If that is the case, no other type of substantiation is required (*başka veçhile sübuta gerek kalmaz*)." The next two articles specify what types of documents should be considered reliable:

> Article 1737: Sultan's orders and entries in imperial registers, if not tinted by fraud, are grounds for [legal] action (*ma'mulun bih*).
>
> Article 1738: The court records, if kept free from acts of deception or corruption, in ways described in the Book of Judicial Administration [in the *Mecelle*], are also grounds for legal action.[24]

1156 / October 26, 1743 in KCR vol. 40. For references to false witnessing in accounts by Western observers of Ottoman justice, see Ergene (2003, chapter 6). For references to false witnessing in the court of eighteenth-century Bursa, see Düzbakar (2009).

[24] We did not find any instructions in the "Book of Judicial Administration" about how to keep the court archives free from "deception and corruption." However, it is possible that the authorities who prepared this code had in mind the "Instructions on the Sharia Court Registers and the Journals for Recording Cases" (Sicillat-ı Şer'iyye ve Zabt-ı Deavi Cerideleri Hakkında Talimat) that was promulgated in 1874 (*Düstur*[1] vol. 4, 83–5). According to this edict, the pages of court registers should be numbered, presumably to determine later whether any pages had been removed or torn off. Also, the documents issued by the court to individual parties should be copied in court registers, and the scribe

Dürer (vol. 4, 252) appears to be reticent to trust the court's archive: "The kadı may not pronounce a judgment based on written records [in the *sicil*s] alone, unless he remembers the relevant testimonies or admissions." It is important here to note that none of the legal texts use the term "evidence," or *beyyine*, when discussing even the most reliable forms of documentation. This term is used specifically to refer to witness testimony.[25] According to *Hidaye* (vol. 3, 182–4), letters containing witness testimonies sent by one kadı to another, although often necessary, are legally consequential only if their origin and content is validated by witnesses to original proceeding. This is because "[one's] handwriting often look like other handwritings, which is why they should be authenticated by evidence," meaning witness testimony (*Hidaye* vol. 3, 183; also see *Mülteka* vol.3, 204–5).[26] Similarly, Article 1739 of the *Mecelle* (390) seems to suggest that no type of documentation in private hands, whether officially produced or not, can be considered on its own as proper grounds for legal judgment. The article states that "no legal action may be taken based on deeds of pious endowments (*vakfiyye*). [However,] if *vakfiyye*s are registered in court's archives that are free from taint, [then] they may be considered as grounds for legal action." One would think that what is true for *vakfiyye*s in private hands must also be true for other types of privately owned documents.

Historians and legal scholars have generally acknowledged the inadequacies of written documents as evidence and consider this to be a characteristic of premodern Islamic legal practice. According to Tyan (1965a, 171), "writing in itself has no evidential value; it is a valid mode of proof only in

who does the copying should be identified both in the registers and on the original documents. In addition, court records should contain no erasures or "scratch-outs," and nothing should be added subsequently between the lines in a particular entry. If such additions are made, the kadı should confirm their accuracy with his seal. Furthermore, the space between individual entries should not be excessive. When the tenure of a judge comes to an end, he should seal the court registers with his personal seal. And whenever these records are not in his possession, they should be kept in a locked and sealed trunk at the courthouse.

25 This being said, the term "*hüccet*," often used in relation to written documentation, could mean "a document constituting proof" according to Brunschvig (1960, 1150), instead of simply "document"; cf. Meshal (2014, Chapter 4).

26 This is what Wael Hallaq (1999, 451) has stated on the topic in his study on the genre of *kitāb al-qādi ilā al-qādi* or the "modalities" of written communications between kadıs: "The Shāfi'ites insist that the legitimacy of the *kitāb* rests upon the two witnesses who attest to the authenticity of the document. Without them the document has no value, but without the document their testimony remains valid ... Generally speaking, this is the position of all the schools, to the exception of the later Mālikites." Baber Johansen agrees with this opinion (1997, 374).

so far as it is orally confirmed by duly qualified witnesses." Also, Peters (1997, 298) suggests that "since under Islamic law documentary evidence is not admitted, the deed itself does not furnish proof, but, in cases of litigation, the testimonies given in court by the witnesses who have signed the deed." Finally, Brunschvig (1960, 1150) observes that in classical Islamic law, "it was only in so far as written evidence could be construed as a *Zeugenurkunde* (cf. the *testatio* of Roman law) that it became generally and more widely accepted, though not without keen discussion, reservations, and precautions, even in the case of notarial acts."[27]

However, the *Mecelle* also demonstrates in one section an atypical attitude compared to those found in premodern interpretations toward at least one type of a document. In the section titled "On Written Admissions," Article 1606 (346) states that "a written admission (*kitabetle ya'ni yazı ile ikrar*) is the same as an oral admission (*lisan ile ikrar*)." Articles 1608 and 1609 explain what types of documents may count as a written admission. The first article states that "a merchant's entries in his books, if properly kept, are also like written admissions" (ibid.). According to the second one, "if a person writes or has a clerk prepare a debt certificate (*deyn senedi*) that contains the person's sign or seal . . . that certificate would constitute an admission in writing and have the same force as oral admission" (347). The same article also includes receipts (*makbuz ilmuhaberleri*) in the same status (ibid.).

As discussed, an admission (*ikrar*) could bring a trial to an immediate conclusion. Given the consequence of such an action, the weight that the Ottoman Civil Code accords written admissions is not entirely consistent with the contents of the later section titled "On Written Documents." Based on what we have already seen in this section, we should expect a confirmation of the contents of these documents by witness testimony. But, as Articles 1610, 1611, and 1612 demonstrate, this is not the case (*Mecelle*, 347–8).

Article 1610: Assume that a person prepares or makes another person prepare a debt certificate that contains the former's signature or seal. If this person first admits ownership of the certificate and then denies the debt contained therein, the denial is

[27] *Zeugenurkunde* and *testatio* refer to documents that contain witness statements. See Johansen (1997) for a fascinating discussion of differing temporal and regional attitudes towards written documents (as evidentiary tools) within Sunni jurisprudential traditions. In this study, Johansen contrasts more accommodating opinions developed in Transoxiana between the tenth and twelfth centuries and more restrictive ones that remained popular in Syria and Egypt until the nineteenth century. For a critical engagement of Johansen's ideas on the status of written documents in the Ottoman context, see Ergene (2004). Also see Hallaq (1995, 1999) for another nuanced perspective on the topic.

disregarded, and the person is expected to pay the debt. If ownership of the certificate is denied, but the handwriting or seal in the certificate is well-known to belong to the person, the denial is disregarded … If the handwriting or seal in the certificate is not recognized, the person is asked to provide handwriting specimens to be submitted to experts. If they report that both scripts belong to the same person, that person is ordered to pay the debt. If the certificate is free from any taint of fraud or forgery, action will be taken in accordance with it. If it is not free from suspicion, however, and should the debtor deny the debt, the debtor shall, if the plaintiff so demands, be made to swear an oath denying both the debt and the acknowledgement.

Article 1611: If a person dies after giving another person a debt certificate and if the person's heirs acknowledge the validity of the certificate, they should pay the debt from the deceased's estate. If the heirs deny that the certificate belongs to the deceased, and should the latter's handwriting or seal in the certificate be well-known, action shall be taken in accordance with the certificate [that is, the debt should be paid from the estate].

Article 1612: If a purse of money is found in the estate of a deceased person and if it is written on the purse that it belongs to another person … the latter has the right to claim the purse from the estate of the deceased; there is no need for any further proof.

Contrary to what the Code states in Article 1736 (above), these articles call for legal action based on the signature or seal alone, at least when these are recognized to belong to the owner of the document. The concern that Merginani had put forward earlier ("handwritings look like handwritings") seems to have given way in this section of the *Mecelle* to a recognition of the intrinsic, independent authority of the document. Indeed, *Dürer*'s (vol. 4, 226) treatment of the same topic is also different: "To order an admission to be recorded is admission."[28] Unlike in the *Mecelle*, the written document does not amount to admission in *Dürer*. It is the *order* to record the admission that is consequential. And *Dürer* does not attribute any special power to the written document to demonstrate whether such an order was given or not. Moreover, there is no reference in *Dürer* to any handwriting or seal as the arbiter of truth. On the contrary, and in line with premodern Islamic legal conventions, the testimony of the clerk who receives the order is recognized as the medium that confirms the order.[29]

[28] This is how this statement is explained in the version that we have used in this study (*Dürer* vol. 4, 226–7): "If a person ('one who admits' or *mukır*) orders another person to write down that the former possesses one thousand *akçe*s of a third party, that order would amount to an admission. The testimony of the person who receives the order from the first person to the admission of the latter would be legal (*helal*). If a person orders a clerk to record that a certain house was sold, whether a certificate is produced or not, that order would amount to an admission. If a party orders a clerk to record that he divorced his wife, whether recorded or not, his wife is divorced."

[29] The apparent inconsistency in the attitudes towards written documents in two separate sections of the *Mecelle* could be a consequence of the limited attempts in the Ottoman

Kastamonu court records confirm the tenuous position of written documents in evidentiary processes (Ergene 2004, 2005). According to Ergene, although litigants occasionally brought written documentation (deeds, receipts, vouchers, legal certificates, and the like) to trials, in almost no case did written documents play any evidentiary role. Often, the existence of these documents is mentioned in the initial phase of the litigation, when the litigants stated their claims and counter-claims. But after the kadı assigned the proof responsibility and requested evidence, documents only rarely factored in the process; cases were usually decided based almost exclusively on the availability of witnesses and their testimonies. Here is an example:

Example 8: Written document in trial

It was legally determined that the estate of the late Esseyyid Mehmed Çelebi of the Albarslan village in Kastamonu should be divided among his wives, Fatma bint Ahmed and Aişe bint Hasan, and adult sons, Esseyyid Mehmed, Esseyyid Mustafa, and Esseyyid İbrahim. Subsequently, the aforementioned Esseyyid Mehmed Beşe accused Şaban Beğzade Mehmed Ağa as follows: "This Mehmed Ağa illegally sold a house that belonged to my father to another person and collected its price. This is a two-storey, single-entry house in good condition. It is located in the Frenkşah quarter and surrounded by Esseyyid Ali Çelebi's property on one side, Şatır [zade] property on one side, and public road on two sides. When I demand my share from the price of the house, he refuses to pay me. I would like him to be questioned."

When questioned, Mehmed Ağa responded as follows: "Indeed, the said house belonged to the plaintiff's father, the late Esseyyid Mehmed Çelebi. However, in the beginning (*evail*) of CII in 1126

judicial system to modernize while retaining some of the most rooted judicial tendencies in Hanafi jurisprudence and legal traditions. Cf. Tyan (1965a, 172), where the author states that "in the final stage of Islamic law in the Ottoman Empire, as represented by the code known as *Mecelle-i ahkam-i ʿadliyye*, ... the old system of daʿwa [litigation] was reformed in a number of particulars, notably the by the recognition of the intrinsic probative value of writing (art. 1736)." While we agree with the author that the *Mecelle* displays a new attitude towards written documentation, we believe that this is evident not in Article 1736, but in Articles 1606 to 1612, as argued above.

Example 8: (cont.)

[14–23 June 1714], the late Esseyyid Mehmed Çelebi gave (*hibe*) the said house to his wife Fatma bint Ahmed, who is my paternal aunt (خالة). Subsequently, Fatma gifted it to me and I sold it to someone else." With these words, Mehmed Ağa submitted to court a legal certificate (*hüccet-i şer'iyye*) that stated that the house was a gifted property of Fatma.

When the plaintiff denied the rebuttal (*def'*) and the contents of the certificate, the court demanded that Mehmed Ağa prove their truthfulness, subsequent to which Mehmed Ağa presented to court two trustworthy Muslims, Ahmed Ağa bin Mustafa Ağa and Hüseyin bin Ali, who testified as follows: "Indeed, in the first ten days (*evail*) of Cemaziyelahir in 1126, the late Esseyyid Mehmed Çelebi, the father of the plaintiff, gifted to Fatma in our presence the two-storey, single-entrance house in good condition, which is located in the Frenksah quarter and surrounded by Esseyyid Ali Çelebi's property on one side, Şatır[zade] property on one side, and public road on two sides. After Fatma accepted the gift, a receipt was prepared by the judge of Kastamonu at that time, Mehmed Efendi. Subsequently, Fatma gifted the house to her nephew, the defendant Mehmed Ağa. We are witnesses to these events and transactions and testify thus."

After the testimonies of witnesses were accepted, the court instructed Esseyyid Mehmed Beşe to cease his contentions. Recorded as requested.

22 Şaban 1152 / 24 November 1739 (KCR vol. 38).

Witnesses . . .

Note in the above example that the defendant's certificate, rather than functioning to corroborate his rebuttal, is presented and treated as a component of his counter-claim and subjected to verification by witness testimony. We noted in Chapter 3 that the notarial functions of the court gained importance during the eighteenth century. While this development may be indicative of a growing concern with documentation via court-produced or -approved written records, our sources force us to take a nuanced position on the ways in which they were used in legal processes. If documents were commonly treated in the way exemplified above (example 8), why did litigants take the trouble of obtaining and bringing them to court? It is possible that documents, which contained the details of past transactions and the names of the witnesses to them, were often used as a memory aid (Ergene 2004, 2005). In the example above, the legal certificate appears to have been used precisely in this way. The term "*evail*," referring to the first ten days of the month, which sounds awkward in an oral statement, is in fact a technical term commonly used in dating the legal documents. The fact that it was used in the defendant's oral statement and in witness testimonies might mean that it functioned as a "cheat sheet" when the above entry was composed. It is also likely that the witnesses who testified on behalf of the defendant were identified and brought to court because their names appeared on the certificate as witnesses to the original transaction that had taken place more twenty years before, a possibility we raised in Chapter 3 when we discussed the strategic importance of *şuhudülhal* choice for possible future contentions. Finally, and as is evident in the case entry, documents might have been useful in identifying the exact dates of initial transactions and describing the original conditions and precise locations of properties subject to dispute after a long period of time.

The court records sometimes provide clues as to why written documents may have been deemed unreliable as evidentiary tools. For example, in a case entry dated 15 Şevval 1104 (19 June 1693, KCR vol. 5), we find a *vakıf* manager (*mütevelli*) testifying in a trial over land possession, against a litigant who had submitted to court a receipt bearing the manager's seal. The manager testified that the receipt was a fake and the seal used to prepare to receipt had been taken from him by force. This being said, there was at least one type of document, copies of imperial registers (*suret-i defter-i hakani*), that served evidentiary purposes without any support from witness testimony (for example, entry of *evail* CI 1104 / 8–17 January 1693; KCR vol. 5). Very rare in Kastamonu *sicil*s, these instances are consistent with Article 1737 of the *Mecelle* (quoted earlier).

Ergene (2005) has noted that the court's own archive did not serve an evidentiary function on a regular basis.[30] For example, there is no indication in the above example (entry of *evail* CI 1104 / 8–17 January 1693; KCR vol. 5) that the court consulted its own archive when the plaintiff questioned the legal certificate's authenticity.[31] While we cannot be sure why this was the case, it is possible that the court records of Kastamonu

[30] On the non-evidentiary purposes that the court's archive might have served see Ergene (2004, 2005) and Hallaq (1998, 424–30).

[31] In only one case, the court relied on *kassam* registers, which contained the estate inventories of government functionaries, to resolve a dispute on inheritance shares (entry of 17 CI 1153 / 25 July 1740 in KCR vol. 38). We do not know whether separate *kassam* registers for Kastamonu exist.

were not considered particularly reliable, perhaps because they were vulnerable to contamination or erroneous recording due to carelessness on the part of the scribes.[32] Indeed, the *sicil*s that we are familiar with are filled with changes, partially or completely crossed-out entries, notes in the margins, and displaced pages. Given the large number of individuals who had authorized or de facto access to the court records, it is nearly impossible to surmise who made these alterations or if the changes were even lawful. Hence, it is not surprising that the court archives did not play any evidentiary role. Furthermore, if the kadı was not supposed to trust the court's archives if he could not remember the processes that generated them, as *Dürer* suggested, he could not possibly have used the records produced under his predecessors (cf. Johansen 1997, 349–52, 374).[33]

Even though written documents did not function as evidence, there are reasons to suspect that they affected trial results. The best documents provided detailed information about and articulate formulations of complex issues relevant to disputes, potentially bolstering litigants' statements. In addition, while documents may not have functioned as evidence, they represented the *promise* of evidence, as they contained the names of witnesses who could support specific claims or counter-claims. Thus, it is possible that they affected litigant strategies and/or influenced the kadı's disposition toward opposing parties' claims to truth. At the very least, we should expect a direct association between document use and litigant sources, sophistication, and competency in the court room. We explore in subsequent chapters how document use impacted litigation results in the court of Kastamonu.

However, it is also likely that the impact of written documents was felt most outside of the courtroom. As a "promise" of evidence, a document may have protected its bearer, at minimum cost, against the possibility that a given conflict would escalate to formal litigation. In an age of economic growth, if this indeed took place in Kastamonu, those who could afford it must have taken advantage of the insurance that written

[32] Our discussion of two registries (Examples 10 and 11) pertaining to client representation in legal processes (below), exemplify such errors in the court records. Feriha Karadeniz reports frequent complaints from all over Anatolia about Ottoman judges who allegedly made illegal additions on or "erased" entries from the *sicil*s, prepared false documents, and forged seals (1996, 46, 47, 71).

[33] This does not mean that the court's archives were of no use to judicial authorities. It is possible that the *sicil*s provided them with a basic understanding of earlier disputes and transactions, and also helped them identify and then locate socially and judicially acceptable information sources – witnesses, mainly – about the cases brought to court.

documents provided in order to protect their interests from possible legal challenge. Thus, the growing notarial responsibilities of the court might have undermined its litigative functions in our period.

Oath in Evidentiary Processes

The *Mecelle* (391) considers oath and the refusal to take oath (*yeminden nükul*) among reasons for legal judgment (*esbab-ı hüküm*). Again, the term *beyyine* is not used with reference to oath or the refusal to take one. In fact, the distinction between the two terms is explicit in the title of the relevant section in the *Mecelle* (373): "The Book of Evidence (*Beyyinat*) and Administration of Oaths (*Tahlif*)." The ontological difference between evidence and oath is also clear in the famous prophetic tradition (*hadith*) that associates the former with making a claim that challenges existing circumstances, and oath with denying this claim and maintaining the status quo.[34] *Dürer* (vol. 4, 158) explains that the word *beyyine* is related to the word *beyan* or "declaration." It also states that "evidence is the most certain indication. By it, truth can be distinguished from untruth" (*Beyyine delalet-i vazıhadır. Hak, batıldan … onunla ayırd edilir*). Oath, however, is not considered a direct, clear sign of truth. It is, rather, a logical deduction, based on a specific assumption regarding the proper priorities in life for a Muslim. That assumption is that a false oath, a major sin, means for a Muslim to sacrifice his or her eternal afterlife, which is much more serious and consequential than sacrificing the material possessions subject to a dispute by refusing to swear such an oath (*Dürer* vol. 4, 159).

As is evident in the case entries provided earlier, an oath is proposed by the party who assumes the proof responsibility in litigation, but fails to provide evidence (*Mecelle*, 391–2).[35] The *Mecelle* (392) prescribes that the oath should be taken formally, in the presence of the judge, and should mention the name of Allah (by saying "by Allah," for example).[36] If an

[34] This hadith is related both in the *Hidaye* (vol. 3, 277–9) and *Dürer* (vol. 4, 158–61). Accordingly, when a man approached the Prophet to make a claim against another man who possessed a field that the former claimed belonged to him, the Prophet responded by asking if he had evidence (*beyyine*). When the man said he did not, the Prophet instructed him to ask his opponent to take an oath.

[35] See note 8 in the present chapter.

[36] *Hidaye* (vol. 3, 284–5), *Dürer* (vol. 4, 167–8), and *Mülteka* (vol. 3, 277) provide more detail about the variations in the manner in which oaths could be administered. For example, we learn from these sources that jurists disagreed whether to place conditions on oaths, such as the automatic divorce of individuals who swore false oaths.

oath is sworn at the request of an opponent, but before the judge formally asks for it, it is not acceptable (*Mecelle*, 393). The wording of the oath should be different for Jews, Christians, and Zoroastrians.[37]

The *Mecelle* contains a number of articles regarding different types of oath, their suitability for different situations, and how litigants should swear them. For example, Article 1748 (393) states that an oath concerning an individual's own action must be phrased categorically, indicating whether the matter is so or is not so. However, an oath sworn in relation to another person's action might testify to the oath-taker's lack of knowledge about it. According to Article 1749 (ibid.), "an oath can be sworn on a cause (*sebeb*) or effect/result (*hasıl*). Swearing an oath that a certain thing has or has not happened is an oath on cause. An oath to argue that a thing or process is still valid or continuing is an oath to an effect." *Hidaye* (vol. 3, 285–6) indicates that these two types of oaths would be appropriate in different types of disputes. For example, in a dispute involving a transaction, an oath on a valid and still effective contract is more appropriate than an oath on whether such a contract had ever been arranged (which might have been later dissolved). A contract from the past is not necessarily still binding. A litigant's silence in response to the judge's request to take an oath is considered a refusal, which is a basis for the kadı's judgment (*Mecelle*, 394). A mute may take an oath or refuse to do so by use of generally recognized signs (ibid.).

In some cases the administration of oath is not allowed. For example, in certain kinds of disputes related to marriage, divorce, marital annulment, manumission, or parental lineage (*neseb*), those who deny the claims against them should not be administered oaths. Similarly, in litigations involving *hadd* crimes oaths should not be administered (*Mecelle*, 392; *Dürer* vol. 4, 161–6; *Mülteka* vol. 3, 276–7).

Before we proceed, we should mention that *karine* (translated by some as "circumstantial evidence") is another basis that could technically produce judgments by the kadı. For example, the smell of alcohol on the breath or the obvious pregnancy of an unmarried woman might trigger punishments. This said, detailed information on *karine* is lacking in jurisprudential sources (Derin 2010, 164–6). Also, judgments based on *karine* not documented through witness testimony do not exist in the

[37] The wordings suggested for oaths administered to the members of these groups should include the following phrases as appropriate: "I swear by God who revealed the Torah to Moses," "the New Testament to Jesus," and "by God who created the fire" (*Hidaye* vol. 3, 284–5; *Mülteka* vol. 3, 277).

litigations we examined in Kastamonu court records. For these reasons, we have excluded *karine* from the forthcoming analysis.[38]

Quantitative Information Found in Court Records

Table 8.1 demonstrates how litigant groups in Kastamonu used various evidentiary and adjudicative tools during litigation. As explained in the preceding section, litigants won trials by submitting witness testimony, by opponents' inability to prove their allegations (almost always followed by an oath), and by opponents' admissions. They lost cases when they were unable to substantiate their cases with witness testimony (again, almost always followed by the opponent's oath), when they admitted the truthfulness of the opponents' allegations, and when they declined to take an oath when urged to do so subsequent to their opponents' failure to submit credible evidence.

In litigations that involved single plaintiffs and defendants, about 29 percent of the litigants used witness testimony, which indicates that about 58 percent of these trials were resolved by witness testimony. Another 16 percent of the trials were decided on the basis of the opponent's inability to submit evidence. A vast majority of these trials also involved oaths administrated to litigants whose opponents failed to provide credible evidence. About 12 percent of the trials were ended by opponents' admission, and another 2 percent by litigants' refusal to swear an oath.

The relatively high rates that we observe for witness testimony among religious titleholders (elite and non-elite), pilgrims, and *zade*s indicates that they assumed the burden of proof more often than other groups, a topic that we explore in detail in subsequent chapters. What is revealing in the Table is the high "inability to provide evidence" (*ityan-ı beyyineden ʻacz*) rates observed among women, titleless men, individuals with no religious status, and non-Muslims. This figure represents the frequency of failure by these groups to substantiate their claims when they assumed the proof responsibility. Thus, it might be seen as a measure of their relative preparedness for trials or litigious competency compared to other groups. Another interesting observation is the relatively high rates

[38] The kadı could also decide a case based on personal knowledge or information reported to him by representatives sent to inspect (*keşif*) a location associated with a dispute. Alternatively, he could base his decision on the opinions of experts (*ehl-i vukuf*) in disputes that required specialized knowledge, such as medicine or architecture (Demir 2010, 172–7). Although occasional references to inspection or expert opinion exist in our sources, in no instance did either of them constitute a basis for judgment.

TABLE 8.1: *Court Clients and Adjudicative Tools*

Litigants	Total	Witness Testimony	Inability to Prove (Followed by Opponent's Oath)	Refusal of Oath (After Opponent's Inability to Prove)	Admission	Opponent's Admission	Document Use
Single	1413	405 (29)	112 (8)	10 (1)	90 (6)	91 (6)	96 (7)
Multiple	272	71 (26)	17 (6)	0 (0)	12 (4)	13 (4)	21 (8)
Corporate bodies	33	10 (30)	2 (6)	0 (0)	4 (12)	5 (15)	4 (12)
Women	282	81 (29)	32 (11)	0 (0)	13 (5)	17 (6)	15 (5)
Elite Religious	55	20 (36)	3 (6)	1 (2)	3 (6)	9 (16)	10 (18)
Non-elite Religious	111	44 (40)	5 (5)	0 (0)	7 (6)	6 (5)	10 (9)
Elite Military	94	27 (29)	4 (4)	0 (0)	5 (5)	7 (7)	11 (12)
Non-elite Military	203	63 (31)	14 (7)	5 (3)	18 (9)	11 (5)	12 (6)
No Title	435	103 (24)	42 (10)	2 (0)	29 (7)	26 (6)	21 (5)
Pilgrim	94	36 (38)	7 (7)	1 (1)	2 (2)	9 (10)	9 (10)
Desc. of Muh.	103	30 (29)	7 (7)	1 (1)	5 (5)	13 (13)	13 (13)
No Religious Status	952	264 (28)	82 (9)	6 (1)	66 (7)	54 (6)	58 (6)
Non-Muslim	31	9 (29)	4 (13)	0 (0)	1 (3)	0 (0)	1 (3)
Prominent	38	15 (40)	0 (0)	0 (0)	1 (3)	6 (16)	8 (21)
Non-prominent	1142	332 (29)	104 (9)	8 (1)	75 (7)	70 (6)	72 (6)

Note: Figures on litigant categories (last 12 rows) are based on trials (590) that involved individual plaintiffs and defendants. Figures in parentheses are percentage values. Percentages may not add up to 100% due to overlaps in the use various evidentiary and adjudicative tools.

observed for "opponent's admission" for *zade*s, elite religious titleholders, descendants of Muhammad, and corporate litigants.

Document use, it seems, was relatively popular among members of prominent families, elite titleholders, descendants of Muhammad, and corporate litigants. It would be interesting to know the extent to which this situation is related to higher literacy rates among these groups, their strategic preferences in adjudicative processes, or the types of disputes in which they became involved.

FETVA AND REPRESENTATION AS ADJUDICATIVE TOOLS

In this final section of the chapter we focus on two adjudicative tools: *fetva*s, and representation by third parties. Unlike witness testimony, oath-taking, or written documents, these did not serve as bases for judgment. Nevertheless, they were very much part of the litigations in Kastamonu and may have influenced trial results in indirect ways. This is a topic that we explore in subsequent chapters. Before we do so, however, we discuss how *fetva*s and representation factored in litigations.

Fetva Use

The term *fetva* refers to an "opinion on a point of law, the term 'law' applying, in Islam, to all civil and religious matters" (Tyan 1965b, 806). Such opinions could technically involve innovative interpretations of specific aspects of legal theory or practice: for example, the *fetva*s issued by the great Ottoman *şeyhülislam*, or chief *müfti*, Ebussuud Efendi on taxation and land ownership in the sixteenth century. In provincial settings, however, they were more often issued by local *müfti*s (jurisconsults) and contained simple reports of preferred judicial opinion on specific legal problems (Heyd 1969, 53–4), sometimes with reference to well-known *fetva* compilations (for example, Fetava-yı Kadıhan or Fetava-yı Tatarhaniyye). In eighteenth-century Kastamonu, *müfti*s were usually members of locally influential families, who possessed religious-legal credentials and enjoyed respect for their piety and other personal qualities. In provincial settings, retired kadıs often served in this capacity (ibid.).[39]

[39] We have identified the estate inventories of four *müfti*s in Kastamonu court records, which belonged to İbrahim, Hüseyin, Numan, and Elhac Mustafa *Efendi*s. The inventories indicate that these were relatively wealthy individuals. The net value of their estates ranged between, approximately, 560 and 1,800 *guruş* in 1713 prices, with the average hovering around 1,060 *guruş* (std. dev. = 530 *guruş*).

The *fetva* included an abstract formulation of a legal question – that is, with no reference to specific incidents or individuals. This question was followed by the *müfti*'s answer, which could range from a brief "Yes" or "No" to a lengthy discussion of the issue at hand and evaluation of different approaches. True, in many cases the object of the person who directed this question to the *müfti* was to simulate a dispute at trial and obtain a favorable legal opinion. Yet the *fetva* was not supposed to be a ruling on an actual case, but, rather, an opinion in response to how the person who sought the *fetva* represented the question from his or her point of view. The *fetva* also did not assess the accuracy or evidentiary merits of various claims made by opposing parties. For these reasons, the *fetva* was not legally binding and did not require the kadı to decide a case one way or another.[40] The *müfti*'s opinion was based on a hypothetical question and it was meant to be informative.

Example 9: *Fetva* use in litigations

Çakıroğlu Mustafa Beşe bin İbrahim of the Arız quarter accused Mehmed bin Elhac Mehmed of the Ak Mescid quarter as follows: "Mehmed refuses to surrender my share in a house located in Ak Mescid quarter. This share belonged to my father's mother, Hadice, and, after her, to my father, İbrahim. I would like the court to question Mehmed and order him to hand over my share."

When questioned, Mehmed denied Mustafa Beşe's allegation: "I do not recognize that Mustafa Beşe owns any share in the aforementioned house. Furthermore, I have been occupying this house for more than thirty years. According to the noble *fetva* in my possession, those disputes that are brought to court fifteen years after they took place should be considered invalid." With these words he submitted to the court the aforementioned *fetva*.

Subsequently, *imam* Mustafa Halife, *müezzin* Hüseyin Çelebi, Ali Hocazade Elhac Ahmed Çelebi and some other inhabitants of the Ak Mescid quarter declared that Mehmed had been occupying the house for more than thirty years and that during this period neither Mustafa Beşe nor his father, İbrahim, made any claims against him. Since jurists agree that disputes that have not been

[40] *Fetvas* by *şehülislams* may be exceptions (Demir 2010, 30).

Example 9: (cont.)

brought to court for fifteen years or more should be considered invalid, the court ordered the plaintiff not to intrude in the affairs of Mehmed. Recorded as requested.

Entry of 20 Rebiyülevvel 1149 / 28 August 1736 (KCR vol. 35). Witnesses . . .

In some court entries, *fetva*s are quoted verbatim, the names of the *müfti*s who issued them are given, and their sources are cited. For example, when the heirs of the late Kalyoncu Ali Beşe sued the inhabitants of Kırk Çeşme quarter over Ali Beşe's blood money (*dem-i diyet*) because the latter had been killed within the boundaries of the quarter,[41] the inhabitants of Kırk Çeşme defended themselves by submitting to court a *fetva* that the *sicil* entry described as follows:

The inhabitants of Kırk Çeşme quarter submitted a *fevta* by the *müfti* of Kastamonu, İsmail Efendi, which stated the following: "If "Zeyd" [a hypothetical person] is attacked and injured in a certain location and afterwards he states that it was "Amr" [another hypothetical person] who was absent at the time of Zeyd's statement, who had attacked and injured him, and he subsequently dies because of his injuries, are the inhabitants of that location required to pay Zeyd's blood money?" The answer is given as, "Not required," It is noted in the *fetva* that a similar *fetva* may be found in the well-respected Tatarhaniyye [*fetva* collection]."

Entry of? Zilhicce 1149 / ? April-May 1737 (KCR vol. 35).

In Kastamonu, religious titleholders and pilgrims were the groups most likely to use *fetva*s in trials involving a single plaintiff and defendant. About 10 to 13 percent of litigants in these groups submitted *fetva*s to the court. Non-Muslims and military titleholders, on the other hand, were the least inclined to use *fetva*s. The proportion of litigants belonging to these groups who used *fetva*s ranges between 0 (non-Muslims and elite military titleholders) to about 3 (non-elite military titleholders) percent. The proportion in other groups (including women) varies from around 5 to 8 percent. *Fetva* use was relatively common among corporate bodies (12.5 percent) but not among smaller parties of multiple litigants (6.3 percent).

41 According to law, the blood money of those found dead in a particular location should be paid by the inhabitants of that location, if the killers cannot be found.

Representation (*Vekalet*) in Litigations

Legal texts treat *vekalet* or representation in trials as a subtopic of legal representation. According to Ronald Jennings (1975b, 149–51), representation can be "general" in the sense that it signifies full control over all legal affairs of the person represented, or "special," as when it constitutes a mandate to carry out a specific service such as selling a house or collecting a debt. A minor or a person of unsound mind is not allowed to appoint a representative in most circumstances (*Mecelle*, 303–4; *Mülteka* vol. 3, 251–2).[42] On the other hand, a representative is expected to be a person of sound mind but not necessarily an adult (*Mecelle*, 304; *Mülteka* vol. 3, 251). This being said, we have not encountered any references to a minor representative in the court records.

References to representation in litigation entries are brief and generally uninformative. For example, we find in the entry dated 24 Rebiyülevvel 1105 / 23 November 1693 (KCR vol. 5) that a "Hasan Çelebi bin Mustafa appeared in court as the representative of Alime bint Elhac Mehmed, a claim that was confirmed by Elhac Hüseyin bin Satılmış and Elhac Ali bin Hasan, who knew Alime personally." Another entry dated 26 Rebiyülevvel 1105 / 25 November 1693 (KCR vol. 5) identifies Ahmed Efendi bin Ali Efendi as the representative of Hasan Beşe bin Mehmed of Taşotalar quarter in the distant city of Edirne, in his trial against Elhac Sefer bin Ahmed of Sarraçlar quarter in Kastamonu. Ahmed Efendi's claim to representative status was confirmed in court by Mehmed Ağa bin Tayyib and Mustafa bin Turmuş.

However, the court records also contain sporadic representation contracts. Here is one example:

Example 10: Representation agreement

Fatma bint Elhac Hasan of Çay quarter in Kastamonu [*sic*] made the following statement in court, in the presence of Mahmud Ağa bin Mehmed Otabaşı: "My husband Varıcıoğlu (واريجي اوغلو) Mehmed left me without providing for any marital support (*nafaka*). He also usurped 300 *guruş* from the inherited estate of my minor son, Ebu

[42] However, a minor may authorize another person as his or her representative in those transactions or legal actions which could generate favorable consequences – for example, in order to accept gifts or alms (ibid.).

Example 10: (cont.)

Bekir, of whom I am the guardian (*vasi*). My husband currently resides in Kastamonu. I designate Mahmud Ağa to claim the aforementioned 300 *guruş* and my marital support from my husband, to collect the goods and property that he [the husband] left in trust of (*emaneten*) Esseyid Ali Çelebi bin Abdullah [*sic*] in the aforementioned location [Kastamonu], and to deliver them to me and my son Ebu Bekir. As my representative, Mahmud Ağa may sue my husband or settle with him over these matters. He also has the authority to release them from future claims by me.

Mahmud Ağa accepted the charge and promised to serve as required. Recorded as requested.

Entry of 1–10 Receb 1149 / 5–15 November 1736 (KCR vol. 35)
Witnesses:
Elhac Süleyman Efendi *el-katib*
Mehmed Efendi bin Ali Efendi
İbrahim Efendi bin Osman Efendi
Ahmed Beşe bin Mehmed
Mehmed Beşe bin Ali
and the rest (*ve gayrihim*)

It is noticeable that the representative, who does not appear to be related to Fatma, is a high-ranking military officer, although we cannot know if this was a deliberate choice on Fatma's part. The document reveals that the role of representative was limited to very specific functions, comparable to what Jennings has called "special" representation. It is, however, not clear why Mahmud Ağa agreed to serve as Fatma's representative, what made him a good choice in this regard, or whether he expected to be compensated for his service. There are also some oddities about the information presented in the entry. It is not obvious what Fatma meant when she stated that her husband left her as they both appear to have resided in Kastamonu. Such agreements of representation were more common when parties lived in distant regions or towns. Also, it is interesting that Fatma chose not to face her husband or Esseyid Ali Çelebi in court personally, although she had no qualms about appearing in court to formalize the representation agreement. Fortunately for us, the very next entry in the register provides some clues about these issues, while also demonstrating how the representative Mahmud Ağa fulfilled at least part of his responsibility.

Example 11: Representative in action

Mahmud Ağa bin Mehmed Otabaşı appeared in the court of Kastamonu as the representative of Fatma bint Elhac Hasan of Çay Müslim/Müsellem (مسلم) [*sic*] quarter in Tokat [*sic*], a claim recognized in a court-prepared legal document witnessed by Mehmed Beşe bin Ali and Ahmed Beşe bin Mehmed [names underlined in the above example], and made the following statement in the presence of Esseyid Ali Çelebi bin Esseyyid Ahmed [*sic*], a grocer (*bakkal*) in the Cibrail quarter in Kastamonu: "When Fatma relocated to Tokat from Kastamonu, she [*sic*] left some household goods and property in trust of Esseyid Ali Çelebi. As her representative, I collected this property from Esseyyid Ali Çelebi in full and released him from future claims related to this issue. There is now nothing in Esseyid Ali Çelebi's possession that belongs to Fatma."

Esseyid Ali Çelebi confirmed this statement. Recorded as requested.

28 Receb 1149 / 2 December 1736 (KCR vol. 35).

Witnesses ...

This entry reveals that Fatma lived in Tokat and not Kastamonu, possibly in a similarly named quarter (Çay vs. Çay Müslim/Müsellem),[43] and that Mahmud Ağa traveled from Tokat to Kastamonu in pursuit of Fatma's husband and Esseyid Ali Çelebi. Apparently, he brought with him a legal certificate that described his arrangement with Fatma, which ended up being recorded in the Kastamonu *sicil*, albeit with significant inaccuracies.[44] The second entry indicates that it took Mahmud Ağa twenty to thirty days to travel to Kastamonu, locate Esseyid Ali Çelebi, and make the practical and legal arrangements necessary to collect the property that Fatma claimed from him. It is, however, not clear how much this may have cost him and whether he was paid by Fatma. Unfortunately, we also do not know if Mahmud Ağa was able to locate Fatma's husband or collect what he owed to Fatma and Ebu Bekir.

43 There was in fact a Çay quarter in Kastamonu, which might have confused the court's scribe.

44 The fact that the entry in the Kastamonu *sicil* contains major errors (Fatma's location at the time, the name of Esseyid Ali Çelebi's father, and whether Fatma or her husband left property in Esseyid Ali Çelebi's trust) gives us additional reasons to suspect the reliability of the court's archive.

Judicial discussions on the topic focus largely on the nature and limits of the representatives' legal responsibilities. For example, according to the *Mecelle*, the representative is authorized to verify the accuracy of allegations made against the represented party (*Mecelle*, 318; also see *Dürer* vol. 4, 70–1). Also, representation in litigation does not amount to representation in control of the property or money subject to dispute (*Mecelle*, 318). The *Mecelle* (319) states that it is the litigant's right to dismiss his or her representative and the representative's privilege to step down from the position at a point they consider to be appropriate. Finally, apostasy or sudden development of insanity on the part of a litigant or representative are both reasons for the dissolution of the relationship between them (*Hidaye* vol. 3, 270–1; *Dürer* vol. 4, 75–6; *Mecelle*, 320).

Ronald Jennings (1975b, 168) has suggested that there was no "professional class of vekils" in seventeenth-century Kayseri, Amasya, or Karaman. Our observations are consistent with this observation. On the other hand, the judicial texts do not completely discount this possibility, a topic we return to in the next chapter.

Representation in litigations was not particularly common in Kastamonu. In litigations that involved individual plaintiffs and defendants, only about 12 percent of the litigants had representatives.[45] A slight majority of the representatives (about 52 percent) were related to the litigants they represented.[46] It was predominantly female litigants who used representatives in trials (about 62 percent of representatives).[47] Of those who represented female litigants, about 64 percent were family members or kin. A great majority of these representatives were the fathers, sons, and husbands of female litigants (cf. Jennings 1975b, 165–6).

Only 38 percent of the representatives acted as proxies for male litigants and the representation rate among male litigants is about 6 percent (54 of 898). Among male litigants, the representation rates for elite titleholders are relatively high (9 and 18 percent for religious and military, respectively), although the rate for elite military titleholders is inflated as a result of *pro-forma* litigations involving the *mütesellim* (deputy district

[45] Jennings (1975b, 165) calculated this rate respectively as 3, 8, 10, and 12 percent, in the court records of early seventeenth-century Kayseri, Amasya, Karaman, and Trabzon.

[46] According to Jennings (1975b, 165), the rates of related representatives ranged between 30 to 42 percent in early seventeenth-century Kayseri, Amasya, Karaman, and Trabzon.

[47] In litigations that involved individual litigants, about 31percent of female litigants used representatives (see Table 8.2). This rate was 33 percent in Kayseri, 37 percent in Amasya, and 53 percent in both Karaman and Trabzon in the early seventeenth century (Jennings 1975b, 164).

TABLE 8.2: *Court Clients and Representation*

Litigants	No Representative	Related Representative	Unrelated Representative
Women	194 (69)	56 (20)	32 (11)
Elite Religious	50 (91)	0 (0)	5 (9)
Non-elite Religious	104 (94)	3 (3)	4 (4)
Elite Military	77 (82)	1 (1)	16 (17)
Non-elite Military	196 (97)	3 (1)	4 (2)
No Title	417(96)	11 (3)	7 (2)
Pilgrim	89 (95)	1 (1)	4 (4)
Desc. of Muh.	91 (88)	6 (6)	6 (6)
No Religious Status	827 (87)	67 (7)	58 (6)
Non-Muslim	31 (100)	0 (0)	0 (0)
Prominent	33 (87)	0 (0)	5 (13)
Non-prominent	1005 (88)	74 (6)	63 (6)

Note: Based on litigations that involved individual plaintiffs and defendants (590). Figures in parentheses are percentage values.

governor) and the relatives of non-locals who had died while in Kastamonu and whose estates had been seized by the authorities for the public treasury. In these trials, the *mütesellim*, who was an Ağa, was almost always represented by someone in his entourage. Remarkably, of all those who represented *zade* and elite titleholder litigants in court, only one was a relative. Non-Muslims brought no representatives to court.

Table 8.3 presents the title, marker, religion, and family affiliation distribution of litigant representatives (a total of 142). What is particularly striking is the large proportion of titleholders and members of prominent families among representatives (compare to the figures provided in the bottom section of the second column [labelled "Litigations"] of Table 3.11).[48] This finding indirectly confirms the likelihood that individuals with higher socioeconomic status were sought to serve as representatives, possibly because status was a factor that influenced adjudicative processes. While titleless men are underrepresented as litigant representatives, women and non-Muslims almost never assumed this role.

[48] The large number of representatives with *Ağa* titles in the table is again partly a result of the trials against the *mütesellim* in disputes over the estates of the non-local deceased. In these occasions, relatives of the deceased arrived in Kastamonu after a period of time and sued the *mütesellim* over the seized property. There are eleven such cases in our sample and in almost all of them the *mütesellim* was represented by an *Ağa*.

TABLE 8.3: *Representative Identities*

	Representatives	
	Number of Representatives	Proportion of Representatives
Women	2	1.4
Elite Religious	12	8.5
Non-elite Religious	14	9.9
Elite Military	33	23.2
Non-elite Military	38	26.8
No Title	43	30.3
Pilgrim	10	7
Desc. of Muh.	12	8.5
No Religious Status	120	85
Non-Muslim	0	0
Prominent	11	7.7
Non-prominent	131	92.3

Note: Based on litigations that involved individual plaintiffs and defendants (590).

Corporate bodies did not utilize representatives. And it is difficult to prepare a table similar to the one presented above for trials that involved multiple plaintiffs and/or defendants. This is mainly because in many such cases plaintiffs also acted as representatives and multiple litigants often represented the plaintiff and defendant sides. Nevertheless, our observations do not indicate major differences in the ways in which representatives became involved in these cases. We have also observed in these cases that the numbers of related and unrelated representatives were very close; and the proportions of elite titleholders and *zade*s among representatives were disproportionally higher than their proportions among litigants. On the other hand, the only non-Muslim representative in our dataset (representing another non-Muslim) appeared within this group of litigations.

This chapter provided theoretical and empirical information about litigation processes, evidentiary procedures followed in court, bases of legal judgment, various tools of litigations, and how litigants utilized these tools. In the next phase of our study of litigations, we first propose a formal theoretical framework for exploring Ottoman litigations (Chapter 9) and, then, test the validity of this framework by using available information on litigations in Kastamonu (Chapter 10).

9

Economics of Litigation: What Affects Success at Trial?

INTRODUCTION

We now turn our attention to trial outcomes and examine influences on the plaintiff's chances of success at trial. This is an inherently difficult task because trials are complex settings that involve two or more parties and the plaintiff's success depends on the strategic interactions of all parties and the underlying facts and applicable laws of the dispute. To reduce the complexity of trials for analysis, we use the simple framework developed in Chapter 6 and build on it by drawing on select insights from the Law and Economics literature on trials and the historical literature on Ottoman courts.[1] Our objective, once again, is not to engage in an exhaustive review of the literature on trials but to combine selective insights for a coherent analysis of trial outcomes in an Ottoman court.

ECONOMIC INSIGHTS ON SUCCESS AT TRIAL

In their work on the selection of cases for trial, discussed in Chapter 6, Priest and Klein (1984) formulated the baseline argument that under certain conditions plaintiff win rates at trial should tend toward 50 percent as the fraction of cases that go to trial approaches zero. This is based on a simple selection effect that follows from the observation that cases that go to trial are not a random selection of all suits. Since trials are costly,

[1] The following arguments are based on Cooter and Rubinfeld (1989), Kaplow (2012), Kessler, Meites, and Miller (1996), Kessler and Rubinfeld (2007), Miceli (2009), Siegelman and Waldfogel (1999), and Spier (2007).

rational litigants would likely settle cases in which one side is likely to be a clear winner, and they would go to trial only in difficult and uncertain cases for which there is greater disagreement. As a result, the cases that go to trial would likely be "toss up" ones which are won about half the time by the plaintiff and the other half by the defendant.

Priest and Klein (1984) were careful to note that the 50 percent hypothesis is a limiting case of a tendency and that in reality the observed average success rates would likely deviate from this benchmark. In the extensive literature that has developed, researchers have examined how actual rates have varied systematically from this limiting case and tried to reconcile the selection hypothesis with observed plaintiff win rates depending on actual trial conditions.[2] In a seminal article on the topic, Shavel (1996) has argued that in cases that go to trial, any probability of plaintiff victory is possible. Starting with the limiting case of 50 percent success rate for the plaintiff, researchers have explored how the trial outcomes change when the conditions differ from those underlying the baseline model. Wittman (1985, 1988), for example, has argued that the plaintiff win rates can deviate substantially from 50 percent when parties have significantly different expectations about the trial award. Studying cases decided by a US court in the 1980s, Kessler, Meites, and Miller (1996) have similarly identified various case characteristics that explain deviations from the 50 percent rule. A key question in the Law and Economics literature on trials has been to determine the factors affecting the plaintiff's chances of winning the suit.

The 50 percent win-rate implication of the Priest and Klein argument is a useful point to start specifying the conditions that lead plaintiff's success to differ significantly from this baseline. The basic model makes three important assumptions about the litigants:

1) Parties have the same knowledge of the facts of the case and expectations about the plaintiff's chances of success. More formally, parties form independent, unbiased estimates of the plaintiff's chances of success such that they are independent random variables with the same expected value of true probability of success and identical standard errors.
2) They have symmetric stakes from trial outcome such that the outcome confers no other (negative or positive) subjective payoff to the parties than the judgment. There are no external effects on either

[2] See, for example, Eisenberg, (1990), Waldfogel (1995, 1998).

party in the form of reputation for future disputes or any other indirect personal cost or benefits.

3) Parties face the same legal uncertainty such that they have the same knowledge of the law governing the case and similar legal capability. They have the same knowledge of trial procedures, including the rules of evidence and tools of litigation, and are equally capable of presenting their case in court.

It follows from these conditions that rational litigants would settle those cases in which the plaintiff's chance deviates significantly from 50 percent, because trial is costly and parties can avoid this cost by implementing the same outcome in a settlement. It also follows under these conditions that plaintiff victories among the cases that wind up at trial will approach 50 percent. To identify the conditions causing the plaintiff win ratios to deviate significantly from 50 percent, we thus need to relax the assumptions of the hypothetical baseline case and determine how changes in these assumptions affect the win rate. More specifically, we need to examine how the plaintiff's chances of success vary when the parties have divergent expectations about their chances of success, asymmetric stakes from trial outcome, and differential ability to take advantage of trial rules and tools.

DIVERGENT EXPECTATIONS ABOUT CASE QUALITY

Consider first the divergence of expectations about the plaintiff's chances of success at trial. As noted earlier, parties may differ in their beliefs about case quality if they have asymmetric information about the facts of a dispute. This could be the case if, for example, the defendant in a criminal case had private information about incriminating evidence or the parties in a civil dispute had differential access to information regarding fault or liability.

In such trials, the selection effect would result in a higher chance of success for the more informed party. For example, suppose in a class of trials the defendants have greater ability to estimate their chances of success. This would mean that the defendants with relatively worse chances at trial would tend to settle their disputes and those with relatively good chances would likely go to trial. Consequently, the pool of defendants who go to trial rather than settle would likely consist of those with a good chance of success, resulting in a higher than 50 percent chance rate of success for them at trial.

To see how the selection effect could affect chances of success in an Ottoman court, consider the difference between elite titleholders and others in estimating the quality of their cases. Based on our knowledge and assumptions of differential access of elite titleholders and others to education, economic resources, and influential connections in Ottoman society, we would expect individuals with elite titles to have greater ability to estimate the strength of their cases because they would be more likely than others to possess pertinent knowledge about the facts of a dispute, have the means to acquire it from others, or, more generally, understand the contextual circumstances that influenced litigation processes. All else being the same, this would mean that among those litigants with low chances of success, the elite titleholders would be more likely to settle than others, resulting in a pool of litigants that includes elites who have a disproportionately higher chance of success at trial than others who chose to go to trial. As a result, facing each other in court, on average elites would be more likely than others to win at trial.

ASYMMETRIC STAKES

Consider next the role of asymmetric stakes on the plaintiff's chances of success at trial. Asymmetric stakes arise when one or both of the parties to a case derive some cost or benefit from the outcome that is not captured entirely by the amount of damages to be paid by the defendant to the plaintiff in this case. This may happen, for example, if one of the parties has higher reputational concerns about the trial outcome than the other, such as when a prominent member of a society faces a relatively unknown individual and similar litigations are possible in the future. In this case, a win for the prominent individual in the initial trial might thwart subsequent legal challenges. In situations of asymmetric stakes, we would expect parties with greater stakes to have a higher chance of success in litigation because of a selection effect that raises the proportion of strong cases that go to trial. By altering the total cost and benefit of court outcomes, asymmetric stakes make settlement more likely in otherwise "toss up" disputes. Since the party with greater stakes would have more to lose from litigation, he or she would be more likely to settle the dispute by making an acceptable offer to the party with the lesser stake than to risk a larger loss at trial. As a result, the cases that go to trial would likely be the ones in which the party with higher stakes has a greater chance for success than would be the case if the stakes were the same.

To imagine how asymmetric stakes can affect the plaintiff win ratio in Kastamonu courts, consider the difference among litigants regarding family status, which can be determined through the presence of the suffix *zade*, typically entered in court records for individuals from prominent families. All else being the same, prominent members of the society would be expected to have greater stakes in a dispute than individuals from non-prominent families because of their concern to protect their reputations, status, and/or family honor. With higher stakes at trial, individuals from prominent families would thus be more likely than others to settle a dispute than to go to court. Such a selection effect would consequently mean a higher expected chance of success for prominent individuals who choose to go to trial.

DIFFERENTIAL KNOWLEDGE ABOUT TRIAL PROCEDURES AND RELATIVE ABILITY

The plaintiff's chances of success can also depend on asymmetric legal uncertainty, differences in the parties' knowledge of the law and procedures governing a case, and differences in their relative mastery of the rules and tools of litigation. This is different from the divergence of expectations about case quality discussed above, because it concerns less the facts of the case or the contextual circumstances surrounding it than the applicable laws and trial procedures. Legal uncertainty could cause plaintiff win rates to deviate systematically from 50 percent in litigation if parties differ in their knowledge of these laws and procedures and in their ability to take advantage of them. To see this, consider the rules of evidence. We would expect the plaintiff win ratio to tend toward 50 percent in the litigations in which the litigants have the same knowledge of the rules regarding admissibility of evidence and the same ability in presenting it at trial. That is, given litigants with identical knowledge of rules and ability, there is nothing about this situation that differs from the basic setup that generated the 50 percent prediction through settlement decisions. If their knowledge is asymmetric, however, the plaintiff win ratio may deviate systematically from 50 percent because we would expect individuals with better knowledge of the rules and formidable legal ability to be more likely than others to take advantage of this differential and win.

The deviation from 50 percent follows from a selection effect that results in a higher chance of success for the party with better knowledge of legal rules and procedures. To see this, consider hypothetically an extreme example of a class of trials in which a specific evidentiary rule allows the plaintiffs to present a certain type of evidence at trial but only the defendants know about this rule. This would mean that the defendants with relatively worse chances at such a trial would tend to settle their disputes and those with relatively good chances would likely go to trial. Since the plaintiffs cannot make the same determination without knowledge of the rule, the pool of defendants who go to trial rather than settle would likely consist of those with a good chance of success, resulting in a higher than 50 percent chance rate of success for them at trial.

To see how differential legal knowledge ability could affect litigations in Ottoman courts, we return below to Islamic trial procedures. Building on the description of these procedures in the preceding chapter, we examine how the assignment of the burden of proof and use of non-evidentiary tools of litigation could affect success at trial.

Importance of Getting the Burden of Proof

According to Islamic law, litigants possessed different evidentiary responsibilities based on the nature of their claims, as discussed in Chapter 8. The law placed the burden of proof on the party whose contention was contrary to the initial legal presumption, an assignment technically decided by the judge. In an unpaid-debt dispute, for example, the judge would first hear the claim by the plaintiff (the alleged creditor) and then demand a response from the defendant (the alleged debtor). He could dismiss the case immediately if he decided that the dispute had no legal merit, or he could decide it based on litigant depositions if no further evidentiary support was required. If the litigation proceeded to the next state, the burden of proof could be assigned to either party. If the defendant denied the debt claim, the judge would require the plaintiff to provide evidence to support his or her claim, since the legal presumption in this case was that the alleged debtor was free from debt. However, if the defendant acknowledged the original debt transaction but also contended that the debt had been paid before the trial, then the court would require him or her to prove it, since in this situation it was the defendant making a counter-claim.

To summarize, the procedure involves the following four phases:

Phase 1: Litigants approach the court without knowing for certain (though perhaps anticipating) which party is going to assume the burden of proof.

Phase 2: They make allegations and counter-allegations in front of the judge, who determines whether the litigation should end at that point or proceed to the next stage, and if so, assigns the burden of proof based on litigants' depositions.

Phase 3: The litigant who fails to seize the burden of proof decides whether to exit litigation, either by conceding defeat or by agreeing to a settlement, or to continue with trial.

Phase 4: Trial resumes.

We would thus expect that in disputes that reach *Phase 4* the procedures favor the party who assumes the burden of proof. In the unpaid-debt case, for example, the judge would decide in favor of the party who assumed the burden of proof as long as this party can present credible evidence to support his or her allegations. If the evidence is credible, the opposing party would have no opportunity to provide evidence supporting his or her own position.[3]

As discussed in Chapter 8, the judge is not supposed to evaluate and choose between the evidence already submitted by both parties. Instead, he first chooses the party whose evidence is considered to be technically relevant ("*evla*," or superior) and then determines the strength and credibility of that party's evidence on its own terms, not in relation to the opposing party's evidence. Under these guidelines, a litigant might have credible evidence that could prove his or her claim but be unable to use this evidence in court, a possibility we raised in the previous chapter.

Based on this discussion, we would expect the average win ratio to be higher for parties cognizant of the benefits of being assigned the burden of proof and ones who were capable of presenting an argument that secured the assignment. A litigant's chance of winning at trial was higher in a litigation in which he or she was cognizant of the higher likelihood of being assigned the burden of proof and could go to court prepared to submit credible evidence when this happened.

Ability to Produce Supporting Documents

Although written documents could not be considered direct evidence, they must have served some purpose for them to be used at trial, a point we made in Chapter 8. Perhaps they contained the names of individuals who observed a business transaction and could serve as witnesses. In complex cases, documents could allow the litigants to state their arguments

[3] On the other hand, if the party bearing the burden of proof fails to produce evidence, or if the evidence is deemed untrustworthy, the judge will rule in the opponent's favor, often after the latter is asked to take an oath of truthfulness. If he or she refuses, the judge will rule for the former, even in the absence of evidence, sometimes after forcing him or her to take an oath as well.

carefully, especially when a dispute involved a series of allegations and counter-allegations, elaborate transactions, or intricate relationships among the parties. Litigants could support their version of the dispute by submitting a written document that substantiated their oral arguments, raised the credibility of witnesses, or established disputed facts. As Jørgen Nielsen (1985, 25) has argued in a different context, documents could even have served as the basis for the initial presumptions of the judges in assigning the burden of proof.

For all these reasons, we may take document use as an indicator of legal proficiency. Those who used documents in their cases were more likely than others to make informed choices about when to settle and when to continue litigation, thereby increasing their chances of success at trial.

*Ability to Secure Legal Opinion (*Fetva*)*

The use of legal opinions issued by *müfti*s (jurisconsults) could have a positive effect on the win ratio, as documents did during trials (Ergene 2003, chapter 8). For one thing, opinions could help the judge in interpreting the law and finding legal justification for siding with one party against the other. Since the *müfti* presumably formulated his opinion by applying the same legal standard as the judge, and presented it with the same judicial terminology, we would expect the judge to welcome the opinion even if he did not agree with it completely. Local politics may have played a role too. Whereas judges served in court districts temporarily, *müfti*s were usually local legal scholars who had influence and commanded respect. Their opinions probably carried weight and made it difficult for the judge to disagree.

Legal opinions could affect the average win ratio through a similar selection effect as in documents. Litigants who brought an opinion to trial were likely better positioned to estimate their chances in litigations compared to those who did not, because they were likely better informed through the opinion. Among the disputes with legal opinions that wound up at trial, therefore, the plaintiff win ratio would tend to be different from 50 percent because of a selection effect. The parties with relatively worse chances (weak opinions) at trial would likely settle their disputes and those with relatively good chances would likely go to trial. Consequently, the pool of litigants with legal opinions who went to trial rather than settle would likely consist of those with a good chance of success, resulting in a higher than 50 percent chance rate of success at trial.

Need for Representation

Court records do not specify why in some cases litigants had representatives and whether they had any influence on the outcome.[4] We would expect litigants to need representation for two general reasons. The first was to increase their chances of success at trial. Islamic law allows litigants to use representation by skilled individuals for the sole purpose of improving their case. *Hidaye* (vol. 3, 266), for example, indicates that one of the criteria for choosing a representative is skill in litigious argumentation. Similarly, *Dürer* (vol. 4, 69) differentiates between representatives chosen for their legal knowledge and experience to assist in litigations and others who serve as trustworthy agents in regular transactions. According to Article 1476 of the *Mecelle* (307), it was legally acceptable for representatives to be compensated for their services (Article 1467). In theory, litigants could use representatives, paid or not, to gain advantage at trial.[5]

Although the court records include no indication of professional lawyers used in litigations, the frequent appearance of a small group of individuals as representatives raises the possibility that they were hired to serve in such a capacity in litigations. We have identified only two or three individuals who acted as representatives multiple times, similar to what Jennings (1975b) observed in seventeenth-century Kayseri.

The second reason we would expect litigants to need representation was simply to ensure appropriate presence at trial. As we saw in Chapter 8, in a high number of cases representatives were related to litigants, indicating representation not for trial strategy but for mere convenience or out of necessity. Those litigants could be absent due to old age, poor health, or even concern for privacy in the case of many women. There is no reason to expect that use of representatives in such cases raised litigants' chances of success. The absence of a litigant could even lower chances at trial if it was crucial for the judge to hear the litigant's own testimony.

4 It is important not to confuse representation in traditional Ottoman courts of law with modern attorneyship. Before the late nineteenth century, "the premodern judicial agent (*vekil*) could be any individual empowered by the litigant through a special contract, with no need for a license, and that the *vekil*s duty was to represent rather than advocate the interests of his client. In other words, while manipulating information and employing rhetorical maneuvers to serve the client's legal interest are considered appropriate practices in modern legal advocacy, the *vekil* was expected to simply provide the necessary information in order for the judge to get to the truth of the matter" (Rubin 2012, 115). Professional attorneyship was introduced into the Ottoman legal system in the 1870s (ibid.).

5 For complaints about presumably hire-for-money *vekil*s accused of manipulating litigations for the benefit of their clients before the nineteenth century, see Demir (2010, 79–80).

Before concluding the chapter, we offer a caveat on some of the less obvious influences on the plaintiff's chances of success, factors left out of the formal framework because of the difficulty of identifying them in our sources.[6] One such factor is the practice of "fictitious litigation" (Agmon 1998). The phrase refers to those litigations that could be brought to court not to resolve genuine conflicts but to register prearranged agreements as verdicts. For instance, a "plaintiff" might make a superfluous claim regarding a previously owned property, and the "defendant" might then prove that this property had been sold to him or her by the "plaintiff." In this case the judge would decide for the "defendant" and order the "plaintiff" to abide by the conditions of the agreement, listed in the court-produced documentation. Since Islamic law maintains that the judge's decision on a particular issue cannot be overturned by a later verdict unless it is deficient because of a legal error, fictitious litigation could serve as a mechanism to protect contractual arrangements from future challenge. Unable to differentiate between fictitious and bona fide litigations in court records, we cannot determine if the former type introduced systematic bias to average win ratios. If, for example, the winners of fictitious litigations in the Kastamonu court were regularly the "plaintiffs," then the overall plaintiff win rates would be biased upwards. We discuss the possibility of fictitious litigation in the next chapter.

CONCLUSION

Using insights from economic analyses of trials, we have discussed the factors expected to influence trial outcomes in Ottoman courts. In the baseline model of litigation, we would expect plaintiff win rates at trial to tend toward 50 percent, because trials were costly and litigants likely settled cases where one side was likely to be a clear winner and went to trial only in difficult and uncertain cases where there was greater disagreement. For this outcome to hold, it must be the case that the litigants had identical expectations about the plaintiff's chances of success, symmetric stakes from trial outcome, and equal ability to take advantage of the rules and tools of litigation. Examining the factors that likely distorted these conditions in Ottoman courts, we have examined how these factors could affect the plaintiff's chances of success at trial.

If parties had divergent beliefs about the quality of the plaintiff's case, the selection effect would result in a higher chance of success for the more

[6] For a comprehensive discussion of these factors, see Coşgel and Ergene (2014a).

sophisticated party, such as those with elite titles. This is because among the litigants with low chances of success, elite titleholders would be more likely than others to settle, owing to their superior ability to assess the situation, resulting in a pool of litigants that includes elites who have a disproportionately higher chance of success at trial than others who choose to go to trial. Asymmetric stakes could have a similar influence on the outcome of trial. If one of the parties derived some cost or benefit from the outcome that was not captured entirely by the amount of the damages, possibly caused by differences in gender and socioeconomic status, we would expect the party with higher stakes to have a greater chance for success than would be the case if the stakes were the same.

Success at trial could also depend on the differential knowledge of the parties about the legal system and their relative ability regarding trial procedures. For example, in Ottoman courts we would expect the party with superior knowledge of the advantages of assuming the burden of proof to be more likely than his or her opponent to win at trial. Similarly, we would expect the average win rate to be higher for those with better knowledge of the benefits of providing a document for support or bringing a legal opinion from a *müfti*. Although representatives were involved in many litigations, we cannot form clear expectations of how they affected the outcome. Whereas some litigants may have used representatives for assistance at trial to raise their chances, others had no choice but to be represented by family members because of old age or poor health. Because we cannot identify these reasons in court records, we would expect the overall effect of representation to be mixed. In the next chapter, we use the information from the Kastamonu court to see how these expectations were realized in litigations decided in Ottoman courts.

10

Who Won? Case-type- and Period-based Analyses

In this chapter we apply the insights developed in preceding chapters to examine the factors that affected the plaintiff's chances of success in the court of Kastamonu. We began systematic analysis of court records in Chapter 4 with the questions of who came to court, against whom, and for what purpose, and examined them quantitatively by differentiating between agreements and disputes. Narrowing the focus on disputes, we next asked which cases went to trial and used the information from court records for a quantitative analysis of case characteristics that raised the likelihood of trial (Chapter 7). We now turn to trials and ask, who won?

For a quantitative investigation of the factors affecting the trial outcome, we follow a procedure similar to that used in Chapter 7 by separating our analysis into two parts. In the first part (Tables 10.1–10.12), we provide descriptive statistics of the relationship between litigant and case characteristics and success at trial. These statistics summarize the information from court records and help us make preliminary observations on how variations across different combinations of litigant and case characteristics affected average plaintiff win ratios and whether this relationship changed between case-types and over time. In the second part (Tables 10.13–10.16), we use multiple regression analysis of influences on the likelihood of the case being ruled in favor of the plaintiff for a more sophisticated investigation that allows us to identify the individual effect of each variable by controlling for others.

This chapter contributes new concepts, theoretical insights, analytical categories, and quantitative methods to the analysis of dispute resolution in Ottoman courts. In Chapters 8 and 9, we examined the rules and tools of litigation in the Ottoman legal system and discussed the importance of being assigned the burden of proof in a trial, the status of *fetva*s and written documents for support, and the potential benefits of representation during trial. Using concepts and insights from the Law and Economics literature, we also discussed how divergent expectations about plaintiff's success, asymmetric stakes with respect to trial outcome, and differential legal knowledge and ability would be expected to affect their chances of success at trial. We now examine these questions quantitatively by determining how the plaintiff's chances of success varied by the size-composition, gender, honorific titles, family status, religion, and religious markers of the parties and the types of evidence and legal support they used at trial. Separating cases by the type and time-period categories introduced in earlier chapters, we examine whether the relationship between litigant characteristics, types of evidence, and trial outcome varied systematically across criminal and civil cases and over time periods.

Our results provide answers to various important yet still unresolved questions regarding dispute resolution in Ottoman courts. One of these questions, originating from the broader literature on the operations of Islamic courts, has addressed the predictability of judicial decisions.[1] Bridging the gap between the largely qualitative literature on Ottoman courts and the theoretical and empirical literature on dispute resolution in Law and Economics, we provide a quantitative analysis of this ultimately empirical question. Another question of great concern in Ottoman historiography has been the relative performance of different segments of society in court. Previous approaches to this question have remained brief and impressionistic, lacking systematic analyses of the relationship between cases, parties, and outcomes.[2] By identifying the personal characteristics of litigants and studying how they fared in court against others, we are able to determine how social groups performed at trial relative to others and whether the courts reproduced or resisted hierarchies in class, gender, and religious affiliation.[3]

[1] The modern academic literature on Ottoman courts developed to a significant extent in reaction to the Weberian notion of *kadijustiz*, which portrayed the operations of Islamic courts as arbitrary and unpredictable (Weber 1978, 891–2, 897, 976). The Weberian characterization of the Islamic courts remained dominant in Western scholarship until the second half of the twentieth century (Peters 2005, 70; Powers 2002, chapter 1; Jennings 1978).

[2] See Chapter 1 for a discussion of how Ottomanists have generally characterized the trial performance of privileged and under privileged court clients.

[3] Coşgel and Ergene (2014c) have explored how plaintiff and defendant success rates varied according to gender, religious affiliation, and socioeconomic status in eighteenth-century Kastamonu. Kuran and Lustig (2012) provided consistent results in the context of

WHO WON AT TRIAL: PRELIMINARY ANALYSES

To obtain preliminary insights into the factors that affected the plaintiff's chances of success, in this section we display various tables of simple statistics that describe the relationship between case characteristics and trial outcome. In Tables 10.1–10.10, we report the relative frequency of various plaintiff–defendant combinations that wound up at trial, the types of evidence presented in court, and the proportions of cases that resulted in a win for the plaintiff. Our objective in this section is modest. Based on simple comparisons of entries, in each table we are seeking to identify interesting patterns in how the frequency of trial and average win ratios varied across case-types and over time. For a more sophisticated investigation of these patterns, we run a multiple regression analysis in the last section of the chapter to see if these patterns hold up when we consider them simultaneously, and we use theoretical insights developed in the preceding chapters to explain their sources.

The data set on litigations consists of 859 cases. Table 10.1 shows the distribution of these litigations across case-types and over time periods. About 60 percent of all litigations were civil cases between unrelated parties, and criminal cases constituted only 11 percent of the total. Although the total number of cases rose significantly over time (by 17 percent in the second period and 30 percent in the third period), the change was not uniform across case-types. While civil cases between related parties almost tripled during this period, those between unrelated parties stayed about the same in the second period and went up by about one-third in the third period. The number of criminal cases, in contrast, actually declined between the first and third periods, despite a sharp increase in the second period, as discussed in earlier chapters.

Interestingly, plaintiffs won 47 percent (standard deviation 0.50) of all cases in our sample, slightly lower than the rate of 50 percent hypothesized by Klein and Priest.[4] The rate varied significantly, however, across the three subject categories. Whereas the plaintiff win ratio was 53 percent ($\sigma = 0.50$) in criminal cases, it was 50 percent ($\sigma = 0.50$) in civil disputes among unrelated parties and 39 percent ($\sigma = 0.49$) in those among related parties.

seventeenth-century İstanbul, although their categories of analysis are different from those employed by Coşgel and Ergene (2014c).

4 The plaintiff win-rate in Kastamonu was significantly lower than the rate of about 60 percent that was observed in İstanbul (Kuran and Lustig 2012, 643).

TABLE 10.1: *Trials across Case-types and over Time*

	Number of Cases				Plaintiff Win Ratio			
TYPE	1684–96	1735–43	1781–90	All	1684–96	1735–43	1781–90	All
Criminal	27	50	20	97	0.63	0.6	0.2	0.53
Civil between related	46	66	126	238	0.46	0.52	0.30	0.39
Civil between unrelated	160	156	208	524	0.58	0.54	0.41	0.50
All	233	272	354	859	0.56	0.54	0.36	0.47

Comparing the plaintiff win ratio over time, we see a sharp decline in the third period in all case-types. In the first two periods, the average win ratio was higher in criminal cases than in civil cases among unrelated parties, followed by those among related parties. Although in the third period the win ratio was lower in criminal cases than in civil cases, the number of observations in the first category is too low to generalize from this comparison.

To see the relationship between the size-composition of parties and plaintiffs' chances of success, in Table 10.2 we examine average win ratios corresponding to various combinations of parties across case-types and over time periods. Although most trials were between two individuals, a significant number were between single and multiple individuals. Of the thirty trials that involved corporate bodies, only three were between two such bodies. Most of the trials involving a corporate body were civil cases between unrelated parties. The number of trials rose steadily over time in most size-combinations of parties.

To identify patterns in the plaintiff win ratio, we compare the four size-combinations of parties for which we have complete averages across case-types and over time periods, namely "Single vs. Single," "Multiple vs. Single," "Multiple vs. Multiple," and "Single vs. Multiple." As in Chapter 7, the party cited first in the size-combinations is the plaintiff. Interestingly, whereas the first three combinations shared the same pattern in average plaintiff win ratios across case-types and over time, the pattern was different in the "Single vs. Multiple" cases. More specifically, in the first three combinations the average win ratio was significantly lower in civil cases among related parties than in other case-types, and it fell steadily over time. The average win ratio in "Single vs. Multiple" cases, in contrast, was about the same in criminal cases as in civil cases among related parties, and it did not rise steadily over time. After approximately doubling between the first and second periods, the ratio fell in the third period but was still significantly higher in the third period than in the first period. A different selection effect must have operated in "Single vs. Multiple" cases than in other combinations for the plaintiff's chances of success to vary systematically across case-types and over time. On the other hand, the win ratios in all size-combinations are lower in civil related trials than in civil unrelated ones, the reasons for which are not immediately clear to us.

Although the trials involving corporate bodies are small in number and cover a limited range of case-types and time periods, the results are interesting. As plaintiffs, corporate bodies took to court mostly civil

TABLE 10.2: *Plaintiff Win Ratio according to Size-composition*

	Number of Cases			Plaintiff Win Ratio			Number of Cases			Plaintiff Win Ratio			N	%
SIZE	Criminal	Civil Related	Civil Unrelated	Criminal	Civil Related	Civil Unrelated	1684–96	1735–43	1781–90	1684–96	1735–43	1781–90	All Cases	
Single vs. Single	67	169	354	0.54	0.38	0.46	162	188	240	0.57	0.51	0.32	590	0.45
Single vs. Multiple	14	32	79	0.43	0.44	0.57	29	33	63	0.38	0.73	0.48	125	0.52
Single vs. Corporate	2		2	0		0.5		2	2		0	0.5	4	0.25
Multiple vs. Single	8	29	54	0.5	0.31	0.56	23	33	35	0.61	0.52	0.34	91	0.47
Multiple vs. Multiple	4	8	11	0.75	0.63	0.64	5	8	10	0.8	0.75	0.5	23	0.65
Multiple vs. Corporate	1		2	1		0	2		1	0		0	3	0
Corporate vs. Single	1		12	1		0.67	9	4		0.78	0.5		13	0.69
Corporate vs. Multiple			7			0.83	2	4	1	1	0.75	1	7	0.86
Corporate vs. Corporate			3			1	1		2	1		1	3	1

cases against unrelated parties and won on average more than two-thirds of these cases. They were similarly successful as defendants, winning three of the four cases initiated by single individuals and two of the three cases initiated by multiple parties.

To narrow the focus on the individual characteristics of parties, we now omit those cases that involved multiple individuals or corporate bodies and examine only trials between two individuals. Table 10.3 shows the aggregate distribution of single vs. single cases across case-types and over time periods. Of the 590 trials between single individuals, 354 (60 percent) were civil cases between unrelated individuals, followed by 169 (29 percent) civil cases between related individuals. The distribution over time periods was very similar to that by the whole sample (Table 10.1), though the overall win ratio was slightly lower (45 percent versus 47 percent) in litigations between individuals than in the whole sample that also included multiple individuals and corporate bodies. Although the total number of trials between individuals rose steadily over time, this was not a uniform pattern across case-types. When we compare the plaintiff win ratio across types and over time periods, a uniform pattern that stands out is the sharp decline in the third period in all case-types. We discuss below the implications of this decline for the possibility of "fictitious" litigations in Ottoman courts of law.

Table 10.4 shows the breakdown of the trials between individuals according to gender. More than half (57 percent) of these cases were between two men, and women brought suits against men in twice as many cases (26 percent) than the other way around (13 percent). Overall, the plaintiff win ratio was higher when the plaintiff was a man, though the ratio varied significantly across case-types and over time. In most gender combinations the win ratio was lower in civil cases between related parties than between unrelated parties, except in "Male vs. Female" cases that had a slightly higher win ratio when the litigants were related. Comparing the win ratio over time periods, we see that the "Male vs. Female" combination was similarly the sole exception to the general pattern of a sharp decline in the third period. This exception clearly raises the question of whether there was a distinct process of selection that applied to "Male vs. Female" cases but not to others.

Going beyond the basic difference between men and women, we can use the honorific titles of men to explore further differences among them in socioeconomic status. Using the same procedures as in Chapters 4 and 7, we created two sets of categories from titles. The first set differentiates between religious and military titles, and the second between elite

TABLE 10.3: *Trials between Individuals*

	Number of Cases				Plaintiff Win Ratio			
TYPE	**1684–96**	**1735–43**	**1781–90**	**All**	**1684–96**	**1735–43**	**1781–90**	**All**
Criminal	19	36	12	67	0.63	0.64	0.08	0.54
Civil between related	35	47	87	169	0.4	0.51	0.31	0.38
Civil between unrelated	108	105	141	354	0.61	0.47	0.35	0.46
All	162	188	240	590	0.57	0.51	0.32	0.45

TABLE 10.4: *Gender and Plaintiff Win Ratio*

	Number of Cases			Plaintiff Win Ratio			Number of Cases			Plaintiff Win Ratio			N	%
GENDER	Criminal	Civil Related	Civil Unrelated	Criminal	Civil Related	Civil Unrelated	1684–96	1735–43	1781–90	1684–96	1735–43	1781–90	All Cases	
Male vs. Male	46	36	253	0.59	0.28	0.47	104	121	110	0.61	0.55	0.25	335	0.47
Male vs. Female	1	35	39	0	0.49	0.46	12	25	38	0.58	0.4	0.47	75	0.47
Female vs. Male	19	81	53	0.47	0.38	0.43	40	34	79	0.47	0.47	0.35	153	0.41
Female vs. Female	1	17	9	0	0.41	0.44	6	8	13	0.5	0.5	0.31	27	0.41

and non-elite titles. Both sets also include women and titleless men as the third and fourth categories.

Table 10.5 shows the number of trials and plaintiff win ratios corresponding to combinations of gender and religious/military titles. As seen in the table, the litigations initiated by men with religious and military titles against other men were mostly civil cases against unrelated individuals. Women as plaintiffs generally had the least success against men with religious titles, presumably individuals with the highest levels of education in religious and legal sciences and with connections to legal personnel. In fact, these men generally had high success as defendants against all groups, and as plaintiffs they achieved some of the highest average win ratios (about 75 percent) reported in the table. Although men with no titles also performed poorly as plaintiffs against men with religious titles, they achieved higher rates of win against men with military titles in criminal cases and in civil cases among unrelated individuals. Women did relatively well as plaintiffs and defendants against titleless man in all case-types compared to other groups. Men with military titles had the lowest success rate against religious titleholders and highest success rates against women, both as plaintiffs and as defendants.

In the second set of categories derived from honorific titles, we reclassified men based on whether one's title indicated membership in the elite category. Table 10.6 shows the distribution of trials and win ratios corresponding to combinations based on whether the litigant is a woman, "Man, elite title," "Man, non-elite title," or "Man, no title."

As seen in the table, when elites came to court as plaintiffs, they mostly litigated civil cases against unrelated individuals and achieved a remarkably high win ratio of about two-thirds against all other groups. They also won often against other groups when they acted as defendants. A majority of cases brought by women, in contrast, were civil cases against related individuals. Women achieved significantly higher win rates in such cases against other women and men with no titles than against men with titles, the lowest rate being against elites. Note also that women achieved the highest win rates in criminal cases against men with non-elite titles and in civil cases against unrelated men with elite titles. Interestingly, men with no titles had the same pattern in their high rates of success, namely a higher-than-average win rate in criminal cases against men with non-elite titles and in civil cases against unrelated elites. In most case-types, however, men with no titles achieved lower win rates on average than women in litigations against the same groups. Finally, whereas men with non-elite titles performed better as defendants against

TABLE 10.5: *Religious/Military Titles and Plaintiff Win Ratio*

	Number of Cases			Plaintiff Win Ratio			Number of Cases			Plaintiff Win Ratio			N	%
GENDER AND TITLE	Criminal	Civil Related	Civil Unrelated	Criminal	Civil Related	Civil Unrelated	1684–96	1735–43	1781–90	1684–96	1735–43	1781–90	All Cases	
Woman vs. Woman	1	17	9	0	0.41	0.44	6	8	13	0.5	0.5	0.31	27	0.41
Woman vs. Men, religious title	3	13	14	0.33	0.23	0.43	9	11	10	0.33	0.36	0.3	30	0.33
Woman vs. Men, military title	5	15	16	0.6	0.4	0.44	6	6	24	0.5	0.5	0.42	36	0.44
Woman vs. Men, no title	11	53	23	0.45	0.42	0.43	25	17	45	0.52	0.53	0.33	87	0.43
Men, religious title vs. Woman		8	5		0.88	0.4	4	4	5	0.75	0.75	0.6	13	0.69
Man, religious title vs. Man, religious title		2	16		0	0.44	7	6	5	0.43	0.67	0	18	0.39
Man, religious title vs. Man, military title	2	1	24	1	0	0.75	6	11	10	1	0.82	0.5	27	0.74
Man, religious title vs. Man, no title	2	1	17	1	0	0.76	9	5	6	1	0.6	0.5	20	0.75
Man, military title vs. Woman		13	14		0.46	0.57	4	10	13	0.75	0.4	0.54	27	0.52
			8			0.38	2	2	4	0.5	0.5	0.25	8	0.38

(continued)

TABLE 10.5: *(continued)*

	Number of Cases			Plaintiff Win Ratio			Number of Cases			Plaintiff Win Ratio			N	%
GENDER AND TITLE	Criminal	Civil Related	Civil Unrelated	Criminal	Civil Related	Civil Unrelated	1684–96	1735–43	1781–90	1684–96	1735–43	1781–90	All Cases	
Man, military title vs. Man, religious title														
Man, military title vs. Man, military title	5		48	0.8		0.56	17	24	12	0.82	0.58	0.25	53	0.58
Man, military title vs. Man, no title	4	5	32	0.5	0.2	0.41	14	11	16	0.57	0.45	0.19	41	0.39
Man, no title vs. Woman	1	14	20	0	0.29	0.4	4	11	20	0.25	0.27	0.4	35	0.34
Man, no title vs. Man, religious title	4	6	22	0.25	0.33	0.27	5	13	14	0.2	0.38	0.21	32	0.28
Man, no title vs. Man, military title	12	6	34	0.75	0.17	0.5	12	25	15	0.58	0.64	0.27	52	0.52
Man, no title vs. Man, no title	17	15	52	0.41	0.4	0.29	32	24	28	0.44	0.38	0.18	84	0.33

TABLE 10.6: *Elite Status and Success at Trial*

	Number of Cases			Plaintiff Win Ratio			Number of Cases			Plaintiff Win Ratio			N	%
GENDER AND ELITE STATUS	Criminal	Civil Related	Civil Unrelated	Criminal	Civil Related	Civil Unrelated	1684–96	1735–43	1781–90	1684–96	1735–43	1781–90	All Cases	
Woman vs. Woman	1	17	9	0	0.41	0.44	6	8	13	0.5	0.5	0.31	27	0.41
Woman vs. Men with elite title	1	7	9	0	0.29	0.56	5		12	0.6		0.33	17	0.41
Woman vs. Men with non-elite title	7	21	21	0.57	0.33	0.38	10	17	22	0.3	0.41	0.41	49	0.39
Woman vs. Men with no title	11	53	23	0.45	0.42	0.43	25	17	45	0.52	0.53	0.33	87	0.43
Elite vs. Woman		5	9		0.6	0.67	4	3	7	0.75	0.33	0.71	14	0.64
Elite vs. Elite			17			0.71	12	3	2	0.58	1	1	17	0.71
Elite vs. Non-elite	3		19	1		0.68	6	9	7	0.83	0.89	0.43	22	0.73
Elite vs. No title	2	1	20	1	0	0.65	13	6	4	0.69	0.67	0.5	23	0.65
Non-elite vs. Woman		16	10		0.63	0.4	4	11	11	0.75	0.55	0.45	26	0.54
Non-elite vs. Elite		1	18		0	0.56	3	11	5	1	0.55	0.2	19	0.53
Non-elite vs. Non-elite	4	2	42	0.75	0	0.48	11	20	17	0.82	0.55	0.18	48	0.48
Non-elite vs. No title	4	5	29	0.5	0.2	0.45	10	10	18	0.8	0.4	0.22	38	0.42
No title vs. Woman	1	14	20	0	0.29	0.4	4	11	20	0.25	0.27	0.4	35	0.34
No title vs. Elite	1	1	18	0	0	0.5	3	6	11	0.67	0.83	0.18	20	0.45
No title vs. Non-elite	15	11	38	0.67	0.27	0.37	14	32	18	0.43	0.5	0.28	64	0.42
No title vs. No title	17	15	52	0.41	0.4	0.29	32	24	28	0.44	0.38	0.18	84	0.33

women and titleless men than against men with elite and non-elite titles, as plaintiffs their record against the same parties was more mixed

Status as plaintiff or defendant was important. For example, whereas the average win ratio was 73 percent in "Elite vs. Non-elite" litigations, it was only 53 percent when the roles were reversed in "Non-elite vs. Elite" litigations. In the same vein, the win ratio went from 65 percent in "Elite vs. No title" cases to 45 percent in "No title vs. Elite" cases, and a similar discrepancy took place in trials between women and non-elite men. This finding may be related to the advantages that we associate with assuming the burden of proof in trials, a topic that we explore shortly in this chapter.

As noted in previous chapters, court records noted the religious affiliation of non-Muslims in a way that makes it easy to distinguish them from Muslims, and we can use religious markers to further distinguish among Muslim litigants based on whether they claimed descent from Muhammad or had made the pilgrimage to Mecca. The latter marker is particularly significant in this context because of its association with wealth (Chapter 2).

Table 10.7 shows the proportions of various plaintiff–defendant combinations according to religious affiliation and markers. Of the 590 litigations between single individuals, only 21 (3.6 percent) involved a non-Muslim, which is noteworthy since non-Muslims constituted about 15 percent of the population. About 30 percent of all cases involved an individual with a religious marker, and about 40 percent of those were against litigants who did not carry such a title.

Although the number of cases in most combinations is too small to justify generalizing from the average win rates reported in the table, in civil cases between unrelated individuals the combinations involving individuals with religious markers against those with no markers are sufficiently large and yield interesting comparisons. More specifically, the average plaintiff win rate is relatively high when the defendant has no religious marker and the plaintiff is a pilgrim (70 percent) or descendant of Muhammad (50 percent), but the average falls significantly when the roles are reversed and the plaintiff has no marker and the defendant is a pilgrim (44 percent) or descendant of Muhammad (31 percent). These observations confirm that the positional roles of litigants as plaintiffs or defendants were important.

We saw in earlier chapters that court records also include information about family affiliation, which allows us to infer from the presence of the suffix *zade* in a litigant's name that he or she was related to an established and prominent family. As seen in Table 10.8, only a small proportion

TABLE 10.7: *Religion, Religious Markers, and Plaintiff Win Ratio*

	Number of Cases			Plaintiff Win Ratio			Number of Cases			Plaintiff Win Ratio			N	%
RELIGION AND RELIGIOUS MARKER	Criminal	Civil Related	Civil Unrelated	Criminal	Civil Related	Civil Unrelated	1684–96	1735–43	1781–90	1684–96	1735–43	1781–90	All Cases	
Muslim vs. Muslim	63	166	340	0.56	0.37	0.46	159	178	232	0.57	0.5	0.32	569	0.45
Muslim vs. Non-Muslim			2			0.5	1		1	1		0	2	0.5
Non-Muslim vs. Muslim	1		8	0		0.63	2	5	2	0.5	0.6	0.5	9	0.56
Non-Muslim vs. Non-Muslim	3	3	4	0.33	1	0.25		5	5		0.8	0.2	10	0.5
Pilgrim vs. Pilgrim		2	7		0	0.57	2	6	1	1	0.33	0	9	0.44
Pilgrim vs. Desc. of Muh.	1		1	1		1	1	1		1	1		2	1
Pilgrim vs. No marker	3	6	23	1	0.5	0.70	10	13	9	0.7	0.62	0.78	32	0.69
Desc. of Muh. vs. Pilgrim			1			0			1			0	1	0
Desc. of Muh. vs. Desc. of Muh.		5	3		0.2	0.67	1	1	6	0	1	0.33	8	0.38
Desc. of Muh. vs. No marker	3	8	26	0.33	0.5	0.5	4	10	23	0.5	0.7	0.39	37	0.49
No marker vs. Pilgrim	4	8	25	0	0.5	0.44	15	7	15	0.67	0.29	0.2	37	0.41
No marker vs. Desc. of Muh.	3	12	32	0.33	0.33	0.31	6	11	30	0.33	0.45	0.27	47	0.32
No marker vs. No marker	53	128	236	0.57	0.38	0.45	123	139	155	0.55	0.50	0.31	417	0.45

TABLE 10.8: *Family Prominence and Plaintiff Win Ratio*

	Number of Cases			Plaintiff Win Ratio			Number of Cases			Plaintiff Win Ratio			N	%
FAMILY AFFILIATION	Criminal	Civil Related	Civil Unrelated	Criminal	Civil Related	Civil Unrelated	1684–96	1735–43	1781–90	1684–96	1735–43	1781–90	All Cases	
Prominent vs. Prominent	1	1	2	1	1	1	2	2		1	1		4	1
Prominent vs. Non-prominent	1	1	10	1	1	0.8	3	6	3	0.67	0.83	1	12	0.83
Non-prominent vs. Prominent	2	2	14	1	0	0.21	4	6	8	0.75	0.33	0	18	0.28
Non-prominent vs. Non-prominent	63	165	328	0.51	0.38	0.46	153	174	229	0.56	0.5	0.32	556	0.44

(about 6 percent) of cases involved members of prominent families. Once again, the numbers are too small to justify generalizations, but when we compare the win rates in civil cases between unrelated individuals we see clearly that family prominence had a significant impact on trial outcome and that the chances of success shifted accordingly when the litigants' roles were reversed. The average win rate is only 21 percent when the plaintiff is a member of a non-prominent family in a case against a member of a prominent family, and the rate rises to 80 percent when the roles are reversed and the plaintiff is from a prominent family.

THE RULES AND TOOLS OF LITIGATION AND SUCCESS AT TRIAL

To enhance their chances of winning at trial, litigants in Ottoman courts could present oral testimony and written documents and use various types of non-evidentiary tools to support their cases. We discussed in Chapter 8 the laws and procedures guiding the use of evidence and other adjudicative tools during trial. Although Ottoman historians have previously examined how parties could use various legal tools at trial, the actual influence of these tools on the outcome has not been systematically studied. By studying the relationship between trial outcome and use of documents, *fetva*s, and representation, we contribute to the literature a quantitative assessment of the role played by these tools.

For reasons given in previous chapters, the relationship between the testimony of credible witnesses and favorable outcomes is direct and unequivocal. Although there were exceptions allowed by jurisprudential rules, in most cases opposing litigants could not submit witness testimony simultaneously. These rules make it redundant to look into the nature of the relationship between credible testimony and court outcome: In Kastamonu court records the parties who appear to have submitted witness testimony almost always won their cases.[5] For this reason, in this section our analysis focuses on how the burden of proof and other litigation tools affected the outcome of trial.

Table 10.9 shows the distribution of who won the burden of proof and the associated rates of success at trial. Overall, the court assigned the

[5] It is possible that (1) testimonies of non-credible witnesses were not transcribed in the records, and that (2) although both parties could have brought witnesses to court, only the witnesses of those who were entitled to submit evidence (and not their opponents) were listened to and had their testimonies recorded.

TABLE 10.9: *Burden of Proof and Success at Trial*

	Total Litigants	Number with Burden of Proof	Number of Those Who Won with Burden of Proof	Win Ratio with Burden of Proof
Multiple Litigants	213	87	80	92
Corporate	16	12	9	75
Women	222	112	80	71.4
Elite Military Titleholders	69	32	29	90.6
Elite Religious Titleholders	32	23	20	87
Non-elite Military Titleholders	160	77	63	81.8
Non-elite Religious Titleholders	88	49	43	87.8
No Title	310	145	107	73.8
Pilgrim	73	43	38	88.4
Descendant of Muhammad	76	37	30	81.1
No Religious Status	734	360	276	76.7
Non-Muslim	19	13	9	69.2
Prominent	26	15	15	100
Non-prominent	874	437	337	77.1

Note: Calculations based on individual litigant categories (bottom 12 rows) are based on litigations that involved individual plaintiffs and defendants.

burden of proof in 452 cases.[6] In about 78 percent of those cases, the litigant with the burden of proof won at trial, confirming our arguments in the previous chapter about the advantage one gained by assuming the burden of proof.

Because we have no detailed, anthropological descriptions of individual litigations, we cannot determine whether the litigants consciously took advantage of the benefits of bearing the burden of proof. However, since we would expect litigants with legal experience and sophistication to be more likely than others to take advantage of evidentiary processes, we

[6] In 138 litigations within this sample (23.4 percent), decisions were reached through means that did not require the assignment of the burden of proof, including confessions, the judge's interpretation of the validity of the complaint, his personal discretion, and considerations based on the statute of limitations.

can infer this indirectly by examining how the burden of proof varied among groups of litigants. Table 10.9 shows to what extent different litigant groups seized the burden of proof and the corresponding win rates at trial.

The figures presented in the column titled "Number with Burden of Proof" reveal that among Muslim gender- and title-groups, it was the groups most educated and experienced in the legal and religious sciences (*ilmiyye*), who managed to assume the burden of proof. Indeed, we found an astonishing rate of about 72 percent for the *Efendis*. Pilgrims and members of prominent families were also more successful than their counterparts.[7]

Two results stand out as surprising. The first is the exceptionally low rate observed among the *Ağas*, elite members of the military-administrative establishment. This finding, along with the low rate that we observed among non-elite military titleholders, suggests that members of the military establishment were less capable of seizing the burden of proof compared to members of the religious establishment. The second surprising result is the remarkably high rate observed among non-Muslims (but see below).

Since the figures presented in the last column represent the litigants' ability to acquire the burden of proof *and* use it to win their trials, they can be viewed as proxies for legal competency. Not surprisingly, our results indicate that privileged parties took advantage of the burden of proof procedures much better than their underprivileged counterparts, as can be seen in the win ratios of elite titleholders (both *ilmiyye* and *seyfiyye*), non-elite religious titleholders, and pilgrims. Remarkably, members of prominent families won all of the litigations in which they assumed the burden of proof! The results show a significant gap between the legal competency of these groups and that of women, titleless men, individuals with no religious markers, and members of non-prominent families. Non-Muslim litigants appear to be the least successful group to take advantage of having the burden of proof, which might explain why they tended to participate mostly in litigations in which they assumed the burden of proof. If they were less discriminating in the choice of litigations, their win rates could possibly be even lower.

The importance of assuming the burden of proof is related to some of our findings regarding settlement-trial decisions in Chapter 7. In many disputes in which privileged and underprivileged parties faced each other

[7] We determined in separate calculations that corporate bodies assumed the burden of proof in about 75 percent of their cases.

as opponents, settlement was likely if underprivileged groups (women, men with no titles, non-Muslims, and non-*zade*s) were potential/actual defendants. When privileged defendants (men with titles, Muslims, and *zade*s) faced underprivileged plaintiffs, however, the chances of trial increased (see Tables 7.11 and 7.12). Our findings in the present chapter help to explain this general tendency. Since it was more likely for litigants to acquire the burden of proof as plaintiffs,[8] and since there existed a positive relationship between the assumption of burden of proof and success at trial for those who could play the legal game well,[9] it made sense for underprivileged groups to settle their disputes with privileged opponents as soon as it became clear that they would assume the role of the defendant in the trial, but before the case was decided. Because privileged groups were more likely to win as defendants compared to underprivileged ones, they were more willing to force trials in disputes that pitted them against plaintiffs with inferior legal skills and resources.[10]

Turning our attention to the use of documents at trial, we examine in Table 10.10 the numbers of litigations in which the parties presented documents and the corresponding win rates. The use and effectiveness of documents followed a similar pattern in all litigations as it did in those between two individuals. It was more common in civil cases between unrelated individuals than between other types. More specifically, in litigations between two individuals, parties used documents in 77 cases (13 percent of the total), only 3 of which involved documents by both parties. A document was used in only one criminal trial, and about 75 percent of the trials in which a document was presented were civil cases between unrelated parties. Over time periods, document use in trials followed an interesting pattern, namely a sharp decline in the second period, followed by a sharp rise in the third. Document use peaked in the third period.

As noted in the previous chapter, although written documents served no direct evidentiary function, they could have a significant impact on trial results. A comparison of average win rates indicates that presenting documents at trial indeed influenced the outcome positively. Whereas

8 Plaintiffs and defendants assumed the burden of proof at significantly different rates: 62.4 and 37.7 percent, respectively.

9 Although plaintiffs were more likely than defendants to assume the burden of proof, when defendants did so, they almost always won their trials. The "Win ratios with Burden of Proof" rates for plaintiffs and defendants are 93.5 and 68.4 percent, respectively.

10 There may be, however, exceptions to this situation. See our discussion of the results presented in Tables Appendix 7.A and Appendix 7.B.

TABLE 10.10: *Document Use and Success at Trial*

	Number of Cases			Plaintiff Win Ratio			Number of Cases			Plaintiff Win Ratio			N	%
DOCUMENT USE	Criminal	Civil Related	Civil Unrelated	Criminal	Civil Related	Civil Unrelated	1684–96	1735–43	1781–90	1684–96	1735–43	1781–90	All Cases	
ALL LITIGATIONS														
Document vs. Document		1	5		1	0.2	2	1	3	0.5	0	0.33	6	0.33
Document vs. No document		7	41		0.86	0.73	21	6	21	0.81	0.67	0.71	48	0.75
No document vs. Document	3	23	37	0.33	0.04	0.08	15	4	44	0.13	0	0.07	63	0.08
No document vs. No document	94	207	441	0.53	0.41	0.52	195	261	286	0.57	0.55	0.38	742	0.49
LITIGATIONS BETWEEN TWO INDIVIDUALS														
Document vs. Document		1	2		1	0	2		1	0.5		0	3	0.33
Document vs. No document		3	24		1	0.67	12	5	10	0.83	0.6	0.6	27	0.70
No document vs. Document	1	15	31	0	0.07	0.10	13	4	30	0.15	0	0.07	47	0.09
No document vs. No document	66	150	297	0.55	0.4	0.49	135	179	199	0.59	0.52	0.35	513	0.47

the average win ratio was 70 percent in litigations between two individuals when the plaintiff presented a document and the defendant did not, the ratio plummeted to below 10 percent when document use was reversed – a clear contrast in favor of using documents.

Consider next the use of *fetva*s in court. Interestingly, the distribution of *fetva*s across case-types and over time periods followed a similar pattern to that of documents in all litigations as well as those between two individuals. Parties presented *fetva*s in only 5 criminal cases, 3 of which were between two individuals. The majority of cases in which *fetva*s were presented were civil litigations between unrelated parties. More specifically, in litigations between two individuals, 39 (58 percent) of the 67 cases in which a *fetva* was used were civil cases between unrelated parties. In only 2 of these cases did both parties present *fetva*s. After a sharp fall in the second period, *fetva* use rose sharply again in the third and reached a peak (a *fetva* was used in about 16 percent of the litigations in the third period).

More importantly, *fetva*s influenced the trial outcome in a fashion similar to written documents. As documents, *fetva*s had no evidentiary function at trial, yet they could affect the outcome indirectly. By presenting *fetva*s in court, parties seem to have indeed raised their chances of success sharply, even more so than was the case for documents. The average win ratio in litigations between two individuals was 79 percent when the plaintiff presented a *fetva* in court but the defendant did not, and the plaintiff had no chance of winning (average win ratio 0 percent) if the defendant presented a *fetva* but the plaintiff did not.

Finally, consider the influence of representation by third parties on trial outcome. As seen in Table 10.12, overall and in litigations between two individuals, representatives were involved in about a quarter of all litigations. The proportion was higher in civil cases between related individuals, probably because of the likely higher proportion of such cases involving women, who were more likely to use representatives compared to male litigants. Most of these were cases in which the plaintiff had a (related or unrelated) representative but the defendant did not. In litigations between two individuals, for example, 43 (40) cases involved a plaintiff represented by someone related (unrelated) through family ties against a defendant who had no representative, constituting 31 (29) percent of all litigations. In another 49 cases, the plaintiff had no representative but the defendant did. In criminal cases, representatives were present in only 8 cases. Over time, the proportion of all litigations with representation rose from 20 percent to 29 percent in the second

TABLE 10.11: Fetva *Use and Plaintiff Win Ratio*

	Number of Cases			Plaintiff Win Ratio			Number of Cases			Plaintiff Win Ratio			N	%
FETVA USE	Criminal	Civil Related	Civil Unrelated	Criminal	Civil Related	Civil Unrelated	1684–96	1735–43	1781–90	1684–96	1735–43	1781–90	All Cases	
ALL LITIGATIONS														
Fetva vs. *Fetva*			2			0	1		1	0		0	2	0
Fetva vs. No *fetva*	4	22	28	1	0.73	0.89	18	4	32	0.89	1	0.78	54	0.83
No *fetva* vs. *Fetva*	1	12	36	0	0	0	16	4	29	0	0	0	49	0
No *fetva* vs. No *fetva*	92	204	458	0.51	0.38	0.52	198	264	292	0.58	0.55	0.35	754	0.48
LITIGATIONS BETWEEN TWO INDIVIDUALS														
Fetva vs. *Fetva*			2			0	1		1	0		0	2	0
Fetva vs. No *fetva*	3	15	15	1	0.67	0.87	13	2	18	0.92	1	0.67	33	0.79
No *fetva* vs. *Fetva*		10	22		0	0	10	3	19	0	0	0	32	0
No *fetva* vs. No *fetva*	64	144	315	0.52	0.38	0.48	138	183	202	0.58	0.51	0.32	523	0.46

TABLE 10.12: *Representation and Plaintiff Win Ratio*

	Number of Cases			Plaintiff Win Ratio			Number of Cases			Plaintiff Win Ratio			N	%
REPRESENTATION	Criminal	Civil Related	Civil Unrelated	Criminal	Civil Related	Civil Unrelated	1684–96	1735–43	1781–90	1684–96	1735–43	1781–90	All Cases	
ALL LITIGATIONS														
No representative vs. No representative	85	153	396	0.53	0.41	0.46	186	192	256	0.55	0.51	0.35	634	0.46
No representative vs. Related representative	1	13	24	0	0.62	0.58	3	13	22	0.67	0.62	0.55	38	0.58
No representative vs. Unrelated representative		8	41		0.38	0.78	10	17	22	0.8	0.82	0.59	49	0.71
Related representative vs. No representative	6	27	32	0.67	0.22	0.56	14	25	26	0.36	0.64	0.27	65	0.43
Related representative vs. Related representative		5	1		0.4	1	2	3	1	1	0.33	0	6	0.5
Related representative vs. Unrelated representative		1	1		1	0	1		1	1		0	2	0.5
Unrelated representative vs. No representative	5	28	27	0.4	0.32	0.56	16	18	26	0.63	0.5	0.27	60	0.43
Unrelated representative vs. Related representative		1			1			1			1		1	1

Unrelated representative vs. Unrelated representative		2	2		0.5	0.5	1	3		0	0.67		4	0.5
LITIGATIONS BETWEEN TWO INDIVIDUALS														
No representative vs. No representative	59	118	276	0.54	0.40	0.43	128	139	186	0.56	0.49	0.31	453	0.44
No representative vs. Related representative	1	8	14	0	0.63	0.36	2	9	12	0.5	0.44	0.42	23	0.43
No representative vs. Unrelated representative		5	21		0.40	0.76	6	10	10	0.83	0.8	0.5	26	0.69
Related representative vs. No representative	5	17	21	0.6	0.18	0.48	13	11	19	0.31	0.64	0.26	43	0.37
Related representative vs. Related representative		3	1		0.67	1	2	2		1	0.5		4	0.75
Related representative vs. Unrelated representative														
Unrelated representative vs. No representative	2	17	21	0.5	0.29	0.62	11	16	13	0.73	0.44	0.31	40	0.47
Unrelated representative vs. Related representative														
Unrelated representative vs. Unrelated representative		1			1			1			1		1	1

period and stayed about the same in the third. In litigations between two individuals, the proportion likewise rose from 21 percent to 26 percent in the second period, but declined to 23 percent in the third.

When we compare the average win ratios across litigant combinations in civil cases, we notice interesting patterns that suggest that representatives were more likely to affect the trial outcome if they were unrelated to litigants. To illustrate this, consider how having a representative influenced the plaintiff's chances of success in civil cases between two individuals. When the plaintiff had a representative but the defendant did not, the win rates were significantly higher if the representative was unrelated to the plaintiff than if he or she was related. This might be because when litigants brought representatives from outside the family or kinship connections, the choice was based on legal skill and experience. Suggestive in this regard is the fact that representatives with the *Efendi* title won eight of the twelve cases in which they appeared.[11] Notice also how in civil litigations between two individuals the win rates differed between cases involving related and unrelated parties: The win rate was generally higher in litigations between unrelated individuals than between related individuals. The only exception to this pattern was those cases in which the plaintiff had no representative and the defendant had a related representative.

A REGRESSION ANALYSIS OF INFLUENCES ON TRIAL OUTCOMES

Although the information presented in Tables 10.1–10.12 provides important insights into the factors affecting the plaintiff's chances of success at trial, we have to be careful to treat these inferences as preliminary until we examine them simultaneously through a procedure similar to that we used in Chapter 7. Just as we used multiple regression analysis there to isolate the individual effects of factors affecting the likelihood of trial, here too we use multiple regression analysis to control for other factors and identify the individual effects of factors affecting success at trial.

The dependent variable is the outcome of trial, a dummy variable that takes the value of 1 if the case was won by the plaintiff. For reasons explained in Chapter 7, we use the probit model for estimation and report

[11] No other title-group had as high a success rate as representatives. Pilgrims also won eight of the ten trials in which they served as representatives.

the estimated coefficients and the corresponding ***p*-value and pseudo R-squared** as measures of significance. Running separate regressions for each case-type (Tables 10.13 and 10.15) and each time period (Tables 10.14 and 10.16), we examine how influences on the trial outcome varied across types and periods. In Tables 10.13 and 10.15, we control for the effect of possible changes in the decision standard over time by including two temporal variables. More specifically, using Period 1 as the omitted category, we include periods 2 and 3 as dummy variables in the regression equation. In Tables 10.14 and 10.16, we replace the temporal variables by two case-types, using "Civil cases between unrelated individuals" as the omitted category and including "Criminal disputes" and "Civil disputes between related parties" as dummy variables. In the last column of these tables, we run the same regression for all observations and control for differences in case-types and time periods through the same dummy variables. To correct for the possibility of correlation of observations within each case-type or period, we divide observations into clusters and use clustered errors in regression analysis. The clusters are the same as in Chapter 7, namely the three time periods in the first three columns of Tables 10.13 and 10.15, the three case-types in the first three columns of Tables 10.14 and 10.16, and the nine combinations of case-types and time periods in the last columns.

To recap, the regression analysis includes three categories of explanatory variables. The first category consists of various plaintiff–defendant combinations corresponding to differences in composition (single vs. group), gender and honorific titles, religion and religious markers, and family status. Each of these is a dummy variable that takes the value of 1 if the parties have the specified characteristic, 0 otherwise. For example, the dependent variable "Single vs. Multiple" is equal to 1 when the plaintiff is a single individual and the defendant is multiple individuals, and 0 if the size-composition of the parties is anything else. By the same token, the dependent variable "Male vs. Female" is equal to 1 when the plaintiff is male and the defendant female, and 0 otherwise.

The second category shows the effects of various rules and tools of litigation – more specifically, the assignment of the burden of proof, the use of documents and *fetva* by the parties, and representation by third parties. These are dummy variables that take on the value of 1 if the plaintiff has the burden of proof, or when document or *fetva* use by the parties or representation by third parties are as specified in the tables, 0 otherwise. Finally, the third category consists of the two time periods and the two case-types, the third period or case-type being the omitted base category.

Following the same procedure as in Chapter 7, we ran separate regressions for each case-type and time period, and we report the results separately for all litigations (Tables 10.13 and 10.14) and those between just two individuals (Table 10.15 and 10.16). For reasons explained in more detail in Chapter 7, although the results are mostly consistent with preliminary observations based on Table 10.2, we also see why multiple regression analysis is necessary to ensure the robustness of tentative inferences based on singleton comparisons. For example, the coefficient of "Multiple vs. Multiple" is significant and positive across equations, which is consistent with simple comparisons of average win ratios in Table 10.2. The coefficients and significance of "Multiple vs. Single," however, calls into question the reliability of singleton comparisons of averages. Although the differential between the average win ratios of "Multiple vs. Single" and "Single vs. Single" seems wider for civil cases than for criminal cases, the coefficient is more significant for the latter, indicating that part of the differential observed in civil cases is captured by some other variable or is attributable to other differences. One would thus be mistaken to conclude, for example, that the seemingly higher win ratio (0.56 vs. 0.46) in "Multiple vs. Single" civil litigations (compared to "Single vs. Single" civil cases) between unrelated parties necessarily means that such litigations were significantly more likely than "Single vs. Single" ones to result in a win for the plaintiff, or that the win differential was more significant in civil cases than in criminal ones, all else being the same.

As already noted in Chapter 7, we have decided to retain in the analysis the variables that perfectly predict success or failure in the dependent variable, even though the probit model would normally drop these variables along with their associated observations. Including them in the analysis allows us to incorporate this information in our tables without affecting our estimates of any of the other coefficients. We have already observed in some of the earlier tables in this chapter that the plaintiffs won all cases in some combinations of parties. This was true, for example, in the "Corporate vs. Corporate" civil litigations between unrelated parties and in periods 1 and 3 and in the "Prominent vs. Non-prominent" litigations in period 3 and in criminal and civil unrelated case-types. Conversely, the plaintiffs did not win any of the following cases: two litigations in the "Multiple vs. Corporate" combination, two civil litigations between men with religious titles, and two civil litigations between Muslims vs. Non-Muslims. To incorporate these unique relationships into our results explicitly, we retained these variables in the regression analysis.[12]

SIZE-COMPOSITION AND CHANCES OF SUCCESS AT TRIAL

Table 10.13 shows the estimated coefficients and ***p*-values** of how various combinations of size-composition of parties, as compared to "Single vs. Single" litigations, affected the plaintiff's chances of success at trial across case-types, and Table 10.14 shows the same effects separately for time periods, controlling for other variables. To interpret the results, we examine whether the signs and coefficients of the variables are consistent with the theoretical arguments developed in the preceding chapter about how differences in expectations, stakes, and legal knowledge and ability would affect the trial outcome. The coefficient of "Single vs. Multiple" is generally negative (though insignificant), indicating that the lower ability of a single person relative to multiple individuals in estimating case strength and/or the higher stakes that multiple individuals likely faced caused single individuals to be less successful than multiple ones, as hypothesized. The results also show that corporate bodies likely won against others, both as plaintiffs and defendants, again consistent with the greater ability and stakes we would expect them to have compared to others. Although the positive and significant coefficient of "Single Individual vs. Corporate Body" in civil cases seems to contradict the argument, there are only two cases in this category – too low to generalize. Recall also from Table 10.2 that single individuals lost both of the criminal cases they litigated against corporate bodies, an outcome that is reflected in the negative and significant coefficient of this variable in Table 10.13.

The results concerning how the rules and tools of litigation affected the outcome are interesting. Based on the discussion in the previous chapter, we would expect litigants to be more likely to win in civil cases if they assumed the burden of proof, and the results confirm this expectation. Asymmetries in the use of documents or *fetva*s in civil litigations generally favored the party who took advantage of these tools against others who did not, as can be seen in the consistently positive and significant coefficients of "*Fetva* vs. no *fetva*" and "Document vs. No document" variables and the negative and significant coefficients of the "No document vs. Document" variable. Recall also from Table 10.11 that plaintiffs who

[12] We used the "asis" option of Stata, the statistical package we have used for probit estimation.

TABLE 10.13: *Probit Analysis of Influences on Plaintiff's Chances of Success at Trial: Size-composition and Case-types*

	(1)	(2)	(3)	(4)
VARIABLES	Criminal	Civil Related	Civil Unrelated	All Cases
Single vs. Multiple	-0.18	-0.04	-0.15	-0.10
	(0.432)	(0.746)	(0.750)	(0.698)
Single vs. Corporate	-6.09***		0.34***	-0.06
	<.001		<.001	(0.902)
Multiple vs. Single	-0.35***	-0.14	0.25	0.08
	<.001	(0.797)	(0.176)	(0.699)
Multiple vs. Multiple	5.62***	0.66**	0.67***	0.61***
	<.001	(0.011)	(0.001)	<.001
Multiple vs. Corporate			-5.89***	-5.86***
			<.001	<.001
Corporate vs. Single	5.39***		0.57	0.48
	<.001		(0.353)	(0.357)
Corporate vs. Multiple	5.39***		1.02**	0.92**
	<.001		(0.045)	(0.038)
Corporate vs. Corporate			5.34***	5.17***
			<.001	<.001
Plaintiff has burden of proof	-0.13	1.76***	1.24***	1.21***
	(0.626)	<.001	<.001	<.001
Document vs. Document		6.89***	-1.04***	0.67
		<.001	<.001	(0.503)
Document vs. No document		6.53***	0.65***	0.85***
		<.001	(0.001)	<.001
No document vs. Document	5.43***	-0.95***	-1.14***	-0.83***
	<.001	<.001	<.001	(0.002)
Fetva vs. *Fetva*			-4.19***	-5.34***
			<.001	<.001
Fetva vs. No *fetva*	10.92***	1.31***	1.58***	1.39***
	<.001	(0.004)	(0.001)	<.001
No *fetva* vs. *Fetva*	-5.47***	-9.85***	-5.26***	-5.26***
	<.001	<.001	<.001	<.001
Representative vs. Representative		0.25	1.04***	0.32
		(0.367)	(0.003)	(0.114)
No representative vs. Representative	-6.09***	0.45**	0.65***	0.52***
	<.001	(0.024)	<.001	<.001
Representative vs. No representative	-0.31	-0.36***	0.42***	0.05
	(0.189)	(0.008)	<.001	(0.747)
Criminal				-0.29*
				(0.086)

(continued)

TABLE 10.13: *(continued)*

	(1)	(2)	(3)	(4)
VARIABLES	Criminal	Civil Related	Civil Unrelated	All Cases
Civil Related				−0.30***
				<.001
Period 2	0.24***	0.45***	−0.31***	−0.09
	<.001	<.001	<.001	(0.460)
Period 3	−5.63***	−0.27***	−0.49***	−0.53***
	<.001	<.001	<.001	<.001
Constant	0.29	−1.28***	−0.47***	−0.46***
	(0.150)	<.001	<.001	<.001
Observations	97	238	524	859
Pseudo R^2	0.289	0.423	0.325	0.296

Notes:

a. See the text for definitions of variables. The dependent variable takes the value of 1 if the case was won by the plaintiff.

b. Standard errors have been adjusted for clustering on case-type and time period.

c. Robust *p*-values in parentheses.

d. The omitted variables are "single vs. single" in the litigant characteristics category; "no document vs. no document," "no *fetva* vs. no *fetva*," and "no representative vs. no representative" in the rules and tools of litigation category; and "civil dispute among unrelated parties" in the case-type category; and "1684–96" in the time-period category.

e. *** indicates significance at 1%, ** at 5%, and * at 10% for a two-tailed test.

did not present a *fetva* lost all forty-nine cases against defendants who did present one.[13] Although the positive and significant coefficient of the "No document vs. Document" variable in criminal cases seems to contradict this trend, there are only three cases in this category – too small to suggest a systematic difference between civil and criminal cases. The results are mixed on representation during trial, which is not surprising because representatives served in this capacity for a variety of reasons, not necessarily as advocates to enhance chances of success.

As suggested earlier, the fall in the plaintiff win ratio in the third period provides some support to arguments recently made in the literature about "fictitious" litigations in Ottoman courts in the eighteenth century. Aykan (2012, 107) has argued that in Diyarbekir, actual criminal disputes were taken to other military-administrative organs of the Empire during this

[13] The negative and significant coefficient of the "*Fetva* vs. *Fetva*" variable is also interesting and may have further implications about how *fetva*-use influenced the litigation process, but the number of observations (2) in this category is too low to generalize.

TABLE 10.14: *Probit Analysis of Influences on Plaintiff's Chances of Success at Trial: Size-composition and Time Periods*

	(1)	(2)	(3)	(4)
VARIABLES	1684–96	1735–43	1781–90	All Cases
Single vs. Multiple	−0.99***	0.20	0.23	−0.10
	<.001	(0.525)	(0.171)	(0.698)
Single vs. Corporate		−4.57***	0.37***	−0.06
		<.001	<.001	(0.902)
Multiple vs. Single	0.24	−0.09	−0.05	0.08
	(0.355)	(0.868)	(0.565)	(0.699)
Multiple vs. Multiple	1.08***	1.04***	0.57**	0.61***
	(0.003)	<.001	(0.011)	<.001
Multiple vs. Corporate	−6.35***		1.25***	−5.86***
	<.001		(0.006)	<.001
Corporate vs. Single	5.11***	−0.25		0.48
	<.001	(0.174)		(0.357)
Corporate vs. Multiple	5.11***	0.42**	6.45***	0.92**
	<.001	(0.019)	<.001	(0.038)
Corporate vs. Corporate	4.31***		5.27***	5.17***
	<.001		<.001	<.001
Plaintiff has burden of proof	0.87***	1.23***	1.59***	1.21***
	(0.009)	<.001	<.001	<.001
Document vs. Document	6.52***	−0.76**	−0.96***	0.67
	<.001	(0.026)	<.001	(0.503)
Document vs. No document	0.86***	−0.01	1.00*	0.85***
	<.001	(0.791)	(0.051)	<.001
No document vs. Document	−1.21***	−4.88***	−0.59	−0.83***
	<.001	<.001	(0.261)	(0.002)
Fetva vs. *Fetva*	−12.00***		−4.16***	−5.34***
	<.001		<.001	<.001
Fetva vs. No *fetva*	1.53*	5.77***	1.41***	1.39***
	(0.052)	<.001	<.001	<.001
No *fetva* vs. *Fetva*	−10.04***	−4.92***	−5.30***	−5.26***
	<.001	<.001	<.001	<.001
Representative vs. Representative	0.84**	0.57***	−3.74***	0.32
	(0.013)	<.001	<.001	(0.114)
No representative vs. Representative	0.76	0.48**	0.46***	0.52***
	(0.223)	(0.020)	<.001	<.001
Representative vs. No representative	0.07	0.17	−0.11	0.05
	(0.813)	(0.454)	(0.754)	(0.747)
Criminal	−0.21*	−0.08	−1.17***	−0.29*
	(0.053)	(0.419)	<.001	(0.086)

(continued)

TABLE 10.14: *(continued)*

	(1)	(2)	(3)	(4)
VARIABLES	**1684–96**	**1735–43**	**1781–90**	**All Cases**
Civil Related	–0.67***	–0.09***	–0.38***	–0.30***
	<.001	<.001	<.001	<.001
Period 2				–0.09
				(0.460)
Period 3				–0.53***
				<.001
Constant	–0.17	–0.65***	–1.17***	–0.46***
	(0.189)	<.001	<.001	<.001
Observations	233	272	354	859
Pseudo R^2	0.304	0.230	0.405	0.296

See notes to Table 10.13.

period, such as the governor's council, where they were decided with or without the involvement of judicial authorities.[14] If this practice also existed in Kastamonu, criminal trials in the late eighteenth century may have served functions other than dispute resolution: When a criminal dispute came to court, the parties could have simply been seeking to register the defendant's innocence for future reference, causing the observed average plaintiffs win rates to be artificially low. This is consistent with the sharp decline of the plaintiff win rate in the Kastamonu court to 20 percent in criminal cases in the late eighteenth century (Table 10.3). It is possible that, by then, the court had ceased to be the real venue for resolving criminal disputes and seemingly weak criminal cases came to court not for resolution but to protect the rights and interests of defendants.

The possibility of "fictitious" litigation – cases that were brought to court for merely contractual purposes – could be prevalent in civil cases as well. The declining average win rates in the third period in civil cases, though not as sharp as that in criminal cases, suggest this possibility at some level. Recall that the number of contracts increased in the third period, as the court's primary function shifted from dispute resolution to notarial registry. This is also consistent with our findings in earlier chapters, altogether indicating that changing socioeconomic conditions affected the court's functions in the second half of the eighteenth century.

[14] Alternatively, such cases might have also been referred to the imperial center. See Tak (2009, 151–3).

INDIVIDUAL CHARACTERISTICS AND CHANCES OF SUCCESS AT TRIAL

We now sharpen our focus on the individual characteristics of litigants. Dropping from analysis the 269 observations that involved multiple litigants and corporate bodies, we take advantage of the rich information recorded about the litigants in the 590 trials between single individuals. Using this information, we introduce several new variables in the first category to measure the influence of gender, honorific titles, religion and religious (pilgrimage) markers, and family affiliation on the plaintiff's chances of success at trial. In all other respects, we follow exactly the same procedure as above in the way we defined the dependent variable, included three categories of explanatory variables, used the probit model for estimation, reported appropriate statistics of significance, ran separate regressions for each case-type and time period, and used clustered errors in regression analysis.

Tables 10.15 and 10.16 show how the individual characteristics of litigants and the rules and tools of litigation affected trial outcome across case-types and over time. Although in previous tables we gave detailed breakdowns of titles in relation to elite status or religious and military affiliation, for the regression analysis reported in the next two tables we lump them into one category for simplicity. For the reader interested in seeing the results with specific categories of titles, we present detailed breakdowns in the separate regressions included in the appendix to this chapter. The variables included in Tables 10.15 and 10.16 simply differentiate between women, men with honorific titles, and men with no titles. The omitted variable in the gender/title category is "Men, no title vs. Men, no title," so the coefficients show the differential effect of each plaintiff–defendant combination from this variable. Recall from Table 10.5 that the average win ratio of the omitted combination was 0.33.

To interpret the estimated signs and coefficients, once again we turn to the theoretical arguments developed in the preceding chapter about how we would expect the divergent expectations, asymmetric stakes, and differential knowledge and ability of litigants to affect the plaintiff's chances of success. For example, the coefficients of variables corresponding to litigant combinations in which men with titles served as plaintiffs is mostly positive as expected, indicating that they were more able than others to estimate the strength of their cases and/or to manipulate the legal system. The same was true in litigations involving members of

TABLE 10.15: *Probit Analysis of Influences on Plaintiff's Chances of Success at Trial: Individual Characteristics and Case-types*

VARIABLES	(1) Criminal	(2) Civil Related	(3) Civil Unrelated	(4) All Cases
Woman vs. Woman	-5.48***	0.16	0.66	0.47
	<.001	(0.567)	(0.267)	(0.106)
Woman vs. Man, title	6.23***	0.09	0.64	0.55
	<.001	(0.873)	(0.365)	(0.157)
Woman vs. Man, no title	0.73	0.28	0.57	0.56**
	(0.444)	(0.361)	(0.226)	(0.023)
Man, title vs. Woman		0.33	0.89	0.82***
		(0.506)	(0.134)	(0.002)
Man, title vs. Man, title	6.27***	-5.17***	1.21***	0.92***
	<.001	<.001	<.001	<.001
Man, title vs. Man, no title	1.14	-0.63*	0.85***	0.66***
	(0.373)	(0.064)	<.001	<.001
Man, no title vs. Woman	-5.37***	-0.69***	0.85	0.51
	<.001	<.001	(0.255)	(0.281)
Man, no title vs. Man, title	0.88**	-1.13**	0.70*	0.40*
	(0.018)	(0.019)	(0.079)	(0.093)
Muslim vs. Non-Muslim			0.11	0.30
			(0.803)	(0.607)
Non-Muslim vs. Muslim	-6.42***		0.33	-0.15
	<.001		(0.385)	(0.666)
Non-Muslim vs. Non-Muslim	6.03***	6.74***	0.42***	1.00***
	<.001	<.001	<.001	(0.008)
Pilgrim vs. Pilgrim		-4.69***	0.10	-0.03
		<.001	(0.896)	(0.964)
Non-pilgrim vs. Pilgrim	-6.33***	0.46	0.04	-0.07
	<.001	(0.151)	(0.918)	(0.813)
Pilgrim vs. Non-pilgrim	5.61***	0.58***	0.34	0.46
	<.001	<.001	(0.497)	(0.117)
Prominent vs. Prominent	-0.10	4.26***	3.77***	6.13***
	(0.868)	<.001	<.001	<.001
Prominent vs. Non-prominent	5.11***	-0.13	1.08*	1.20**
	<.001	(0.852)	(0.097)	(0.017)
Non-prominent vs. Prominent	-0.32	-3.94***	-0.62*	-0.33
	(0.310)	<.001	(0.074)	(0.316)
Plaintiff has burden of proof	0.12	1.74***	1.37***	1.27***
	(0.798)	<.001	<.001	<.001
Document vs. Document		6.80***	1.05*	6.57***
		<.001	(0.079)	<.001

(continued)

TABLE 10.15: *(continued)*

	(1)	(2)	(3)	(4)
VARIABLES	Criminal	Civil Related	Civil Unrelated	All Cases
Document vs. No document		6.92*** <.001	0.27 (0.534)	0.54 (0.149)
No document vs. Document	−0.08 (0.820)	−0.60 (0.349)	−1.27*** <.001	−1.01*** <.001
Fetva vs. *Fetva*			−5.14*** <.001	−12.19*** <.001
Fetva vs. No *fetva*	16.98*** <.001	1.22*** <.001	1.78*** <.001	1.35*** <.001
No *fetva* vs. *Fetva*		−3.97*** <.001	−5.62*** <.001	−11.64*** <.001
Representative vs. Representative		0.76** (0.020)	5.75*** <.001	1.36*** (0.008)
No representative vs. Representative	−5.37*** <.001	0.42 (0.248)	0.36*** <.001	0.35*** <.001
Representative vs. No representative	−0.60 (0.150)	−0.69*** <.001	0.44* (0.070)	−0.00 (0.983)
Criminal				−0.16 (0.641)
Civil Related				−0.24 (0.243)
Period 2	−0.05 (0.733)	0.80*** <.001	−0.75*** <.001	−0.28 (0.232)
Period 3	−11.38*** <.001	−0.03 (0.730)	−0.69*** <.001	−0.66*** <.001
Constant	−0.39 (0.461)	−1.53*** (0.001)	−1.08*** <.001	−0.97*** <.001
Observations	67	169	354	590
Pseudo R^2	0.565	0.465	0.382	0.323

Notes:

a. See the text for definitions of variables. The dependent variable takes the value of 1 if the case was won by the plaintiff.

b. Standard errors have been adjusted for clustering on case-type and time period.

c. Robust *p*-values in parentheses.

d. The omitted variables are "Man with No Title vs. Man with No Title" in the Gender–Title category; "Muslim vs. Muslim" in the Religious Affiliation category; "Non-pilgrim vs. Non-pilgrim" in the Religious Marker category; "Non-prominent vs. Non-prominent" in the Family Affiliation category; "No Document vs. No Document," "No *Fetva* vs. No *Fetva*," and "No Representative vs. No Representative" in the Rules and Tools of Litigation category; "Civil Dispute among Unrelated Parties," in the Case-type category; and " 1684–96" in the Time Period category.

e. *** indicates significance at 1%, ** at 5%, and * at 10% for a two-tailed test.

f. For simplicity, the Religious Marker category includes only the pilgrim status.

prominent families, as they were more likely than others to win as plaintiffs and defendants. As an exception to this argument, the coefficient of "Men, title vs. Men, no title" in civil cases between related individuals is negative and somewhat significant, an indication that other differences between men with titles and others offset the influence of differential ability within family and kin networks.

TABLE 10.16: *Probit Analysis of Influences on Plaintiff's Chances of Success at Trial: Individual Characteristics and Time Periods*

	(1)	(2)	(3)	(4)
VARIABLES	**1684–96**	**1735–43**	**1781–90**	**All Cases**
Woman vs. Woman	0.34	0.64	0.57	0.47
	(0.668)	(0.361)	(0.269)	(0.106)
Woman vs. Man, title	-0.15	0.66	1.36**	0.55
	(0.567)	(0.184)	(0.026)	(0.157)
Woman vs. Man, no title	0.58	0.70*	0.97**	0.56**
	(0.107)	(0.050)	(0.048)	(0.023)
Man, title vs. Woman	0.41	0.79***	1.58***	0.82***
	(0.383)	(0.001)	<.001	(0.002)
Man, title vs. Man, title	1.04***	1.30***	0.30	0.92***
	<.001	<.001	(0.707)	<.001
Man, title vs. Man, no title	0.83***	0.70***	0.48	0.66***
	<.001	<.001	(0.524)	<.001
Man, no title vs. Woman	-0.13	-0.28	1.16	0.51
	(0.724)	(0.491)	(0.252)	(0.281)
Man, no title vs. Man, title	-0.14	0.73***	0.10	0.40*
	(0.742)	(0.003)	(0.913)	(0.093)
Muslim vs. Non-Muslim	4.58***		-4.56***	0.30
	<.001		<.001	(0.607)
Non-Muslim vs. Muslim	-4.96***	0.04	3.81***	-0.15
	<.001	(0.812)	<.001	(0.666)
Non-Muslim vs. Non-Muslim		1.77**	0.35**	1.00***
		(0.016)	(0.019)	(0.008)
Pilgrim vs. Pilgrim	5.58***	0.37	-8.03***	-0.03
	<.001	(0.333)	<.001	(0.964)
Non-pilgrim vs. Pilgrim	0.30	-0.47	-0.19	-0.07
	(0.424)	(0.463)	(0.743)	(0.813)
Pilgrim vs. Non-pilgrim	0.34**	0.22	1.49*	0.46
	(0.047)	(0.107)	(0.074)	(0.117)

(continued)

TABLE 10.16: *(continued)*

	(1)	(2)	(3)	(4)
VARIABLES	1684–96	1735–43	1781–90	All Cases
Prominent vs. Prominent	4.45***	4.53***		6.13***
	<.001	<.001		<.001
Prominent vs. Non-prominent	0.64***	0.98***	7.44***	1.20**
	(0.005)	(0.005)	<.001	(0.017)
Non-prominent vs. Prominent	9.07***	−0.64	−5.27***	−0.33
	<.001	(0.139)	<.001	(0.316)
Plaintiff has burden of proof	0.83**	1.18***	1.98***	1.27***
	(0.032)	<.001	<.001	<.001
Document vs. Document	6.70***		10.31***	6.57***
	<.001		<.001	<.001
Document vs. No document	1.01***	−0.26***	0.68	0.54
	<.001	<.001	(0.408)	(0.149)
No document vs. Document	−1.33***	−9.53***	−0.70**	−1.01***
	<.001	<.001	(0.014)	<.001
Fetva vs. *Fetva*	−11.61***		−4.38***	−12.19***
	<.001		<.001	<.001
Fetva vs. No *fetva*	1.83***	5.58***	1.97***	1.35***
	(0.002)	<.001	<.001	<.001
No *fetva* vs. *Fetva*	−11.12***	−4.90***	−9.23***	−11.64***
	<.001	<.001	<.001	<.001
Representative vs. Representative	5.95***	5.24***		1.36***
	<.001	<.001		(0.008)
No representative vs. Representative	0.91	0.25	0.16***	0.35***
	(0.239)	(0.104)	<.001	<.001
Representative vs. No representative	0.28	−0.01	−0.14	−0.00
	(0.586)	(0.980)	(0.598)	(0.983)
Criminal	0.04	0.46***	−2.46***	−0.16
	(0.492)	(0.002)	<.001	(0.641)
Civil Related	−0.70***	0.38***	−0.76***	−0.24
	<.001	<.001	<.001	(0.243)
Period 2				−0.28
				(0.232)
Period 3				−0.66***
				<.001
Constant	−0.74***	−1.60***	−1.99***	−0.97***
	(0.001)	<.001	(0.001)	<.001
Observations	162	188	240	590
Pseudo R^2	0.370	0.298	0.494	0.323

See notes to Table 10.15.

Our results for positional differences in religious marker and family status suggest that asymmetric stakes may have also affected trial outcomes. Note, for example, the positive and significant coefficients of "Pilgrim vs. Non-pilgrim" and "Prominent vs. Non-prominent," and the negative and significant coefficients of "Non-pilgrim vs. Pilgrim" and "Non-prominent vs. Prominent." Since these results are also consistent with the divergence of expectations and differential legal ability among pilgrims and non-pilgrims and among *zade*s and non-*zade*s, we cannot isolate with precision the influences of individual factors that likely affected trial results.

For variables in the category of differential use of the rules and tools of litigation, the results are consistent with expectations and preliminary observations based on Tables 10.9–10.12. More specifically, our results show that the parties who assumed the burden of proof had better chances in litigations, and that those who presented *fetva*s or documents were more likely to win at trial against those who did not take advantage of these opportunities, regardless of their status at trial as plaintiff or defendant.

Representation by third parties had mixed effects on trial outcome and seemed to depend on case-type, as was the case in Table 10.13. In civil cases between unrelated individuals, the plaintiff's chance of success was generally higher in all other combinations of representation as compared to the reference category of no representation by either party. Interestingly, the positive coefficient remained the same regardless of the reversal of differential representation between the plaintiff and the defendant. In civil cases between unrelated individuals, however, whereas the effect was positive and significant when both parties were represented, it was negative and significant when the plaintiff had representation but the defendant did not. In criminal trials, the plaintiff's chances were hurt by having no representation against defendants who came with a representative.

Our results confirm our earlier finding that litigant roles affected success at trial. In many cross-group pairings, litigants with higher status dominated as plaintiffs but not as defendants, or not as much in this role.[15] Nevertheless, when the parties differed in social status, the

[15] A fee-for-service compensation regime in courts might have led to a pro-plaintiff bias, which may be relevant here (Coşgel and Ergene, 2014a, 138; cf. Kuran and Lustig 2012, 10). Such a bias, if it really existed in the Ottoman context, may not be fully accounted for by the variables included in our analysis, which, for example, does not explore if trial results based solely on the kadıs' discretion (see p. 216) were inclined for the plaintiffs. Although, in principle, defendants should be able to adjust their settlement-trial decision thresholds to accommodate a pro-plaintiff bias, there might have been obstacles for such a correction in actual practice.

coefficients estimated for pairings in which the plaintiff had a higher status (for example, "Man, title vs. Man, no title," "Man, title vs. Woman," or "Prominent vs. Non-prominent" in Tables 10.15 and 10.16) are larger and more significant than the coefficients for pairings in which low-status parties were plaintiffs (for example, "Man, no title vs. Man, title" "Woman vs. Man, title," or "Non-prominent vs. Prominent"). The fact that such differences continue to exist among groups of unequal stature even when we control for many factors that could have generated advantages for privileged parties (*fetva*s, written documents, the knowledge of probable success associated with the assumption of burden of proof) is remarkable. Although Tables 10.4 to 10.8 collectively provide a better depiction of the overall differences in trial performance among client groups, the analysis presented in Tables 10.15 and 10.16 suggests that privileged litigants had a multitude of mechanisms that helped them dominate their trials, some of which are not directly detectable in the court records.

In the appendix to this chapter, we provide further detail regarding the effects of holding titles, broken into subcategories based on religious-military affiliation and elite status. For example, regression results in Appendix 10.A show that plaintiffs with elite and non-elite titles mostly won against other defendant groups. In the same vein, Appendix 10.B shows that plaintiffs with religious titles likely won against defendants with other title affiliations and plaintiffs with military titles against everybody else except for religious titleholders. Noteworthy in both sets of regressions is the fact that some of the coefficients for litigant combinations with elite and religious titleholding plaintiffs are the largest that we have observed for all title, gender, status, and religious pairings (with large numbers of observations) in all regressions, revealing these groups' superior success in winning their cases. Remarkably, religious titleholders do not appear to have been disadvantaged even in trials where they appeared as defendants.

CONCLUSION

In this chapter we offered a quantitative analysis of how size-composition and individual characteristics of the parties, rules and tools of litigation, and temporal and categorical variations of the legal environment influenced the outcome of litigations. Using insights from the theoretical and historical arguments developed in previous chapters, we discussed whether the results confirm expectations.

Overall, our results indicate that affluent and socially prominent litigants, presumably skilled in estimating case strength and knowledgeable about legal rules and procedures, performed well against their poorer, less prominent, and less informed opponents, when the former group acted as plaintiffs. Stakes from trial outcome were also important, as seen in the higher likelihood of success for pilgrims against non-pilgrims and members of prominent families against others.

Differential use of the rules and tools of litigation affected the outcome significantly and, assuming that litigants were informed about this fact, might have influenced prior settlement-trial decisions. Individuals who assumed the burden of proof were generally more likely than others to win, as were those who presented *fetva*s or documents against those who did not take advantage of these opportunities. Representation by third parties had mixed effects on trial outcome. The average win ratio varied systematically across case-types, and was generally lower in civil cases between related parties than between unrelated ones. Although the overall win ratio fell gradually over time, case-types followed different patterns.

Our results suggest that Kastamonu judges made decisions that can be grasped by the tools and concepts of modern scholarship on dispute resolution, and their decisions displayed quite a few systematic patterns that are consistent with those identified by quantitative analysis of court outcomes in modern societies. The results also challenge the widely shared perception in Ottoman legal scholarship that the court may have subscribed to an egalitarian legal ideology. Contrary to presumptions, based largely on impressionistic observations, that judges protected or favored the interests of the poor and the underprivileged, trial outcomes were neither impartial to the individual characteristics of litigants nor did they systematically favor women or titleless or non-elite men against more privileged elites. On the contrary, our results indicate that titleholders (religious and elite ones, in particular), pilgrims, and members of prominent families generally performed better in trials than other groups.

APPENDIX 10.A: *Individual Characteristics (Including Breakdown by Elite Status) and the Plaintiff Win Ratio across Case-types and over Time*

	(1)	(2)	(3)	(4)	(5)	(6)	(7)
VARIABLES	Criminal	Civil Related	Civil Unrelated	1684–96	1735–43	1781–90	All Cases
Woman vs. Woman	–5.50***	0.23	0.69	0.40	0.61	0.59	0.47
	<.001	(0.123)	(0.256)	(0.599)	(0.395)	(0.259)	(0.113)
Woman vs. Man, elite title	5.76***	0.18	0.83***	5.46***		1.29**	0.79***
	<.001	(0.782)	(0.005)	<.001		(0.013)	<.001
Woman vs. Man, non-elite title	6.18***	0.14	0.60	–0.65*	0.59	1.51*	0.48
	<.001	(0.849)	(0.471)	(0.067)	(0.267)	(0.056)	(0.286)
Woman vs. Man, no title	0.73	0.33	0.58	0.61*	0.67**	0.98*	0.55**
	(0.445)	(0.397)	(0.193)	(0.074)	(0.041)	(0.070)	(0.024)
Man, elite title vs. Woman		0.07	1.13**	1.22***	0.85***	1.03*	0.67**
		(0.850)	(0.022)	<.001	<.001	(0.052)	(0.012)
Man, elite title vs. Man, elite title			1.16**	0.47***	5.60***	4.21***	1.04***
			(0.014)	(0.001)	<.001	<.001	(0.002)
Man, elite title vs. Man, non-elite title	6.19***		1.69***	1.04***	1.89***	1.33**	1.50***
	<.001		<.001	<.001	<.001	(0.023)	<.001
Man, elite title vs. Man, no title	6.12***	–4.79***	1.26**	1.15***	1.08***	1.72	1.07***
	<.001	<.001	(0.022)	(0.008)	<.001	(0.154)	<.001
Man, non-elite title vs. Woman		0.59	0.71	0.38	0.82*	1.86***	0.93**
		(0.400)	(0.428)	(0.688)	(0.076)	<.001	(0.010)

Man, non-elite title vs. Man, elite title		−5.24***	1.63***	7.85***	1.43***	−0.53	1.00***
		<.001	<.001	<.001	<.001	(0.353)	(0.001)
Man, non-elite title vs. Man, non-elite title	6.20***	−5.06***	0.94***	1.45***	0.96***	0.17	0.64***
	<.001	<.001	<.001	<.001	<.001	(0.842)	(0.002)
Man, non-elite title vs. Man, no title	0.93	−0.13	0.57***	0.76***	0.42***	0.10	0.43***
	(0.405)	(0.774)	<.001	<.001	<.001	(0.878)	<.001
Man, no title vs. Woman	−5.43***	−0.64**	0.85	0.06	−0.35	1.20	0.50
	<.001	(0.020)	(0.243)	(0.835)	(0.410)	(0.270)	(0.289)
Man, no title vs. Man, elite title	0.62	−6.45***	1.05	−4.89***	1.45	0.11	0.51
	(0.652)	<.001	(0.108)	<.001	(0.222)	(0.907)	(0.348)
Man, no title vs. Man, non-elite title	0.85**	−0.77***	0.60*	−0.04	0.61***	0.11	0.37*
	(0.020)	(0.004)	(0.083)	(0.925)	<.001	(0.903)	(0.070)
Muslim vs. Non-Muslim			0.23	4.52***		−3.90***	0.40
			(0.447)	<.001		<.001	(0.422)
Non-Muslim vs. Muslim	−6.35***		0.21	−5.28***	−0.28	3.68***	−0.21
	<.001		(0.718)	<.001	(0.662)	<.001	(0.572)
Non-Muslim vs. Non-Muslim	5.97***	6.80***	0.39***		1.71**	0.40***	0.97***
	<.001	<.001	<.001		(0.027)	(0.002)	(0.010)
Pilgrim vs. Pilgrim		−4.59***	−0.02	6.04***	0.23	−8.01***	−0.09
		<.001	(0.985)	<.001	(0.498)	<.001	(0.875)
Non-pilgrim vs. Pilgrim	−6.12***	0.67	−0.00	0.32	−0.64	−0.17	−0.11
	<.001	(0.232)	(0.999)	(0.376)	(0.308)	(0.767)	(0.693)
Pilgrim vs. Non-pilgrim	5.66***	0.31	0.28	0.28	0.20	1.54	0.46
	<.001	(0.244)	(0.585)	(0.408)	(0.220)	(0.105)	(0.118)

(continued)

	(1)	(2)	(3)	(4)	(5)	(6)	(7)
VARIABLES	Criminal	Civil Related	Civil Unrelated	1684–96	1735–43	1781–90	All Cases
Prominent vs. Prominent	−0.06	4.09***	3.70***	5.66***	4.60***		4.88***
	(0.927)	<.001	<.001	<.001	<.001		<.001
Prominent vs. Non-prominent	0.07	−0.27	0.96*	0.46***	0.81**	6.75***	1.09**
	(0.930)	(0.878)	(0.054)	<.001	(0.048)	<.001	(0.022)
Non-prominent vs. Prominent	−0.26***	−4.01***	−0.88**	14.79***	−0.63	−5.04***	−0.42
	<.001	<.001	(0.029)	<.001	(0.182)	<.001	(0.286)
Plaintiff has burden of proof	0.07	1.76***	1.40***	0.63*	1.16***	2.11***	1.28***
	(0.876)	<.001	<.001	(0.076)	(0.001)	<.001	<.001
Document vs. Document		7.12***	1.02*	5.95***		10.92***	5.19***
		<.001	(0.082)	<.001		<.001	<.001
Document vs. No document		6.86***	0.19	1.08***	−0.44***	0.59	0.46
		<.001	(0.724)	<.001	<.001	(0.525)	(0.259)
No document vs. Document	−0.14	−0.61	−1.36***	−2.00***	−9.75***	−0.76**	−1.05***
	(0.697)	(0.355)	<.001	<.001	<.001	(0.012)	<.001
Fetva vs. *Fetva*			−5.12***	−11.61***		−3.97***	−9.55***
			<.001	<.001		<.001	<.001
Fetva vs. No *fetva*	16.92***	1.22***	1.79***	2.16***	5.68***	2.10***	1.35***
	<.001	<.001	<.001	<.001	<.001	(0.001)	<.001
No *fetva* vs. *Fetva*		−4.00***	−5.95***	−22.42***	−4.85***	−8.97***	−8.68***
		<.001	<.001	<.001	<.001	<.001	<.001
Representative vs. Representative		0.76**	5.71***	6.30***	5.30***		1.35***
		(0.018)	<.001	<.001	<.001		(0.006)

No representative vs. Representative	−5.43***	0.31	0.26**	0.75***	0.07	0.23***	0.31***
	<.001	(0.128)	(0.047)	(0.004)	(0.343)	<.001	<.001
Representative vs. No representative	−0.53	−0.73***	0.38	0.16	−0.02	−0.15	−0.01
	(0.290)	<.001	(0.102)	(0.703)	(0.960)	(0.528)	(0.952)
Period 2	0.00	0.75***	−0.75***				−0.26
	(0.990)	<.001	<.001				(0.275)
Period 3	−11.26***	−0.01	−0.69***				−0.64***
	<.001	(0.908)	<.001				(0.001)
Criminal				0.07	0.47***	−2.53***	−0.16
				(0.133)	(0.006)	<.001	(0.653)
Civil Related				−0.66***	0.40***	−0.73***	−0.25
				<.001	(0.001)	<.001	(0.229)
Constant	−0.39	−1.59***	−1.06***	−0.67***	−1.53***	−2.12***	−0.97***
	(0.444)	(0.003)	<.001	(0.001)	<.001	(0.002)	<.001
Observations	67	169	354	162	188	240	590
Pseudo R^2	0.570	0.473	0.396	0.421	0.318	0.512	0.332

Notes:

a. See the text for definitions of variables. The dependent variable takes the value of 1 if the case was won by the plaintiff.

b. Standard errors have been adjusted for clustering on case-type and time period.

c. Robust *p*-values in parentheses.

d. The omitted variables are "Man with No Title vs. Man with No Title" in the Gender–Title category; "Muslim vs. Muslim" in the Religious Affiliation category; "Non-pilgrim vs. Non-pilgrim" in the Religious Marker category; "Non-prominent vs. Non-prominent" in the Family Affiliation category; "No Document vs. No Document," "No *Fetva* vs. No *Fetva*," and "No Representative vs. No Representative" in the Rules and Tools of Litigation category; "Civil Dispute among Unrelated Parties," in the Case-type category; and "1684–96" in the Time Period category.

e. *** indicates significance at 1%, ** at 5%, and * at 10% for a two-tailed test.

f. For simplicity, the Religious Marker category includes only the pilgrim status.

APPENDIX 10.B: *Individual Characteristics (Including Breakdown by Religious and Military Titles) and the Plaintiff Win Ratio across Case-types and over Time*

	(1)	(2)	(3)	(4)	(5)	(6)	(7)
VARIABLES	Criminal	Civil Related	Civil Unrelated	1684–96	1735–43	1781–90	All Cases
Woman vs. Woman	–5.69***	0.28	0.52	0.15	0.29	0.65	0.38
	<.001	(0.131)	(0.303)	(0.881)	(0.562)	(0.130)	(0.192)
Woman vs. Man, religious title	6.50***	0.26	0.22	–0.34	0.10	1.25	0.20
	<.001	(0.585)	(0.774)	(0.289)	(0.850)	(0.119)	(0.650)
Woman vs. Man, military title	6.97***	0.21	0.70	–0.61**	0.76	1.54***	0.69
	<.001	(0.809)	(0.343)	(0.048)	(0.462)	(0.004)	(0.105)
Woman vs. Man, no title	0.66	0.42	0.36	0.42	0.36	1.06**	0.48*
	(0.519)	(0.176)	(0.536)	(0.314)	(0.444)	(0.020)	(0.088)
Man, religious title vs. Woman		0.60***	–0.60	–0.07	0.39	1.21***	0.42
		(0.004)	(0.155)	(0.846)	(0.686)	(0.007)	(0.380)
Man, religious title vs. Man, religious title		–5.10***	0.43	0.04	–0.08	–2.26***	0.12
		<.001	(0.270)	(0.299)	(0.156)	<.001	(0.652)
Man, religious title vs. Man, military title	6.99***		1.53***	6.52***	1.72***	1.17**	1.28***
	<.001		<.001	<.001	<.001	(0.037)	<.001
Man, religious title vs. Man, no title	6.28***	–4.11***	1.51**	6.40***	0.51**	2.42**	1.23***
	<.001	<.001	(0.019)	<.001	(0.036)	(0.018)	(0.001)
Man, military title vs. Woman		0.44	1.43***	1.88***	0.36	1.93***	0.91***
		(0.631)	<.001	<.001	(0.498)	<.001	(0.009)

Man, military title vs. Man,			0.11	−0.24	−0.39	0.01	−0.08
religious title			(0.733)	(0.298)	(0.348)	(0.962)	(0.733)
Man, military title vs. Man,	7.05***		1.08***	1.40***	0.86**	0.03	0.89***
military title	<.001		<.001	<.001	(0.027)	(0.935)	<.001
Man, military title vs. Man, no	0.99	−0.33	0.30***	0.37***	0.27**	−0.24	0.29***
title	(0.461)	(0.375)	(0.005)	<.001	(0.048)	(0.735)	(0.002)
Man, no title vs. Woman	−5.80***	−0.55**	0.73	−0.17	−0.50	1.30	0.44
	<.001	(0.013)	(0.364)	(0.611)	(0.229)	(0.207)	(0.383)
Man, no title vs. Man, religious	−5.82***	−0.46	0.72***	−1.88***	0.40*	−0.22	0.20
title	<.001	(0.230)	(0.002)	<.001	(0.097)	(0.685)	(0.542)
Man, no title vs. Man, military	1.40*	−1.44***	0.39	0.11	0.44*	0.26	0.39
title	(0.068)	<.001	(0.202)	(0.860)	(0.087)	(0.779)	(0.109)
Muslim vs. Non-Muslim			−0.30	4.67***		−6.10***	−0.03
			(0.655)	<.001		<.001	(0.966)
Non-Muslim vs. Muslim	−7.29***		0.41	−5.71***	−0.15	3.36***	−0.25
	<.001		(0.330)	<.001	(0.378)	<.001	(0.553)
Non-Muslim vs. Non-Muslim	6.41***	6.77***	0.37**		1.52*	0.44***	0.95***
	<.001	<.001	(0.024)		(0.083)	<.001	(0.009)
Pilgrim vs. Pilgrim		−4.60***	0.02	5.80***	0.20	−8.11***	−0.06
		<.001	(0.984)	<.001	(0.532)	<.001	(0.917)
Non-pilgrim vs. Pilgrim	−6.96***	0.56	−0.11	0.17	−0.60	−0.20	−0.12
	<.001	(0.133)	(0.770)	(0.485)	(0.230)	(0.772)	(0.652)
Pilgrim vs. Non-pilgrim	6.34***	0.32	0.46	0.22*	0.14	1.95	0.50
	<.001	(0.238)	(0.394)	(0.094)	(0.598)	(0.130)	(0.150)

(continued)

APPENDIX 10.B: *(continued)*

	(1)	(2)	(3)	(4)	(5)	(6)	(7)
VARIABLES	Criminal	Civil Related	Civil Unrelated	1684–96	1735–43	1781–90	All Cases
Prominent vs. Prominent	–0.09***	4.31***	3.40***	2.09*	4.78***		5.23***
	<.001	<.001	<.001	(0.052)	<.001		<.001
Prominent vs. Non-prominent	0.09***	–0.14	1.14	–0.37	1.61***	7.66***	1.21**
	<.001	(0.834)	(0.120)	(0.295)	<.001	<.001	(0.016)
Non-prominent vs. Prominent	–0.26***	–3.99***	–0.68*	9.10***	–0.70*	–4.93***	–0.45
	<.001	<.001	(0.085)	<.001	(0.052)	<.001	(0.152)
Plaintiff has burden of proof	–0.12	1.75***	1.51***	0.85**	1.26***	2.15***	1.31***
	(0.327)	<.001	<.001	(0.024)	<.001	<.001	<.001
Document vs. Document		6.70***	0.09***	7.49***		11.79***	5.52***
		<.001	<.001	<.001		<.001	<.001
Document vs. No document		6.99***	0.41	0.91***	–0.29	0.88	0.57*
		<.001	(0.205)	<.001	(0.103)	(0.272)	(0.090)
No document vs. Document	–0.06***	–0.60	–1.56***	–2.26***	–9.10***	–0.91*	–1.07***
	<.001	(0.309)	<.001	<.001	<.001	(0.064)	<.001
Fetva vs. *Fetva*			–5.25***	–12.85***		–3.69***	–10.09***
			<.001	<.001		<.001	<.001
Fetva vs. No *fetva*	19.10***	1.14***	1.74***	1.99***	5.40***	2.28***	1.29***
	<.001	<.001	<.001	<.001	<.001	(0.003)	<.001
No *fetva* vs. *Fetva*		–4.02***	–6.22***	–10.38***	–4.77***	–8.07***	–8.30***
		<.001	<.001	<.001	<.001	<.001	<.001
Representative vs. Representative		0.75**	6.05***	6.41***	4.85***		1.35***
		(0.020)	<.001	<.001	<.001		(0.007)

No representative vs. Representative	−5.80***	0.40	0.32***	1.56**	0.41	0.17***	0.36***
	<.001	(0.249)	<.001	(0.042)	(0.163)	(0.009)	(0.003)
Representative vs. No representative	−0.77**	−0.70***	0.55*	0.54	0.02	−0.12	0.03
	(0.018)	<.001	(0.068)	(0.398)	(0.968)	(0.685)	(0.918)
Period 2	−0.20***	0.79***	−0.83***				−0.30
	(0.007)	<.001	<.001				(0.231)
Period 3	−12.82***	−0.06	−0.83***				−0.71***
	<.001	(0.722)	<.001				<.001
Criminal				0.11	0.28***	−2.51***	−0.22
				(0.257)	(0.001)	<.001	(0.482)
Civil Related				−0.76***	0.37**	−0.76***	−0.25
				<.001	(0.015)	<.001	(0.235)
Constant	−0.08	−1.65***	−0.91***	−0.64***	−1.28***	−2.22***	−0.87***
	(0.900)	(0.001)	(0.001)	<.001	<.001	<.001	<.001
Observations	67	169	354	162	188	240	590
Pseudo R^2	0.637	0.466	0.413	0.425	0.308	0.530	0.339

See notes to Appendix 10.A.

Conclusion

This book examined legal practice in the sharia court of Ottoman Kastamonu in the late seventeenth and eighteenth centuries. More specifically, we investigated how the legal and judicial functions of the court changed over time and how its clients, as representatives of various segments of the society, interacted and fared in these encounters. Applying theoretical insights from the Law and Economics scholarship to the Ottoman socio-legal environment, we utilized sophisticated quantitative techniques to examine court documents. To classify court clients, we introduced novel categories of analysis that allowed us to evaluate how differences in gender, religious affiliation, and socioeconomic status influenced legal interactions and consequences. The result is a systematic depiction of Ottoman legal practices in one Anatolian setting that offers fresh insights and new possibilities for Islamic–Ottoman legal scholarship.

Little direct historical information exists about the inhabitants and socioeconomic conditions of pre-nineteenth-century Kastamonu, as is typical for many locations in Ottoman lands for the same period. We know that Kastamonu was a small- to medium-sized town by contemporary standards, and that its geographic limits and population did not change significantly during our period of study. Sporadic information about the region's economic circumstances indicates little if anything special about Kastamonu's agrarian, commercial, or industrial characteristics. The region may have experienced a transition from prebendal revenue extraction to short- and longer-term tax-farming in the agrarian sector, like many locations in the empire during the seventeenth and eighteenth centuries. It is not immediately clear, however, how this shift influenced Kastamonu's general conditions. In our attempts to understand the socioeconomic circumstances in Kastamonu, we filled some major historiographical gaps by using information from probate estate inventories. Our analysis indicated that economic conditions deteriorated for most inhabitants during the eighteenth century, as average real wealth fell and overall inequality rose, though men and women experienced these changes somewhat differently and some socioeconomic groups fared better than others. The recent historical literature on the Ottoman Empire has characterized the seventeenth and eighteenth centuries as a period of major socioeconomic dynamism. While this may have been true for many places in the Empire, there is little evidence of this trend for Kastamonu.

This book has provided important empirical information about the place and operations of the sharia court in this historical context. For one, we demonstrated that the court played a limited role in the legal and judicial affairs of the district, as is evident in the modest number of documents pertaining to litigations, settlements, and contractual arrangements relative to the size of the local population. This particular finding should caution students of Ottoman court records who might be tempted to amplify the representativeness of their source base with respect to major socioeconomic and political dynamics in provincial locales. Only further research can demonstrate whether our findings for Kastamonu can be generalized to other settings; however, our study suggests that the court in Kastamonu was not the primary venue for dispute resolution and that many (possibly most) Kastamonians avoided use of the court for management of settlements or contractual arrangements.

At the same time, we also observed some significant changes in the court's operations during our period. First, the court's involvement in the disputes and contractual interactions of the local population increased over time, as is clear in the growing amount of court-produced documentation during the eighteenth century, when the population of the region remained stable. Also, the residents of Kastamonu became less hesitant to bring to court intra-family and intra-kin affairs for resolution or registration. Second, by the late eighteenth century, the court was less of a venue for dispute resolution compared to earlier times, as its notarial workload had increased. While litigations also rose in number, contractual and settlement activities grew proportionally more. Third, the court became increasingly focused on disputes and transactions related to immovable property and land transactions, which may be indicative of the local population's growing preoccupation with property ownership, usufruct rights, and/or revenue collection. Fourth, the court became less involved in criminal disputes during our period, to the extent that the court's function of crime prevention had been taken over by non-judicial authorities by the late eighteenth century, possibly by the subgovernor and/or his representatives.

Although our sources do not include direct and unequivocal information regarding the reasons for these temporal variations in court-use patterns, we suggested that they could be related to the history of the court in Kastamonu – reflecting changes in local attitudes toward dispute resolution and court-produced documentation or institutional transformations in the administration of justice and wider social, economic, and financial trends in the empire. More specifically, the proportional changes that we observed in the number of litigations, settlements, and contracts may be related to the growing economic tensions in the region, as we explain below, when we deliberate on the results of Part IV. In addition, we proposed a connection between the spread of long-term tax-farming, the probable commercialization of the economy (if in fact this happened), and the growing notarial functions of the court and its frequent involvement in immovable property and land transactions. More research is necessary to substantiate both of these claims.

One of our main objectives in this book has been to identify how various client groups used the court. To accomplish this task, we differentiated among various types of legal affairs and looked at *all* parties involved in specific legal interactions, instead of examining the actions of individual groups of court clients in isolation. As our discussion progressed, we narrowed our focus by successively studying smaller subsets of the court's business. We first examined the differences between contractual agreements and disputes (settlements and litigations), then the characteristics of disputes that likely wound up at trial, and finally the factors that may have enhanced the plaintiff's chances of success in litigations.

Our preliminary observations on court-use patterns in Chapters 3 and 4 indicated that women, non-Muslims, and lower classes were underrepresented among court clients. Although female representation increased during the eighteenth century, there is little evidence that court use became more democratic otherwise. Our analysis also revealed important gender- and class-based court-use patterns. Women appeared more often in settlements than in contracts or litigations, and their legal interactions in court often involved male relatives. Moreover, women's legal interactions with related men were more likely to be disputes than contractual agreements, compared to their interactions with unrelated men. Upper-class men, including elite religious and military titleholders, pilgrims, and members of prominent families, were better represented in contracts than in litigations or settlements compared to non-elite titleholders and titleless men. Significant segments of the upper classes (in particular, elite and religious titleholders, pilgrims, and members of prominent families) were underrepresented in legal interactions that involved kin and family members. Our analysis also revealed major variations in court-use patterns among gender, title, religious marker, and family groups over time, indicating dynamic and temporally sensitive patterns of court use, a topic that has received no scholarly attention until now.

Part III focused on settlements and litigations. After we surveyed the legal, historical, and anthropological literature on dispute resolution in various Islamic settings, we offered a formal economic approach to trial-settlement decisions that was informed by the realities of the socio-legal environment of the Ottoman Empire. The analytical framework that we introduced in Part III (and continued in Part IV) draws from the modern Law and Economics literature and challenges Ottomanists to think about disputing in novel ways. Specifically, this framework compels us to consider litigations and settlements not as isolated events, but in relation to each other, as phases of complex dispute resolution processes.

In our empirical analysis of trial-settlement decisions, we first observed basic patterns in the way average trial ratios (i.e., proportions of disputes that ended up in trial) varied across case-types and over time. Since the gender, religious, and class characteristics of parties must have also influenced trial-settlement decisions, we ran regression analysis to isolate the individual effects of each characteristic-combination of parties by controlling for others. Our results showed systematic patterns in trial-settlement decisions that are generally consistent with expectations based on economic models of dispute resolution and historical knowledge of Ottoman Kastamonu during our period. The analysis confirmed our expectations regarding how differences among court clients in gender, class, and religious characteristics influenced the likelihood of trial by causing parties to have asymmetric reputational stakes from losing the case, divergent estimates of their chances of success at trial, and differential social and economic costs of attending litigation.

To be specific, trial rates varied according to the size-combinations of parties, the personal characteristics of individuals, and the nature of their relationships with each other. For example, religious and elite titleholders were more likely to litigate their disputes than to settle, compared to other client groups. Whether a dispute was civil or criminal in nature also influenced the choice of how to resolve it. For example, while trial was less likely than settlement in criminal cases between two women than those between two titleless men, in civil disputes against unrelated individuals this likelihood was reversed. More generally, we discovered that trial rates were lower in disputes between men with titles and between two women, compared to those between titleless men. Lower trial rates also held for disputes between pilgrims as compared to those between non-pilgrims. On the other hand, trial was more likely in disputes between titleless men and other gender and title groups. The position of parties as (actual or potential) plaintiffs or defendants was also important in the likelihood of trial. Overall, the results indicated that the conflicts that went to trial were not a random sample of all disputes – a consideration with important historical implications, but also one that has received little attention in Ottoman legal scholarship.

In Part IV, we examined the likelihood of success in litigations. In general, the plaintiff's chances would depend not just on the facts of the case but on the evidentiary standards and trial procedures that applied to the presentation of these facts and on the actions and strategies of the defendant. To examine the factors that influenced win rates in litigations, we first reviewed the rules and procedures of Islamic–Ottoman jurisprudence, including some of its unique features with respect to evidentiary standards, document use, jurisprudential opinions, and legal representation. We also discussed theoretical insights from the Law and Economics literature on trials to develop a basic framework that identified a trial's basic parameters and the factors influencing the plaintiff's chances of success.

The empirical analysis revealed systematic patterns in plaintiff win rates across case-types and over time, as well as interesting exceptions to these patterns. For example, the size-compositions of parties – that is, whether the litigant was a single individual or a group of individuals or a corporate body (e.g., a village or neighborhood community) – influenced trial results. In regards to litigations between single individuals, our results showed how trials, as in trial-settlement decisions, reflected gender and socioeconomic hierarchies in late seventeenth- and eighteenth-century Kastamonu. Although the position of the litigants in trials (as plaintiffs or defendants) had an impact on the results, titleholders (in particular elite and religious titleholders) and members of prominent families generally dominated litigations. Also, while female plaintiffs often won against titleless male defendants, they frequently lost as defendants and against titleholding opponents. Overall, the plaintiff win rate was higher when the plaintiff was a man. Our investigation showed no systematic patterns regarding the outcomes of the few trials between Muslims and non-Muslims.

As mentioned, titleholders and members of prominent families were generally more successful in trials against their less-privileged opponents. We also noted earlier that Kastamonu experienced an intensifying economic impoverishment and polarization during the eighteenth century, which possibly amplified existing socioeconomic tensions. One question in both regards is whether these tensions are reflected in trial results observed for successive subperiods. Could it be that the court became more (or less) inclined to support specific groups – for example, the poor and the underprivileged (as many of our Ottomanist colleagues would assume) – in response to changing circumstances?

Although the question is interesting, we have to be careful where we look for an answer. One might be tempted to examine the effects of judicial bias in trial results: whether the win ratios rose for groups suspected of being supported by the court. As our analysis shows, however, the relationship between judicial standards and trial results can be far from obvious if the standards, including biases appearing over time, were known to the public. Even if the court had developed an inclination to protect the interests of particular groups, we would expect the parties negatively impacted by this bias to have responded by settling those cases which they no longer had a reasonable chance of winning and by continuing to litigate only those cases in which they felt confident of success. As a result, the average win rates would have remained relatively constant over time, all else being the same.[1] Put differently, we would expect any bias emerging from the court's sensitivity toward rising tensions to be reflected in the changing proportions of settlements over time, but not necessarily in the average win rates of favored groups.[2] As we have seen, the proportions of settlements and contracts increased faster than the proportions of litigations in Kastamonu during the eighteenth century. Although we have no direct evidence to link this tendency with the

[1] Such a change might also have altered the prevailing attitudes towards contractual arrangements, which served the function of thwarting future disputes, and, thus, the proportional representation of contracts in the court records.

[2] Of course, when the judicial standard is altered, some cases that previously would have been settled might end up litigated. The proportion of litigations and of settlements should remain constant before and after the change in judicial standard only if the number of would-be litigated settlements is equal to that of would-be settled litigations.

proclivities of the court toward any group, we simply note that our analysis allows us to identify the appropriate place to look for the answers to such questions.

Finally, Part IV revealed that a litigant could gain an advantage by assuming the burden of proof since it prevented the opponent from substantiating his or her position. Among all client groups, religious titleholders were most successful in claiming proof responsibility. In addition, we observed a higher likelihood of success for parties who presented documents or *fetva*s in trials. Overall, our results indicated a significant gap in legal competency between religious titleholders, pilgrims, and members of prominent families on the one hand, and other client groups on the other. In general, our findings confirmed once again the expectation that the litigants' chances of success at trial depended on their divergent assessments of case strength, asymmetric stakes from losing at trial, and unequal legal knowledge and ability.

The analysis provided in Part IV fills an important gap in Ottoman legal research by providing insights on factors affecting the litigants' chances of success in court. We contribute to the literature the first systematic analysis of why we should expect certain groups to have dominated litigations and whether socioeconomic privilege translated into wins and losses in sharia courts. Lacking the theoretical framework and quantitative methodologies used in this analysis, previous research has been unable to explain not just why men, Muslims, or upper classes could dominate trials, but also under which circumstances women, non-Muslims, and the underprivileged could sometimes stand their ground against privileged opponents. Our analytical framework allowed us to examine how litigants could affect the trial outcome through their own decisions and how their class, gender, and religious identity also affected their chances of success in court.

In terms of the wider implications of this study, our research represents a shift in the treatment of legal practice in the Ottoman Empire. Until recently, most studies of the Ottoman legal system displayed a state-centric perspective by focusing on the institution of the court, its place in the provincial administration, and its functions within a system of checks-and-balances that aimed to represent the imperial center in the local setting. It is because of the significance that Ottomanists have attributed to the relationship between the imperial government and the provincial court that we know much about the court's non-judicial responsibilities, such as the collection of taxes and the mobilization of troops in wartime.

In judicial terms, the scholarship has emphasized the role of the court in containing provincial power-holders, including executive administrative officials, and in providing the local population with a means of redress against abuse inflicted by parties associated with the state. Since the court functioned as a legal venue in which common people could challenge local power-holders and have them punished for transgressions, most historians have insisted that it helped legitimize the entire system of imperial governance. No other topic has received as much attention in the scholarship on legal practice in the Ottoman Empire.

As is clear from our findings, this study takes a different orientation. Instead of treating the court as a body that represented the state and acted on its behalf, we considered it as a local venue in which social differences and hierarchies were revealed. In this book, we focused on court clients, depicted their judicial experiences, and discussed their attempts to use the court to their benefit. We discussed how clients may have strategized their legal interactions and uncovered the ways in which gender-, religion- and class-based power disparities influenced court processes. We demonstrated not only how specific client groups performed in litigations but also *why* they tended to dominate or fail in these processes.

Our choice of a pluralistic methodology that combined insights from multiple disciplines has significantly enhanced the contributions of this book to legal studies and Ottoman historiography. This approach has allowed us to freely cross artificial disciplinary boundaries and pragmatically apply the concepts and theories that are best suited to our objective of understanding the workings of the Kastamonu court in the seventeenth and eighteenth centuries. In our collaborative experience, just as the perspective and comparative advantage of the historian was essential in interpreting the court records and identifying the socioeconomic status of court participants, so too was the economic approach essential in applying theoretical concepts and quantitative tools to analyze this information systematically. By softening the boundaries across disciplines, we were able to expand our overall capacity for historical interpretation and answer hitherto unanswered questions in Ottoman legal history. We believe that similar opportunities exist for collaborative and multidisciplinary research within our field and within Ottoman history-writing in general. All that we need is the will to seize these opportunities. The result of our efforts will no doubt be a richer appreciation of the archives and a more sophisticated understanding of the past.

Bibliography

ARCHIVAL SOURCES

Microfilms of Kastamonu Court Records (KCR) stored in the National Library in Ankara, Turkey.

Information on estate inventories (*terekes*) are from fifty-nine volumes of court registers, from volumes 428/18 (1125 H./1713 C. E.) to 486/76 (1217 H./1802 C. E.).

Information on contracts, settlements, and litigations are from three groups of Kastamonu court registers. The first group, which includes volumes 413/3, 411/1, 414/4, 415/5, 416/6, 417/7, and 465/55, covers between 1095 H./1684 C. E. and 1107 H./1696 C. E., with the exception of 1084–6 H./1673–5 C. E. The second group includes volumes 444/34, 445/35, 446/36, 447/37, 448/38, 449/39, and 450/40, and covers between 1148 H./1735 C. E.–1156 H./1743 C. E. The third group includes volumes 472/62, 473/63, 474/64, 475/65, and 476/66 and covers between 1195 H./1781 C. E.–1204 H./1790 C. E.

In addition, KCR vol. 418/8 (1109 H./1698 C. E.–1110 H./1699 C. E.) was also consulted for the purposes of comparison and documentation.

PUBLISHED AND SECONDARY SOURCES

Abou-El-Haj, R. A. (1991a). *Formation of the Modern State: The Ottoman Empire, Sixteenth to Eighteenth Centuries*. Albany: State University of New York Press.

(1991b). Power and Social Order: The Uses of the Kanun. In D. Preziosi and R.A. Abou-El-Haj (eds.). *The Ottoman City and Its Parts: Urban Structure and Social Order* (pp. 77–99). New Roschelle and New York: A.D. Caratzas.

Abu Nimer, M. (1996). Conflict Resolution Approaches: Western and Middle Eastern Lessons and Possibilities. *American Journal of Economics and Sociology*, 55 (1), 35–52.

Agmon, I. (1996). Muslim Women in Court according to the Sijill of Late Ottoman Jaffa and Haifa: Some Methodological Notes. In A. E.-A. Sonbol (ed.), *Women, Family and Divorce Laws in Islamic Society* (pp. 126–40). Syracuse: Syracuse University Press.

(1998). Women, Class, and Gender: Muslim Jaffa and Haifa at the Turn of the 20th Century. *International Journal of Middle East Studies*, 30 (4), 477–500.

(2004a). Social Biography of a Late Ottoman Shari'a Judge. *New Perspectives on Turkey*, 30, 83–113.

(2004b). Women's History and Ottoman Sharia Court Records: Shifting Perspectives in Social History. *Hawwa*, 2 (2), 171–209.

(2006). *Family and Court: Legal Culture and Modernity in Late Ottoman Palestine*. Syracuse: Syracuse University Press.

Agmon, I., and Shahar, I. (2008). Introduction to the Theme Issue: Shifting Perspectives in the Study of Shari'a Courts: Methodologies and Paradigms. *Islamic Law and Society*, 15 (1), 1–19.

Ainsworth, W. F. (1842). *Travels and Researches in Asia Minor, Mesopotamia, Chaldea and Armenia* (vol. 2). London: Parker.

Akdağ, M. (1974). *Türkiye'nin İktisadi ve İctimai Tarihi*. İstanbul: Cem Yayınevi.

Akgündüz, A. (1988). *Şer'iye Sicilleri: Mahiyeti, Toplu Kataloğu ve Seçme Hükümler*. 2 vols. İstanbul: Türk Dünyası Araştırmaları Vakfı.

(1990). *Osmanlı Kanunnameleri ve Hukuki Tahlileri*. Vol. 1. İstanbul: FEY Vakfı Yayınları.

Akiba, J. (2013). *Uniformity and Diversity of Legal Practices in Late Eighteenth-Century Ottoman Anatolia: A Case Study on Missing Husband*. Unpublished Paper presented at MESA Annual Meeting New Orleans, LA.

Antoun, R. (1990). Litigant Strategies in an Islamic Court in Jordan. In D. H. Dwyer (ed.), *Law and Islam in the Middle East* (pp. 35–60). New York: Bergin and Garvey.

Antoun, R. T. (1980). The Islamic Court, the Islamic Judge, and the Accommodation of Traditions: A Jordanian Case Study. *International Journal of Middle East Studies*, 12 (4), 455–67.

Arrondel, L. and Grange, C. (2006). Transmission and Inequality of Wealth: An Empirical Study of Wealth Mobility from 1800 to 1939 in France. *Journal of Economic Inequality*, 4 (2), 209–32.

Aydelotte, W. O. (1966). Quantification in History. *The American Historical Review*, 71 (3), 803–25.

Aydelotte, W. O., Bogue, A. G., and Fogel, R. W. (1972). *The Dimensions of Quantitative Research in History*. Princeton: Princeton University Press.

Aykan, Y. (2012). *Les acteurs de la justice à Amid et dans la province du Diyarbekir d'après les sicil provinciaux du 18e siècle*. Unpublished PhD dissertation. EHESS, Paris, France.

Baldwin, J. (forthcoming). *Islamic Law and Empire in Ottoman Cairo*. Edinburgh: Edinburgh University Press.

Barbir, K. (1992). Wealth, Privilege, and Family Structure: The `Askaris of 18th Century Damascus according to the Qassam `Askari Inheritance Records. In T. Philipp (ed.), *The Syrian Land in the Eighteenth and Nineteenth Century: The Common and the Specific in the Historical Experience* (pp. 179–95). Stuttgart: Franz Steiner Verlag.

Barkan, Ö. L. (1943). *XV ve XVIıncı Asırlarda Osmanlı İmparatorluğunda Zirai Ekonominin Hukuki ve Mali Esasları: Kanunlar*. İstanbul: Burhaneddin Matbaası.

(1968). Edirne Askeri Kassamına ait Tereke Defterleri (1545–1659). *Belgeler*, III, 1–479.

Barkey, K. (1996). *Bandits and Bureaucrats: The Ottoman Route to State Centralization*. Ithaca: Cornell University Press.

(2008). *Empire of Difference: The Ottomans in Comparative Perspective*. Cambridge: Cambridge University Press.

Başar, F. (1997). *Osmanlı Eyalet Tevcihatı (1717–1730)*. Ankara: Türk Tarih Kurumu Yayınevi.

Bayerle, G. (1997). *Pashas, Begs, and Effendis: A Historical Dictionary of Titles and Terms in the Ottoman Empire*. İstanbul: Isis Press.

Baykara, T. (2015). *Anadolu'nun Tarihi Coğrafyasına Giriş -1- Anadolu'nun İdari Taksimatı*. 3rd edn. İstanbul: Bilge Kültür Sanat Yayınları.

Bayındır, A. (1986). *İslam Muhakeme Hukuku: Osmanlı Devri Uygulaması*. İstanbul: İslami İlimler Araştırma Vakfı.

Bebchuk, L. A. (1984). Litigation and Settlement under Imperfect Information. *RAND Journal of Economics*, 15 (3), 404–15.

Behar, C. (1996). *Osmanlı İmparatorluğu'nun ve Türkiye'nin Nüfusu, 1500–1927: The Population of the Ottoman Empire and Turkey, 1500–1927*. Ankara: T. C. Başbakanlık Devlet İstatistik Enstitüsü.

Berki, A. H. (ed.) (1986). *Açıklamalı Mecelle (Mecelle-i Ahkām-ı Adliyye)*. İstanbul: Hikmet Yayınları.

Bouckaert, B., and De Geest, G. (ed.) (2000). *The History and Methodology of Law and Economics*. Cheltenham: Edward Elgar.

Bowen, J. R. (2003). *Islam, Law, and Equality in Indonesia: An Anthropology of Public Reasoning*. Cambridge: Cambridge University Press.

Brunschvig, R. (1960). Bayyina. *Encyclopedia of Islam* (2nd edn., vol. 1, pp. 1150–1). Leiden: E. J. Brill.
Canbakal, H. (2005). On the Nobility of Urban Notables. In A. Anastasopoulos (ed.), *Provincial Elite in the Ottoman Empire* (pp. 39–50). Rethymno: Crete University Press.
(2007). *Society and Politics in an Ottoman Town: 'Ayntāb in the 17th Century*. Leiden: Brill.
(2012). Wealth and Inequality in Ottoman Bursa, 1500–1840. Unpublished paper presented at Conference on New Perspectives in Ottoman Economic History. Yale University.
Canbakal, H., and Filiztekin, A. (2013). Wealth and Inequality in Ottoman Lands in the Early Modern Period. Unpublished paper presented at AALIMS – Rice University Conference on the Political Economy of the Muslim World Rice University.
Cezar, Y. (1986). *Osmanlı Maliyesinde Bunalım ve Değişim Dönemi: XVIII. yy'dan Tanzimat'a Mali Tarih*. İstanbul: Alan Yayıncılık.
Clark, G., and Cummins, N. (2009). The Origins of Modern Growth: Fertility and Human Capital in England, 1500–1914. Unpublished paper available at: http://economics.barnard.edu/sites/default/files/clark_cummins_nov2009.pdf (accessed at 8/7/2015).
Cohen, A. (1994). *A World Within: Jewish Life as Reflected in Muslim Court Documents from the Sijill of Jerusalem*. Pennsylvania: Centre for Judaic Studies.
Cooter, R. D., and Rubinfeld, D. L. (1989). Economic Analysis of Legal Disputes and Their Resolution. *Journal of Economic Literature*, 27 (3), 1067–97.
Coşgel, M. M. (2004). Ottoman Tax Registers (Tahrir Defterleri). *Historical Methods*, 37(2), 87–100.
(2005). Efficiency and Continuity in Public Finance: the Ottoman System of Taxation. *International Journal of Middle East Studies*, 37 (4), 567–586.
(2006). Taxes, Efficiency, and Redistribution: Discriminatory Taxation of Villages in Ottoman Palestine, Southern Syria, and Transjordan in the Sixteenth Century. *Explorations in Economic History*, 43 (2), 332–56.
(2011). The Political Economy of Law and Economic Development in Islamic History. In J. L. Van Zanden and D. Ma (eds.), *Law and Long-Term Economic Change: A Eurasian Perspective* (pp. 158–77). Stanford: Stanford University Press.
(2015). The Fiscal Regime of an Expanding State: Political Economy of Ottoman Taxation. In A. Monson, and W. Scheidel (eds.), *Fiscal Regimes and the Political Economy of Premodern States* (pp. 404–28). Cambridge, United Kingdom; New York: Cambridge University Press.

Coşgel, M. M., and Ergene, B. A. (2011). Intergenerational Wealth Accumulation and Dispersion in the Ottoman Empire: Observations from Eighteenth-Century Kastamonu. *European Review of Economic History*, 15 (2), 255–76.

(2012). Inequality of Wealth in the Ottoman Empire: War, Weather, and Long-term Trends in Eighteenth Century Kastamonu. *Journal of Economic History*, 72 (2), 308–31.

(2014a). Law and Economics Literature' and Ottoman Legal Studies. *Islamic Law and Society*, 21 (4), 114–44.

(2014b). Dispute Resolution in Ottoman Courts: A Quantitative Analysis of Litigations in Eighteenth Century Kastamonu. *Social Science History*, 38 (1–2), 183–202.

(2014c). The Selection Bias in Court Records: Settlement and Trial in Eighteenth Century Ottoman Kastamonu. *Economic History Review*, 67 (2), 517–34.

Cosgel, M. M., Ergene, B. A., Etkes, H., and Miceli, T. J. (2013). Crime and Punishment in Ottoman Times: Corruption and Fines. *Journal of Interdisciplinary History*, XLIII (3), 353–76.

Coşgel, M. M., Etkes, H., and Miceli, T. J. (2011). Private Law Enforcement, Fine Sharing, and Tax Collection: Theory and Historical Evidence. *Journal of Economic Behavior and Organization*, 80 (3), 546–52.

Coşgel, M. M., and Miceli, T. J. (2005). Risk, Transaction Costs, and Tax Assignment: Government Finance in the Ottoman Empire. *Journal of Economic History*, 65 (3), 806–821.

(2009). Tax Collection in History. *Public Finance Review*, 37 (4), 399–420.

Coşgel, M. M., Miceli, T., and Ahmed, R. (2009). Law, State Power, and Taxation in Islamic History. *Journal of Economic Behavior and Organization*, 71 (3), 704–17.

Cosgel, M. M., Miceli, T. J., and Rubin, J. (2012a). The Political Economy of Mass Printing: Legitimacy and Technological Change in the Ottoman Empire. *Journal of Comparative Economics*, 40 (3), 357–71.

(2012b). Political Legitimacy and Technology Adoption. *Journal of Institutional and Theoretical Economics*, 168 (3), 339–61.

De Bellefonds, Y. L. (1971). Iqrār. *Encyclopedia of Islam* (2nd edn., vol. 3, pp. 1078–131). Leiden: E.J. Brill

Demir, A. (2010). *Osmanlı Mahkemesi: Medeni Yargılama Hukuku*. İstanbul: Işık Yayıncılık.

Dörtok Abacı, Z. (2006). Bir Sorun Çözme Yöntemi Olarak Sulh: 18. Yüzyıl Bursa Kadı Sicillerinden Örnekler ve Düşündürdükleri. *Ankara Üniversitesi Osmanlı Tarihi Araştırma ve Uygulama Merkezi Dergisi*, 20, 105–15.

Dupret, B. (2006). The Practice of Judging. In M. K. Masud et al. (eds.), *Dispensing Justice in Muslim Courts: Qadis, Procedures and Judgments* (pp. 143–68). Leiden, Boston: Brill.

Duxbury, N. (1995). *Patterns of American Jurisprudence*. Oxford: Oxford University Press.

Düzbakar, Ö. (2009). Bribery in Islam-Ottoman Penal Codes and Examples from the Bursa Shari'a Court Records of 18th Century. *Bilig* (51), 55–84.

Eisenberg, T. (1990). Testing the Selection Effect – A New Theoretical Framework with Empirical Tests. *Journal of Legal Studies*, 19, 337–58.

Eisenberg, T., and Lanvers, C. (2009). What is the Settlement Rate and Why Should We Care? *Journal of Empirical Legal Studies*, 6 (1), 111–46.

El-Nahal, G. H. (1979). *The Judicial Administration of Ottoman Egypt in the Seventeenth Century*. Minneapolis and Chicago: Bibliotheca Islamica.

Ergene, B. A. (2001). On Ottoman Justice: Interpretations in Conflict (1600–1800). *Islamic Law and Society*, 8 (1), 52–87.

(2002). Costs of Court Usage in Seventeenth-and Eighteenth-Century Ottoman Anatolia: Court Fees as Recorded in Estate Inventories. *Journal of the Economic and Social History of the Orient*, 45 (1), 20–39.

(2003). *Local Court, Provincial Society and Justice in the Ottoman Empire: Legal Practice and Dispute Resolution in Çankırı and Kastamonu (1652–1744)*. Boston and Leiden: Brill

(2004). Evidence in Ottoman Courts: Oral and Written Documentation in Early-Modern Courts of Islamic Law. *Journal of American Oriental Society*, 124 (3), 471–91.

(2005). Document Use in Ottoman Courts of Law: Observations from the Sicils of Seventeenth- and Eighteenth-Century Çankırı and Kastamonu. *Turcica*, 37, 83–111.

(2008). Social Identity and Patterns of Interaction in the Sharia Court of Kastamonu (1740–44). *Islamic Law and Society*, 15 (1), 20–54.

(2010). Why Did Ümmü Gülsüm Go to Court? Ottoman Legal Practice between History and Anthropology. *Islamic Law and Society*, 17 (2), 215–44.

Ergene, B. A., and Berker, A. (2008). Wealth and Inequality in 18th-century Kastamonu: Estimations for the Muslim Majority. *International Journal of Middle East Studies*, 40 (1), 23–46.

Ergene, B. A., and Kaygun, A. (2011). Intergenerational Mobility in the in the Ottoman Empire: Observations from Eighteenth-Century Kastamonu. *The History of the Family*, 16 (1), 30–46.

(2012). Spouse Selection and Marital Mobility in the Ottoman Empire: Observations from Eighteenth-Century Kastamonu. *Historical Methods: A Journal of Quantitative and Interdisciplinary History*, 45 (1), 3–20.

Ergene, B. A., Kaygun, A., and Coşgel, M. M. (2013). A Temporal Analysis of Wealth and Inequality in Eighteenth-Century Ottoman Empire. *Continuity and Change*, 28 (1), 1–26.

Establet, C., and Pascual, J.-P. (1994). *Familles et fortunes `a Damas: 450 foyers damascains en 1700*. Damascus: Institut français de Damas.

(2011). *La gent d'état dans la société ottomane damascène: les 'askar à la fin du XVIIe siècle*. Paris: Institut français du Proche-Orient.

Establet, C., Pascual, J.-P., and Raymond, A. (1994). La mesure de l'inégalité dans la société ottomane: utilisation de l'indice de Gini pour Le Caire et Damas vers 1700. *Journal of the Economic and Social History of the Orient*, 37 (2), 171–82.

Eyüpgiller, K. K. (1999). *Bir Kent Tarihi: Kastamonu*. İstanbul Eren Yayınları.

Farge, A. (1989). *Le goût de l'archive*. Paris: Le Seuil.

Faroqhi, S. (1984). *Towns and Townsmen of Ottoman Anatolia: Trade, Crafts and Food Production in an Urban Setting, 1520–1650*. Cambridge: Cambridge University Press.

(1992). Anatolian Townsmen as Pilgrims to Mecca: Some Evidence from the XVIth–XVIIth centuries. In G. Veinstein (ed.), *Soliman le Magnifique et son temps: Recontres de l'École du Louvre* (pp. 309–325). Paris: La Documentation Française.

(2006). Declines and Revivals in Textile Production. In S. Faroqhi (ed.), *The Cambridge History of Turkey: The Later Ottoman Empire, 1603–1839 (vol. 3)*. Cambridge: Cambridge University Press.

Fadel, M. (1995). Adjudication in the Maliki Madhhab: A Study of Legal Process in Medieva Islamic Law. Unpublished Ph.D. Dissertation, University of Chicago.

Fodor, P. (2009). Fur of Lynx and Arable Land: The Wealth of an Ottoman Tax Farmer in Early Seventeenth Century. *Oriens*, 37, 191–208.

Fogel, R. W. (1964). *Railroads and American Economic Growth*. Cambridge: Cambridge University Press.

Fogel, R. W., and Elton, G. L. (1983). *Which Road to the Past?* New Haven: Yale University Press.

Genç, M. (1973). Osmanlı Maliyesinde Malikane Sistemi. In O. Okyar and Ü. Nalbantoğlu (eds.), *Türkiye İktisat Tarihi Semineri: Metinler/ Tartışmalar* (pp. 231–91). Ankara: Hacettepe Üniversitesi Yayınları.

(1994). Ottoman Industry in the Eighteenth Century: General Framework, Characteristics, and Main Trends. In D. Quataert (ed.),

Manufacturing in the Ottoman Empire and Turkey, 1500–1950. Albany: State University of New York Press.
Gerber, H. (1981). Sharia, Kanun, and Custom in the Ottoman Law: The Court Records of 17th Century Bursa. *International Journal of Turkish Studies*, 2 (1), 131–47.
(1988). *Economy and Society in an Ottoman City: Bursa, 1600–1700.* Jerusalem: The Hebrew University Press.
(1994). *State, Society, and Law in Islam: Ottoman Law in Comparative Perspective.* Albany: SUNY Press.
Ghazzal, Z. (1996). Review of Familles et Fortunes à Damas: 450 Foyers Damascains en 1700 by Colette Establet; Jean-Paul Pascual. *International Journal of Middle East Studies*, 28 (3), 431–2.
(1998). A Reply to André Raymond. *International Journal of Middle East Studies*, 30 (3), 474–5.
(2007). *The Grammars of Adjudication: The Economics of Judicial Decision Making in Fin-de-siecle Ottoman Beirut and Damascus.* Beirut: Institut Français du Proche-Orient.
Ginio, E. (1998). The Administration of Criminal Justice in Ottoman Selanik (Salonica) during the Eighteenth Century. *Turcica*, 30, 185–209.
Göçek, M. (2005). The Legal Recourse of Minorities in History: Eighteenth Century Appeals to the Islamic Court of Galata. *Princeton Papers*, (12), 47–69.
Gökçe, T. (1994a). Anadolu Vilayeti'ne Dâir 919 (1513) Tarihli Bir Kadı Defteri. *Ege Üniversitesi Edebiyat Fakültesi Tarih İncelemeleri Dergisi*, 9, 215–59.
(1994b). 934 (1528) Tarihli Bir Deftere Göre Anadolu Vilayeti Kadılıkları ve Kadıları. In İ. Aka-Turan (ed.), *3 Mayıs 1944 50. Yıl Türkçülük Armağanı Akademik Kitabı* (pp. 77–94). İzmir: Akademi Kitabevi.
Gradeva, R. (1997). Orthodox Christians in the Kadı Courts: The Practice of Sofia Sheriat Court, Seventeenth Century. *Islamic Law and Society*, 4 (1), 37–69.
(2005). Towards a Portrait of 'the Rich'in Ottoman Provincial Society: Sofia in the 1670s. In A. Anastasopoulos (ed.), *Provincial elite in the Ottoman Empire* (pp. 147–97). Rethymno: Crete University Press.
(2006). On Judicial Hierarchy in the Ottoman Empire: The Case of Sofia, Seventeenth – Beginning of Eighteenth Century. In M. K. Masud, et al. (eds.), *Dispensing Justice in Islam: Qadis and Their Judgments* (pp. 271–98). Leiden: Brill.
Grossman, G. M., and Katz, M. L. (1983). Plea Bargaining and Social Welfare. *American Economic Review*, 73 (4), 749–57.

Hallaq, W. (1995). Model Shurut Works and the Dialectic of Doctrine and Practice. *Islamic Law and Society*, 2 (2), 109–34.

(1998). The Qadi's *Diwan* (*Sijill*) before the Ottomans. *Bulletin of the School of Oriental and African Studies*, 61 (3), 415–36.

(1999). Qadi's Communicating: Legal Change and the Law of Documentary Evidence. *Al-Qantara*, 20 (2), 437–66.

Halebi, İ. (n.d.). *İslam Fıkhında Tahkikli ve Tahriçli el-Hidaye Tercemesi*. A. Meylani, trans. İstanbul: Kahraman Yayınları.

Hanna, N. (1995). Administration of Courts in Ottoman Cairo. In N. Hanna (ed.), *The State and Its Servants* (pp. 44–59). Cairo: American University Press.

The Hedaya or Guide: A Commentary on the Mussulman Laws. (1982). C. Hamilton, trans. Delhi: Islamic Book Trust.

Heyd, U. (1969). Some Aspects of the Ottoman Fetva. *Bulletin of the School of Oriental and African Studies*, 32 (1), 35–56.

(1973). *Studies in Old Ottoman Criminal Law*. Oxford: Clarendon Press.

Heywood, C. (1978). Kastamonu. *Encyclopedia of Islam* (2nd edn., vol. 4, pp. 738). Leiden: E.J. Brill.

Hill, E. (1979). *Mahkama! Studies in the Egyptian Legal System: Courts and Crimes, Law and Society*. London: Ithaca.

Hirsch, S. (1998). *Pronouncing and Persevering: Gender and the Discourses of Disputing in an African Islamic Court*. Chicago: University of Chicago Press.

Hourani, A. (1981). *The Emergence of the Modern Middle East*. Berkeley: University of California Press.

Hudson, P. (2000). *History by Numbers: An introduction to Quantitative Approaches*. London: Hodder Arnold Publication.

Hüsrev, M. (1980). *Gürer ve Dürer Tercümesi (Islam Fıkhı ve Hukuku)*. A. Erkan, trans. İstanbul: Eser Neşriyat.

Ianeva, S. (2009). Financing the State? Tax-farming as a Source of Individual Wealth in the Nineteenth Century. *Oriens*, 37, 209–24.

Issawi, C. P. (1966). *The Economic History of the Middle East, 1800–1914*. Chicago: University of Chicago Press.

İnalcık, H. (1977). Centralization and Decentralization in Ottoman Administration. In T. Naff and R. Owen (eds.), *Studies in Eighteenth Century Islamic History* (pp. 27–52). Carbondale: Southern Illinois University Press.

İnalcık, H. (1978a). Ḳānūn. *Encyclopaedia of Islam* (2nd edn. vol. 4, 558–62). Leiden: E.J. Brill.

(1978b). Ḳānūnnāme. *Encyclopaedia of Islam* (2nd edn. vol. 4, 562–66). Leiden: E.J. Brill.

(1986). Mahkama. *Encyclopedia of Islam* (2nd edn., vol. 6). Leiden: E.J. Brill.

(1988a). Şikayet Hakkı: `Arz-ı Hal ve `Arz-ı Mahzarlar. *Osmanlı Araştırmaları*, 7–8, 33–45.
(1988b). The Ruznamçe Registers of the Kadıasker of Rumeli as Preserved in the İstanbul Müftülük Archives. *Turcica*, 20, 251–75.
İpşirli, M. (1992). Beylerberi. *Türkiye Diyanet Vakfı İslam Ansiklopedisi* (vol. 6, pp. 69–74). İstanbul: Türkiye Diyanet Vakfı Yayınları.
(1991). Aşir Efendi. *Türkiye Diyanet Vakfı İslam Ansiklopedisi* (vol. 4, pp. 7–8). İstanbul: Türkiye Diyanet Vakfı Yayınları.
İslamoğlu-İnan, H. (1994). *State and Peasant in the Ottoman Empire: Agrarian Power Relations and Regional Economic Development in Ottoman Anatolia during the Sixteenth Century*. Leiden: E.J. Brill.
Jennings, R. C. (1975). Women in Early 17th Century Ottoman Judicial Records: The Sharia Court of Anatolian Kayseri. *Journal of the Economic and Social History of the Orient*, 18 (1), 53–114.
(1978a). Kadi, Court, and Legal Procedure in 17th C. Ottoman Kayseri: The Kadi and the Legal System. *Studia Islamica*, 48, 133–72.
(1978b). Zimmis (Non-Muslims) in Early 17th Century Ottoman Judicial Records: The Sharia Court of Anatolian Kayseri. *Journal of the Economic and Social History of the Orient*, 21 (3), 225–93.
(1979). Limitations of the Judicial Powers of the Kadi in 17th c. Ottoman Kayseri. *Studia Islamica*, 50, 151–84.
(1992). *Christians and Muslims in Ottoman Cyprus and the Mediterranean world, 1571–1640*. New York: NYU Press.
Johansen, B. (1997). Formes de langage et fonctions publiques: stéréotypes, témoins et offices dans la preuve par l'écrit en droit musulman. *Arabica*, 44 (3), 333–76.
Jolls, Christine, Cass R. Sunstein, and Richard H. Thaler (2000). "A Behavioral Approach to Law and Economics." In Cass R. Sunstein (ed), *Behavioral Law and Economics* (pp. 13–58). Cambridge Series on Judgment and Decision Making; Cambridge; New York and Melbourne: Cambridge University Press.
Kahneman, D. and A. Tversky (1984). Choices, Values, and Frames *American Psychologist*, 39 (4), 341–50.
Kahneman, Daniel, Paul Slovic, and Amos Tversky (1982). *Judgment under Uncertainty: Heuristics and Biases*. Cambridge; New York: Cambridge University Press.
Kaldy-Nagy, G. (1978). Kadi. *Encyclopedia of Islam* (2nd edn., vol. 4, pp. 373–5). Leiden: E.J. Brill.
Kankal, A. (2004). *Türkmen'in Kaidesi Kastamonu (XV-XVIII. Yüzyıllar Arası Şehir Hayatı)*. Ankara: Zafer Matbaası.
Kaplow, L. (2012). Burden of Proof. *Yale Law Journal*, 121 (4), 738–859.
Karadeniz, F. (1996). "Complaints against the Kadis and Abuses of Their Authority." Unpublished M.A. Thesis. Ankara: Bilkent University.

Karagöz, M. (2009). XVII. ve XVIII. Asırlarda (1650–1750) Kayseri: İktisat Tarihinde Şehir İktisadiyatı Denemesi. *Fırat University Journal of Social Science*, 19 (1), 259–79.

Kasaba, R. (1988). *The Ottoman Empire and the World Economy: The Nineteenth Century*. Albany: SUNY Press.

Katip, Çelebi (2013). *The Book of* Cihannüma. İstanbul: Boyut Yayıncılık.

Kerkmeester, H. (2000). Methodology: General. In B. Bouckaert and G. De Geest (eds.), *Encyclopedia of Law and Economics, Volume I. The History and Methodology of Law and Economics* (pp. 383–401). Cheltenham: Edward Elgar.

Kessler, D., Meites, T., and Miller, G. (1996). Explaining Deviations from the Fifty-Percent Rule: A Multimodal Approach to the Selection of Cases for Litigation. *Journal of Legal Studies*, 25 (1), 233–59.

Kessler, D. P., and Rubinfeld, D. L. (2007). Empirical Study of the Civil Justice System. In A. M. P. a. S. Shavell (ed.), *Handbook of Law and Economics* (vol. I, pp. 343–402). Oxford: Elsevier B.V.

Kinneir, J. M. (1818). *Journey Through Asia Minor, Armenia and Koordistan, in the Years 1813 and 1814; With Remarks on the Marches of Alexander and Retreat of the Ten Thousand*. London: John Murray.

Klerman, D. (2012). The Selection of 13th-Century Disputes for Litigation. *Journal of Empirical Legal Studies*, 9 (2), 320–46.

Kousser, J. M. (1984). The Revivalism of Narrative: A Response to Recent Criticisms of Quantitative History. *Social Science History*, 8 (2), 133–49.

Kunt, I. M. (1983). *The Sultan's Servants: The Transformation of Ottoman Provincial Government, 1550–1650*. New York: Columbia University Press.

Kuran, T., and Lustig, S. (2012). Judicial Biases in Ottoman İstanbul: Islamic Justice and Its Compatibility with Modern Economic Life. *Journal of Law and Economics*, 55 (3), 631–66.

Landes, W. M. (1971). An Economic Analysis of the Courts. *Journal of Law and Economics*, 14 (1), 61–107.

Layish, A. (1975). *Women and Succession in the Muslim Family in Israel*. New Jersey: Transaction Books.

(1991). *Divorce in the Libyan Family: A Study Based on the Sijills of the Sharia Courts of Ajdābiyya and Kufra*. New York: New York University Press

Lewis, B. (1958). Some Reflections on the Decline of the Ottoman Empire. *Studia Islamica*, 9, 111–27.

Ma, D., and van Zanden, J. L. (ed.) (2011). *Law and Long-Term Economic Change: A Eurasian Perspective*: Stanford: Stanford University Press, Stanford Economics and Finance.

MacGowan, B. (1981). *Economic Life in Ottoman Europe: Taxation, Trade and the Struggle for Land, 1600–1800*. Cambridge: Cambridge University Press.
MacKaay, E. (2000). History of Law and Economics. In B. Bouckaert and G. De Geest (eds.), *Encyclopedia of Law and Economics, Volume I. The History and Methodology of Law and Economics* (pp. 63–117). Cheltenham: Edward Elgar.
Maden, F. (2007). XVIII. Yüzyıl Sonu, XIX. Yüzyıl Başlarında Kastamonu'da Esnaf Grupları: Zanaatkarlar ve Ticari Faaliyetler. *Karadeniz Araştırmaları*, 15, 149–67.
(2012). *XVIII. Yüzyılın Sonlarında Kastamonu*. İstanbul: Roza Yayınları.
Mallon, F. E. (1994). The Promise and Dilemma of Subaltern Studies: Perspectives from Latin American History. *The American Historical Review*, 99 (4), 1491–515.
Marcus, A. (1989). *The Middle East on the Eve of Modernity: Aleppo in the 18th Century*. New York: Columbia University Press.
Mattei, U. (1997). Three Patterns of Law: Taxonomy and Change in the World's Legal Systems. *American Journal of Comparative Law*, 45 (1), 5–44.
McCarthy, J. (1997). *The Ottoman Turks: An Introductory History to 1923*. London and New York: Longman.
Mehmed Süreyya (1996). *Sicill-i Osmani*. 6 volumes. İstanbul: Tarih Vakfı Yurt Yayınları.
Mercuro, N., and Medema, S. G. (2006). *Economics and the Law: From Posner to Postmodernism and Beyond*: 2nd edn. Princeton and Oxford: Princeton University Press.
Merginani, B. E. l. H. A. b. E. B. (1986). *İslam Fıkhında Tahkikli ve Tahriçli el-Hidaye Tercemesi*. A. Meylani, trans. İstanbul: Kahraman Yayınları.
Meshal, R. (2010). Antagonistic Sharīʿas and the Construction of Orthodoxy in Sixteenth-Century Ottoman Cairo. *Journal of Islamic Studies*, 21 (2), 183–212.
(2014). *Shaira and the Making of the Modern Egyptian: Islamic Law and Custom in the Courts of Ottoman Cairo*. Cairo and New York: American University in Cairo Press.
Messick, B. (1993). *The Calligraphic State; Textual Domination and History in a Muslim Society*. Berkeley: University of California Press.
(2008). Legal Narratives from Shari'a Courts. In B. Dupret, B. Driskens and A. Moors (eds.), *Narratives of Truth in Islamic Law* (pp. 51–68). London: I.B. Tauris.
Miceli, T. J. (2009). *The Economic Approach to Law*. 2nd edn. Stanford, Calif.: Stanford Economics and Finance.

(2014). Economic Models of Law. University of Connecticut Working Paper.
Miller, R. (2005). *Legislating Authority: Sin and Crime in the Ottoman Empire and Turkey*. New York and London: Routledge.
Mir-Hosseini, Z. (2000). *Marriage on Trial: A Study of Islamic Family Law*. London: I.B. Tauris.
Moors, A. (1995). *Women, Property and Islam: Palestinian Experiences, 1920–1990*. Cambridge: Cambridge University Press.
Mutaf, A. (2004). Amicable Settlement in Ottoman Law: Sulh System. *Turcica*, 36, 125–40.
Nader, L. (1969). Styles of Court Procedure: To Make the Balance. In L. Nader (ed.), *Law in Culture and Society* (pp. 69–91). Chicago: Aldine.
Nielsen, J. (1985). *Secular Justice in an Islamic State: Maẓālim under the Baḥrī mamlūks 662/1264-789/1387*. Istanbul: Nederlands Historisch-archaeologisch Instituut.
Othman, A. (2005). *And Sulh is Best: Amicable Settlement and Dispute Resolution in Islamic Law*. Unpublished Ph.D. Dissertation. Harvard University, Cambridge, USA.
(2007). "And Amicable Settlement Is Best": Ṣulḥ and Dispute Resolution in Islamic Law. *Arab Law Quarterly*, 21 (1), 64–90.
Özel, O. (2004). Population Changes in Ottoman Anatolia during the 16th and 17th Centuries: The "Demographic Crisis" Reconsidered. *International Journal of Middle East Studies*, 36 (2), 183–205.
Özkaya, Y. (1985). *XVIII. Yüzyılda Osmanlı Kurumları ve Osmanlı Toplum Yaşantısı*. Ankara: Kültür Bakanlığı Yayınları.
Özmucur, S., and Pamuk, S. (2002). Real Wages and Standards of Living in the Ottoman Empire, 1489–1914. *The Journal of Economic History*, 62 (2), 293–321.
Pamuk, S. (2000). *A Monetary History of the Ottoman Empire*. Cambridge: Cambridge University Press.
(2004). Institutional Change and the Longevity of the Ottoman Empire, 1500–1800. *Journal of Interdisciplinary History*, 35 (2), 225–47.
Peters, R. (1997). Shahid. *Encyclopedia of Islam* (2nd edn., vol. 9, pp. 297–8). Leiden: E.J. Brill.
(2005). *Crime and Punishment in Islamic Law: Theory and Practice from the Sixteenth to the Twenty-First Centuries*. Cambridge: Cambridge University Press.
Peirce, L. (2003). *Morality Tales: Law and Gender in the Ottoman Court of Aintab*. Berkeley: University of California Press.
Peletz, M. G. (2002). *Islamic Modern: Religious Courts and Cultural Politics in Malaysia*. Princeton: Princeton University Press.

Pitcher, D. E. (1972). *An Historical Geography of the Ottoman Empire, from Earliest Times to the End of the Sixteenth Century*. Leiden: E. J. Brill.

Posner, R. A. (1973). *Economic Analysis of Law*. Boston: Little Brown and Company.

Powers, D. S. (1994). Kadijustiz or Qadi-Justice? A Paternity Dispute from Fourteenth-Century Morocco. *Islamic Law and Society*, 1 (3), 332–66.

(2002). *Law, Society and Culture in the Maghrib, 1300–1500*. Cambridge: Cambridge University Press.

Priest, G. L., and Klein, B. (1984). The Selection of Disputes for Litigation. *The Journal of Legal Studies*, 13 (1), 1–55.

Al-Qattan, N. (1996). Textual Differentiation in the Damascus Sijill: Religious Discrimination or Politics of Gender. In A. Sonbol (ed.), *Women, the Family, and Divorce Laws in Islamic History* (pp. 191–201). Syracuse: Syracuse University Press.

(1999). Dhimmis in the Muslim Court: Legal Autonomy and Religious Discrimination. *International Journal of Middle East Studies*, 31 (3), 429–44.

Rabb, T. K. (1981). Coherence, Synthesis, and Quality in History. *Journal of Interdisciplinary History*, 12 (2), 315–32.

(1983). The Development of Quantification in Historical Research. *Journal of Interdisciplinary History*, 13, 591–601.

Raymond, A. (1998). A Response to Zouhair Ghazzal's Review of Colette Establet and Jean-Paul Pascual, Familles et fortunes à Damas: 450 foyers damascains en 1700. *International Journal of Middle East Studies*, 30 (3), 473–4.

(2000). *Cairo*. Cambridge, MA: Harvard University Press.

Reilly, J. A. (1992). Property, Status, and Class in Ottoman Damascus: Case Studies from the Nineteenth Century. *Journal of the American Oriental Society*, 112 (1), 9–21.

Repp, R. (1988). Qanun and Shari'a in the Ottoman Context. In A. Al-Azmeh (ed.) *Islamic Law: Social and Historical Contexts* (pp. 124–45). London: Routledge.

Roded, R. (1984). Ottoman Service as a Vehicle for the Rise of New Upstarts among the Urban Elite Families of Syria in the Last Decades of Ottoman Rule. In G. R. Warburg and G. G. Gilbar (eds.), *Studies in Islamic Society: Contributions in Memory of Gabriel Baer*. Haifa: Haifa University Press.

(1986). Social Patterns among the Urban Elite in Syria in the Late Ottoman Period. In D. Kushnered (ed.), *Palestine in the Late Ottoman Period* (pp. 146–71). Jerusalem: Yad Izhak Ben-Zvi.

Rosen, L. (1984). *Bargaining for Reality: The Construction of Social Relations in a Muslim Community*. Chicago: University of Chicago Press.

(1990). *The Anthropology of Justice*. Cambridge: Cambridge University Press.

(1995). Law and Custom in the Popular Legal Culture of North Africa. *Islamic Law and Society*, 2 (2), 194–208.

(2000). *The Justice of Islam: Comparative Perspectives on Islamic Law and Society*. Oxford: Oxford University Press.

Rubin, A. (2007). Legal Borrowing and Its Impact on Ottoman Legal Culture in the Late Nineteenth Century. *Continuity and Change*, 22 (2), 279–303.

(2008). Judicial Change in the Age of Modernity: A Reappraisal. *History Compass*, 7 (1), 119–40.

Rubin, A. (2011). *Ottoman Nizamiye Courts: Law and Modernity*. New York: Palgrave MacMillan.

(2012). From Legal Representation to Advocacy: Attorneys and Clients in the Ottoman Nizamiye Courts. *International Journal of Middle East Studies*. 44 (1), 111–27.

Şahin, B. (2009). Osmanlı'dan Cumhuriyet'e Kastamonu Nüfusu. *Akademik Bakış*, 17, 1–10.

Saler, M. (2006). Modernity and Enchantment: A Historiographic Review. *The American Historical Review*, 111 (3), 692–716.

Salzmann, A. (1993). An Ancien Regime Revisited: "Privatization" and Political Economy in the Eighteenth-Century Ottoman Empire. *Politics and Society*, 21 (4), 393–423.

(1995). *Measures of Empire: Tax Farmer and the Ottoman Ancien Régime, 1695–1807*. Unpublished Ph.D. Dissertation. Columbia University, New York, USA.

(2004). *Tocqueville in the Ottoman Empire: Rival Paths to the Modern State*. Leiden: Brill.

Sartori, P. (2011a). The Birth of a Custom: Nomads, Sharīʿa Courts and Established Practices in the Tashkent Province, ca. 1868–1919. *Islamic Law and Society*, 18 (3), 293–326.

(2011b). The Evolution of Third-Party Mediation in Sharīʿa Courts in 19th- and early 20th-century Central Asia. *Journal of the Economic and Social History of the Orient*, 54 (3), 311–52.

Schatkowski Schilcher, L. (1985). *Families in Politics: Damascene Factions and Estates of the Eighteenth and Nineteenth Centuries*. Wiesbaden: F. Steiner.

Scheele, J. (2010). Councils without Customs, Qadis without States: Property and Community in the Algerian Touat. *Islamic Law and Society*, 17 (3), 350–74.

Schneider, M. A. (1993). *Culture and Enchantment*. Chicago: University of Chicago Press.
Scott, J. (2000). Rational Choice Theory. In G. Browning, A. Halcli and F. Webster (eds.), *Understanding Contemporary Society: Theories of the Present* (pp. 126–38). London: Sage Publications.
Shaham, R. (1994). Judicial Divorce at the Wife's Initiative: The Sharīʿa Courts of Egypt, 1920–1955. *Islamic Law and Society*, 1 (2), 217–57.
(1997). *Family and the Courts in Modern Egypt: A Study Based on Decisions by the Sharīʿa Courts, 1900–1955*. Leiden: Brill.
Shahar, I. (2006). *Practicing Islamic Law in a Legal Pluralistic Environment: The Changing Face of a Muslim court in Present-Day Jerusalem*. Unpublished Ph.D. Dissertation. Ben-Gurion University of the Negev, Be'er Sheva, Israel.
Shavell, S. (1982). Suit, Settlement, and Trial – A Theoretical-Analysis under Alternative Methods for the Allocation of Legal Costs. *Journal of Legal Studies*, 11 (1), 55–81.
(1996). Any Frequency of Plaintiff Victory at Trial Is Possible. *Journal of Legal Studies*, 25 (2), 493–501.
Sicillat-ı Şer'iyye ve Zabt-ı Deavi Cerideleri Hakkında Talimat (1874). *Düstur*[1]. Vol. 4. 15 Zilhicce 1290/3 February 1874, 83–5.
Siegelman, P., and Waldfogel, J. (1999). Toward a Taxonomy of Disputes: New Evidence through the Prism of the Priest/Klein Model. *Journal of Legal Studies*, 28 (1), 101–30.
Simon, H. A. (1957). *Models of Man: Social and Rational; Mathematical Essays on Rational Human Behavior in a Social Setting*. New York: Wiley.
Spier, K. E. (2007). Litigation. In A. M. P. a. S. Shavell (ed.), *Handbook of Law and Economics* (vol. I, pp. 259–342). Oxford: Elsevier B.V.
Stiles, E. E. (2006). Broken Edda and Marital Mistakes: Two Recent Disputes form an Islamic Court in Zanzibar. In M. K. Masud et al. (eds.), *Dispensing Justice in Islam: Qadis and Their Judgments* (pp. 95–116). Leiden: Brill.
(2009). *An Islamic Court in Context: An Ethnographic Study of Judicial Reasoning*. New York: Palgrave Macmillan.
Tabakoğlu, A. (1985). *Gerileme Dönemine Girerken Osmanlı Maliyesi*. İstanbul: Dergâh Yayınları.
Tak, E. (2009). *Diplomatik Bilimi Bakımından XVI.-XVII. Yüzyıl Kadı Sicilleri ve Bu Sicillerin İhtiva Ettiği Belge Türlerinin Form Özellikleri Ve Tanımlanması*. Unpublished Ph.D. Dissertation. Marmara University, İstanbul Turkey.
Tamdoğan, I. (2008). Sulh and the 18th Century Ottoman Courts of Üsküdar and Adana. *Islamic Law and Society*, 15 (1), 55–83.

Tekgül, N. (2012). *Comments on Ottoman Provincial Courts in the Classical Period*. Unpublished paper presented at *La justice dans la société Ottomane: institutions, acteurs et practiques (16ème – 18ème siecles)*. İstanbul.

Tezcan, B. (2012). *The Second Ottoman Empire: Political and Social Transformation in the Early Modern World*. Cambridge: Cambridge University Press.

Tucker, J. (1998). *In the House of Law: Gender and Islamic Law in Ottoman Syria and Palestine*. Berkeley: University of California Press.

(1991). Ties that Bound: Women and Family in Eighteenth- and Nineteenth-Century Nablus. In N. Keddie and B. Baron (Eds.), *Women in Middle Eastern History* (pp. 233–53). New Haven: Yale University Press.

Tülüveli, G. (2005). Honorific Titles in Ottoman Parlance: A Reevaluation. *International Journal of Turkish Studies*, 11 (1–2), 17–28.

Tyan, E. (1960). `Adl. *Encyclopedia of Islam* (2nd edn., vol. 1, pp. 209–210). Leiden: E.J. Brill.

(1965a). Da'wā. *Encyclopedia of Islam* (2nd edn., vol. 2, pp. 170–172). Leiden: E.J. Brill.

(1965b). Fatwā. *Encyclopedia of Islam* (2nd edn., vol. 2, pp. 806–807). Leiden: E.J. Brill.

Ursinus, Michael (2004). *Grievance Administration (Şikayet) in an Ottoman Province: The Kaymakam of Rumelia's 'Record Book of Complaints' of 1781–1783*. New York: Routledge Curzon.

Uzunçarşılı, İ. H. (n.d.). Naip. *İslam Ansiklopedisi* (vol. 9, pp. 50–2). İstanbul: Türkiye Diyanet Vakfı Yayınları.

Uzunçarşılı, İ. H. (1965). *Osmanlı Devletinin İlmiye Teşkilâtı*. Ankara: Türk Tarih Kurumu Basımevi.

Waldfogel, J. (1995). The Selection Hypothesis and the Relationship between Trial and Plaintiff Victory. *Journal of Political Economy*, 103 (2), 229–60.

(1998). Reconciling asymmetric information and divergent expectations theories of litigation. *Journal of Law and Economics*, 41 (2), 451–476.

Weber, M. (1978). *Economy and Society: An Outline of Interpretive Sociology*. Vol. 3. New York: Bedminster Press.

Welchman, L. (2000). *Beyond the Code: Muslim Family Law and the Shari'a Judiciary in the Palestinian West Bank*. Leiden: Brill.

White, S. (2011). *The Climate of Rebellion in the Early Modern Ottoman Empire*. Cambridge, UK: Cambridge University Press.

Wittman, D. (1985). Is the Selection of Cases for Trial Biased? *Journal of Legal Studies*, 14(1), 185–214.

(1988). Dispute Resolution, Bargaining, and the Selection of Cases for Trial – a Study of the Generation of Biased and Unbiased Data. *Journal of Legal Studies*, 17 (2), 313–52.

Wooldridge, J. M. (2003). *Introductory Econometrics: A Modern Approach*. 2nd edn. Cincinnati, Ohio: South-Western College Pub.

Wrigley, E. A., and Schofield, R. S. (2002). *The Population History of England, 1541–1871: A Reconstruction* Cambridge: Cambridge University Press.

Yaman, T. M. (1941). Küre Bakır Madenine Dair Vesikalar. *Tarih Vesikaları*, 1 (4), 266–82.

Yi, E. (2004). *Guild Dynamics in Seventeenth-Century İstanbul: Fluidity and Leverage*. Leiden: Brill.

Yurdakul, İ. (2008). *Osmanlı İlmiye Merkez Teşkilatı'nda Reform (1826–1876)*. İstanbul: İletişim Yayınları.

Yücel, Y. (1970). XVIII. Yüzyılda Mütesellimlik Müessesesi. *Ankara Üniversitesi Dil ve Tarih-Coğrafya Fakültesi Dergisi*, XXVIII (3–4), 369–85.

Zarinebaf, F. (2010). *Crime and Punishment in İstanbul: 1700–1800*. Berkeley: University of California Press.

Ze'evi, D. (1998). The Use of Ottoman Sharia Court Records as a Source for Middle Eastern Social History: A Reappraisal. *Islamic Law and Society*, 5 (1), 35–56.

(2006). *Producing Desire: Changing Sexual Discourse in the Ottoman Middle East, 1500-1900*. Berkeley: University of California Press.

Ziadeh, F. J. (1990). Integrity (`Adalah) in Classical Islamic Law. In N. I. L. a. J. Heer (Ed.) *Islamic Law and Jurisprudence* (pp. 73–93). Seattle: University of Washington Press.

Index

Entries in bold typeface denote figures or tables.

Other Titles in the Series

Popular Culture in Medieval Cairo Boaz Shoshan
Early Philosophical Shiism: The Ismaili Neoplatonism of Abū Ya'qūb al-Sijistānī Paul E. Walker
Indian Merchants and Eurasian Trade, 1600–1750 Stephen Frederic Dale
Palestinian Peasants and Ottoman Officials: Rural Administration around Sixteenth-Century Jerusalem Amy Singer
Arabic Historical Thought in the Classical Period Tarif Khalidi
Mongols and Mamluks: The Mamluk–Īlkhānid War, 1260–1281 Reuven Amitai-Preiss
Hierarchy and Egalitarianism in Islamic Thought Louise Marlow
The Politics of Households in Ottoman Egypt: The Rise of the Qazdağlis Jane Hathaway
Commodity and Exchange in the Mongol Empire: A Cultural History of Islamic Textiles Thomas T. Allsen
State and Provincial Society in the Ottoman Empire: Mosul, 1540–1834 Dina Rizk Khoury
The Mamluks in Egyptian Politics and Society Thomas Philipp *and* Ulrich Haarmann *(eds.)*
The Delhi Sultanate: A Political and Military History Peter Jackson
European and Islamic Trade in the Early Ottoman State: The Merchants of Genoa and Turkey Kate Fleet
Reinterpreting Islamic Historiography: Hārūn al-Rashīd and the Narrative of the 'Abbāsid Caliphate Tayeb El-Hibri
The Ottoman City Between East and West: Aleppo, Izmir, and Istanbul Edhem Eldem, Daniel Goffman, *and* Bruce Masters
A Monetary History of the Ottoman Empire Şevket Pamuk
The Politics of Trade in Safavid Iran: Silk for Silver, 1600–1730 Rudolph P. Matthee
The Idea of Idolatry and the Emergence of Islam: From Polemic to History G. R. Hawting
Classical Arabic Biography: The Heirs of the Prophets in the Age of al-Ma'mūn Michael Cooperson
Empire and Elites After the Muslim Conquest: The Transformation of Northern Mesopotamia Chase F. Robinson
Poverty and Charity in Medieval Islam: Mamluk Egypt, 1250–1517 Adam Sabra
Christians and Jews in the Ottoman Arab World: The Roots of Sectarianism Bruce Masters
Culture and Conquest in Mongol Eurasia Thomas T. Allsen
Revival and Reform in Islam: The Legacy of Muhammad al-Shawkani Bernard Haykel
Tolerance and Coercion in Islam: Interfaith Relations in the Muslim Tradition Yohanan Friedmann
Guns for the Sultan: Military Power and the Weapons Industry in the Ottoman Empire Gábor Ágoston
Marriage, Money and Divorce in Medieval Islamic Society Yossef Rapoport
The Empire of the Qara Khitai in Eurasian History: Between China and the Islamic World Michal Biran
Domesticity and Power in the Early Mughal World Ruby Lal
Power, Politics and Religion in Timurid Iran Beatrice Forbes Manz
Postal Systems in the Pre-Modern Islamic World Adam J. Silverstein

Kingship and Ideology in the Islamic and Mongol Worlds Anne F. Broadbridge
Justice, Punishment and the Medieval Muslim Imagination Christian Lange
The Shiites of Lebanon Under Ottoman Rule, 1516–1788 Stefan Winter
Women and Slavery in the Late Ottoman Empire Madeline Zilfi
The Second Ottoman Empire: Political and Social Transformation in the Early Modern World Baki Tezcan
Non-Muslims in the Early Islamic Empire: From Surrender to Coexistence Milka Levy-Rubin
The Legendary Biographies of Tamerlane: Islam and Heroic Apocrypha in Central Asia Ron Sela
Law and Piety in Medieval Islam Megan Reid
The Origins of the Shi'a: Identity, Ritual, and Sacred Space in Eighth-Century Kufa Najam Haider
Politics, Law, and Community in Islamic Thought: The Taymiyyan Moment Ovamir Anjum
The Power of Oratory in the Medieval Muslim World Linda G. Jones
Animals in the Qur'an Sarra Tlili
The Logic of Law Making in Islam: Women and Prayer in the Legal Tradition Behnam Sadeghi
Empire and Power in the Reign of Süleyman: Narrating the Sixteenth-Century Ottoman World Kaya Şahin
Law and Piety in Medieval Islam Megan H. Reid
The New Muslims of Post-Conquest Iran Sarah Bowen Savant
Women and the Transmission of Religious Knowledge in Islam Asma Sayeed
The Mamluk City in the Middle East: History, Culture, and the Urban Landscape Nimrod Luz
The Holy City of Medina: Sacred Space in Early Islamic Arabia Harry Munt
Disability in the Arab Ottoman World, 1500–1800 Sara Scalenghe
Muslim Midwives: The Craft of Birthing in the Premodern Middle East Avner Giladi
The Second Formation of Islamic Law: The Hanafi School in the Early Modern Ottoman Empire Guy Burak
Doubt in Islamic Law: A History of Legal Maxims, Interpretation, and Islamic Criminal Law Intisar A. Rabb
Sexual Violation in Islamic Law: Substance, Evidence, and Procedure Hina Azam
Gender Hierarchy in the Qur'an: Medieval Interpretations, Modern Responses Karen Bauer